Beyond the Second Sophistic

Beyond the Second Sophistic

Adventures in Greek Postclassicism

Tim Whitmarsh

UNIVERSITY OF CALIFORNIA PRESS
Berkeley   Los Angeles   London

University of California Press, one of the most distinguished university presses in the United States, enriches lives around the world by advancing scholarship in the humanities, social sciences, and natural sciences. Its activities are supported by the UC Press Foundation and by philanthropic contributions from individuals and institutions. For more information, visit www.ucpress.edu.

University of California Press
Berkeley and Los Angeles, California

University of California Press, Ltd.
London, England

© 2013 by The Regents of the University of California

First Paperback Printing 2020

Library of Congress Cataloging-in-Publication Data

Whitmarsh, Tim.
  Beyond the Second Sophistic : adventures in Greek postclassicism / Tim Whitmarsh.
      p.   cm.
  Includes bibliographical references and index.
  ISBN 978-0-520-34458-7 (pbk.: alk. paper)
  1. Greek literature—Rome—History and criticism.   I. Title.
PA3086.W55   2013
880.9′001—dc23   2013002937

10, 9, 8, 7, 6, 5, 4, 3, 2, 1
24, 23, 22, 21, 20

CONTENTS

Preface vii
Acknowledgments ix
Abbreviations xi

Introduction: Beyond the Second Sophistic and into the Postclassical   1

PART ONE. FICTION BEYOND THE CANON

1. The "Invention of Fiction"   11
2. The Romance of Genre   35
3. Belief in Fiction: Euhemerus of Messene and the *Sacred Inscription*   49
4. An I for an I: Reading Fictional Autobiography   63
5. Metamorphoses of the *Ass*   75
6. Addressing Power: Fictional Letters between Alexander and Darius   86
7. Philostratus's *Heroicus*: Fictions of Hellenism   101
8. Mimesis and the Gendered Icon in Greek Theory and Fiction   123

PART TWO. POETRY AND PROSE

9. Greek Poets and Roman Patrons in the Late Republic and Early Empire   137
10. The Cretan Lyre Paradox: Mesomedes, Hadrian, and the Poetics of Patronage   154

| 11. Lucianic Paratragedy | 176 |
| 12. Quickening the Classics: The Politics of Prose in Roman Greece | 186 |

PART THREE. BEYOND THE GREEK SOPHISTIC

| 13. Politics and Identity in Ezekiel's *Exagoge* | 211 |
| 14. Adventures of the Solymoi | 228 |

References 249
Index 275

PREFACE

This volume consists of ten substantially revised and updated essays and five previously unpublished. I am immensely grateful to the original editors and publishers, all of whom have graciously permitted republication. It would be tedious, even if it were possible, to list all who deserve thanks for shaping the ideas in here, but at the risk of invidious omission let me record that my ideas about the Second Sophistic and its limitations have been formatively shaped by discussions with Jaś Elsner, Simon Goldhill, Constanze Güthenke, Brooke Holmes, Richard Hunter, Larry Kim, Helen Morales, Dan Selden, and Froma Zeitlin. I owe a huge debt also to those who have offered me the opportunity for discussion of these ideas in variously inchoate forms, among them Eran Almagor, Alain Billault, Peter Bing, Barbara Borg, Bracht Branham, Jésus Carruesco, Honora Chapman, Katharine Earnshaw, Marco Fernandelli, Tom Habinek, Owen Hodkinson, Marko Marinčič, Emeline Marquis, Francesca Mestre, Teresa Morgan, Maren Niehoff, Michael Paschalis, Jim Porter, Jonathan Price, Tessa Rajak, Zuleika Rodgers, Kim Ryholt, Thomas Schmitz, Eva Subias, Ruth Webb, and Nicolas Wiater. My wonderful friends and colleagues at Corpus Christi College—Ewen Bowie, Ursula Coope, Jaś Elsner (again), Peter Haarer, Stephen Harrison, John Ma, Anna Marmodoro, Neil McLynn, and Tobias Reinhardt—have been an ever-present source of inspiration and advice both intellectual and practical during the shaping of this project. I am also indebted to a number of my former colleagues at the University of Exeter (where I worked for the years 2001–7), especially Chris Gill, Rebecca Langlands, Francesca Stavrakopoulou, and John Wilkins: without their support, tolerance of crude experimentation, and tough quizzing the ideas in this book would never have made it to this stage. Erich Gruen, Fergus Millar, Thomas

Schmitz, and Stephanie West have saved me from various egregious misprisions, although others will surely remain. Special thanks to my amazingly patient and forgiving parents (Judy and Guy) and children (India and Soli); this book is for them all.

All translations, unless otherwise indicated, are my own.

ACKNOWLEDGMENTS

The following chapters are revisions of previously published material; permission from the various publishers to revisit that material is gratefully acknowledged.

Chapter 1, "The 'Invention of Fiction,'" revised from "Prose Fiction," in *A Companion to Hellenistic Literature*, edited by M. Cuypers and J. Clauss (Oxford: Blackwell, 2010), 395–411.

Chapter 4, "An I for an I: Reading Fictional Autobiography," revised from the article of the same name in *Cento Pagine* 3 (2009): 56–66 (available online at http://www2.units.it/musacamena/iniziative/SCA2009_Withmarsh.pdf [*sic*]); appears in slightly different form in *The Author's Voice in Classical and Late Antiquity*, edited by A. Marmodoro and J. Hill (Oxford: Oxford University Press, 2013), 233–47.

Chapter 5, "Metamorphoses of the *Ass*," revised from the chapter of the same name in *Lucian of Samosata: Greek Writer and Roman Citizen*, edited by F. Mestre and P. Gómez (Barcelona: Universitat de Barcelona, 2010), 73–81.

Chapter 6, "Addressing Power: Fictional Letters between Alexander and Darius," revised from the chapter of the same name in *Epistolary Narratives in Ancient Greek Literature*, edited by O. Hodkinson, P. Rosenmeyer, and E. Bracke (Leiden: Brill, forthcoming).

Chapter 7, "Philostratus's *Heroicus*: Fictions of Hellenism," revised from "Performing Heroics: Language, Landscape and Identity in Philostratus' *Heroicus*," in *Philostratus*, edited by E. Bowie and J. Elsner (Cambridge: Cambridge University Press, 2009), 205–29.

Chapter 8, "Mimesis and the Gendered Icon in Greek Theory and Fiction," revised from "The Erotics of *Mimēsis*: Gendered Aesthetics in Greek Theory and

Fiction," in *The Construction of the Real and the Ideal in the Ancient Novel*, edited by M. Paschalis and S. Panayotakis (Groningen: Barkhuis, forthcoming).

Chapter 9, "Greek Poets and Roman Patrons in the Late Republic and Early Empire" revised from "Greek Poets and Roman Patrons in the Late Republic and Early Empire: Crinagoras, Antipater, and Others on Rome" in *The Struggle for Identity: Greeks and Their Past in the First Century BCE*, edited by T. Schmitz and N. Wiater (Stuttgart: Franz Steiner, 2011), 189–204.

Chapter 10, "The Cretan Lyre Paradox: Mesomedes, Hadrian, and the Poetics of Patronage," revised from the chapter of the same name in *Paideia: The World of the Second Sophistic*, edited by B. E. Borg (Berlin: de Gruyter, 2004), 377–402.

Chapter 12, "Quickening the Classics: The Politics of Prose in Roman Greece," revised from the chapter of the same name in *Classical Pasts: The Classical Traditions of Greco-Roman Antiquity*, edited by J. I. Porter (Princeton: Princeton University Press, 2005), 353–74.

Chapter 13, "Politics and Identity in Ezekiel's *Exagoge*," revised from "Pharaonic Alexandria: Ezekiel's *Exagoge* and Political Allegory in Hellenistic Judaism," in *The Space of the City in Graeco-Roman Egypt: Image and Reality*, edited by E. Subias, P. Azara, J. Carruesco, I. Fiz, and R. Cuesta (Tarragona: Institut Català d'Arqueologia Clàssica, 2011): 41–48.

ABBREVIATIONS

AC L'antiquité classique.
AJPh American Journal of Philology.
ANRW Aufstieg und Niedergang der römischen Welt. Berlin, 1972–.
ASNP Annali della Scuola Normale Superiore di Pisa.
BICS Bulletin of the Institute of Classical Studies.
CA J. Powell, Collectanea Alexandrina: reliquiae minores poetarum Graecorum aetatis Ptolemaicae 323–146 A.C., epicorum, elegiacorum, lyricorum, ethicorum. Oxford, 1925.
CCJ Cambridge Classical Journal.
CJ Classical Journal.
ClAnt Classical Antiquity.
CPh Classical Philology.
CW Classical World.
CQ Classical Quarterly.
DK H. Diels and W. Kranz, Die Fragmente der Vorsokratiker. 6th ed. Berlin, 1951–52.
EA Epigraphica Anatolica.
EG G. Kaibel, Epigrammata Graeca ex lapidibus conlecta. Berlin, 1878.
EGF M. Davis, Epicorum Graecorum Fragmenta. Göttingen, 1988.
EMC Echos du Monde Classique/Classical Views.
FGE D. L. Page, Further Greek Epigrams: Epigrams before A.D. 50 from the Greek Anthology and Other Sources, not Included in Hellenistic Epigrams or "The Garland of Philip." Revised and prepared for publication by R. D. Dawe and J. Diggle. Cambridge, 1981.

FGrH	F. Jacoby et al., *Die Fragmente der griechischen Historiker*. Berlin and Leiden, 1876–1959; continued Leiden, 1998–.
FHJA	C. Halladay, *Fragments from Hellenistic Jewish Authors*. 4 volumes. Chico, 1983–2003.
GDRK	E. Heitsch, *Die griechischen Dichterfragmente der römischen Kaiserzeit*. 2 vols. Göttingen, 1961–64.
GGM	C. F. W. Müller, *Geographi graeci minores*. 2 vols. Paris, 1855–82.
GRBS	*Greek, Roman, and Byzantine Studies*.
HSCPh	*Harvard Studies in Classical Philology*.
HThR	*Harvard Theological Review*.
IG	*Inscriptiones Graecae*.
IGRR	R. Cagnat, *Inscriptiones Graecae ad res Romanas pertinentes*. Rome, 1964.
IJCT	*International Journal of the Classical Tradition*.
JHS	*Journal of Hellenic Studies*.
JRS	*Journal of Roman Studies*.
JSJ	*Journal for the Study of Judaism*.
JTS	*Journal of Theological Studies*.
LCM	*Liverpool Classical Monthly*.
LGPN	P. M. Fraser et al., *A Lexicon of Greek Personal Names*. Oxford, 1987–.
LIMC	H. C. Ackermann, J.-R. Gisler, and L. Kahil, *Lexicon iconographicum mythologiae classicae*. Zurich, 1981–.
LSJ	H. G. Liddell, R. Scott, et al., *A Greek-English Lexicon*. 9th ed. with supplement. Oxford, 1996.
MD	*Materiali e discussioni per l'analisi dei testi classici*.
OCD^3	S. Hornblower and A. Spawforth, *The Oxford Classical Dictionary*. 3rd rev. ed. Oxford, 2005.
OLD^2	P. G. W. Glare, *The Oxford Latin Dictionary*. 2nd ed. Oxford, 2012.
PCG	R. Kassel and C. Austin, *Poetae comici Graeci*. Berlin, 1983–.
PCPhS	*Proceedings of the Cambridge Philological Society*.
P.Hamb.	*Griechische Papyri der Hamburger Staats- und Universitäts-Bibliothek mit einigen Stüchen aus der Sammlung Hugo Ibscher*. Hamburg, 1954.
P.Herc.	*Herculaneum Papyri*.
PLG	T. Bergk, *Poetae lyrici Graeci*. 4th ed. Leipzig, 1878–82.
PMG	D. Page, *Poetae melici Graeci*. Oxford, 1962.
P.Mich.	D. S. Crawford, *Papyri Michaelidae: Being a Catalogue of the Greek and Latin Papyri, Tablets and Ostraca in the Library of G. A. Michaïlidis of Cairo*. Aberdeen, 1955.
P.Oxy.	*The Oxyrhynchus Papyri*. London, 1898–.
PSI	*Papiri greci e latini: pubblicazioni della Società Italiana per la ricerca dei papiri greci e latini in Egitto*. Florence, 1912–79.

QUCC	Quaderni Urbinati di Cultura Classica.
RE	Paulys Realencyclopädie der classischen Altertumswissenschaft. 1st ed. Munich, 1903–78.
REA	Revue des Études Anciennes.
RFIC	Rivista di filologia e di istruzione classica.
RhM	Rheinisches Museum für Philologie.
SEG	Supplementum epigraphicum Graecum. Leiden, 1923–1971; continued Amsterdam, 1979–.
SH	H. Lloyd-Jones and P. Parsons, Supplementum Hellenisticum. Berlin, 1983.
SIFC	Studi Italiani di Filologia Classica.
SO	Symbolae Osloenses.
SVF	H. von Arnim, Stoicorum veterum fragmenta. Leipzig, 1923–24.
TאPhA	Transactions of the American Philological Association.
TEGP	D. W. Graham, The Texts of Early Greek Philosophy: The Complete Fragments and Selected Testimonies of the Major Presocratics. 2 vols. Cambridge, U.K., 2010.
TGrF	B. Snell, S. L. Radt, and R. Kannicht, Tragicorum graecorum fragmenta. 5 vols. Göttingen, 1971–2004.
UPZ	U. Wilcken, Urkunden der Ptolemäerzeit (ältere Funde). 2 vols. Berlin, 1927–57.
WJA	Würzburger Jahrbücher für die Altertumswissenschaft.
WS	Wiener Studien: Zeitschrift für Klassische Philologie und Patristik und lateinische Tradition.
YCS	Yale Classical Studies.
ZPE	Zeitschrift für Papyrologie und Epigraphik.

Introduction

*Beyond the Second Sophistic and
into the Postclassical*

This book represents a series of experiments in alternative ways of thinking about ancient Greek literature, which I shall identify by the term (to which I lay no exclusive claim) *postclassicism*.[1] With this neologism I mean, principally, to mark an aspiration to rethink classicist categories inherited from the nineteenth century. It is not intended to proclaim any sharp rupture with existing theories and practices within the discipline, for clearly there are many theoretically informed approaches (literary and cultural theory, feminism, reception, Marxism, postcolonialism, queer theory . . .) that share in that labor of reconstructing the humanities legacy, but it seems to me that finding a progressive label that is specific to classical literary studies should be a useful reminder that (despite what is sometimes claimed) battle lines are still drawn up fiercely around the study of ancient texts.

Postclassicism is not, however, merely a matter of updating political and ethical mores. Classics as a discipline was, for sure, more than most humanities subjects forged in the white heat of imperialist, nationalist, elitist, disciplinarian, androcentric imperatives, but collective self-congratulation on "our" liberal progressiveness is lazy and too easy. Rather, what I aim to do in this book is attack some of the conventional ways of categorizing literature, all of which are to some extent rooted in nineteenth-century, postromantic ideas of classical *value*. Classicists' organization of literary history has tended to be dominated by an unspoken aesthetic that places certain kinds of texts in the center and hence privileges certain kinds of

---

1. I have benefited from rich and ongoing discussions with Brooke Holmes and Constanze Güthenke of Princeton University, and from contributors to the "Postclassicisms" seminar at Oxford in the autumn of 2012.

narratives of "what the Greeks thought." It is at this kind of assumption, most of all, that this book takes aim. The literary production of the ancient Greeks (and others) is understood here not in terms of an intrinsic worth that is to be adulated—for *value* only ever indicates what the buyer is willing to pay—but as a plural cultural system. Despite the ever-increasing sophistication of our strategies for reading individual texts, classicists in general still seem to cling to unreconstructed narratives that privilege early Greece as a site of cultural, intellectual, and indeed religious purity. This creates a historical matrix that not only overaestheticizes material from the early period (particularly the tough, manly stuff: Homer, Pindar, and Aeschylus) but also dooms later literary traditions to being comprehended in terms only of replication and emulation of prior glories. This assessment, it seems to me, works only if we ignore the majority of the surviving evidence.

Any area of classical culture can be considered from a postclassical vantage. There are, of course, brilliantly innovative readings of (for example) Sappho and Herodotus that reshape our ideas about literary history. This book, however, focuses on literary texts that are also chronologically postclassical. All are located somewhere on that slippery slope toward decadence that (so some might argue) began in the aftermath of the fourth century B.C.E. I choose this material not just because it has been understudied relative to earlier texts (true though that is) but also because it offers the best opportunities for confronting the larger questions of historical change, linear versus plural traditions, and cultural conflict.

The material I consider, moreover, will (I hope) challenge many readers' ideas about what counts as Greek literature. Some of it was written by Egyptians or Jews. Some of it is "subliterary." Some of it, for sure, fits a more conventional template of Greek literature, but in those cases the disruption comes in in different ways. The range is designedly diverse, cutting as it does across temporal, cultural, and generic boundaries, precisely to pose sharp questions about how and why we think of Greek literary history in the way that we do. It is not my aim, let me make clear, simply to erase all the contours and lineaments that give shape and meaning to our maps of postclassical Greek culture; rather, I wish to demonstrate (i) how these intellectual frameworks can constrict as well as enable our thinking; (ii) how much more richness and variety there is to the postclassical world than conventional accounts suggest; and (iii) a more general point of methodology, on which I wish to insist. Boundaries should be seen not as barriers, the limits of our inquiry—but as crossing points, the spaces that prompt the most interesting questions. This is the nub of postclassicism as methodology: think not of the well-wrought urn but of the working of it, its breaking, its contents, its storage, the points of juncture between it and abutting objects.

Much of my work over the past fifteen years or so has focused on Greek literature of the time of the Roman Empire, roughly 50–300 C.E., a period that is sometimes known as the Second Sophistic. I have inveighed against the inaccuracies and (more importantly) blighted history of this term on a number of occasions,² but at the risk of trying patiences let me return to the question here, for it offers a nice illustration of the general problematics sketched above and gets us to the very heart of the postclassical project. It is not the term *Second Sophistic* itself that is the problem—all terminology has limitations as well as advantages—but the way that unexamined adherence to nineteenth-century categories can still blinker us now. The phrase is first found in the third-century C.E. Greek writer Philostratus, where it denotes a particular oratorical style; since its reappropriation in the late nineteenth century, however, it has been associated with a supposed Hellenic revivalism calqued on the model of postindustrial nationalism.³ Erwin Rohde's *zweite Sophistik* was imagined as a reassertion of "a national Hellenic element" in the face of a double threat to identity, from both "orientals" and Rome.⁴ (Rohde, a friend of Friedrich Nietzsche's, was preoccupied with questions of cultural vigor in his own era too.) More recent scholarship has, perhaps understandably, preferred to speak in anthropological terms of Greek "culture" or "cultural identity" rather than "nationality."⁵ But *culture* too is a tricky word, and arguably even more problematic: it not only risks simply repackaging the old product (that is, committing to the same metaphysics of unbroken, linear continuity)⁶ but also tacitly activates the idea of a Jaegerian model of idealized aristocratic solidarity (Greek literature as "high culture"). Nationalism through the back door, in other words. The Second Sophistic has been—and remains in much current scholarship—a modern fantasy projected back on to the ancient world, an *objet petit a*, an impossible idealization of pure, untainted aristocratic Greek tradition.

Now, it is of course not hard to find expressions of aristocratic Hellenocentrism in the postclassical Greek world. My argument, however, is that such expressions should be seen as local and tactical rather than as absolute paradigms of the spirit of the age. The enthusiasm with which classicists have embraced Plutarch,⁷ for instance, should give us pause: an extraordinarily rich and varied author, to be sure, but also one who shapes (or has been taken to shape)⁸ a very conservative vision of Greek identity in terms of a dialogue with the classical greats, particularly

---

2. See especially Whitmarsh 2001, 42–45; 2005a, 4–10.

3. Philostr., *VS* 481, 507; see, e.g., Rohde 1876, which is in part a polemic against the hypothesis of Eastern influence on the development of the Greek novel. On the nationalist, and arguably anti-Semitic, context of Rohde's work, see Whitmarsh 2011b.

4. Rohde 1914, 310–23, at 319.

5. So Swain 1996, Whitmarsh 2001, and Goldhill 2001b.

6. See the pertinent critique of McCoskey 2012, 93.

7. Witness the success of the International Plutarch Society, its multiple publications, and its journal, *Ploutarchos*. Let me stress that reflection on the phenomenon does not imply any criticism of this fine institution or its wonderful members!

8. As ever, such generalizations risk oversimplifying. There is much more that could be said about Plutarch's multifaceted relationship with non-Greek cultures, particularly Roman. His (surely ironic)

the nonfictional prose authors. If we take Plutarch as paradigmatic of postclassical Greece, we miss so many dimensions of Greek writing: lateral engagement with other peoples' cultures, poetics and imaginative literature, the continuity with Hellenistic Greek culture. Much the same could be said of Dio Chrysostom and Aelius Aristides, both of whom loom large in the standard accounts of Greek identity in the Roman Empire. I am not, of course, arguing against their value for cultural historians, merely observing that selecting a limited evidentiary range leads to oversimplified claims about "the Greeks" and "the Roman Empire."[9]

This picture of seamless panhellenism is, ultimately, a scholarly fiction, resting on a circular process of exclusion of evidence to the contrary. Standard accounts of postclassical Greek literature (I include my own earlier work) have, for example, little room for Jewish[10] or Christian literature (although here the tide is beginning to turn).[11] They scarcely acknowledge the competitor traditions that were contemporaneously devising, reimagining, and commentating on literary canons (viz. rabbinical Hebrew[12] and Christian Syriac). They present the Hellenistic era as dominated by poetry and the imperial era by prose, usually by simply failing to refer to the full range of surviving material. Nor do they accommodate much demographic range within mainstream Greek society. It is rare to find mention of paraliterary works such as the *Alexander Romance* or the *Life of Aesop*, whose strata range from Hellenistic to imperial dates, or, indeed, of the so-called *Acts of the Pagan Martyrs* or *Secundus the Silent Philosopher*, works that clearly operate at some considerable remove from the Atticizing classicism of Aristides or Philostratus. We should note too the relative marginalization of the voluminous technical literature of the later era.[13] While the physiognomical works of Galen (antiquity's most productive author, to judge by what we have) and Polemo have to an extent been brought into the fold,[14] little awareness is

---

claim to know minimal Latin (*Demosthenes* 2, carefully unpacked by Zadorojnyi 2006) has been given far too much prominence, at the expense of such extraordinarily hybridized texts as *On the Fortune of the Romans* and the *Roman Questions*. Strobach 1997 opens up these questions interestingly.

9. A case in point is Veyne 2005, 195–310, magisterial but largely unencumbered by awareness of the voluminous scholarship on the complexity of Greek identity, and hence prone to unsustainable generalization (e.g., p. 238: "The Greeks are tacitly considered, in the Roman Empire, as foreigners. The Greeks equally considered themselves superior, which is why their identity remained irreducible").

10. Goldhill 2001b is an exception, containing an excellent essay by Maud Gleason on Josephus.

11. König 2009 is exemplary in this regard; see also, from the side of Christian studies, especially Lieu 2004, Nasrallah 2010 (with 28–30 specifically on this issue), and now Perkins 2010 and Eshleman 2012.

12. Linked to the Second Sophistic by, e.g., Jaffee 2001, 128–40, with further bibliography at 202 n. 9, 203 nn. 24–25.

13. König and Whitmarsh 2007 represents an attempt to bridge this particular gap.

14. Galen receives a chapter in Bowersock 1969; see further Gill, Whitmarsh, and Wilkins 2009. Gleason 1995, 55–81, situates Polemo's *Physiognomics* within rhetorical agonistics; for a fuller discussion of this question see Swain 2007.

shown of—to take but a few examples—Hero of Alexandria on mechanics, Apollonius Dyscolus the grammarian, Aristides Quintilianus on musicology, Aelian on animals,[15] astrologers, or alchemists. No wonder the stereotype of imperial Greeks as flouncy, elitist orators persists, when texts that present an alternative image are not pictured. How different our conception of the period would be had Philostratus not survived.

It is clearly beyond the scope of a single volume to survey the full range of postclassical literary production, and this in any case is not my aim here.[16] That being said, there is certainly a primary intention to expand the range of material that scholars of the Hellenistic and early imperial periods have traditionally covered. Part 1 treats Greek fiction proposing that the span extends well beyond the "Greek novel" (or "romance") as conventionally understood—that is, the works of Chariton, Achilles Tatius, and so forth. These, I argue in chapter 2, represent a very limited window onto the world of ancient fictional production, and indeed they play by very different rules than those of the generality of "novelistic" literature. My wider narrative of prose fiction begins early in the Hellenistic era, with Euhemerus (sometime after 300 B.C.E.), and gives a central berth to a series of texts too often relegated to "the fringe":[17] the *Alexander Romance,* the pseudo-Lucianic *Ass,* Philostratus's *Heroicus,* and even the literary-critical writings of Dionysius of Halicarnassus. Part 2 attempts to remedy the general neglect of poetics in the scholarship of the early imperial period (a neglect that is certainly prompted by certain ancient sources themselves, which diagnose the imperial era as a prosaic one: see chapter 12). There are signs here and there that the corner is being turned,[18] albeit slowly, but even so the emphasis is too often placed on subordinating poetics to a supposed context where rhetorical prose dominates, rather than reading the material on its own terms, as poetry. My chapters on the early imperial epigrammatists (chapter 9), Mesomedes (chapter 10), and Lucian's paratragedies (chapter 11) seek to show how these cunning poems resonate against both the rich tradition of classical poetics and contemporary culture. Part 3 marks the end of the book's adventures, in Hellenistic Judaism: Ezekiel's tragic retelling of the Exodus story (chapter 13) and the various attempts to integrate the biblical and the Homeric traditions (chapter 14). This material is unusually rich and sophisticated, and with its concern to root a distinct identity politics in the revivifying and transforming of an ancient literary culture it can

---

15. A deficit that Steven Smith will correct in an eagerly anticipated study.
16. For an excellent survey of Hellenistic literature that adopts a more pluralistic perspective see Cuypers and Clauss 2010; the forthcoming *Cambridge History of Later Greek Literature,* edited by Robert Shorrock, promises to be a milestone.
17. The phrase used and explored in Karla 2009.
18. See especially Baumbach and Bär 2007, on Quintus of Smyrna and the Second Sophistic.

be said to preempt many of the concerns of the Greek Sophists of the early Roman Empire.

As will be clear, this book does more than simply expand the canon. My aim is to do away entirely with the idea of the culturally central, the paradigmatic, to dispense with hierarchies of cultural value. The Jewish epic poets Theodotus and Philo may be fragmentary, for example, and may not have spawned an entire tradition of Jewish epic poetics (although perhaps they did? We have lost so much Jewish literature of the era), but to me they are potentially as significant in cultural terms as Vergil. I say *potentially* because thinking more pluralistically involves a hypothetical rewiring of literary history: let us bracket the subsequent reception that made Vergil (in T.S. Eliot's famous phrase) "the classic of all Europe" and Philo and Theodotus footnotes in literary history; let us recall instead that when each of these poets wrote, the future was entirely up for grabs. Philo and Theodotus did not know that Jerusalem would be sacked in 70 C.E. and that Judaism would as a result turn its back on the Greco-Roman tradition: for all they knew, they were composing poems that might change the world. This kind of utopian (or, better, uchronic) intellectual experiment with literary history seeks not only to unsettle our deeply embedded metanarratives of classical "value" but also to restore some of the local vitality, urgency, and conflict that is endemic to all literary production.

Issues of centrality and marginality cluster particularly around fiction and the novel, which is why part 1 focuses on this area. The issue here is not just the familiar one that the Greeks themselves apparently set little store by fictional production; it is, more pertinently, that there is a hierarchy of sorts among the novels themselves. The five "romances" of Chariton, Xenophon, Achilles, Longus, and Heliodorus seem to work together as a unit and hence as a bullyboy gang excluding all those that do not fit. Scholars, however, have been too easily magnetized by the imperial romances' apparent generic coherence, so that we tend to read other prose fictions in terms primarily of their deviation from the romance paradigm (see chapters 1-2). The imperial romances do indeed work as a genre, but I propose that this sense of shared form coalesced only partially, gradually, and in a sense retrospectively: thus the first-century *Callirhoe* became a "romance" as we understand the term (that is, a participant in the genre) only as a result of the later formation of a tradition. We need a much more plural model of what Greek fiction is and was, a model that includes works such as the pseudo-Lucianic *Ass*, the *Alexander Romance*, and Philostratus's *Heroicus*.

The book's second major theme, already adverted to above, is that poetry gives us a very different point of entry into the world of the Greeks under the Roman Empire. Perhaps surprisingly, much of the poetry is written "from below": whereas prose authors tend to project their relationship with empire in terms of parity—a projection that feeds the nineteenth-century preoccupation with noble Greeks preserving their cultural traditions—poets mobilize a stock of topoi, drawn from patronal poets such as Pindar, Bacchylides, and Theocritus, that emphasize a difference of status. Poets do not necessarily give us a truer picture of Greeks' feelings about Rome: these we will never know. But they do capture a different facet of that relationship, where the hierarchy and exploitation are much more visible.

The third thematic locus is Hellenistic Judaism. Literary classicists have in general neglected material that is not perceived to be echt Greek; the lionization of Lucian, the Hellenized Syrian of the second century C.E., is the exception (but Lucian plays almost entirely by "classical" rules, apart, perhaps, for in *On the Syrian Goddess*). The reasons for this are in many ways understandable. We have lost entire cultural traditions: Greco-Phoenician culture is in effect represented only by Philo of Byblos, who is himself excerpted in Eusebius; likewise Greco-Mesopotamian literature, where Berossus survives (again) primarily in Eusebius's paraphrase. Demotic Egyptian texts do survive (usually in fragments), and there were clearly numerous points of cultural contact between Egyptian and Hellenistic Greek culture, but the material is difficult to work with, given how much primary editorial work remains to be done.[19] With Second Temple Jewish literature, however, we have (thanks to late-antique Christians, who treated biblical matter with predictable reverence) a rich, albeit incomplete, body of literature: it presents classicists with a wonderful opportunity to test the ways in which sophisticated Greek speakers deployed the traditional Greek forms of tragedy and epic as vehicles for non-Greek narrative traditions. These texts, indeed, seem to preempt much of the ingenious play with issues of identity, self-fashioning, and cultural bivalence that scholars have detected in the Second Sophistic. It may be a provocation, but it is no exaggeration to speak of a "Jewish Sophistic" already in the second and first centuries B.C.E.

There are other threads running through this book: the figure of metalepsis, the (dis)appearances of authors, the intersection between literary production and literary criticism, and my unflagging preoccupation with the power of the human imagination to transform. These are best left to emerge organically, in the reading. This book was, as I have said, conceived in an adventurous spirit; there are many alternative tracks and trails for "off-roaders." With that same desire for openness and accessibility, I have kept the endnoting relatively light and used Greek letters only where they have seemed impossible to avoid (and only in endnotes). I hope the writing is accessible to nonspecialists.

---

19. Whitmarsh and Thomson, forthcoming, covers much of this Hellenistic intercultural material.

PART ONE

Fiction beyond the Canon

1

The "Invention of Fiction"

"Invention" is one of the central tropes of classical, particularly Greek, scholarship: it seems that even in this methodologically hyperaware, post-postmodern age, we are still addicted to romanticizing narratives of origination (however contested). When it comes to the (discrete but interlocking) categories of fiction, prose literature, and the novel, recent years have seen originomania in overdrive. Can we attribute to Chariton, in the first century C.E., "the invention of the Greek love novel"?[1] Or was Theocritus responsible for "the invention of fiction"?[2] Or was it rather a question of "the birth of literary fiction," thanks to philosophical innovations culminating in Plato and Aristotle?[3] Or is "die Entdeckung der Fiktionalität"[4] perhaps to be attributed to the development of relatively widespread literacy, in the fifth century B.C.E.? Yet a sense of fictionality has already been credited, by different scholars, to the poetry of Homer and Hesiod.[5] "The invention of Greek prose," meanwhile, might be sought in stories around and reflections on the figure of Aesop, which for us surface to visibility in the fifth century B.C.E.[6] Clearly at one level these are merely rhetorical claims, *façons de parler*: few scholars, I imagine,

---

This chapter contains material drawn from Whitmarsh 2010d; I am grateful to Wiley-Blackwell for permission to reuse it.
  1. Tilg 2010.
  2. Payne 2007.
  3. Finkelberg 1998. The extent to which Plato's Atlantis story is self-consciously fictional has been much debated: see ch. 3, n. 9.
  4. Rösler 1980.
  5. See, e.g., Goldhill 1991.
  6. Kurke 2010.

would if pressed argue that fiction, the novel, or literary prose was actually "invented," definitively, at a specific historical juncture. Partly because these are our categories, not those of the Greeks or the Romans, ancient ones map only inexactly onto them. It makes no more sense to ask when in antiquity "fiction" was invented than "economics," "stress management," or "technology." More than this, however, fiction is a cultural universal, and storytelling is an intuitive human activity; all cultures have, and always have had, a developed sense of the power of fictive creativity. All literature is to an extent fictional. Its social and aesthetic role may shift at different times, as may the manner of its presentation, but there is—I suggest—never a point in any culture's history when fiction is "yet to be invented."

At the same time, however, literature does have its own history, and certain practices and constructions come into (and indeed out of) focus at certain times. Literary history, moreover, is not simply about the discovery of new techniques, genres, or conceptual apparatuses; it also has an embodied, physical, institutional history. For example, in the Greek world, shifting conceptions of literature are bound up with the changing relationship between orality and the book,[7] with the emergence of an archival culture in Hellenistic Alexandria (building on foundations laid in Athens), and with wider shifts in the political culture of the Greek world.[8] So while, as we have said, fiction is not "invented" like the process of uranium enrichment or "discovered" like the moons of Jupiter, it should be possible to track its changing inflection throughout Greek literary history.

In this chapter, I aim to describe how prose fiction emerged as a marked category through the classical and Hellenistic periods. In so doing, I am deliberately avoiding the familiar questing after the "precursors" of the Greek novel. The novel as conventionally understood—that is to say, the romance form as practiced by Chariton, Xenophon of Ephesus, Achilles Tatius, Longus, Heliodorus, and various fragmentary writers—is almost certainly a product entirely of Roman times.[9] The formative work of modern scholarship on Greek prose fiction—still subtly influential—was Erwin Rohde's *Der griechische Roman und seine Vorläufer* (The Greek novel and its forerunners), first published in 1876.[10] Rohde's interest lay primarily in the imperial romance, a phenomenon he sought to explain by revealing its "forerunners" in the Hellenistic period: principally erotic poetry and prose travel narrative. The novel, in his view, was the hybrid offspring of these two Hellenistic forms. Rohde's work inspired a number of other attempts to locate the

---

7. Here Karen Ní Mheallaigh's forthcoming book on Lucian and fiction is keenly anticipated.
8. I attempt to follow many of these threads in Whitmarsh 2004a.
9. See Bowie 2002a, which places the earliest novels in the first century C.E.; there is also much useful discussion in Tilg 2010, 36–78.
10. Rohde 1876, which I cite below from the 1960 reprint of the third edition (1914).

origins of the imperial romance,[11] but in general this kind of evolutionary narrative has fallen out of favor.[12] There are, however, two consequences of his argument that are still with us. The first is a general reluctance to consider Hellenistic prose narrative on its own terms. Despite a number of studies of individual works,[13] scholars of ancient fiction have generally been too fixated on the paradigm of the imperial romance to acknowledge the existence of any culture of Hellenistic fiction. If, however, we cease to view Hellenistic prose culture teleologically—that is to say, simply as a stepping stone en route to the novel—then we can begin to appreciate a much more vibrant, dynamic story world, which we can understand on its own terms. As we shall see below, there are indeed elements of continuity between Hellenistic prose and the imperial romance, but the novel also marks a real break from its Hellenistic predecessors (see particularly chapter 2).[14]

The second fallacy I wish to identify is the belief that Greek culture was insulated from non-Greek influence. A veiled racism drives Rohde's project, which seeks to defend the novel against the charge (as he saw it) of Eastern influence; like his friend Friedrich Nietzsche, he was keen to distinguish the idealized Greek *Geist* from the corrupting effects of the East, which culminated in the success of Christianity. "What hidden sources," he asks programmatically (but, it turns out, ironically), "produced in Greece this most un-Greek of forms?"[15] The identification of echt Hellenistic precursors allows him to preserve the Greekness of this superficially "un-Greek" form. Of course, few nowadays would formulate their views like this. Nevertheless, scholars of Greek tend (understandably) to emphasize Greek sources and hence tacitly to exclude the possibility of cultural fusion.

This chapter is principally designed to contest both these assumptions. The first half argues against the retrojection of anachronistic concepts of fiction, proposing that we should instead look for challenges to dominant modes of narrative authority (conveyed particularly through the genres of epic and history). The second claims that frictions both within Greek culture and between Greek and other cultures energized Hellenistic narrative.

ANCIENT FICTION?

The category of fiction is not only philosophically complex but also culture specific: each society, in each historical phase, has its own way of conceptualizing narratives that are accepted as not literally true but as vehicles for a kind of moral

---

11. Lavagnini 1921; Giangrande 1962; Anderson 1984.
12. Especially in light of the influential critique of Perry 1967, 14–15.
13. E.g., Lightfoot 1999 on Parthenius; Brown 2002 on Conon; Winiarczyk 2002 on Euhemerus.
14. See further Whitmarsh 2005b on the specific nature of the imperial romance.
15. Rohde 1914, 3.

or cultural truth. Fiction, as I see it, is not a linguistic pathology but primarily and most fundamentally a way of expressing a culture's view of the logic of the cosmos in narrative form;[16] it is, hence, responsive to changing ideas around the nature of the cosmos and humanity's place within it.

Although eternally aware of the potentially fictive properties of all discourse, Greeks only rarely acknowledged fiction as a genre: partial exceptions can be found in forms of rhetoric and New Comedy (discussed below), but it was not until the emergence of the novel in the imperial period that one particular literary form became definitively fictive.[17] In the Archaic, classical, and Hellenistic periods, on the other hand, literary "fictions" were rather communicated through established narrative forms that hovered ambiguously between truth and falsehood.

From the earliest times it was accepted that poetry could mislead as well as pronounce authoritatively. Hesiod's Muses know how to tell "lies like the truth," as well as the truth (*Theogony* 27). A similar phrase is used of Homer's Odysseus (*Odyssey* 19.203), who prefaces his narration to the Phaeacians with a reminder that he is "famous among all for my deceptions" (9.19–20). Lyric poetry from Archilochus to Pindar is also full of reflections upon the truth status of stories and myths.[18]

The fifth century, however, saw a set of cultural developments that increased consciousness of fictitious narrative.[19] When drama emerged as a major form in the fifth century, it too became a prime site for exploring questions of truth and fiction. The Sicilian Sophist Gorgias famously claimed that in tragedy "the deceiver is more just than the nondeceiver, and the deceived wiser than the undeceived" (fr. 23 DK). Drama also presents the earliest examples of what critics would later call plasmatic narrative: that is to say, stories based on neither historical nor mythical but on invented characters and events.[20] This kind of plot can be found in mime and even occasionally in tragedy (see, e.g., Arist., *Poet.* 1451b), but is most prominent in comedy. Old Comedy often blends real figures (e.g., Cratinus's Pericles or Aristophanes's Cleon) with fictional and uses scenarios that are fantastical distortions of contemporary reality. Hellenistic New Comedy, however, is based entirely around invented figures and (at least after Menander) set in a hazy, idealized version of the democratic city.

Comedy is thus one preimperial literary genre that consistently handles people and events that are—and are recognized by the audience as—entirely conjured from the author's imagination. The boundaries between fictive and "real" worlds

---

16. Pavel 1989; Newsom 1988; Currie 1990.
17. Morgan 1993, 176–93; similarly Schirren 2005, 15–37.
18. Pratt 1983; Bowie 1993.
19. Finkelberg 1998; Rösler 1980, although the connection between textuality and fiction seems less direct than he claims.
20. Sext. Emp., *Adv. gramm.* 1.263; for Latin versions, see *Rhet. ad Her.* 1.13; Quint., *Inst.* 2.4.2; see further Barwick 1928.

are constantly and knowingly traversed: for example, in the *parabaseis* of Aristophanic comedies (when the chorus "steps aside" and addresses the audience directly), or in the scene in the same poet's *Women at the Thesmophoria* where interjections relating to the here and now punctuate Euripides's and Mnesilochus's attempts to conjure the world of Euripides's *Andromache*.[21] Another case is rhetoric: the scenarios of invented declamatory exercises (*progymnasmata* like Lucian's *Tyrannicide* and *Disowned*), acted out by a speaker who adopts the persona of another (a prosecutor, defendant, or famous figure from the past), involve impersonation and make-believe.[22] Both set-piece rhetoric and comic drama are indeed, as has long been acknowledged, key intertextual reference points for the imperial romance, invoked as literary precedents.[23]

Whether such dramatic and rhetorical acting actually constitutes fiction, however, is a matter of definition. Certainly the reader is contracted into a willing suspension of belief concerning the text's veracity, but that fictionality may be said to be a coefficient factor rather than central to the text's purpose. Yet it pays, as we have already said, to remain aware that fiction is not an ontologically solid quality that either is or is not in a text. If (as I have claimed above) all literature contains an element of fictionality, then the history of fictionality is also the history of literature. That, clearly, is beyond the scope of a humble chapter, so for the present purposes, I will concentrate instead on narrative forms, particularly prose narrative. In fictional prose narrative, we might say, the fiction is embodied in the discourse itself rather than the performance. In drama and rhetorical logography, the founding "untruth" is perhaps the act of impersonating another: the fictionality flows from the brute disjunction between a performer with a real identity and the identity he claims. This is the case particularly, but not exclusively, when such texts are received through oral performance, a scenario that allows for complex "disjunctural" effects, such as in the famous case of the actor Polus, who carried his own son's ashes when performing in Sophocles's *Electra*.[24] Fictional narrative, however, operates in a very different way: there is no disjunction between true and false identities, because (with the partial exception of the author)[25] such texts contain no true identities at all. This distinction is, avowedly, slippery, especially when we accept that narrative forms sometimes may have been accessed through public recitation—that is, through a form of impersonation. But without wishing to shut

---

21. Ar., *Thesm.* 871–928.
22. Webb 2006, especially 43–44; Van Mal-Maeder 2007 explores the fictionality of the declamations while resisting the temptation to see them as genetic ancestors of the novel: see pp. 115–46.
23. Fusillo 1989, 43–55, 77–83; Whitmarsh 2005a, 86–89; see, however, Van Mal-Maeder, previous note, for reservations.
24. Aul. Gell. 6.5.1–8.
25. See ch. 4.

off such avenues for future investigation, I shall for now keep the focus centrally on the fictional narrative book, which defines its fictionality in a distinctively absolutist and discursive way.

Epic and Fiction

Preimperial fiction, understood in this way, emerges not as a freestanding category but as an ontologically ambiguous subcategory of existing narrative forms. Of these, the most evident is traditional hexameter epic. I wish to turn now to consider briefly the reception of Hesiod and Homer from the classical into the Hellenistic period. Their poems became particular targets of scorn in the early classical period, when the so-called Ionian revolution shifted the burden of cosmic explanation from mythical narrative to physiological speculation. Xenophanes (early fifth century) mocks epic "inventions [*plasmata*]" about centaurs (fr. 1.22 DK) and naïve anthropomorphisms (frs. 13–14 West), chiding Homer and Hesiod for their depictions of divine immorality (frs. 10–11 West). Heraclitus too castigates his epic predecessors vigorously (frs. 42, 56–57, 105, 106 DK). This process of decentering the cultural authority of epic continued within the philosophical tradition, most notably in Plato's famous critiques (in *Ion* and especially *Republic* II–III and X).

Much of the anxiety, as the above examples show, focused on the role of the gods, who were held to behave in ways that were either unbecoming or incredible.[26] For some ancient writers, the Homeric gods themselves were fictions. In a dramatic (perhaps satyric) fragment of the late fifth century, Critias or Euripides has Sisyphus claim that "a shrewd and thoughtful man" invented the gods, in order to terrify other humans into social conformity (fr. 19.11–13 *TGrF*). Whether this heretical belief was disproved later in the narrative we do not know, but it is clearly designed to reflect (or refract) contemporary Sophistic beliefs, mimicking the patterns of social-constructionist anthropological etiology elsewhere attributed to Prodicus and Protagoras.[27]

This form of theological debunking is most fully realized in a Hellenistic text, the *Sacred Inscription* attributed to Euhemerus of Messene (early third century B.C.E.; discussed more fully in "Imaginary Worlds" below and in chapter 3), which survives principally in summary via books 5 and 6 of Diodorus of Sicily.[28] The author claims to have visited the Panchaean Islands (supposedly off the eastern coast of Arabia), where he saw a golden pillar inscribed with the deeds of Uranus, Cronos, and Zeus, three Panchaean kings (Diod. Sic. 6.1.7–10). The Greek gods were, it transpires, originally historical mortals, who were accounted gods because

---

26. Feeney 1991.
27. *P.Herc.* 1428 fr. 19, with Henrichs 1975, 107–23; Plat., *Prot.* 320C–323A.
28. Testimonia in Winiarczyk 1991; discussion in Winiarczyk 2002.

of Zeus's great achievements. As I argue more fully in chapter 3, the Euhemeran narrative predicates its sense of its own status as a fictional text on a knowing, intellectualized tradition of commentary on Homeric and Hesiodic misrepresentations, particularly of the gods.

This kind of fiction thus emerges as reflexive rather than autonomous, nesting as it does in the periphery of the epic tradition. The *Sacred Inscription* is in one sense the least "Euhemeristic" of such mythological rationalizations, if we take that label to point to the careful sanitization of traditional myth so as to exclude implausible elements.[29] It does not deal at all, so far as we can tell, with the explication of Homeric and Hesiodic narrative; the travels of Zeus related on the inscription proper are not presented as the kernel of truth underlying traditional mythology. But there were plenty of other writers engaged in the project of stripping away poetic embellishment. Already in the celebrated opening of Herodotus we find the stories of the thefts of Europa, Helen, Medea, and Io presented in a pared-down, "realistic" mode (1.2.1–1.5.2). In an equally famous passage, Thucydides scales back the Greek expedition to Troy, arguing that while it may have been the largest up to that point, it was considerably smaller than anything in his own time (1.10). Significantly, Thucydides here makes mention of the principle of poetic exaggeration: "It is likely that, being a poet, he [Homer] adorned [*kosmēsai*] his poetry with a view to magnification [*epi to meizon*]" (1.10.3; see too the following section). This is an early example of the prose "position statement," marking the rivalry between prose and verse as veridical genres.[30]

Herodotus and Thucydides were aiming at communicating a type of truth—even if, in Herodotus's case at least (see the following section), in a strikingly polyphonic medium. We cannot, however, assume this of all such "rationalists." It is extremely difficult to assess the tone of, for example, Palaephatus (possibly fourth century B.C.E.), whose jejune narrative style and simplistic procedure can, depending on one's vantage, seem either naïve or ludic:

> They say that Diomedes's mares were man-eating. How laughable! Horses eat hay and barley, not human flesh. The truth is as follows. In ancient times, people labored for themselves and got food and wealth by working the land themselves. But one man started to rear horses. He took pleasure in these horses up until the point when he lost his possessions. He sold them all and used the money to feed his horses, so his friends started to call these horses "man-eating." That is was happened, and the myth was generated thereby. (7)

---

29. Winiarczyk 2002, 136.
30. See ch. 12.

The word *laughable* discloses the stakes: what version of the story we choose to believe will determine whether we laugh with or are laughed at. But is this radical banalization of the Diomedes legend not in itself ludicrous? Certainly the pretext has something of an Old Comedy plot about it: Aristophanes's *Clouds*, notably, centers on the ruinous state of the household thanks to Pheidippides's obsession with horses. But while it is always attractive to posit a hypersophisticated, self-deconstructive motive that will rescue a text like this from its own apparent inconsequentiality, there are no explicit triggers: it is invariably possible to read Palaephatus, as indeed most people have, as a simple monomaniac. Yet as I have hinted above and argue at greater length in chapter 3, the *Sacred Inscription* seems different: there is every reason to believe that the original text was avowedly and playfully fictional. This seems to go too for the work of Euhemerus's successor Dionysius "Scytobrachion" (The leather arm), who in the second century B.C.E. composed prose versions of the Argonautic and Trojan events shorn of mythological apparatus.[31] In both cases, as far as one can tell from the fragments and summaries that survive, there is a playful tension between claims to narrative realism and the outrageously bathetic treatment of canonical myth.[32]

Further challenge to the veridical authority of epic came from the development of forensic oratory, beginning in fifth-century Athens. Particularly critical was the role of "plausibility [*to eikos*]": invoking or impugning the credibility of a particular account was a way of buttressing or assailing a speaker's trustworthiness.[33] Rhetoric opened up a new language for assessing narrative: Do we believe Homer's version of affairs? Is he a credible witness? Questions of narrative plausibility thus become central to literary criticism (they are famously prominent in Aristotle's discussion of tragic plotting in the *Poetics*). These debates persisted into the Hellenistic period. In the early third century, the scholar-poet Callimachus protests that "the ancient poets were not entirely truthful" (*Hymn to Zeus* 60) in their account of the gods' drawing of lots for Heaven, Earth, and Hades: "It is plausible [*eoike*] that one should draw lots for equal things," not on such asymmetrical terms (ibid., 63–64).[34] Later, in the first century C.E., Dio Chrysostom would argue that Troy was not captured, making heavy use of the criterion of *to eikos* in his argument (11.16, 20, 55, 59, 67, 69, 70, 92, 130, 137, 139). Were such rhetorical confabulations promoted in the intervening Hellenistic period? We can, appropriately enough, appeal only to plausibility.

---

31. *FGrH* 32; Rusten 1982 adds three other fragments. For the influence of Euhemerus see Winiarczyk 2002, 139–42.
32. As emphasized by Rusten 1982, e.g., p. 112 (on the Libyan stories): "A work of fiction."
33. Goldhill 2002a, 49–50.
34. On the wiles of this poem see especially Hopkinson 1984.

Let us return to late-fifth-century Athens. The decentering of Homeric authority also allowed Sophists to begin experimenting with alternative Homeric "realities." Hippias claimed to have an authoritative version of Trojan events, based not on Homer alone but on a synthesis of multiple sources (fr. 6 DK). Gorgias, followed in the mid-fourth century by Isocrates, defended Helen on the count of willing elopement and composed a defense speech for Palamedes. Homer's most notorious woman could thus be reappraised, and a figure who does not appear in the *Iliad* could be wedged into the narrative. Sophistry also fostered a relativistic approach to storytelling. Around the turn of the fourth century, Antisthenes composed versions of Ajax's and Odysseus's speeches for the arms of Achilles. Once forensic rhetoric had permitted the idea that a single event could be narrated from multiple perspectives, then the Muse-given authority of the epic narrator ceased to be wholly authoritative.

This development allowed for the possibility of versions of the Trojan narrative told from alternative angles. The best-known examples are imperial in date: in addition to Dio's *Trojan Oration*, noted above, we also have Philostratus's *Heroicus* (see chapter 7), which impugns Homer's version of events for its pro-Odyssean bias, and the diaries of Dares and Dictys, which purport to offer eyewitness accounts of the Trojan War.[35] This phenomenon has its roots in the numerous Hellenistic prose texts attempting to establish the truth of the Trojan War, now largely lost to us: philological works such as those of Apollodorus and Demetrius of Scepsis and synthetic accounts such as those of Idomeneus of Lampsacus and Metrodorus of Chios. Other versions seem to have come closer to the fictionalizing accounts of the imperial period. Palaephatus, whom we met above, composed a *Trōika* that seems to have been full of the wonders better known from his extant *On Incredible Things*. A particularly alluring figure is Hegesianax of Alexandria Troas, a polymath of the third to second centuries B.C.E. who composed a prose *Trōika* pseudonymously ascribed to one Cephalon (sometimes called Cephalion) of Gergitha. "Cephalon" was probably not presented as a contemporary of the Trojan action, as is sometimes claimed: his account of the foundation of Rome by Aeneas's son Romus (*sic*), two generations after the war, seems to rule that out (*FGrH* 45 F 9). Nevertheless, the narrator certainly did pose as a voice from the distant past, and convincingly enough to persuade Dionysius of Halicarnassus, writing not much more than a century later, that he was an "extremely ancient" authority (*AR* 1.72 = *FGrH* 45 F 9; see also *AR* 1.49 = *FGrH* 45 F 7).

Hellenistic texts also demonstrate a different kind of relativization of narrative authority, based on the conflict between local traditions. Callimachus's *Hymn to*

---

35. On this trend in imperial literature see especially Kim 2010a.

Zeus begins by noting the clash over Zeus's birthplace between two versions, the Cretan and the Arcadian. The poet professes himself "in two minds" before deciding on the Arcadian version on the grounds that "Cretans are always liars" (4–9). The rejection of the "lying" tradition does not by itself guarantee that the other is true; in fact, the more emphasis one places on partiality in traditional narrative, the less likely it becomes that any of it is true. "May my own lies be such as to persuade my listener!" (65), the Callimachean narrator expostulates when contesting the story of the divine drawing of lots, discussed above. A dense and cryptic wish, to be sure, but hardly one that strives to conceal the fictiveness of mythological narrative.

Let us note finally in this section that the poet Callimachus represents a rare intrusion into this predominantly prose landscape, and even he is adopting a prosaic voice at this juncture. This kind of fiction is intimately bound up with the questioning of verse and, in particular, epic's claims to divinely inspired authority.

History and Fiction

These cultural shifts in the nature of narratorial authority also had implications for the writing of history. Prose records emerged in the fifth century out of the same adversarial climate that produced cosmologists, scientists, and philosophers: a claim to speak the truth was at the same time a rejection of the falsehoods spoken by predecessors.[36] As early as Hecataeus of Miletus (early fifth century) we find an author's programmatic assertion that he will deliver "the truth," in explicit contrast to the "many ridiculous [*geloia*] stories" told by the Greeks (*FGrH* 1 F 1a). Herodotus (1.1–5) and particularly Thucydides (1.1–22) begin with rationalized, scaled-down accounts of the Trojan War that programmatically announce each author's factual reliability. Thucydides's austere rejection of "the mythical element [*to muthōdes*]" (1.22.4) in favor of "accuracy [*akribeia*]" (1.22.2, 5.20.2, 5.26.5, 5.68.2, 6.54–55) marks his predecessors as inherently untrustworthy. Indeed, extant authors of Greek history (Xenophon, the Oxyrhynchus Historian, Polybius, Dionysius, Arrian, Appian, and so forth) do seem generally to replicate his fondness for relatively unadorned, linear narration.

Yet there was also a different tradition, stemming from Herodotus, which privileged storytelling, exoticism, and wonder (*thauma*). *Thauma* is, indeed, a key term in the history of fictional thought. Wonders occupy a peculiarly indeterminate epistemological position, between the plausible and the impossible.[37] Moreover, wonders standardly form part of a discourse of geographical otherness,

36. Lloyd 1987, 56–70.
37. Packman 1991.

located at the margins of Greek ken.[38] *Thaumata* within a narrative are culturally or physiologically exotic, or both: they thus serve as a challenge to "our" received ideas as to what is plausible and what not.

Collections of *thaumata* and paradoxes become a genre in their own right in the Hellenistic period (thanks, apparently, to Callimachus's lead): such authors as Palaephatus, Antigonus of Carystus, Archelaus (*SH* 125–29), Aristocles, Isigonus of Nicaea, and Apollonius compiled catalogues of wonderous plants, animals, and events. Wonders also played an important role in the narrative texture of the now-fragmentary fourth-century historians Theopompus, Ephorus, and Timaeus. Dionysius of Halicarnassus remarks of Theopompus that "he tells of the inaugurations of dynasties and goes through the foundations of cities, he reveals the life-styles of kings and the peculiarities of their habits and includes in his work any wondrous paradox produced by land or sea" (*Pomp.* 6 = *FGrH* 115 T20a [4]). These writers—famously excoriated by the austere Polybius (12.4a)—seem to have raised Herodotus's digressiveness (*FGrH* 115 T29–31 [Theopompus], 70 T23 [Ephorus], 848 T19 [Timaeus]) and prurience (*FGrH* 115 T2 [Theopompus], 79 T18b [Ephorus]) to new heights. Rather than seeing this habit of collecting wonders in Polybian terms, as a deficiency of seriousness, it is preferable to see it as the sign of a distinctive literary aesthetic celebrating narrative polymorphousness—an aesthetic that seems to have exerted continued influence in swaths of Hellenistic history now largely lost (composed by figures such as Eudoxus of Rhodes, Myrsilus of Lesbos, and Zeno of Rhodes) and whose influence can be seen everywhere in the imperial romance (particularly in Antonius Diogenes's *Implausible Things beyond Thule*), as well as in the *Alexander Romance* (discussed below, in "Greece and Egypt").

Allied to this textural experimentation was a willingness to embrace diverse content, including erotic narrative. Polybius's disapproving gaze also falls on a more centrally Hellenistic historian, Phylarchus (third century), whom he famously accuses of untruth and of presenting his narrative more like a tragedy than a history (2.34 = *FGrH* 81 T3). What Polybius actually means here has been vigorously debated,[39] but other sources indicate that the reference might well be to content as well as form. Phylarchus's histories certainly included erotic, and indeed mythological, narrative. The manchette of one of Parthenius's *Love Stories* (see next section), a distinctive version of the attempted rape of Daphne by Apollo, claims it derives from "Diodorus of Elaea and the fifteenth book of Phylarchus" (Parth. XV = *FGrH* 81 F 32). Plutarch attributes another of these stories (XXIII), detailing the love of Cleonymus of Sparta (third century) for his unfaithful wife Chilonis, to "Phylarchus and Hieronymus" (*Pyrrh.* 27.8 = *FGrH* 81 F 48, 154 27.9 F 14).

---

38. Romm 1992.
39. Walbank 1960.

Undoubtedly the most "romantic" of historians, however, was Ctesias of Cnidos, who served as the doctor to the Persian king Artaxerxes II (ca. 436–358 B.C.E.). Ctesias's principal compositions were the *Persian Affairs* and the *Indian History*, the former of which survives in summaries by Diodorus and Photius, as well as numerous fragments.[40] These works were known in antiquity for their scurrility and exaggeration. Plutarch in his *Artaxerxes*, while using the *Persian Affairs* as a source for his narrative, refers to the "all sorts of nonsense with which Ctesias filled his book" (1.4 = Ctesias T 11d *FGrH*), which "turns away from the truth toward the dramatic and mythical [*to muthōdes*]" (6.9 = Ctesias T 11e *FGrH*). Lucian, in the prologue to his fantastical *True Stories*, cites Ctesias as one of his literary precursors: "He wrote things about India and its customs that he had neither seen nor heard from anyone truthful" (1.3 = Ctesias T 11h *FGrH*).

The surviving testimonia on Ctesias are uniformly critical of his mendacity, but he was clearly widely read in antiquity, particularly for his orientalizing perspective on Persia and the Middle East. (If more of Ctesias survived, then our understanding of the Persian scenes in Chariton and Heliodorus would no doubt be richer.) Nor is his significance confined to this. He is our earliest known source for the story of the union between the (historical) Syrian Semiramis and the (mythical) Assyrian king Ninus (*FGrH* 688 F 1), which captivated later writers including Cornelius Alexander "Polyhistor" (*FGrH* 273 F 81) and the author of the fragmentary proto-novelistic work that modern scholars call *Ninus*, probably of the first century C.E.[41] This story clearly took on a narrative life of its own: Semiramis could be a hyperpowerful queen with divine elements, as in Ctesias, who makes her the daughter of the Syrian goddess Derceto (≈ Atargatis) and implicitly associates her with Astarte/Ištar; in the novel, she is transformed into a blushing maiden;[42] elsewhere we read that she was a prostitute who tricked Ninus out of his kingdom (*FGrH* 690 F 7, 681 F 1; Plut., *Mor.* 753d–e).[43]

Ctesias is also the source of an erotic intrigue between the Mede Stryangaeus and the Sacian Zarinaea, alluded to in a later source (ps.-Demetr., *De eloc.* 213; see also *P.Oxy.* 2230 [= *FGrH* 688 F 8b]). This story has a range of motifs that will reappear in the imperial romance: threatened suicide, a love letter, the bewailing of fortune.[44] Again, the influence on the later novels is arguably direct. Stryangaeus's letter to Zarinaea contains the phrase "I saved you—and although you were saved

---

40. Text: *FGrH* 688; see also the Budé edition of Lenfant 2004 and Stronk 2010. On Ctesias's importance in the history of fiction see especially Holzberg 1993 and Whitmarsh, forthcoming a.
41. Stephens and Winkler 1995, 23–71.
42. Billault 2004.
43. These traditions are discussed in Whitmarsh, forthcoming a.
44. Holzberg 1993, 81–82. And indeed the summary of the story preserved by Nicolaus of Damascus and, since Felix Jacoby, included among the Ctesian fragments (F 8C Stronk) is considerably more "romantic."

by me, I have been destroyed by you" (ps.-Demetr., *De eloc.* 213). Chariton and Achilles Tatius (perhaps via Chariton) seem to have picked up the phrasing in their letters of aggrieved lovers (Char. 4.3.10; Ach. Tat. 5.18.3–4).

Works like these raise difficult questions. They are not plasmatic: they deal with figures and events that already existed within the broad span of traditional records of the past. Moreover, while Lucian may cite Ctesias as a liar, and Polybius may reprove Phylarchus for mixing lies and truth, there is nothing to suggest that such texts were "fictional" at the level of contract between reader and narrator. Ancient readers presumably turned to historians for truths, even if there were discrepancies between different kinds of truth and the different narrative registers through which they were communicated. Even so, neither is this history in the Thucydidean sense, of "realist" chronological sequence and meticulous accuracy. Ctesias, Theopompus, Ephorus, and Phylarchus, in their different ways, seem rather to have privileged (what they understood as) the Herodotean tradition of thrilling, episodic narrative; they reinstated "the mythical element [*to muthōdes*]" so famously excoriated by Thucydides (1.22.4; see also 1.21.1). It is in the margins of historiography that Hellenistic prose culture developed its most vigorous storytelling.

LOCAL HISTORIES

In order to approach Hellenistic fiction, then, we need—paradoxically—to set aside the concept of fiction and turn instead to the gray areas between history, mythology, and creative storytelling, for it is here that Hellenistic culture typically locates its most exuberant narratives. I want to examine first of all the local history of cities. ("Local history" is, of course, not a coherent genre but a modern label covering everything from verifiable recent history to the fantastic mythography of origin narratives.) Such works were widely composed throughout Greek antiquity, particularly in those periods when regional identity was under pressure from larger, "globalizing" (i.e., usually imperial) forces:[45] I count in Jacoby's *Fragmente der griechischen Historiker* (*FGrH*) more than eighty-five titles from the Hellenistic period alone that allude to specific locales. Here more than anywhere, however, we are hampered by the fragmentary nature of sources. In the overwhelming majority of cases we have only brief snippets preserved in later sources, and reflecting the interests (often narrowly lexicographical) of the transmitting author.

Nevertheless, there are good reasons to focus on local history as a locus for fictional thinking. Greek accounts of the past that survive intact from antiquity are as a rule the synthesizing overviews that were too culturally authoritative for Christian late antiquity and Byzantium to ignore. Below this visible tip, however,

---

45. For this phenomenon see Whitmarsh 2010a.

lies a huge iceberg of diversity. Many of these stories may have circulated orally, whether jealously preserved as part of local culture or intermingled with more exotic stories thanks to cross-cultural traffic among travelers, traders, prostitutes, and soldiers. Oral culture is of course lost to us now, but some of its vibrancy can be detected in written texts that survive.

The political organization of Greek society was highly conducive to generating stories. Each community advanced its claims to prominence through local myths, often in the form of *ktistic* (dealing with foundation) or colonial narratives. For the classical period, the works of Pindar and Bacchylides testify to this phenomenon in abundance. Epigraphy in particular exemplifies the genuine, ongoing importance to individual cities of ktistic myth in the Hellenistic period. Far from being simply a parlor game for intellectuals, as was once thought, local myth-history was a politically important medium, through which a city might advance its particular claim to preeminence. Poets might be commissioned to add the luster of verse: Apollonius of Rhodes and Rhianus were active in this field.[46] Narratives might be inscribed on stone: an excellent example is the inscription recently discovered in the harbor wall of Halicarnassus, which connects the city's foundation with the nymph Salmacis and Hermaphroditus, "the inventor of marriage."[47] Another medium for preserving and disseminating local history was religious cult. The guides (exegetes) whose role was to explain the sacred history of epichoric cult sites are more familiar from imperial texts such as Plutarch's *On Why the Pythia No Longer Prophesies in Verse*, Pausanias, and Longus,[48] but the practice is already attested in Strabo (17.1.29) and would almost certainly have existed in the Hellenistic period.

What do these stories have to do with fiction? The first point to make is that local myths are both endowed with an intrinsic cultural authority and conceded (at least by the elite sophisticates who tend to record them) a licence to confabulate, free from the rationalist strictures of more urbane narrative. Local history is expected to be bizarre, exotic: it tolerates stories of immortal intervention, of metamorphosis, of improper passion. It is no doubt for this reason, in part, that Longus's faux-naïf *Daphnis and Chloe* (second–third century c.e.) is dressed in the garb of a local myth, as told to the narrator by the exegete of a Lesbian cult of the Nymphs.

There is also a recurrent linkage between erotic narrative and local history: sexual union seems often to betoken some kind of foundational event.[49] Consequently, a number of texts emerged that used this form as a cover for scurrillity

---

46. *CA*, 5–8, 12–18; Cameron 1995, 47–53.
47. Lloyd-Jones 1999a, 1999b.
48. C. P. Jones 2001a, and below, chapter 6.
49. Rohde 1914, 42–59.

and titillation. The most notorious example is the *Milesian Events* (*Milēsiaka*) of Aristides: "lascivious books," according to Plutarch (*Crass.* 32.3).[50] Ovid refers to Aristides in the same breath as one Eubius, "the author of an impure history" "who recently wrote a *Sybaritic Events*" (*Tristia* 2.413–16). The *Suda* also attests to such works. Philip of Amphipolis (of unknown date) composed *Coan Events*, *Thasian Events*, and *Rhodian Events*, the last of which is styled "totally disgraceful" (*Suda*, s.v. "Philip of Amphipolis"; see also Theodorus Priscianus, *Eupor.* 133.5–12).

Late-Hellenistic prose collections of local narratives (by Nicander, Parthenius, Conon, and others)[51] point to the fact that they were increasingly perceived to have intrinsic narrative interest, independent of their original (or supposedly original) function in local ideology. Such collections are often united by narrative theme: Parthenius gathers love stories (like the pseudo-Plutarchan assemblage, which is probably later in date), and other later examples include the collection of metamorphosis stories of Antoninus Liberalis. What this suggests is that local histories came to be viewed as repositories for arresting and alluring narrative, independent of their political, cultural, or religious value to their communities. Parthenius, indeed, dedicates his collection to his patron Cornelius Gallus for use in his (Latin) hexameters and elegiacs.

Local history is not "fictional" in the same way as the imperial romance.[52] Its subject matter veers from obscure mythology to central mythology to recent history, with plenty of indeterminate areas between. It is not, however, plasmatic, like the novel or New Comedy: the stories are never presented as wholly invented. Indeed, the function of the manchettes that accompany many of Parthenius's narratives is precisely to identify the sources of the stories. For these reasons, it is misleading to present local history as a genetic predecessor of the imperial romance.[53] To grasp the fictionality of local history, we need to resist, once again, conceptions of fiction that are shaped by the imperial period.

Greek and Near Eastern Narratives

The forms of local history and mythology emerging into view during this period were not just Greek.[54] We have already discussed the multiple versions of the story of the Syrian Semiramis and the Assyrian Ninus, which (for Greeks at least) stemmed ultimately from Ctesias. As the doctor of Artaxerxes II, Ctesias is likely to have had access to Persian narratives, perhaps even the "royal parchments" of

---

50. Bowie, forthcoming.
51. See Lightfoot 1999, 224–34.
52. Ibid., 256–63.
53. As, e.g., Lavagnini 1921 does.
54. On this material see Whitmarsh and Thomson, forthcoming; Whitmarsh, forthcoming a, discusses Ctesias and the *Cyropaedia* in terms of cultural bifocality.

which he makes mention,[55] and he may well have spoken the language. Similarly culturally bifocal was Xenophon, whose experiences with the mercenary army of ten thousand who fought to support Cyrus—in his rebellion against Ctesias's patron Artaxerxes—will have brought him into contact with different traditions. Xenophon's most "novelistic" work was the *Cyropaedia*, an idealized biography of the king who united the Persians and Medes. Interwoven with the central section is a subnarrative dealing with the constant, enduring love between Panthea and Abradatas, before the latter is tragically killed in battle (4.6.11–12, 5.1.2–18, 6.1.31–51, 6.3.35–6.4.11, 7.1.15, 7.1.24–32, 7.1.46–49, 7.3.2–16). Critics have rightly emphasized the influence of this episode on the imperial romance, particularly on the Persian episodes of Chariton's *Callirhoe*.[56] We also have a report in Philostratus (third century C.E.) of a work called *Araspes in Love with Panthea* (Araspes being a suitor of the Xenophontic Panthea), which (so says Philostratus) some attribute to Dionysius of Miletus but is in fact the work of a certain Celer (*Lives of the Sophists* 524). Whether this was a "novel" (as modern critics mostly assume) or (more likely, in my view) a rhetorical declamation, it shows the iconic significance of the Panthea sequence in amatory literary history. We also read of a now-lost *Pantheia the Babylonian* by Soterichus of Oasis (writing under Diocletian), which was quite probably a romance (*FGrH* 641).

Indeed, erotic prose seems to have been associated with Eastern storytelling from the very beginning. Herodotus's *Histories* begins with the intriguing assertion that Persian *logioi*—the term seems to mean something like "prose chroniclers" (see Nagy 1987)—tell the story of the Trojan War as an escalation in tit-for-tat woman stealing after the Phoenician abduction of Io (1.1–4). The Phoenicians' version, Herodotus proceeds to tell us, is different: Io left willingly, having fallen pregnant by the captain of a Phoenician ship (1.5). Whether Herodotus is accurately reporting Persian and Phoenician traditions is simply unknowable: it is possible, but it is equally possible that this represents an Orientalist mirage. The central point for our purposes, however, is that he is presenting himself as someone with access to Persian and north-Semitic cultural traditions—and also, crucially, that these traditions are preserved in a form alien to the Greek generic taxonomy, as "realist" (i.e., nonmythological) erotic prose.

The allure of glamorous Oriental eroticism remains evident throughout the Hellenistic period. The Ninus and Semiramis story was undoubtedly the most popular "Orientalist" narrative, but we can identify others. Particularly notable is the association between (particularly erotic) prose fiction and Semitic culture.

---

55. Diod. Sic. 2.32.4 = *FGrH* 688 T3, F 5; Diod. Sic. 2.22.5 = *FGrH* F 1b. On the question of the historicity of the "royal parchments" see Llewellyn-Jones 2010, 58–63; Stronk 2010, 15–25. For *diphtherai* as parchment books see Hdt. 5.58.3.

56. Perry 1967, 166–73; Reichel 2010, 425–30.

One striking example is the complex of narratives around Stratonice, the wife of Alexander's successor Seleucus, and her stepson Antiochus (later to be Antiochus I): according to the story, he fell in love with her and began wasting away; the doctor Erasistratus diagnosed the problem, and then Seleucus ceded to him not only Stratonice but also his kingdom.[57] Despite the historical characters, the main theme of the story is clearly folkloric: an inversion of the motif of the lusty older woman and the virtuous younger man, familiar from the Greek Hippolytus myth and the Hebrew story of Potiphar's wife (Genesis 39). Lucian's version strongly underlines the Semitic overtones of the story, segueing into an etiology of the cult of the Syrian goddess Atargatis at Hierapolis.[58] It looks very much as though the historical story has been blended with a Syrian myth in order to explain the distinctive nature of the Hierapolitan cult.

This interpenetration of Greek and Semitic erotic narrative is paralleled elsewhere. A certain Laetus composed a *Phoenician Events*, including accounts of the abduction of Europa and Eiramus's (Hiram's) presentation to Solomon of his daughter (together with an amount of wood—presumably Lebanese cedar—for shipbuilding; *FGrH* 784 F 1[b]). The latter story was also told by Menander of Ephesus, who was widely held (no doubt on his own testimony) to have learned Phoenician to access his sources (*FGrH* 783 T3[a]–[c]). According to the *Suda*, Xenophon of Cyprus (undatable but probably Hellenistic and perhaps Ovid's source for the relevant stories in the *Metamorphoses*) composed a *Cypriot Events*, glossed as "a history of erotic plots" including the stories of Cinyra, Myrrha, and Adonis. All of these figures are Semitic in origin and no doubt reflect Cyprus's partially Phoenician heritage. We can point also to the *Nachleben* of the Phoenician setting in the imperial romance, in Lollianus's *Phoenician Events*, and in Achilles Tatius's *Leucippe and Clitophon*.

Another erotic story that may have a Semitic source is the notorious love between the children of Miletus, either of Caunus for his sister Byblis or the reverse. The major Hellenistic versions are in the fragmentary works of the epic poets Apollonius of Rhodes and Nicaenetus[59] and the prose mythographers Parthenius[60] and Conon.[61] The Semitic case[62] is based partly on the incest motif (which superficially resembles that of the Cypro-Phoenician Myrrha narrative) and partly on the name *Byblis*, which looks like an eponym for the Phoenician city

---

57. Val. Max. 5.7 ext.; Plut., *Demetr.* 38; Luc., *DDS* 17–18; App., *Syr.* 308–27; further sources at Lightfoot 2003, 373–74.
58. Luc., *DDS* 19–27; see Lightfoot 2003, 373–402, with copious reference to Semitic parallels.
59. *CA*, 5, 1.
60. Parthenius 11, incorporating his own hexameter version, fr. 33 Lightfoot = *SH* 648.
61. Brown 2002. Sources discussed at Rohde 1914, 101–3; Lightfoot 1999, 433–36.
62. Brown 2002, 59–60.

of Byblos. It is also possible that *Caunus* is an originally Phoenician name, given that Caria absorbed Phoenician influence. (Armand d'Angour points out to me, additionally, the Phoenician town known to the author of the biblical 1 Chronicles as *KWN* [18.8].) Again, a Semitic erotic myth seems to have entered the Greek tradition; as it has done so, its etiological aspects have been gradually pared away to emphasize the erotic narrative.

A different kind of Semitic narrative hove over the Greek horizon with the translation of the Septuagint: a number of the so-called Apocrypha have been claimed as "novels" (including Esther, Susanna, Judith, and Daniel—the Greek version of which is longer than the Hebrew, having taken on a life of its own).[63] Whether Greek gentiles actually read them is difficult to ascertain: beyond the famous reference to Genesis in the treatise *On the Sublime* (9.9)—which is itself impossible to date—there is little evidence for a "pagan" Greek readership of Jewish texts. It is, indeed, hard to see how the Jewish novels could appeal directly to gentiles: they primarily express faith in God's ability to rescue his chosen people from foreign oppression. Even at the stylistic level, they manifest a certain intractability, their paratactic style (which renders the *vav* ["and"] constructions distinctive to the Hebrew language) marking their difference from "native" Greek. But direct influence is only one form of cultural contingency, and they do in fact share motifs with Greco-Roman story culture. In particular, the focus on the preservation of female integrity in the face of predatory monarchs (found in Judith and Esther) is a theme in both Latin (Lucretia) and Greek (Chariton, Xenophon, Achilles, Heliodorus) narrative.

Certainly, the Greek erotic tradition seems to have influenced Jewish narrative. Retellings of the erotic segments of the Torah by Josephus and Philo inflect them with Greek narrative motifs.[64] The convergences between Greek and Jewish are closest in the extraordinary *Joseph and Aseneth* (perhaps Hellenistic), which elaborates on the biblical story of Joseph's marriage to a young Egyptian maiden (Genesis 41:45; see also 26:20). The date is extremely controversial—estimates range from the second century B.C.E. to the fourth century C.E.[65]—but the safest guess seems to be that it is a Hellenistic Jewish text overlain with Christian material. Whatever the truth of the matter, the history of this text is clearly interwoven with the rise of the erotic novel. This narrative plays repeatedly on the substitution of erotic with righteous motifs. Aseneth is egregiously beautiful like a goddess (4.2); she is immediately stupefied by the sight of Joseph (6.1), grieves when they are

---

63. See especially Wills 1995, 2002.
64. Braun 1934.
65. Bohak 1996 argues for the second century B.C.E. on the basis of claimed links with the temple of Onias IV at Heliopolis; Kraemer 1998, 225–85, sees the work as late antique. Further discussion of this dating (and other issues) in Whitmarsh, forthcoming a; see also Whitmarsh 2012.

separated after their initial meeting (8.8), and weeps in her room that night (10.2).⁶⁶ Yet their relationship is built around not erotic obsession but pious reverence of the Jewish god. Although this text is aimed at Jews and is probably a translation from the Hebrew (it displays the same paratactic style as the Apocrypha, discussed above), it is clearly designed for a readership also familiar with the Greek literary (and particularly erotic) repertoire.

Greece and Egypt

The existence of significant Hellenistic prose stories on pharaonic themes, Egypt's prominence in the later, imperial romance, and the significance of Hellenistic Alexandria as a point of intersection between Greek and Egyptian traditions⁶⁷ have together led some to believe that the novel first developed in Egypt.⁶⁸ (Traces of narrative motifs from the pharaonic period have even been detected in imperial romances.)⁶⁹ While any crude hypothesis of a single cultural origin for the novel is unconvincing (in light of the evidence discussed above for local Greek and Semitic elements), it is clear that Egypt played an important role in the novelistic *imaginaire*.⁷⁰

Two major traditions are of critical importance. The first is that surrounding the legendary pharaoh Sesonchosis (sometimes called Sesostris or Sesoosis), credited with numerous conquests in Asia and Europe. In addition to the various historical (or quasi-historical) accounts of this figure,⁷¹ we also have three papyrus fragments that seem to derive from a "novelistic" version of his story, composed in unassuming Greek.⁷² Two are military (one names the king's adversaries as an "Arab" [i.e., Palestinian?] contingent, led by one Webelis); a third, however, is erotic, describing the handsome young king's relationship with a girl Meameris, the daughter of a vassal king. This episode does not appear in any of the "historical" versions of the narrative, and the themes of young love, wandering, infatuation, erotic suffering, and distraction at a banquet (Stephens and Winkler 1995, 262) invite obvious comparisons with the imperial romance. Thematically, the narrative resembles the fragmentary, novelistic version of the *Ninus* romance (discussed above): each deals with a great national leader from the distant past, focusing on both military exploits and erotic vulnerability.

---

66. See further Philonenko 1968, 43–48; S. West 1974.
67. Selden 1998; Stephens 2003.
68. Barns 1956.
69. I. Rutherford 2000. On the issue as a whole see I. Rutherford, forthcoming; Stephens, forthcoming.
70. Nimis 2004.
71. Hdt. 2.102–11; Maneth. fr. 34 Robbins; Diod. Sic. 1.53.
72. Stephens and Winkler 1995, 252–66.

What we are to conclude from these similarities is less clear: is *Sesonchosis* an influential Hellenistic text (or, at any rate, part of an influential but now lost Hellenistic tradition)? Or does it represent a specifically local-Egyptian, populist variant on the imperial romance? A third alternative, no doubt the safest, is to rephrase the terms of the question. "The Greek novel" and "the Sesonchosis tradition" were not monolithic and wholly independent, nor was any traffic between the two necessarily unidirectional. As in the case of the Phoenician and Jewish material discussed above, Greek narrative prose proves to be a flexible and capacious medium, able to incorporate numerous cultural perspectives.

This is nowhere truer than in relation to the most important Egyptian-centered text, the text we call the *Alexander Romance*.[73] The work survives in numerous recensions, some prose and some (Byzantine) in verse; in all, there are more than eighty versions from antiquity and the middle ages, in twenty-four languages (including Pahlavi, Arabic, Armenian, and Bulgarian). Different versions contain different episodes, sequences, and cultural priorities: the *Alexander Romance* is a prism through which cultural light is sharply refracted.

The earliest recension is referred to as A and represents a text probably compiled between the second and fourth centuries C.E. The raw materials for this earliest stratum of the complete text were, however, Hellenistic: a bedrock of (creatively) historical narrative, an epistolary novel (manifested in the various letters that dapple the text, most notably Alexander's letters to his mother Olympias, 2.23–41), and a work of Egyptian propaganda. The last is the motivation behind the identification of Alexander as the son, and hence continuator, of the last pharaoh, Nectanebo (1.1–12). The Persian invasion can thus be reinterpreted as a minor blip in the otherwise unbroken tradition of wise, powerful, and autonomous Egyptian kingship. On seeing a statue of Nectanebo, Alexander is told that a prophecy was delivered to his father: "The exiled king will return to Egypt, not as an old man but as a youth, and will beat down our enemies, the Persians" (1.34.5). Alexander's pharaonic credentials, indeed, are more deeply rooted than this. He visits monumental obelisks set up by Sesonchosis (1.33.6, 3.17.17), is hailed as a new Sesonchosis (1.34.2), and even receives a dream visitation from the man himself, who announces that Alexander's feats have outdone his own. These episodes function on two levels: Alexander is appropriated into Egyptian history, as the restorer of Egypt's self-determination, and the *Alexander Romance* presents itself as a rejuvenated version of the Sesonchosis tradition.

In the substance of the narrative, however, Alexander represents a figure with whom all peoples can identify: a wise, brave, questing prince, seeking out the

---

73. Which I cite from Kroll's 1926 edition of the A recension. Fuller discussion of the *Romance* is in Whitmarsh, forthcoming a, and below chapter 6.

edges of the earth. As so often in Greek narrative of this period, he is also a lover: a section toward the end, perhaps originally a separate romance, details his (entirely fictitious) liaison with Candace, queen of Meroë (3.18–23). Here too there is a hint that the author is weaving together different traditions: Candace lives in the former palace of Semiramis (3.17.42–3.18.1). What is striking is not so much the tweaking of the Ninus and Semiramis story (which is not as great as one might suppose: the Ctesian Semiramis did in fact visit Nubia) but the author's self-conscious concern to portray this section of his narrative as a metamorphosed version of it. If the fidelity to tradition is dubious, the negotiation of the anxiety of cultural influence is artful. The *Alexander Romance* presents itself as the summation of that tradition, outdoing each of its predecessors, just as its subject outdid all others in conquest.

Imaginary Worlds

The primary locations for such narrative confections were, then, Egypt and the Phoenician/Palestinian coast. Others did exist (e.g., the Black Sea littoral in the fragmentary *Calligone*, of uncertain date), but I want to conclude by focusing briefly on two "utopian" narratives set in imaginary worlds, the *Sacred Inscription* attributed to Euhemerus of Messene (early third century B.C.E.), mentioned above, and Iambulus's *Islands of the Sun* (ca. second–first century B.C.E.).[74] Each is preserved primarily in a summary by Diodorus of Sicily (2.55–60 and 6.1.3–10, respectively) that gives little flavor of the tone or style of the originals and moreover appropriates the content to suit Diodorus's own agenda: a universal history in which all the individual elements cohere. Euhemerus's and Iambulus's narratives are geographically similar: both involve sea journeys beginning in Arabia (via Ethiopia in Iambulus) and continuing into the Indian Ocean. It is tempting, given our discussion above, to see these journeys as self-conscious attempts to outdo the Semitic and Egyptian narrative traditions, by progressing geographically beyond.

Despite the difficulties in peering through the Diodoran fug, certain features are evident. Euhemerus, as we have seen in "Epic and Fiction," was concerned primarily to provide human, historical identities for the Homeric/Hesiodic pantheon. He seems not to have described the journey to Panchaea in any detail; the process of geographical dislocation is primarily a device allowing him to offer a perspective that is radically alternative to traditional Greek thought. In this respect, Euhemerus is a forerunner of authors like Jonathan Swift, the Samuel Butler of *Erewhon* and *Erewhon Revisited*, Edwin Abbott, Jules Verne, and Pierre Boulle.

---

74. There are useful summaries of scholarship on utopias in Holzberg 2003; see also ch. 3.

Iambulus is more difficult. Some have detected a philosophical, even political, promotion of a communist society "according to nature [*kata phusin*]."[75] Certainly the islanders "do not marry, but hold their wives in common, rearing any children that are born as common to them all, and love them equally.... For this reason no rivalry arises among them, and they live their lives free of faction, extolling like-mindedness to the highest" (2.57.1). Iambulus (or Diodorus) describes a society that embodies the ideals of Greek politics (no "faction [*stasis*]," only "like-mindedness [*homonoia*]") by following the priciples of common property laid out in Plato's *Republic*.[76] Yet the sociopolitical aspects of the island in fact receive far less attention than its bountiful nature and the extraordinary health, size, and longevity of its inhabitants. Diodorus prefaces his summary by promising to recapitulate in brief the "paradoxes" (2.55.1) found on the island, a strong signal that he, at any rate, conceived of Iambulus as a purveyor of marvels rather than a systematic political theorist. Lucian too refers to Iambulus's "paradoxes," adding that "it is obvious to everyone that he fabricated a falsehood [*pseudos*]" (*True Stories* 1). Iambulus seems to have found room enough within a supposedly veridical genre, the geographical travel narrative, to create a "fictional" work.

As recent scholarship has noted, there is an intrinsic connection in the ancient world between travel and fiction: alternative geographies are home to alternative realities.[77] Names of Hellenistic authors such as Antiphanes of Berge—who famously claimed to have visited a climate so cold that words froze in the air (Plut., *Mor*. 79a)—and Pytheas of Massilia became bywords for literary confection. It is important, however, to reemphasize that there was no firm generic dividing line between "factual" report and "fiction." The writers we have discussed in this section inhabited the same literary space as more sober geographical writers, such as Strabo—which is why Diodorus felt licensed to include such material in his own purportedly historical work.

CONCLUSIONS

This chapter has partly been about how not to write the history of Greek fiction. I have argued against linear, "smoking gun" models that seek to pinpoint moments of invention or discovery. Fictionality inheres in all literary discourse; the question to ask is thus not when it was invented but how it was differently inflected over time. In particular, it is crucial not to attempt to write the history of fiction simply by reverse-engineering the imperial romance.

---

75. See, e.g., Dawson 1992.
76. Pl., *Rep*. 449c–50a.
77. Romm 1992, especially 172–214.

I conclude with two positive observations. My first is this: the kind of fictional discourse I have traced in this chapter (and I freely concede there are other types) is intimately tied to the emergence of a prose culture built around the book, which—in contrast to earlier poetic texts whose authority was predicated on that of the inspired performer, the *maître de vérité*—places the accent more on the power of language to create its own plausible world. Plausibility—*to eikos*, this concept so closely tied to the forensic culture of the law courts—at first sight implies realism, approximation to reality (the root verb *eoika* means "I resemble"). In this sense, a plausible story is one that coheres with what we know to be true about the world in which we live, and indeed, as we have seen, much of the fictional material we have been discussing emerges from critiques of the "unreality" of traditional poetic claims. Yet there is another dimension to *to eikos*: a plausible story is also one that is internally coherent, true on its own terms. In other words, plausibility is manufactured discursively, within the confines of the narrative itself. What is at issue, when fictional worlds are being made, is not realism but a constructed reality effect. The contained world of the prose book, then, makes for an entirely different experience of fictionality than that of the performed song.

Second point. When I write of a "world-making" power, I am doing more than invoking a classic text in the modern philosophy of fiction;[78] I am also referring to the trend toward geographical relocation, moving away from the familiar urban landscapes that had served as backdrops for much earlier narrative and into spaces that were felt as exotic, whether for their distant, marginal location, for a perception of cultural otherness, or for their out-of-the-way oddity within Greece itself. This alienation of narrative setting relates to a historical process that we might call Hellenistic but in fact begins already in the fifth century B.C.E. (and the roots of which are indeed already visible in the Homeric and Hesiodic poems): a gradual mapping out of a wider *oikoumene*, and its incorporation into the Greek imaginary. A work such as Euhemerus's *Sacred Inscription* bears the same relationship to the Indian Ocean as *The Tempest* bears to the New World or *2001: A Space Odyssey* to space. Narrative fiction has assumed the shape of real journeys of exploration, particularly in the context of the competitive imperialism of the successor empires (and we should note that Euhemerus's expedition is explicitly cast as a voyage mandated by King Cassander of Macedon).

Yet Euhemerus's phantasmatic projections of other worlds represent only one variety of prose fiction's encounter with the other, and should not be generalized. Greeks did not merely peek at other peoples over the crenellations of their own cultural traditions. The prose literature of (particularly but not exclusively) the postclassical period also represents genuine contact zones, spaces where Greek,

---

78. Pavel 1989.

Egyptian, and Semitic discourses can hybridize to yield new, distinctive forms. The works discussed in this chapter do not simply rehash barbarian stereotypes. Rather, people with an impressive range of cultural competence composed them: figures like Ctesias, Laetus, Alexander Polyhistor, and the authors of *Joseph and Aseneth*, the *Alexander Romance,* and *Sesonchosis*. Matters, indeed, become still more interesting when the empire starts (to borrow Salman Rushdie's phrase) "writing back," when Semitic and Egyptian peoples begin to compose in Greek and insert their own priorities and values into the Greek literary tradition. Although (as we shall see in chapters 13 and 14) there certainly were Jewish poets, it is striking that prose fiction, with its in-built attraction to other worlds, proved the most fertile space in which to explore this particular variety of colonial encounter.

2

The Romance of Genre

The previous chapter sought to sketch a large-scale narrative of the development of Greek prose fiction, a venture that involved setting aside the paradigm of the "imperial romance." Cultural history cannot proceed by reverse engineering: we cannot comprehend ideas of fiction in the classical and Hellenistic periods if we view them simply as proleptic of later developments. That is teleological thinking of the most unhelpful kind. The previous chapter, then, sought to provide a narrative with no metanarrative, in which developments occur locally and adventitiously rather than according to some higher plan.

This book as a whole is about experimenting with precisely that kind of decentering motion. If we adjust the parameters, if we rewrite some of the received "certainties," if we explore alternative literary genealogies, what kind of picture do we come up with? Yet while my interest elsewhere in the book is exclusively in the noncanonical, it seems unthinkable to present an account of prose fiction that ignores the imperial romance.[1] In this chapter I consider how this particular galaxy might be located within the complex firmament of Greek fiction. There is, I believe, an answer to this question. But the crucial point (in view of the themes of this book) is a larger one, which should be borne in mind throughout: among Greek fictional texts the coherence of the romances as a body of texts is an exception rather than the norm.

Whatever phrase we use—my *imperial romance* corresponds to others' *ideal novel, ideal romance*, or even just *Greek novel*—there is little ambiguity as to what we are talking of. Almost all scholars recognize a discrete grouping of texts, within the wider field of the ancient novel, consisting of the five surviving Greek prose

---

1. I return to the romance, from a different perspective, in ch. 8.

romances: Xenophon of Ephesus's *Anthia and Habrocomes*, Chariton's *Callirhoe* (both probably first century C.E.), Achilles Tatius's *Leucippe and Clitophon* (probably second century C.E.), Longus's *Daphnis and Chloe* (second or perhaps early third century C.E.), and Heliodorus's *Charicleia and Theagenes* (probably fourth century C.E.); there are also a number of now-fragmentary novels such as those known to modern scholars as *Metiochus and Parthenope* and *Ninus*. Yet to be able to itemize individual examples of the form is not the same thing, as Socrates might have said, as giving an account of it. How do we know, as readers, that these texts belong to the same category? What difference does this make to the reading experience? These are the questions that I aim to address in this chapter.

Let us begin with the much-debated issue of genre.[2] For a long time it was simply taken for granted that these five surviving texts, and probably much of the fragmentary material, operate generically. All are built around an aristocratic, gorgeous, heterosexual pair, who undergo trials and separations of various kinds before being reunited at the end. Marriage plays a central role, whether at the start (in Chariton and Xenophon) or at the end (in Achilles, Longus, and Heliodorus). They are all set in a classicizing world, sometimes an explicitly classical one (in Chariton and Heliodorus). As has often been noted, moreover, the romances recycle a number of set-piece topoi: love at first sight (preferably at a festival), separation, kidnap by pirates, intense experience of conflicting emotions, the false appearance of death (*Scheintod*), courtroom scenes.[3] Further evidence for genericity can be sought in the titling conventions, which (I have argued) take a distinctive form: "Events concerning [*ta kata* or *ta peri*] *x* girl," or more usually ". . . *x* girl and *y* boy."[4]

---

2. For recent sharp discussion of the genre question (discussed in more detail later) see Goldhill 2008 and Morales 2009.

3. Létoublon 1993 offers a full catalogue.

4. Whitmarsh 2005b. The recent Loeb editor of Xenophon and Longus accepts my arguments (Jeffrey Henderson 2009, 200). Tilg 2010, 2 n. 1, by contrast, declares himself "not convinced" but offers no explanation or counterargument. Henrichs 2011 also registers some skepticism, but his grounds do not seem secure. His claim at 308 n. 23 that I do not "distinguish adequately between pre-Byzantine and Byzantine conventions of quoting or fabricating such titles" is, I think, misleading, since the principal evidence is securely ancient—the texts themselves (e.g., the endings of Chariton and Heliodorus), as well as *P.Mich.* 1, a second-century papyrus of *Callirhoe*, which carries a colophon: "tōn peri Ka[llirhoēn / diēgēm[a]tō[n logos b'." I do not deny that *Ephesiaka* and *Aithiopika* were fully integral to the titles of Xenophon and Heliodorus, but here they were used in conjunction with the name formula; nor, incidentally, do I deny that certain kinds of nonromantic fiction such as Petronius's *Satyrica* and Lollianius's *Phoenicica* had titles only of this form (see Henrichs 2011, 314–15, with n. 37, where a casual reader might deduce that I have not accepted this point). My claim is rather that the romances really are in a category of their own vis-à-vis other works of ancient fiction when it comes to titling conventions and (I hope to make clear in this chapter) to other features. Henrichs's claim that Lollianus's *Phoinikika* is "the one attested title" (314) is contradicted by *P.Mich.* 1 (quoted above), which he himself elsewhere accepts as transmitting Chariton's correct title (311).

Because of the relative consistency of the form over some three hundred years, critics have sometimes presented the generic identity of the romance in terms of adherence to a schematic narrative template.[5] This approach, however, risks downplaying the degree of variation. Each of the surviving five romances is actually very different: if Chariton, quite possibly the earliest, represents the "norm," then Xenophon contrasts with his low-grade style, Achilles with his first-person narrative and emphasis on gore and lechery, Longus with the pastoral setting, and Heliodorus with his sanctity and African location. With repetition of narrative motifs, moreover, come improvisation and variation too: so, for example, Longus's miniaturized pastoral romance has a failed kidnapping in which the abductors do not make it out of the bay (1.30.2), while Achilles's exuberantly over-the-top text features three different false deaths (each of which his credulous protagonist and narrator believe in), and so forth. Genres are not schematic; more recent commentators have, instead, preferred the language of "family resemblance," a Wittgensteinian term first applied to genre theory by Alastair Fowler in 1982.[6] Members of a family are often visibly identifiable as related without sharing identical features; the same model might be used for the romances. The family analogy is also useful in that it gives a role to genetic admixture. Families, if they are not entirely incestuous, propagate themselves by mixing in new DNA; similarly, new texts within literary genres show difference as well as sameness.

This model, however, raises new problems. Families are social constructs rather than straightforward mirrors of biological truth: not all children are the natural offspring of those whom society recognizes as their fathers and mothers. Similarly, identifying the "ancestry" of literary texts can be a more complex issue than it initially appears. This is all the more so in relation to the imperial romances, which are radically intertextual, cannibalizing other forms voraciously: they absorb features from classical epic, tragedy, historiography, New Comedy, rhetoric, lyric, and so forth. What is more, they have numerous points of contact with other "nonclassical" varieties of contemporary literature: a case in point are Christian martyrologies, which often follow a similar pattern of quasi-erotic infatuation leading to obstacles and challenges and finally redemption (although in the self-denying world of early Christianity, it is death rather than sex that marks

---

5. E.g., Holzberg 1995, 9: "Such fixed notions meant that, within the framework of the story, their choice both of individual motifs and of the various devices by which these were to be represented followed an almost stereotype pattern.... The mere presence of elements which are recurrent in all examples of this literary form itself also provides a basis for our attempt to define the genre." See also Lalanne 2006, 47: "All the Greek romances tell the same story of love and adventures, with variations that (for all their number) do not affect the structure as a whole."

6. A. Fowler 1982, followed by, e.g., S. Heath 2004. For the general point see, e.g., Reardon 1991, 3: "Romance will not necessarily follow a recipe, rather it will exhibit typical features."

the telos).⁷ For some, the romance's innumerable points of literary reference point to an absence of coherent generic identity. For Steve Nimis, for example, the romance is "anti-generic, unable to be specified as a single style of discourse."⁸ Helen Morales has recently developed this claim at greater length. "The evidence that we have suggests that there was no 'traditional genre' of the ancient novel," she argues, using Anders Petterson's phrase denoting "a type of literary work which is generally recognised within a culture, as a special type of work."⁹ Rather than defining genre in formalist terms, she argues, we should be viewing the "novel" as an "imaginative mode" with various recurrent features: a concern with boundaries and limits, an attempt to map out morality, an opposition between chastity and prostitution. A "'novelistic' mode of imagination is one that both heightens and exaggerates things, that simultaneously reveres and degrades women, and that suggests that the domestic . . . as opposed to the mythic is a place for the instauration of significance."¹⁰ Once we view "the novelistic" in this way, then we can begin to see new points of connection with, for example, Nonnus's *Dionysiaca* and Musaeus's *Hero and Leander*, and with Roman declamations.

This approach, I think, offers both opportunities and risks. Opportunities, because it challenges the misleading view that genres are somehow ontologically nonnegotiable, a view that the disciplinary practices of the modern academy perpetuate. How many undergraduate courses on the ancient novel include Seneca the Elder, Christian martyrology, and Nonnus? Yet as Morales rightly observes, there are all sorts of points of contact between these different works, and a rich cultural history of the imperial age would need to map out the contraflowing traffic between these many different types of text. That very formulation, however, points to the problem: we need to account for difference as well as identity, for it is intuitively implausible to imagine that ancient readers would turn from Longus to a declamation to a hexameter epic without registering any generic jolt. It might be countered that this jolt occurs because of the generically determined nature of declamation and epic and not of novel/romance, which lacks decisive formal (e.g., epic's meter and diction) and contextual markers (e.g., a sophistic auditorium, in the case of declamation). Here I would agree up to a point: novelistic writing in general is uniquely fluid and multifarious, generically speaking. But within the broad category of "the novelistic," the romance is, I think, coherently generic. This, indeed, is precisely why we can feel the hybridity of an erotic epic like Musaeus's *Hero and Leander*, which imports motifs (and the titling convention) from the

---

7. See now Konstan 2009.
8. Nimis 1994, 398. Fusillo 1989 tracks the romances' many intertextualities; see also Zimmermann 1997.
9. Morales 2009, 9–10.
10. Ibid., 10–11.

romance:[11] the effect depends on the reader's ability to perceive that process of generic cross-pollination, which itself implies an awareness of romance as a distinct literary identity. My argument, then—yet to be fully substantiated—is that Morales is right about "the novelistic" as a general category, but that romance operates according to tighter generic rules. This does not mean that there are no ambiguous cases: clearly Iamblichus's *Babyloniaca*, for example, was a heterosexual romance but also a radical experiment in setting and content (and length). But as with *Hero and Leander*, the fact of the *Babyloniaca*'s generic experimentation reinforces the argument that there was a genre to experiment with.

My discussion above has, in fact, effected a small but significant shift in definition. What Morales resists, quite rightly, is a conservative, rigid, formalist conception of genre. Yet genre should not be thought of in this way, as an intrinsic property of individual texts, like a gene that can be sequenced; it is, rather, a relationship between texts, a relationship invoked for specific, tactical reasons and to shape the reader's literary reception of the work in question. It is—this is Fowler's central point—a communicative device rather than a classificatory one.[12] Indeed, it might be said that genre is essential to all human communication, to the extent that (as Mikhail Bakhtin argued) speech has its own genres, each with their own sets of expectations that can be met, intermixed, flouted, or rewritten (greeting, thanking, joking, etc.)[13] Literature, in a similar but arguably much more complex way, rests on a contract of accepted rules between author and reader: a contract that is unwritten, certainly, and can be reneged on or rewritten, but is always there. It is this contract that dictates whether a particular action or utterance within a text is received as *vraisemblable* or transgressive. "Our intuitive sense of this *vraisemblance* is extremely powerful," writes Jonathan Culler. "We know, for example, that it would be totally inappropriate for one of Corneille's heroes to say, 'I'm fed up with all these problems and shall go and become a silversmith in a provincial town.' Actions are plausible or implausible with respect to the norms of a group of works."[14] Corneille's fed-up hero would be acting in much the same way as a real-life person who, when offered a hand to shake, responded with a punch to the belly: both would be in effect breaching a generic contract (or perhaps in the second case refusing to accept one).

---

11. For the influence of Achilles on Musaeus, see Kost 1971, 29–30, and more fully Lehmann 1910, 12–25; also Morales 1999, 42–43, and Bowie 2003, 95, both with further references. Orsini 1968, xv–xvii, also discerns the influence of Chariton. The generic affiliation to the novel suggested by the title is noted by Kost 1971, 117–18; Schmid at Rohde 1914, 618; Hopkinson 1994, 138; Whitmarsh 2005b, 603.
12. A. Fowler 1982.
13. Bakhtin 1986.
14. Culler 1975, 145.

Let us at this stage dispose of a potential objection. It is true that extant Greek lacks any consistently attested word for designating the ideal romance.[15] In fact, there is not even any consistent word for *novel*: the best candidate, *dramatikon* (*diēgēma*) (dramatic [story]), does not appear before Photius in the ninth century C.E. and even then seems to refer to the "dramatic" aspects of the plot (sufferings and reversals of fortune) rather than to anything distinctive to this kind of text.[16] At first blush the absence of any name for or theorization of the novels or the romances would seem to support the view that the boundaries of the genre were not clearly defined. Yet we can plausibly explain the absence of any explicit label in our pre-Byzantine sources by other means. As one recent critic has observed (in the context of a different kind of argument), the labor of classification was the legacy of Hellenistic Alexandria, an earlier phase in the cultural history of Greek literature. Genre names are not attached to other innovations of the imperial period either: for example Lucian's comic dialogues and Aristides's prose hymns.[17] The absence of an attested ancient name, therefore, is not decisive, and we can proceed with the hypothesis that ideal romance thus constitutes a genre in much the same way that (e.g.) Latin love elegy does: although undertheorized in ancient criticism, indiscriminately cannibalistic in its approach to other literatures (in respect to both form and content), and tolerant of all kinds of hybridizations (e.g., Ovid's *Fasti*), it nevertheless rests on distinctive and recognizable conventions of generic *vraisemblance*.

So what is the positive evidence for a romance genre? The answer lies in the texts themselves, but we shall not find it through exhaustive itemization of *lieux communs*. The best place to look for generic thinking is, as I have already intimated, in those moments where the generic contract is transgressed: where the effect depends on perceptible refusal to meet readerly expectations or on contamination of different generic codes. Indeed, I would submit that it is here, at the borders, that generic identities are at once most securely determined and most open to revision. They are securely determined, on the one hand, in that acts of transgression reinforce our awareness of the very norms they transgress. Let's return to Culler's example of the fed-up hero of Corneille who wishes to retrain as a silversmith: this example highlights the classicizing, aristocratic conventions of action in the French tragic theater. But at the same time (this is where the revision comes in) such an instance would effectively rewrite the rules of the genre for future tragedians. Such cases of aggressively ostentatious rule breaking are relatively rare: Euripides's *Alcestis* represents one example from literary history. But minor adjustments of generic codes happen all the time: this is what makes

---

15. See, e.g., Morales 2009, 9–10; Henrichs 2011, 303–5.

16. See, e.g., *Bibl.* cod. 73 = Hld. test. IV Colonna; 87 = Ach. Tat. test. 2 Vilborg. See further Rohde 1914, 376–79; Agapitos 1998, 128–30.

17. Bowie 1994, 442.

literature fresh, nimble, and inventive rather than repetitively hidebound. And as a result, generic codes are always in process. "Every literary work," writes Fowler, "changes the genres it relates to.... Consequently, all genres are continuously undergoing metamorphosis."[18]

This, I think, is the crucial point, and it bears emphasizing. Classicists have been far too prone to assess the validity of the romance genre synchronically, as though we should be asking the same questions of the earliest texts as of the later ones. It is (to exaggerate, but only marginally) as if we were to put together a magic lantern show, *Casablanca,* and *Avatar* and ask whether the category "Hollywood blockbuster" worked for all of them. What we need instead is an account of genre that respects the diachronic fluctuations and the way in which each new novel both projects its predecessors as paradigmatic and signals its own generic reinventions.

I cannot, in the compass of a single chapter, map out this process in its entirety, but let me make some general observations and visit some particular instances. For the remainder of this chapter, I shall consider three stages in the history of the romance: the initial phase, namely Chariton's *Callirhoe* and Xenophon's *Anthia and Habrocomes;* Achilles Tatius's subversive *Leucippe and Clitophon;* and finally Heliodorus's *Charicleia and Theagenes,* the last of the surviving romances. (Longus, for present purposes, is a marginal case.) I shall proceed not with exhaustive analyses but with a few exemplary discussions of key passages.

There are two enormous questions that confront anyone considering the earliest romances. The first is "Where did they come from?" The second is "Who came first, Xenophon or Chariton?" Let us come to the first via the second, although I do not propose a conclusive answer (which would call for fresh evidence). One recent scholar, Stefan Tilg, has assembled all of the arguments and asserted strenuously that Chariton belongs in the mid-first century.[19] That may well be right, but none of the evidence is conclusive: the linguistic criteria are imprecise (and who says that Atticism spread at the same rate everywhere across the empire?), the supposed references to real people implausible, the identification of the addressee Athenagoras hypothetical, and the claimed relationships between Chariton and other first-century writers unconvincing.[20] All we can say is that one papyrus from

---

18. A. Fowler 1982, 23.
19. Tilg 2010.
20. I am in particular unconvinced that the Neronian poet Persius refers to our text at 1.134: "His mane edictum, post prandia Calliroen do"; see Tilg 2010, 69–78, which cautiously accepts the reference. I argue at Whitmarsh 2005b, 590 n. 14, that some kind of poetic text is needed to make sense of the passage, specifically a competitor to Persius's aggressive satire. It is not impossible, however, that *Calliroe* was a pantomime, a genre introduced to Rome with great fanfare under Augustus: note the story at Paus. 7.21.1 about the Calydonian Coresus, who kills himself for love of Callirhoe. There is another Callirhoe story at 8.24.9–10.

the mid-second century (*P.Mich.* 1) offers a *terminus ante quem*. The evidence for dating Xenophon, meanwhile, is even more exiguous. Far too much has been made of the apparent mention of an *eirenarch* ("the man in charge of peace [*eirēnēs*]," 2.13.3; see also 3.9.5), an office first attested epigraphically under Trajan. It should not need saying that the first inscriptional mention of such an office does not necessarily mark its first institution.[21]

It is, however, possible to model the implications, in generic terms, of imagining precedence. Let us consider the well-known fact that (among the many similarities between them)[22] the two texts open in very similar ways, with a meeting contrived by Eros between the two beautiful young people at or near a festival. The similarities of motif and even language are so close that it is unthinkable that there is no connection[23]—but what is the nature of that connection? There is in fact a long and inglorious history of scholarship exploring the question, but in a desperately naïve fashion: ultimately what is at issue is simply establishing chronological priority, which critics determine according to their aesthetic preconceptions about the process of literary succession, or—to use a particularly misleading word beloved of this kind of criticism—imitation.[24] According to most critics of this school (and indeed to romantic literary criticism, to which it is indebted), an imitation is inherently inferior to an original. The challenge is thus to demonstrate which text is consistently "better" in those areas of similarity and posit it as the prior one.

This model is evidently outdated, both methodologically and in its estimation of the romances' sophistication: nowadays we speak not of (passive) imitation but of (dynamic) allusion. The effect generated by the later text depends on the reader's ability to acknowledge the similarity and to explore the tension between generic identification and local deviation from the model. Let me take just one example, perhaps the best-known point of convergence between Xenophon and Chariton. In both texts, there is a public festival: in Xenophon the phrase is *epikhōrios heortē* (1.2.2), in Chariton *heortē dēmotelēs* (1.1.4). This in itself is not

---

21. So, rightly, J. N. O'Sullivan 1995, 4–9, and Bowie 2002a, 57. Ruiz Montero 2003 argues persuasively that Xenophon shows stylistic similarities with archaizing local legends of the kind found in the second-century pseudo-Plutarch's *Love Stories* and Pausanias, but this affinity cannot date him absolutely since we lack comparable material from earlier periods.

22. See especially Garin 1909, 423–29; Gärtner 1967, 2081–87; J. N. O'Sullivan 1995, 145–70.

23. I tabulate the similarities at Whitmarsh 2011a, 35. There is, of course, the possibility of a common shared source (so, e.g., Hägg 1983, 20–21), but this seems to me unlikely given the extent of the echoing (see above, n. 21).

24. For criticism of the romance along these lines see, e.g., Schnepf 1887; Garin 1909. For this older material, www.archive.org is invaluable, but I have not been able to access either a print or an electronic copy of Kekkos 1890. More recent criticism tends to take Chariton as the prior text (e.g., Bowie 2002a, 56–57; Tilg 2010, 85–92; but contrast J. N. O'Sullivan 1995, 145–70), but there is no real basis for this assumption.

surprising: infatuation at a festival is found widely in New Comedy, in Hellenistic love poetry (e.g., in Callimachus's story of Acontius and Cydippe: *Aetia* 1.67.6), and indeed already at Lysias 1.20.[25] But note that Chariton gives the topos a tweak. The lovers do not meet at the festival, but they bump into each other afterward: "By chance [*ek tukhēs*] the two met in a passageway at a corner and fell into each other" (1.1.6). This reorientation is, indeed, significant and programmatic: as has often been noted, Chariton tends to minimize direct divine intervention, preferring instead to offer psychological motivations.[26] If we interpret Chariton in this way, then the little phrase *by chance* takes on additional resonances. First, it is heavily ironic: the festival encounter is, of course, so far from being accidentally, instead generically predetermined. *Tukhē* (fortune), readers of *Callirhoe* will discover, is a marker of self-conscious authorial intervention in the plot.[27] Alternatively, the "accidental" nature of the collision can be read as a commentary on the misfiring topos: one would expect a meeting at the festival proper, but "by chance" they meet elsewhere.

None of this proves that Xenophon is prior to Chariton (though it is of course consistent with that claim). Chariton, indeed, could be playing with the topical status of the amorous meeting at a festival in preromance texts. But if we do hypothesize Xenophon's priority, or at least the priority of another romance featuring a festival meeting, then we can see instantly how the model of genre bending that I have been proposing may work. Chariton treats the festival encounter as characteristic of the romance *au degré zéro* and self-consciously marks his own innovation within that frame.[28]

My second example comes from Achilles Tatius, who wrote in the next generation (a second-century papyrus confirms the *terminus ante quem*).[29] In book 5 of *Leucippe and Clitophon*, the hero Clitophon—now remarried to Melite—discovers by letter that Leucippe is still alive (5.18.4–5). In a parallel episode in Chariton, as commentators have noted, Callirhoe—now remarried to Dionysius—learns from a letter from Chaereas that he is still alive (4.4.7–10).[30] Although it serves a similar narrative

---

25. Harder 2012, 2.555, gives primary and secondary sources; discussion at Whitmarsh 2011a, 37, with n. 62.

26. Weissenberger 1997; Whitmarsh 2011a, 27.

27. See Whitmarsh 2011a, 246–51, on aleatory *tukhē* versus teleological plotting.

28. Additional, albeit indirect, evidence for the connection between the festival topos and the romance genre comes from Josephus's account of the Potiphar story, where he levers in this extrabiblical detail (*Ant.* 2.45) as part of his program of eroticizing biblical narrative. See Braun 1934 on this process of *Erotisierung*; Whitmarsh 2007a, 88–89, on the passage in question.

29. *P.Oxy.* 3836, which as Henrichs 2011, 308–9, observes is now the only papyrus of Achilles that can be securely dated to the second century.

30. Hunter 1994, 1059–60. More generally on correspondences between Achilles and Chariton see Garin 1909, 433–37.

function, however, Leucippe's letter shows no signs of intertextual engagement with Chaereas's: stylistically speaking, it is ambitious and rhetorical where Chaereas's letter is sparse and pared down, following (as Konstantin Doulamis has shown) the rhetorical theorists' precepts of *saphēneia*, or clarity.[31] In terms of vocabulary and phrasing, Leucippe's letter in fact reworks and amplifies a slightly earlier passage in Chariton, where Chaereas addresses an imaginary reproach to Callirhoe. I give the two passages here in English translation, with the key similarities identified:[32]

> Thanks to you [*dia se*], I left my mother and took up a life of wandering; thanks to you [*dia se*], I was shipwrecked and put up with bandits; thanks to you [*dia se*], I was sacrificed as an expiation and have now died a second time; thanks to you [*dia se*], I have been sold [*pepramai*] and bound in iron, I have wielded [*ebastasa*] a mattock, dug the earth, been whipped—was all this for me to become to another man what you have become to another woman [*gegonas allēi gunaiki*]? Never! No, I [*egō men*] had the strength to hold out in the midst of so many trials—while you [*su de*], unenslaved and unwhipped, you are married! (Ach. Tat. 5.18.4–5)

> I [*egō men*] have been sold [*eprathēn*] thanks to you [*dia se*], have dug, have wielded [*ebastasa*] a cross and been delivered into the hands of the executioner. And you [*su de*] were living in luxury and celebrating your marriage while I was in chains! It was not enough for you to become the wife of another [*gunē gegonas allou*] while Chaereas was still alive, but you had to become a mother as well! (Chariton 4.3.10)

Now, clearly speeches and letters of reproach are to an extent generic in themselves. Powerful contrasts between one person's claims to fidelity and the other's perceived betrayal, particularly in erotic contexts, can be found all over Greek literature, for example in Medea's speech to Jason in Euripides's play (*Med.* 483–89).[33] Moreover, certain elements in Chariton's original ("egō men," "dia se") seem to allude to Stryangaeus's reproachful letter to Zarinaea in Ctesias, a fact that I shall presently argue to be significant.[34] Yet the overall density of similarities between the two passages strongly suggests that Achilles wishes his reader to bear Chariton's passage in mind and read his own against it. This in turn suggests that Achilles is identifying the "lover's reproach" as a signpost of romance genre, so his negotiations of this model can also be taken as indicators of his claimed position at once within and against the genre.

The first point to make is that Leucippe's letter is markedly more elaborate than Chaereas's monologue: it repeats "Thanks to you [*dia se*]" three times, in accordance with Achilles's taste for rhetorical and thematic overkill (compare Leucippe's

---

31. Doulamis 2002, 209–16.
32. Some of the similarities are noted by Garin 1909, 435–36, and Yatromanolakis 1990, 673. My list here is modeled on Whitmarsh 2011a, 165.
33. McClure 1999 discusses the play's remarkable preoccupation with blaming.
34. *P.Oxy.* 2330 = *FGrH* 688F8b = Ctesias fr. 8b in Stronk 2010.

three false deaths, mentioned above). Chaereas's sufferings are limited (!) to enslavement and crucifixion, whereas Leucippe is shipwrecked, delivered to bandits, sacrificed, enslaved, bound in iron, forced into manual labor, and whipped. The excess of lurid detail, inflicted on a woman, betokens Achilles's transformation of the genre into an exuberantly sexist fantasia.[35] There is more, indeed, to be said about gender. At one level, we can read Achilles's passage as a corrective of Chariton's use of Ctesias: by replacing Chariton's monologue with a letter, Achilles is being truer to his Ctesian source. The choice of a letter, then, is an implicit dig at Chariton and marker of Achilles's sophistication. But where Achilles departs from both Chariton and Ctesias is in giving the reproach to a woman. This is all the more striking in that Achilles's romance is narrated almost entirely by Clitophon, in flashback. The reproach is thus a rare occasion where as readers we hear Leucippe's voice (though mediated by Clitophon); in general she speaks very little. The force of the letter—it has a profound impact on Clitophon, who (like the incautious reader) believes her to be dead at this point—lies precisely in this irruptive power. The miraculous reanimation of Leucippe is figured by her authorship of a new text, a female-centered text protesting vigorously against the androcentric worldview of Clitophon's (and Achilles's) monopolized narrative, wherein self-absorbed males turn a blind eye to the horrendous violence inflicted on women. Leucippe's letter, then, turns out to be more than just a claim on Achilles's part of generic proximity to Chariton; it also articulates Achilles's most important revision of the genre, the limiting (more or less) of narrative authority and subjectivity to a single male.

Let me turn finally to Heliodorus—arguably the most intertextual of all the romancers, particularly in his use of other romances[36]—and once more to festival encounters. In *Charicleia and Theagenes,* the lovers again meet and fall in love at a festival, but the event is ingeniously postponed to the third book, where the narrator-priest Calasiris tells it in flashback (3.1–6). Heliodorus's account of the festival procession clearly draws heavily on Xenophon's Ephesian procession (1.2): the linguistic parallels are many and close.[37] Once more this is not simply a case of a later writer covertly recycling another's words; Heliodorus surely expects his readers to identify his use of Xenophon and to explore the dynamic relationship between the two texts. In particular, we are to register the disjunction between Xenophon's bald, terse style and Heliodorus's rich, complex description.[38] Here, by way of illustration, are the two accounts of the female protagonists:

---

35. See Morales 2004, especially 156–83, on Achilles's fantasies of misogynistic violence.
36. See Neimke 1889, 22–57, on Heliodorus and Achilles, although he wrongly posits the latter as the later "imitator."
37. Listed and discussed at Schnepf 1887, 10–14; Gärtner 1967, 2080; Whitmarsh 2011a, 117.
38. Schnepf 1887, 11, contrasts Xenophon's and Heliodorus's festival descriptions in these terms ("The one writes simply.... The other is verbose").

Heading the line of girls was Anthia, the daughter of two locals, Megamedes and Euippe. Anthia was wondrously beautiful, far beyond the other girls. She was fourteen, her body blooming with shapeliness, and her comeliness was increased by the rich adornment of her costume. Her hair was blond, mostly [*hē pollē*] free-flowing (though some was plaited), moving as the wind took it. Her eyes were gorgeous, clear like a beautiful girl's but forbidding like a virtuous girl's. Her clothing was a purple tunic [*khitōn alourgēs*], girdled [*zōstos*] and knee length, loose down the arms, with a fawn skin draped around, a quiver fitted with bows, arrows, javelins in her hand, dogs in train. (*Anthia and Habrocomes* 1.2.5–6)

[Charicleia] was conveyed on a chariot drawn by a pack of white cows, dressed in a purple tunic [*khitōna alourgon*] down to her feet, embroidered with golden sunbeams. Her chest was encircled with a girdle [*zōnēn*], which the creator had imbued with all his skill: he had never before forged such a thing, nor would he ever be able to again. [For brevity's sake I omit the long description of the girdle.] . . . Her hair was neither completely braided nor unbound; most of it [*hē . . . pollē*] fell down her neck and billowed over her shoulder and back, while the remainder, on her head and her brow, was garlanded with tender twigs of laurel, which bound her rosy, sun-colored locks and would not permit them to flutter in the breeze more than was decorous. In her left hand she bore a golden bow, while a quiver hung from her right shoulder. In her right [hand], she carried a lit torch, but in that state her eyes were blazing more light than the flames were. (*Charicleia and Theagenes* 3.4.2–6)

This example shows how Heliodorus extends and amplifies Xenophon's description, filling it out not only with extra details (the cow-drawn chariot and the twigs bound in the hair, for example) but also with narratorial commentary: the observations on the girdle's creator, for example, and on the differential amounts of light coming from the torch and Charicleia's eyes. This tactic is conscious and deliberate, as we can tell from a crucial passage at the start of book 3. Book 2 ends with the Delphians "all aflutter in their eagerness to see the magnificently arrayed procession" (2.36.2), a clear prompt to readers (and to Calasiris's internal addressee Cnemon) that they are to expect a showcase description in the following book. Book 3, however, begins, "When the procession and the entire sacrifice was over . . ." (3.1.1)—at which point Cnemon butts in and asks for a full description and to be made a "viewer [*theatēs*]."[39] The amplification of description and the focus on vivid, visual depiction are therefore highlighted before the procession proper. Heliodorus's intertextual use of Xenophon, then, implicitly casts their relationship in terms of a contest of descriptive prowess, a contest that Heliodorus of course wins. One small detail corroborates this reading. When Calasiris refers to the skill (*tekhnē*) of the artist (*ho tekhnēsamenos*) who created Charicleia's girdle, it is surely

---

39. For more on this episode and the scholarship on it see my discussion at Whitmarsh 2011a, 172–76.

a prompt to think about the process of literary creation too. In this context, the claim that "he had never before forged such a thing, nor would he ever be able to again" takes on a new light: in the context of an intertextual dialogue with a predecessor in the genre, it points to the uniqueness of Heliodorus's description at exactly the point where it is also most generic.

There is much more that could be said about intrageneric reference in the romances; a full study is needed, one moreover that moves beyond the naïve, nineteenth-century accounts of "imitation" and brings in new methodologies of allusion and intertextuality. Enough has been said, however, to show that ancient writers did work with a sense of romance as genre. Let me finish by reemphasizing the point that genre is not a static, synchronic template that can be mapped out typologically but a dynamic relationship between texts, a relationship that shifts and develops over time. Heliodorus's use of Xenophon's procession scene exemplifies this excellently. He casts as naïve, bare, and primitive the generic reference point that he invokes intertextually, but he reinvents the motif sensationally, and with that the genre itself. The genre transforms before our very eyes.

By the time when Heliodorus wrote, there was, I submit, a well-established sense of the romance genre: he could expect his readers to notice his modifications, innovations, and amplifications and interpret them as generic transformations. It is hard to find such traces of generic self-consciousness in Xenophon (although that may of course be simply because he is a less self-conscious writer). Chariton, I have argued, can already be seen to be manipulating topoi self-reflexively, but whether he sees such topoi as constitutive of romance as an independent genre is a more difficult question. The difficulty lies partly in the uncertainty of dates: if Xenophon is older, then Chariton will have had at least one romance to play with.[40] But in any case, lying behind *Callirhoe* is a rich hinterland of Hellenistic narrative erotica embedded in nonromance genres, of which only a few traces survive. Ctesias's famous story of Zarinaea and Stryangaeus, for example, was evidently an important reference point for Chariton (and hence for later romancers). When Nicolaus of Damascus, writing in the Augustan era, produced a version of it, he already larded it richly with motifs that would later be thought of as distinctive to the romance: a weepy, dispirited male threatens suicide and writes a reproachful letter to his beloved, while a counselor attempts to dissuade him from his course.[41] Whether or not he had read anything approximating to what we call prose romances, Chariton was evidently responding to this broader

---

40. Mention should also be made of the biblical romance *Joseph and Aseneth*, which some scholars (e.g., S. West 1974; Bohak 1996) date as early as the second century B.C.E. If that dating is right, some form of prose romance evidently long preexisted Chariton and Xenophon.

41. Recent books have accepted as Ctesian the five fragments of Nicolaus preserved in the tenth-century *Excerpta de virtutibus et vitiis*: for example, the Zarinaea story appears as fr. 8c in Stronk 2010.

range of narrative material as well. In other words, he is likely to have worked with a much looser and more fissiparous sense of generic identity than the later romancers did, or, to put it another way, *Callirhoe* probably became a "romance" only thanks to the co-optation of later romancers. This much is speculation, inevitably so given the uncertainties of dating and the limited amount of surviving Hellenistic prose fiction. Yet what is clear, it seems to me, is that the romance really did develop a strong sense of generic identity, and that fact sets them apart from the more amorphous body of prose fiction to which I turn in the subsequent chapters.

3

Belief in Fiction

Euhemerus of Messene and the Sacred Inscription

In this chapter I consider in more detail a figure who (as we saw in chapter 1) plays a pivotal role in the history of Greek fiction. Euhemerus of Messene is associated predominantly in the modern imagination with the rationalization of myth, of the kind that we find in the opening paragraphs of Herodotus, in Palaephatus, or in Dionysius Scytobrachion, and which may have had its ultimate roots in Hecataeus. Yet the *Sacred Inscription*[1] attributed to him seems to have had little to do with "euhemerism" in the current sense: so far as we can tell from the testimonies refracted in later sources, it made no attempt to launder traditional heroic narrative.[2] Euhemerus's narrator claimed, rather, to have found an island in the Arabian Sea, Panchaea, where a tradition survived that the figures known to the Greeks as the Olympian pantheon were in fact once mortals, whose egregious acts had led to their divination. The text centers on a heterodox anthropology of religion, promoting a particular theory of Olympian divinities (as opposed to the "eternal and

---

1. *Hiera anagraphē*, which I take to mean "sacred inscription" rather than "sacred narrative" (so Winiarczyk 2002, 17, with further references), since Diodorus refers to the inscription itself as an *anagraphē*: cf. *anagegrammenai, prosanagegrammenai,* 5.46.7 = T 37, cited below. Testimonia are cited from Winiarczyk 1991. Note too that there is divergence over Euhemerus's origin, with some traditions claiming Messene (without specifying which particular Messene) and others Acragas (T1C Winiarczyk, with the note ad loc.); elsewhere he is claimed to be Coan (Ath., *Deipn.* 14.658e–f = T 77 Winiarczyk). See most recently De Angelis and Garstad 2006, arguing for Sicilian Messene. I suggest later, however, that Euhemerus may not have been the text's author and that the confusion over his provenance may reflect his fictionality.

2. Winiarczyk 2002, 136–37.

imperishable" sun, moon, and stars) as having originated in the deification of euergetists.³

What kind of text was this, then? The religious-philosophical dimension seems undeniable. A Herculaneum papyrus shows that Prodicus had already in the fifth century B.C.E. argued for two kinds of gods, the elemental and the deified culture bringers; Albert Henrichs in particular has argued for Prodicus's direct influence on Euhemerus (and indeed their names are connected already in antiquity).⁴ It is also worth noting that Sextus Empiricus's brief account of the *Sacred History* at *Adversos mathematicos* 9.17 (T27 Winiarczyk) quotes the opening line of the famous religious anthropology of Critias's (or Euripides's) *Sisyphus*: "Euhemerus, surnamed 'the atheist,' says: 'When the life of humans was unordered...'" Even if the connection was Sextus's own rather than explicit in the *Sacred Inscription*, that itself is instructive, given that Sextus knew the Euhemeran text better than we do.

So the *Inscription* is likely to have had philosophical content. It probably had a political point too, as has long been noted: the elevation of humans to gods for their *euergesiai*, their "great achievements," seems highly likely to have spoken to the emergent practice of deifying rulers.⁵ Yet these observations tell us nothing about the genre and tone of the framing narrative. After all, Aristophanes's *Clouds* and the Aristotelean *Constitution of Athens* contain both philosophical and political content, but they are very different types of text. Let us reemphasize the question: what kind of text was this? The tendency has been to classify it generically as a "utopia,"⁶ but while there clearly was an emerging interest at the time in the description of idealized societies (a tradition that began with Plato's Atlantis and eventually led to Iambulus's *Islands of the Sun*), this label is of course not an ancient generic category, and in any case, to the extent that it has any purchase on the three texts in question, it describes (once again) content rather than form. In other words, the bare ascription *utopia* is nonspecific and (more to the point) does not begin to disclose how earnest or ludic is the presentation. More precise is the claim, which goes back to Erwin Rohde, that the *Sacred Inscription* was a utopian *novel*, a designedly fantastic romance (even if "the fabulous is reduced to a subordinate role" relative to "more serious instruction").⁷ What does

---

3. Meteorological elements as *aidious kai aphthartous*: T25 = Diod. Sic. 6.1.2.

4. Henrichs 1984; further Winiarczyk 2002, 51–52. Prodicus and Euhemerus appear together at Cicero, *DND* 1.118–19 = T14 Winiarczyk (apparently deriving from the "atheist catalogue" of Clitomachus: Winiarczyk 1976); Minucius Felix, *Octavius* 21.1–2 = T9 Winiarczyk.

5. Winiarczyk 2002, 43–69, addresses the history of this line of interpretation.

6. Giangrande 1976–77; Kytzler 1988; Colpe 1995. For a reading of Panchaea in less flattering terms see Dochhorn 2000, 288–89; analogies with the Soviet Union, however, are distracting and potentially misleading.

7. Rohde 1876, 220–24, at 224. Holzberg 2003, 621–26, discusses the "utopian novel" interpretation and concludes that the *Inscription* was "a forerunner of the utopian novel" but not necessarily a travel novel (626). See also Winiarczyk 2002, 23–25.

novel mean in this context? The assumption, though it is rarely stated, is that the label is justified by a substantial narrative element, detailing among other things the narrator's voyage to Panchaea (and perhaps back again). But as Sylvie Honigman observes in a recent article, the identifier *novel* also implies fictionality.[8] To describe the *Inscription* in these terms suggests that ancient readers would have entered knowingly into a fictional contract with the text.

How fictional was the *Inscription*? And fictional how? Honigman's argument is that, to the contrary, the text cleaved to the rhetoric of historiographical truth telling, which permitted a certain amount of elasticity for texts that conveyed general truths; it is thus a text that, while not necessarily true at the level of precise details, demands to be believed for the wider truths it encodes. Her discussion has, assuredly, taken criticism of the *Inscription* to a new level, drawing out the nexus of intertextual links to earlier literature, particularly Plato's Atlantis narrative, which (following Thomas Johansen) she takes as the prototype for this kind of "general truth" historiography. Yet it seems wrong to assume that allusion implies equivalence. Even if it were true that the Atlantis story presented no self-conscious fictionality (which seems far from self-evident),[9] it would not therefore follow that a later text that made reference to it operated according to the same principles. What is more, by limiting the framework of Euhemeran reference to historiography and (as she sees it) related genres such as the Atlantis myth, Honigman risks an etiolated account of the resonances that would have been available to readers at the time. My aim in this chapter is not, in fact, to argue straightforwardly that the *Inscription* operated in a register that was immediately identifiable as fictional, not least because (as we have seen) "fiction" was no more an immediately identifiable category in the early Hellenistic period than was "utopia."[10] Yet there are numerous hints at a more ludic reading, which will lead us to a more experimental and less normative assessment of this extraordinary text.

WHO WAS EUHEMERUS?

The matter is complicated immeasurably by the fact that we have not a single word of the original *Inscription*; everything we know about it is filtered through

---

8. Honigman 2009.

9. After all, this is a story told at the Apatouria festival (Pl., *Tim.* 21b). On the "fictional" elements in the Atlantis narrative, see notably the nuanced discussions of Gill 1973; Gill 1979; Gill 1993, especially 62–66; also K. A. Morgan 2000, 261–71, which argues that the Atlantis myth functions as a kind of "noble lying" charter myth for a philosophical Athens. Less inclined to concede fictionality overall is Johansen 2004, 24–47 ("not simply a lie" but "an illustration of a general truth," 46). Vidal-Naquet 2007 genially discusses the reception of the Atlantis story.

10. A huge topic, of course. For orientation see ch. 1.

later sources, particularly Diodorus Siculus (with extra content provided by Lactantius, who filters Ennius's lost Latin version). Diodorus, as recent scholarship has emphasized,[11] is much more an independent creative force and much less a compiler of tralatitious sources than he was once thought to be. We can test the principle with a brief sideways glance at recent scholarship on Ctesias, for whom Diodorus is again the primary source but where we have more evidence for the nature of the original. Here the tendency has been to resist the assumptions of earlier generations and to see much more of Diodorus in his account of Ctesian material.[12] By the same token, it seems dangerous to assume that Diodorus's use of the *Inscription* offers anything like a pellucid window onto the original.

So what we can say with confidence about the original *Inscription* and its author? According to Diodorus (as paraphrased by Eusebius), Euhemerus was "a friend of King Cassander and required by him to fulfill certain royal tasks and great journeys abroad" (DS 6.1.4 = T3 Winiarczyk); one of these took him to the island of Panchaea, in the Arabian Sea. Cassander was the king of Macedon from 305 to 297 B.C.E., a narrow window that dates the supposed expedition. If we are considering the date of the text's composition, this chronology evidently offers us a *terminus post quem*. It also provokes a fundamental question: are we to reckon that Euhemerus really was a historical figure in the Macedonian court? Or, to put it in crisper literary-critical terms, is the homodiegetic narrator of the voyage to Panchaea to be identified with the real-life author of the text?

This bears on the question of fictionality in a double sense. Let us first unpack some of the implications of the question that are more complex than they might initially appear. The author, of course, did not actually go to Panchaea, since the island does not exist and never has done.[13] There is, then, even at an immediate level, a separation between the flesh-and-blood author and the narrator of this imaginary visit. Of course, it is possible to argue that this level of skepticism was not available to ancient readers, who might have taken the visit at face value, but this is, in general, not borne out by the ancient reception. Diodorus, for sure, seems to take the *Sacred Inscription* as describing real space, but primarily because it fits his philosophically antitheist agenda.[14] It has been claimed that Polybius too put faith in the text's veracity, but in fact the passage in question (a testimonium preserved in Strabo) is ambiguous to say the least and in fact seems to me to imply

---

11. See especially Sacks 1990; Wiater 2006 argues that Diodorus has a cogent historiographical method.
12. Stronk 2010, 64–70.
13. On the misguided tradition of identifying Panchaea with Sri Lanka see Winiarczyk 2002, 21–22.
14. On which see Sacks 1990, 70–72.

considerable skepticism.¹⁵ There are, conversely, explicit references to Euhemeran "lies" from Eratosthenes onward.¹⁶ Honigman's explanation for this general mistrust is that the *Sacred Inscription* failed, methodologically, on two grounds: first, on the absence of external corroboration; second, in adopting a historiographically unconventional form. Both observations are true enough, but they invite the obvious, Occam's razor objection: rather than as a failed attempt to persuade, could we not take the *Inscription* as a successful attempt to discomfit?

Second, there is the deeper question of the identity of the original author. As Niklas Holzberg observes, it is quite possible that "Euhemerus" is merely the name of the fictional narrator rather than that of the historical author.¹⁷ The striking uncertainty over his provenance, we might tentatively suggest, may support this conclusion.¹⁸ That the later tradition did not distinguish the two is not in itself remarkable: as a parallel we could point to Photius's attribution of one of the *Ass* narratives to "Lucius of Patrae," the fictional narrator (*Bibl.* cod. 129 = 96b). Again, the ramifications are more complex. I argue elsewhere that the default position for the reception of Greco-Roman narrative was to assume that a homodiegetic (or "first-person") narrator was also the author, even in situations where the narrative in question was obviously fictional; hence, for example, Augustine's notorious assertion that Apuleius "claimed, whether truthfully or fictitiously," to have been transformed into an ass (*Civ.* 18.18).¹⁹ Homodiegetic fiction is a particularly marked species within the wider fictional genus because of the deeply ingrained presumption that an utterance in the first-person singular is deictically indexed to the author of the utterance, or, in the case of a literary work, the author proper. It thus inevitably invokes the figure of metalepsis, the conflation of different levels of narrative such that, for example, a primary narrator enters a secondary narrative, or an author enters her own narrative.²⁰ It may even be possible to speculate as to why the name *Euhemerus* (which is, admittedly, common enough)²¹ was chosen. A

---

15. Polyb., *Hist.* 34.4 = Strab. 2.4.2 (Euhemerus T5 Winiarczyk): "He [Polybius] says that it is better to trust the Messenian than him [Pytheas of Berge]. The former says that he sailed to only one land, Panchaea, whereas Pytheas toured as far as the limits of the cosmos." This seems to me to be an a fortiori critique of Pytheas: even the author of the *Sacred Inscription*, Polybius implies, is more trustworthy than him, since one made-up land is less of an offense to historiography than many. See contra (but I think wrongly) Honigman 2009, 34: "Polybius . . . was convinced: in his view, the fact that Euhemerus claimed to have sailed to a single island constituted a parameter of credibility." To the contrary, the very pairing of Euhemerus with Pytheas implies considerable skepticism.
16. T4–7 Winiarczyk (especially 7A = Strab. 2.3.5 [*pseusmatōn*]; 7B = *Chrest.* Strab. 2.8 [*pseustai*]).
17. Holzberg 2003, 621 n. 3: "'Euhemerus' could be a fictitious name for the person of the narrator."
18. Above, n. 1.
19. See ch. 5.
20. Genette 2004.
21. The online *LGPN* gives 115 hits.

hēmeroas or *hēmerodromēs* is a courier; the latter is the word Herodotus uses, for example, of Phidippides the Marathon runner (6.105.1). So *Euhemerus* may simply mean "trusted emissary"—perfect for the role this personage plays in the text.

What evidence do we have for the identity of the author as (potentially) discrete from the narrator? The only credible allusion from the early Hellenistic period[22] comes in Callimachus's *Iambi*, where the revivified Hipponax commands the Alexandrian elite: "Come here, all of you, to the temple beyond the wall, where the man who fabricated [*plasas*] Panchaean Zeus of yore [*ton palai Pankhaion . . . Zana*], a blathering old man, scratches away at his improper books [*adika biblia*]" (*Iambi* 1.9–11 = fr. 191 Pf = T1A Winiarczyk). Sextus Empiricus associated this scratcher of improper books with "Euhemerus" (*Adv. math.* 9.50–52 = T23 Winiarczyk), and this seems right (notwithstanding the doubts raised above over whether the name attaches to the author or the narrator).[23] But what else can Callimachus tell us? Not, for sure, the name of the author as distinct from the narrator, since the allusion is oblique rather than direct. But there is a further clue here. If the author in question was, in fact, Euhemerus the friend of King Cassander, then what was he doing writing in Alexandria, the capital of a rival kingdom? It is not, of course, at all impossible that he left Macedon for Egypt, or that Callimachus's allusion is, in a way that we can no longer divine, figurative rather than biographically true. But it is at least equally plausible, and certainly more economical, to see the author of the *Sacred Tale* as an Alexandrian writer, well known enough to be identified allusively, who concocted the narratorial figure of the Macedonian Euhemerus.

The Callimachean allusion yields another couple of hints. The scratcher of improper books is said to have "fabricated" Panchaean Zeus. The verb for "fabricate," *plattein*, is used for literary fictions too. As Arnd Kerkhecker notes in his discussion of this passage, we might take Callimachus to be alluding to the fictionality of the *Inscription* itself, albeit fixating narrowly on its impious theology.[24] There may be an echo too of Xenophanes's famous description of "battling Titans, giants, and centaurs" as the "fabrications [*plasmata*] of former men" (F 1.22–23 DK), a line that is conventionally (and plausibly) taken as part of a wider critique

---

22. Winiarczyk 2002, 3, 16–17, retracts the implication in his 1991 edition of the testimonia that T2 = Call., *Hymn.* 1.8–9 is genuine.

23. Aëtius, *Plac.* 1.7.1 (ps.-Plut., *Plac. phil.* 880d–e = T16 Winiarczyk) cites the couplet with *khalkeion* (bronze) in the place of *Pankhaion*, as does a Byzantine scholiast (Schol. ad Tzetz., *Alleg. Iliad.* 4.37 = T1B Winiarczyk). Yet it is surely right to see this as a reference to the *Sacred Inscription* rather than to a statue maker. For a start, *palai* makes no sense for a statue, whereas it works perfectly as an allusion to the historicization of the gods on Panchaea. Secondly, the archaizing form *Zana* seems to point to the inscription *Zan Kronou*, which, according to Ennius via Lactantius (*Div. inst.* 1.11.46; *Epit. div. inst.* 13.5 = T69A–B Winiarczyk), stood on Zeus's tomb.

24. Kerkhecker 1999, 25.

not just of Homer's and Hesiod's theology but also of their narrative trustworthiness in general.[25] Is Callimachus—or, rather, his speaker Hipponax—turning the tables on the author of the *Sacred Inscription*, critiquing his divine fiction with the same language that rationalists wielded against theists? If we accept the extended sense of Callimachus's *plattein*, then the passage offers further evidence that the *Sacred Inscription* was received, early on, as a fictional text.

The reference to *adika biblia* is also suggestive. I have translated the adjective as "improper," which may be all that it means. But *dikē* also suggests legality, which might imply that the author's works have fallen foul of the law. Lying in the background here are the *asebeia* (impiety) trials of Socrates and (perhaps) Anaxagoras, cultural memories of the penalties for religious heterodoxy. Maybe the aggressive Hipponax is implying that the author of the *Inscription* deserved such a fate. But is there a more direct allusion at work here? Could the "blathering old man" have been, in fact, Theodorus of Cyrene, known as "the godless" for his denial of the existence of conventional gods? The tradition surrounding Theodorus is confused indeed, but he seems to have been tried for *asebeia* in Athens at the very end of the fourth century and thereafter to have relocated to the court of Ptolemy Soter in Alexandria before retiring to Cyrene (Diog. Laert. 2.102).[26] This can only be speculation, but it is not impossible that Theodorus was the aged heretic to whom his fellow Cyrenaean refers.[27] Particularly suggestive is the fact that Theodorus was known in his lifetime as Theos, "God," on the basis of a captious mode of argumentation (Diog. Laert. 2.102). If Theodorus could become a god through an act of linguistic designation, why not suppose that the entire pantheon came into being thus?[28]

---

25. See, e.g., Feeney 1991, 6–8, especially 7 ("This type of poetry is a πλάσμα, depicting not something real or actual, but something fabricated").

26. The details are sketchy: see L.-L. O'Sullivan 1997, 142–46; more fully on the evidence for Theodorus's life, Winiarczyk 1981 (largely a study in uncertainty).

27. If Theodorus really was the author of the *Sacred Inscription*, then the reascription from him to "Euhemerus" will have happened early on. By the time of Arnobius, *Adv. Nat.* 4.29 (T21 Winiarczyk), certainly, Euhemerus and Theodorus are classed separately in the list of atheists. Theodorus's most famous work, *On the Gods*, is unlikely to have been the *Inscription*; this would be incompatible with the assertion of Diogenes Laertius (who claims to have read it and found it "not contemptible") that "Epicurus is said to have taken most of his ideas from it" (2.97; see Winiarczyk 1981, 84, on this passage, arguing against emendation of *Epicurus* to *Euhemerus*). Winiarczyk 1981, 84–85, speculates on the nature of *On the Gods*, suspecting (largely on the basis of the Epicurean analogy) that it was a critique of *Volksreligion* rather than a statement of "extreme atheism."

28. The dating initially may be thought problematic. The publication of Callimachus's *Iambi* is usually placed around 270 B.C.E. The last attested event in Diogenes's biography of Theodorus is his retirement to Cyrene, "where he lived with Magas and continued to be held in high honor" (2.102). Magas conquered Cyrene for Ptolemy I soon after 301 but revolted against Alexandria after the latter's death (probably between 279 and 275). If Theodorus really was to be found working just outside Alexandria at

THEOLOGICAL FICTIONS

I have argued that the *Inscription* is likely to have arisen from a particular commingling of cultural streams, the Athenian tradition of Sophistic/philosophical critique of divinity and the emergent literary self-consciousness of Ptolemaic Alexandria. This cultural hybridization, I suggest, lent itself to the development of modes of writing that were simultaneously highly allusive to earlier texts and radically innovative. I turn now to consider how the *Inscription* may have fused two particular kinds of writing while also rerouting them in new directions.

The first point to make is that the *Inscription* draws on the genre of the traveler's tale, and more specifically the sailor's tale.[29] Strabo (1.3.1 = T4 Winiarczyk), picking up the phrasing of Eratosthenes (T5 Winiarczyk), may have called Euhemerus "Bergaean," an allusion to the notoriously inventive traveloguer Antiphanes of Berge.[30] Together with Pytheas of Massilia, Antiphanes and Euhemerus made—in the eyes of some ancient commentators—an unholy trinity of lying sea travelers.[31] It is in general impossible to judge just how deliberately and knowingly these other lost writers played with categories of truth and falsehood, but there is surely a strong case to be made that unverified accounts of sea journeys carried a presumption of fiction.[32]

Indeed, the ultimate paradigm for the fictional sea voyage will have been the *Odyssey*, a resonant hypotext for the readers of the *Inscription*. Parallels can be detected between Diodorus's account of the temple of Zeus Triphylios and Homer's description of Alcinous's palace in book 7 of the *Odyssey*. Diodorus's insistent emphasis on magnificent architecture and fittings of gold, silver, and bronze looks to Alcinous's palace.[33] Closer still are the links between the trees surrounding the

---

the time of the composition of the *Iambi*, he must have relocated from Cyrene once again—perhaps in the aftermath of worsening relations between the two states. (Note that Diogenes refers to Theodorus's expulsion from Cyrene in his youth with the phrase "when he was banished from Cyrene for the first time" [2.103]; does this imply that there was a second banishment, in later life? Or is it looking forward to his subsequent banishment from Athens? Or does "for the first time" [*to prōton*] simply mean "originally," marking the analepsis?) But all the details are so sketchy that hypotheses are fruitless.

29. Winston 1976; Romm 1992, 196–202.

30. The transmitted passage of Strabo reads, "τοῦ καλοῦντος μάρτυρα τὸν Βεργαῖον ἢ τὸν Μεσσήνιον Εὐήμερον"; editors delete "ἢ τὸν Μεσσήνιον" to yield the description of Euhemerus as Bergaean, but this is hardly certain.

31. Strab. 2.3.5 (T7a Winiarczyk); similarly Polyb. 34.5 (Strab. 2.4.2 = Euhemerus T5 Winiarczyk).

32. Romm 1992; Wiseman 1993, 131–32.

33. The analogies can be traced only in the original Greek: "χαλκεῖα μεγάλα" (Diod. Sic. 5.44.1–3 = T 38 Winiarczyk); "ἀναθήματα . . . χρυσᾶ καὶ ἀργυρᾶ πολλὰ καὶ μεγάλα" (Diod. Sic. 46.5 = T 37 Winiarczyk); "τὰ . . . θυρώματα τοῦ ναοῦ θαυμαστὰς ἔχει τὰς κατασκευὰς ἐξ ἀργύρου καὶ χρυσοῦ καὶ ἐλέφαντος" (Diod. Sic. 46.6 = T 37 Winiarczyk); "ἡ . . . κλίνη τοῦ θεοῦ . . . χρυσῆ τὰ . . . θυρώματα τοῦ ναοῦ θαυμαστὰς ἔχει τὰς κατασκευὰς ἐξ ἀργύρου καὶ χρυσοῦ καὶ ἐλέφαντος" (Diod. Sic. 46.7 = T 37 Winiarczyk); "στήλη χρυσῆ" (Diod. Sic. 46.7 = T 37 Winiarczyk); compare with "χάλκεον οὐδόν"

precinct in Diodorus, and Alcinous's magic garden. Both are egregiously lush and fertile.[34] In each description there is a list of trees and plants, with the emphasis on their size and variety (and with several linguistic correspondences): in Diodorus, cypresses, the inevitable plane trees, laurel, and myrtle—and then, in a second list, date palms, nut trees, and vines; in Homer, pears, pomegranates, apples, figs, and olives, followed by vines and a kitchen garden.[35] In both cases there is a spring channeled so as to water the garden throughout; water also has a secondary purpose, for human use.[36]

There are of course other models woven into the *Inscription*'s *locus amoenus*, most notably the celebrated topography of Plato's *Phaedrus*, yet the underappreciated allusions to Homer's Scheria are crucially significant in thematic terms.[37] The Phaeacians are, after all, "near to the gods [*agkhitheoi*]" (*Od.* 5.35) and indeed used to have the gods dining among them (7.201–3).[38] They thus represent a significant literary prototype for the Panchaeans, who in their different way have historically offered hospitality to "the gods."

If the general assimilation of the temple of Zeus Triphylios to the palace of Alcinous is accepted, then we may push further. The narrative on the golden *stēlē*, the Sacred Inscription itself, now corresponds to Odysseus's *apologoi*; let us note too the formal correspondences, both being embedded analepses, (travel) stories within (travel) stories. The *stēlē* narrative is, like the *apologoi*, a first-person account, authored this time by Zeus. As one would expect, the correspondences between the two accounts are, in outline, suggestive rather than exact: each narrator establishes a family on an island (Crete/Ithaca), fights battles (with the Titans and Uranus / in the Trojan War), then proceeds on a long voyage, both

---

(Hom., *Od.* 7.83), "χάλκεοι ... τοῖχοι" (7.86), "χρύσεαι ... θύραι" (7.88), "ἀργύρεοι σταθμοί" (7.89), "χαλκέωι ... οὐδῶι" (7.89), "ἀργύρεον ... ὑπερθύριον" (7.90), "χρυσέη ... κορώνη" (7.90), "χρύσεοι ... καὶ ἀργύρεοι κύνες" (7.91), "χρύσειοι ... κοῦροι" (7.100).

34. "εὐφυΐαν ... πολυτέλειαν" (Diod. Sic. 5.42.6 = T 38 Winiarczyk); "καταγέμει" (Diod. Sic. 5.43.1 = T 38 Winiarczyk); "δένδρεα μακρὰ πεφύκασι τηλεθόωντα" (Hom., *Od.* 7.114).

35. Diod. Sic. 5.43.1 = T 38 Winiarczyk; Hom., *Od.* 7.115–16. Linguistic correspondences (Diodorus first, Homer second): "παντοίοις" ~ "παντοῖαι"; "καρποφόροις"/"καρποφόρα" ~ "ἀγλαόκαρποι"; "κυπαρίττων ... ἀξαισίων τοῖς μεγέθεσι" / "στελέχη μεγάλα" ~ "δένδρεα μακρά"; "θαυμαζόμενον" ~ "θηεῖτο ... Ὀδυσσεύς."

36. Diod. Sic. 5.43.2 = T 38 Winiarczyk, where a stream waters the plain ("εἰς πολλὰ μέρη τοῦ ὕδατος διαιρουμένου") but is also used for sailing; at *Od.* 7.129–31, one stream is used for the garden ("ἀνὰ κῆπον ἅπαντα / σκιδνᾶται"), the other for watering the populace.

37. Winiarczyk 2002, 93–96, discusses various sources for the temple/garden description without mentioning the *Odyssey*.

38. The phrasing is ambiguous as to whether the theoxeny has now ended: "'have always in the past appeared <and still do>', hence the present tense; see also 8.36. γε, however, raises the possibility that such divine appearances may have ended" (Garvie 1994, 205).

receiving hospitality and encountering conflict,[39] before finally returning home. Especially significant is the claim in Diodorus that Zeus "came among very many races, and was honored [*timēthēnai*] among all, and named a god" (6.1.10–11 = T63 Winiarczyk). This picks up on two Odyssean motifs. The first and most obvious is at 1.1–3, where the hero is said to have "wandered far and wide ... and [seen] the cities and learned the mind of many men." The second is subtler. At three points, the Phaeacians are said to "honor [*timēsanto*, or *timēsousi* in Zeus's prediction]" Odysseus "like a god [*theon hōs*]."[40] Indeed, Odysseus, especially in his traveling aspect, has much of the god about him. Modern scholars have studied the *Odyssey*'s theme of theoxeny, whereby the hospitality that Odysseus receives is predicated on the presupposition that he might be a disguised god.[41] What is more, one of his epithets is *dios*; whatever the Homeric word actually means (and it is, to be sure, not used distinctively of Odysseus), the view that Odysseus might be "Zeus-like" had become available by the time that the *Inscription* was composed.[42]

Crucially, however, Odysseus's narration to the Phaeacians also served as a byword for fictionality. Already in the *Odyssey*, there are strong metafictional signals suggesting that the account may not be straightforwardly true.[43] By the time of Plato's *Republic*, "an *apologos* to Alcinous" had become proverbial for an untruth (614b, with the ancient commentator's scholion). For Lucian at the start of his *True Stories*—a homodiegetic narrative that is avowedly fictitious—"the leader of this crowd [of literary charlatans, the group Lucian's narrator wishes to join] and teacher of such nonsense [*bōmolokhias*] is Homer's Odysseus, who narrates to Alcinous and his court stories of winds in chains; one-eyed, savage cannibals; animals with many heads; his comrades metamorphosed by drugs—lots of that kind of thing, with which he bamboozled the uncultured Phaeacians" (1.3). Let us recall, finally, that the paradigm cases of Odyssean lying narrative are the "Cretan lies" of the latter half of the poem.[44] Even more than Odysseus, Cretans were by the time of the *Inscription*'s composition proverbial

---

39. See Diod. Sic. 6.1.10 = T 61 Winiarczyk ("He went to Babylon and was entertained [*epixenōthēnai*] by Belos"); Diod. Sic. 6.1.10–11 = T 63 Winiarczyk for the war with Cilix.

40. Hom., *Od.* 5.36, 19.280, 23.339. "Honoring like a god" occurs relatively frequently in the *Iliad*: see, e.g., 9.155, with J. Griffin 1995, 93.

41. Kearns 1982; Louden 2011, 30–56 (reading the *Odyssey* against the Hebrew Bible).

42. See LSJ, s.v. "dios," for its later, tragic meaning, "of Zeus." Note too the adjective *diogenēs*, used in the *Iliad* particularly of Odysseus, Ajax, and Patroclus but in the *Odyssey* only of Odysseus (especially in the address formula "Diogenēs Laertiadē, polumēkhan' Odusseu").

43. See especially Goldhill 1991, 30–36; on the reception of the *Odyssey* as fiction see further Romm 1992, 182–96; Georgiadou and Larmour 1998, 23 n. 69, gives a fuller bibliography.

44. Hom., *Od.* 13.256–86, 14.199–359, 17.415–44, 19.165–202, 19.221–48, 19.262–307.

liars.[45] For the author of the *Inscription* to have turned an Odyssean Zeus into a Cretan, then, will have been a highly provocative act; in effect, this would double the covert insinuation of mendacity.

HISTORICAL FICTIONS

I turn now to the second intertextual thread. Honigman, we recall, argues that the *Inscription* should be taken as a variety of historiography, within the category of narratives designed to express general truths rather than specific facts. This claim, I submit, should be modified in light of the Odyssean resonances, which pull in the opposite direction, toward dissemblance and irony. Historiography forms a significant part of the *Inscription*'s weft, to be sure, but even here we should be cautious before assuming that this directs readers toward veridicality. Historians may have (usually) protested their truthfulness, but their works also had an inbuilt awareness of the possibility of critical counterreaction.[46] In fact, thanks to the agonistic structure common to most "scientific" discourse in the formative classical period,[47] it is in effect a generic demand that Greek historiography should balance truth claims with (implicit or explicit) attacks on the falseness of one's competitors. Thus even as individual historians promote their own trustworthiness, the genre as a whole becomes more self-consuming.

The most important historical repertory for the author of the *Inscription* was book 2 of Herodotus's *Histories*, a treasure-house of alternative perspectives on religion. Notable, for example, are chapters 42–45, which deal with the vexatious question of Heracles's ambivalent identity as both mortal and god:[48] "some sacrifice to him as an immortal, others as a hero" (2.44.5).[49] Herodotus claims to have come across two *stēlai* in Tyre in a temple of Heracles, one of gold and the other of emerald (2.44.2); he then learns from the priests of the extreme antiquity of the cult site, from which he concludes that Heracles is indeed an "ancient god [*palaion theon*]" (2.44.5). Although there is no indication that the story of Heracles's deeds is recorded on the *stēlai* (as at Panchaea), the passage surely will have formed part of the intertextual complexion of the original *Inscription*. What is more, this passage is one of a series of modifications of Greek cultural memory, especially in the

---

45. Most famously at Call., *Hymn.* 1.8, conventionally taken as an allusion to Epimenides (fr. 5 Kinkel). In an as yet unpublished paper, however, Stuart Thomson casts doubt on this ascription. This Callimachean line has, indeed, sometimes been taken as an allusion to the *Sacred Inscription* (see above, n. 22).

46. See in general Wiseman 1993.

47. Lloyd 1987.

48. A *zētēma* already implied at Hom., *Od.* 11.601–4.

49. On the prototypical importance to the *Inscription* of Heracles qua divinized human being see Winiarczyk 2002, 30–32.

religious sphere, reversals motivated by texts and traditions found in foreign places. Herodotus opines that the Greeks "say many things injudiciously [*anepiskeptōs*]" on the subject of Heracles and in particular cultivate the "foolish myth [*euēthes . . . muthos*]" of the story of his birth (2.45.1).[50] Again we can see how the *Sacred Inscription* seems to have drawn on this rhetoric of encounter with an older, wiser culture (even if the theological conclusion in the Euhemeran text is much different).

This sense of paradoxical confrontation with alternative truths memorialized in stone intensifies as we proceed to Egypt, finally peaking in the section on the legendary conquering pharaoh Sesostris, beginning at chapter 102. Again we find this account legitimized by columns, this time inscribed: Sesostris, we read, set up *stēlai* whenever he was victorious, recording his name and his victims (with a depiction of women's genitals if he thought they were cowards).[51] This then leads into a rationalizing account of the sanctuary of "the foreign Aphrodite" (2.112), whom Herodotus takes to be Helen, when she was brought to Egypt during the Trojan War; as in the *Sacred Inscription*, we see a deity "unmasked" as a mortal. But most important of all, Herodotus now embarks on the famous "alternative" version of the Helen narrative, derived (so he says) from Egyptian priestly traditions: Helen ended up staying with Proteus as a refugee from Paris (chapters 113–20). As with the earlier revision of the myth of Heracles's birth, this is presented as a corrective to received versions: the priests confirm that "the Greeks' story is vapid [*mataion*]" (2.118.1).

Let us return to the theme of fiction, and take a step back to assess. I am not arguing that Herodotus is a fictional writer—although there is certainly space for a polyphonic Herodotus, well aware of the fictionality of some of his stories ("Anyone who finds this plausible is welcome to do so," he says after the Rhampsinitus story. "My task is just to record the oral history of each people" [2.123.1]),[52] and of course "fictionalizing" is a more charitable way of interpreting some of the features of his text that Detlev Fehling and others have interpreted as deceptive.[53] My substantial point has less to do with the design of Herodotus's text, how many "grains" it has, and which way they run. The crucial point is that in developing a series of devices for narrative legitimation, Herodotus also paves the way for the expropria-

---

50. Echoing the famous opening of Hecataeus that ridicules the "many ludicrous stories" of the Greeks (*FGrH* 1 F 1a).

51. Hdt. 2.102.4–5; see also 2.106. S. West 1992 argues that the Palestinian inscriptions referred to at 2.106 were in reality Hittite rather than Egyptian.

52. Similarly Hdt. 7.152. For a survey of places where Herodotus professes disbelief or belief in a given story see Asheri et al. 2007, 23. On Herodotus's "nascent conception of fiction" see Kim 2010a, 30–37, at 33.

53. Fehling 1989.

tion of these very devices for the creation of irony, distance, and fictional self-consciousness. After all, "I met some priests who told me what really happened to Helen" and "I found a *stēlē* that told me the truth about Heracles" are fundamentally the same trope as "I discovered a manuscript written by Adso of Melk." Critics of ancient fiction refer to this textual strategy as "pseudo-documentarism,"[54] and it becomes widespread in later texts. Examples include Dictys of Crete's *Diaries of the Trojan War* (supposedly discovered in the time of Nero, after an earthquake broke open a Cretan cave) and Antonius Diogenes's *Wonders beyond Thule*, which claims to be modeled on a narrative found in a tomb by Alexander's soldiers after the capture of Tyre.

The line between history and fiction is further blurred in the case of Ctesias's *Persica*, which sits chronologically (and perhaps generically) between the *Histories* and the *Inscription*. According to one later testimony, Ctesias accused Herodotus of "being a liar [*pseustēn*], calling him a fabricator of tales [*logopoion*],"[55] apparently basing his claim on the grounds that he himself had had access to more accurate authentication, in the form of Persian royal records (*basilikai diphtherai*), and had been an eyewitness (*autoptēn*) of events he described and an "earwitness [*autēkoon*]" of Persians who took part in these events.[56] Yet by raising the stakes in this way, Ctesias also increased the risk of rebound. Time and again ancient sources describe him as lying, mythologizing, inventing. Photius explicitly describes him as hoisted by his own anti-Herodotean petard: "As for myths, the pretext for his vitriol against [*loidoreitai*] him [Herodotus]—well, he does not abstain from these."[57] How self-aware Ctesias was, the extent to which he knowingly raised the question of his own fictionality, is a question we cannot address when we have so little of his writing. But it seems at the very least probable that he was attempting to artifice a new kind of history, which was stronger on narrative and romance than on source criticism.[58]

By the time that the *Inscription* was written, then, the device of the discovered source was already freighted with considerable fictional baggage—especially in cases where the line of transmission runs through a single figure. It is thus far likelier that the *Inscription* designedly provoked skepticism in its ancient readers

---

54. See in general Ní Mheallaigh 2008, with the accent on ludic ironies; Hansen 2003; on the motif of the "discovered book" Speyer 1970.

55. Phot., *Bibl.* 72, 45a = FGrH 688 T13. If the phrasing is Ctesias's own, the accusation has a particular piquancy, since *logopoios* is Herodotus's word for "tellers of tall tales" such as Aesop and Hecataeus: see Kurke 2010, 376–82.

56. Phot., *Bibl.* 72, 35b = FGrH 688 T8.

57. Phot., *Bibl.* 72, 45a = FGrH 688 T13.

58. Stronk 2010, 47–48; more generally on Ctesias's relationship to the novel see Holzberg 1993, 79–84.

than that (as Honigman claims) it tried and failed to persuade readers of a general (historical) truth. Does this mean that the text was presented as a mere fiction, a fantasy whose philosophical content might be discarded along with its fictional setting? This too seems wrong, partly because there was no strong sense within Greek culture at this time of fiction as an ontologically discrete category and partly because the work's links to fifth-century Sophistic and philosophical thought are so strong. We should see the *Inscription*'s "fictionality" as ironic accentuation rather than in the full sense of a narrative whose untruth is its dominant feature.

Why, finally, might the author of the *Inscription* have chosen this form of fiction in which to clothe his philosophical experiment? Two interlocking answers suggest themselves. The first builds on Callimachus's Xenophanes-like reference, discussed earlier, to the author having "fabricated" Panchaean Zeus. This observation, we noted, takes the language of literary fiction and cross-applies it to theology. But this was a short leap for Greeks, who often took Homer's and Hesiod's depictions of gods as the most conspicuous signs of their fictionalizing.[59] The fictionality of the *Sacred Inscription* thus, so far from undermining, in a sense corroborates its philosophical content: the *Inscription* puts into practice, self-reflexively, its central claim that stories about gods are fictional. The second reason to opt for fiction was no doubt more pragmatic. Proferring a perspective on the gods that could be deemed atheistic was dangerous, as numerous philosophers had discovered to their cost (among them Theodorus of Cyrene, whom I have tentatively proposed as the *Inscription*'s author). Fiction offered (as David Sedley argues)[60] a safer way of expressing philosophical ideas about the gods, in a "refined intellectual game"[61] that disguised their full import. Still, if the *Inscription*'s philosophical significance lies primarily in its dramatization of older, fifth-century religious anthropologies, its importance as fiction is largely forward-looking, since it points the way both to more self-consciously fictive travel narratives (such as Iambulus's *Islands of the Sun,* Lucian's *True Stories,* and Antonius Diogenes's *Wonders beyond Thule*) and to the pseudo-documentary imbroglios of Dictys and (again) Antonius Diogenes.

---

59. See especially Feeney 1991, 5–56.
60. Sedley, forthcoming.
61. Müller 1993, 300.

4

An I for an I

Reading Fictional Autobiography

Let us pause to develop a thread from the previous chapter. One of the questions posed there is whether Euhemerus was the author of the *Sacred Inscription* or whether this is merely the name of the narrator; I speculatively proposed that Theodorus of Cyrene may have been the author. But even if we discount that hypothesis and keep Euhemerus as the author, there is still an obvious sense in which Euhemerus the author is not Euhemerus the narrator, since the latter went to Panchaea and the former did not. The words in a text (any text) have issued from the consciousness of one individual (or collective). But at the same time, those words are always costumed, dressed for a role. The words you are reading now are mine to the extent that you can hold me to them; you can accost me in the street or email me to protest, and I will (to the best of my abilities) reply. But in another sense, this is not the "real me" speaking: I do not adopt this persona when buying fish, talking to my children, or playing soccer. Perhaps it is better to say that all of those separate verbal identities are facets of the same person, different roles that are assumed in the performance of everyday life.

But the literary "I" in fact poses a distinctive type of cognitive challenge. As a writer of nonfiction I may adopt stylistic mannerisms that are peculiar to this type of writing, but I do not introduce claims I know to be counterfactual; if I am found to have done so, reviewers will take me to task. When we read literary fiction, however, we know that the speaking "I" may make claims we must not expect to be true for the author. This is an obvious point, certainly, but I have belabored it because if we step back and think about the phenomenon, it begins to appear very strange: the author of a work of fiction simultaneously is the narrator (since she or he is responsible for every word) and is not (for the narrator is an unreal character).

In this chapter I argue that the Greeks and Romans were fully aware of this apparent contradiction. Let us begin with a quick look at Catullus's famous poem 16, which takes two readers, Aurelius and Furius, to task for assuming that his "softy [*molliculi*]" poems betoken a "less than virtuous [*parum pudicum*]" author. No, replies Catullus: the poet himself should be moral (*castum*), but there is no need for his verses to be (16.1–6). The ethical identities of the poet and the character he plays in his poems are to be kept well apart. Yet Catullus also mischievously subverts this distinction: for the "me" that is claiming to be "moral" is itself a poetic construct, and so (according to his own argument) not to be automatically associated with the real Catullus. In any case, the poet's insistence on his virtue is undermined by the notoriously obscene threat toward Aurelius and Furius, repeated for effect, that "I'll bugger you and fuck your face" (16.1, 14): hardly words likely to convince anyone of the speaker's sanctity. This in turn raises another problem at a different level: who is making this threat, the real author or the poetic narrator? The confusion between the two initiated by Aurelius and Furius is, it would seem, harder to dispel than one might expect; the poem, indeed, depends for its effect on the conflation of the two.

This conflation is entirely characteristic of ancient practice. Ancient critics regularly took narrators' words as authors', even in instances where it often seems to us absurd to do so. In a rare case where an ancient author discusses an ancient novel, Augustine seems to make an embarrassing error:

> . . . *sicut Apuleius in libris, quos asini aurei titulo inscripsit, sibi ipsi accidisse, ut accepto ueneno humano animo permanente asinus fieret, aut indicauit aut finxit.*

> . . . just as Apuleius, in the books he wrote with the title of *The Golden Ass*, has claimed, or feigned: that it happened to his own self that, on taking a potion, he became an ass, while retaining his human mind. (*City of God* 18.18)

Augustine appears to have taken Apuleius's *Metamorphoses* (in which the narrator Lucius tells of turning into a donkey) as some kind of serious claim on the part of the author. Like Aurelius and Furius, he conflates author and narrator. The story was written by Apuleius, but the protagonist is, of course, Lucius of Corinth. This is one of those moments when modern critics cringe. We so deeply want the ancients to be sophisticated, sensitive readers of literature, but Augustine, one of antiquity's shrewdest minds, seems here to have fallen into the most elementary of elephant traps, by confusing author and narrator.[1] There may be mitigating

---

A version of this chapter appeared as Whitmarsh 2009c; I am grateful to the editors of *Cento Pagine* and to Oxford University Press for permission to reuse this material.

1. It is worth emphasizing that the author/narrator distinction that I am discussing has nothing to do with John Winkler's *auctor/actor*: *auctor* for Winkler means the narrator Lucius, not the author Apuleius (e.g., 1985, 135–40).

circumstances. Augustine was much troubled by Apuleius, whom he saw as a demonologist and apologist for magic.[2] Like his predecessor Lactantius and other early patristic writers,[3] Augustine considered Apuleius an embodiment of all that was false in pagan thaumaturgy, a diabolic opposite number to Christ the miracle worker. There was also a personally competitive edge in his denigration of another North African composer of conversion narratives in sparkling Latin prose— perhaps too a guilty disavowal of the literary pleasures of his pre-Christian youth. At any rate, when, in the passage from which the quotation above is drawn, he comes to decry the "wicked arts" of living metempsychosis, he does not waste the opportunity to berate the author of the *Metamorphoses* (or *The Golden Ass*, as he titles the work) for his claims to have transformed himself into a donkey.

But Augustine was not alone in presuming "without question that Apuleius is claiming to relate his own experience—that he is the Lucius of his novel"; according to a recent account of the reception of the novel, the "assumption continued to be unquestioned for at least a thousand years, and the identity of Apuleius and Lucius was to play a major role in the interpretation of the *Golden Ass*."[4] Similar problems arise, indeed, when we look to the Greek *Ass* tradition. Bishop Photius of Constantinople was no fool, and no one could accuse him of not being widely read, but he likewise seems to ascribe the authorship of the longer version of the Greek *Ass* (now lost) to "Lucius of Patrae" (*Bibl.* cod. 129 = 96b). Lucius of Patrae is the central figure and narrator of the novel and presumably not its real author.[5] It is far from impossible, of course, that this ascription predated Photius and even that it went back to an original pseudonymy in the text. The fact remains, however, that the redoubtable bishop shows no sign of skepticism or even suspicion.

Are these really cases of naïveté? At one level, surely not. Nothing indicates that Augustine actually believes that Apuleius's first-person narrative is, or indeed is intended to be, a factual account of the author's experience (the same is true of Photius vis-à-vis Lucius of Patrae).[6] The phrase *aut indicauit aut finxit* (has claimed, or feigned), with its implicit weighting toward the second option, suggests that he knows full well that he is dealing with a fiction (*fictio*) in the guise of a factual utterance (an *indicatio*, which can mean a "statement" in a forensic

---

2. Generally on the Christian reception of Apuleius see Carver 2007, 17–30, with 26–29 on our passage; Gaisser 2008, 20–39, with 33–34 on our passage. Hunink 2003 discusses Augustine's view of Apuleius.
3. Lact., *Inst.* 5.3.19, discussed at Carver 2007, 18–19, and Gaisser 2008, 22–23.
4. Gaisser 2008, 33.
5. Discussed in more detail in ch. 5.
6. Photius emphasizes the level of quasi-Lucianic "miracle mongering [*terateia*]" in the text and indeed entertains (if he finally rejects) the notion that "Lucius" may have derived the story from Lucian.

context).⁷ Augustine's formulation, indeed, captures the distinctiveness of Apuleius's narrative technique. As Andrew Laird has demonstrated, the chatty, discursive style and use of free indirect discourse in the *Metamorphoses,* coupled with the first-person form, are unprecedented in narrative literature; such features were more typically employed in veridical genres of literature.⁸ In other words, the text is precisely a *fictio* (Apuleius impersonating another person) in the guise of an *indicatio* (a testimony about one's own life). Augustine's conflation of author and narrator is, moreover, already seeded in Lucius's notorious self-identification as "a man from Madaura" —Apuleius's hometown (9.27).⁹

But if we can accept that Augustine was a sophisticated and attentive reader of Apuleius,[10] the question poses itself all the more urgently: how did he manage to make such an elementary confusion? My hypothesis is that the problem lies not with Augustine but with a particular configuration of modern critical practice. The narrator/author divide has become so central to literary criticism that to disturb it seems transgressive, in a way that it clearly was not in premodern times.[11] Narratology is now such a dominant and all-pervasive intellectual idiom that it is easy to forget that antiquity had no dedicated vocabulary to describe the "narrator" (narratology's central category)[12] in the strict, critical sense of a narrating persona within the textual fiction (as distinct from the "poet," "singer," or "writer" who created it).[13] Hence, for example, the well-known tendency of ancient biographers to

---

7. *OLD*², s.v. "indicatio" 2, citing Ulp., *Dig.* 19.1.13.3.
8. Laird 1990.
9. For different readings of this passage see Van der Paardt 1981; Harrison 1990; de Jong 2001. Laird 1990, 156–57, aptly compares ch. 55 of the pseudo-Lucianic *Ass,* where the fictional Lucius reveals that he is "a writer of histories"; see further ch. 5.
10. Augustine's developed, protophenomenological ideas about reading are the subject of Stock 1996.
11. "That it is essential not to confuse author and narrator has become a commonplace of literary theory" (Chatman 1978, 147).
12. Bal 1997, 19: "The narrator is the most central concept in the analysis of narrative texts. The identity of the narrator, the degree to which and the manner in which that identity is indicated in the text, and the choices that are implied lend the text its specific character."
13. Plato's Socrates influentially distinguished "narrator text," in the voice of the Homeric narrator, from "mimetic text," containing characters' words (*Rep.* 393d–94d; for a recent discussion of the influence see Nünlist 2009, 94–115), but crucially it is always "Homer" who is said to be doing the narration (see, e.g., *Rep.* 393d for the distinction between Homer speaking "as Chryses" and "as Homer"). Aristotle's *Poet.* 1460a 5–11 makes the same distinction, even if it is not quite clear why he apparently limits "Homer speak" to proems. See Rabel 1999 for a recent discussion of this problem. I am not, however, convinced that Aristotle necessarily saw the narratorial passages after the proems in terms of impersonation of the voice of the Muses, as Rabel suggests; that even if he did, he was necessarily right to do so (how would this account for the second invocation of the *Iliad,* in book 2?); or that even if he did and was right, that this is an ancient version of the author/narrator distinction (as Rabel 1999, 169–170, seems to imply).

take statements of narratorial self-identification more or less literally, rather than (as modern critics would prefer) as circumscribed by the demands of genre and literary context.[14]

From one perspective this it is clearly right to describe the ancient critical practice in terms of the absence of a term. The more concepts and tools we have at our disposal, the subtler and sharper we are as critics. But it is always awkward when moderns start lording it over their benighted pre-Enlightenment predecessors: partly because this smacks of "presentist" arrogance but more seriously because too heavy a dependence on modern critical schemes risks inattention to the reading instincts and habits of the ancients themselves. Apuleius, "Lucius of Patrae," and their peers, of course, were writing for readers who were closer to Augustine and Photius than to Gérard Genette and Mieke Bal: they surely anticipated the kind of confusion that they generated. And, conversely, it is likely that Augustine and Photius entered this fictional contract willingly and with their eyes open, attuned as they were to the conventions.

This discussion will focus on the phenomenon of first-person fictional narratives, which attract this kind of problematic more than any other type of literary text. In this category I include alongside Apuleius's *Metamorphoses* and the Greek *Ass* texts[15] Petronius's *Satyrica*, Lucian's *True Stories*, Lollianus's now-fragmentary *Phoenician Affairs*, and the framing narrative of Achilles Tatius's *Leucippe and Clitophon*. Not all of these will be discussed here in any kind of detail. For example, Petronius's *Satyrica* seems to me a relatively straightforward case of fictivity: the figure of Encolpius is so obviously not Petronius (especially if this Petronius was Nero's *arbiter elegantiae*) that the issue becomes not so much how to distinguish the two as how to locate the "hidden" authorial slant that ironizes Encolpius's narration (a process that seems more complex than Gian Biagio Conte's and similar readings admit).[16] In *Leucippe and Clitophon*, by contrast, an ancient audience would (I imagine) immediately have identified the figure we tend to call the unnamed narrator of the prologue with Achilles himself, but the narrator plays such a small role that little depends directly on that identification.[17] Lollianus is too fragmentary to admit much discussion. My emphasis, then, will be primarily on

---

14. Lefkowitz 1991, 113: "When ancient poets start to write about themselves in the first person, it has been natural to want to think of them as speaking directly about their feelings and their lives. But it is a mistake to take these 'I'-statements as naïve, direct expressions about some particular development in time, rather than as the formal utterance of some professional person."

15. Excluding *P.Oxy.* 4762, which is apparently narrated in the third person (or heterodiegetically).

16. Conte 1996. See Rimell 2007, 114: "We cannot, as Auerbach, Sullivan and Conte propose, ally ourselves securely with a sophisticate Author (Petronius) and condescend to a buffoonish Narrator (Encolpius) from a position of objectivity and superiority 'outside' the text: it is ultimately impossible to disentangle narrator from author, or even narrator from protagonist."

17. I explore some of the possible consequences in Whitmarsh 2011a.

the various Greek and Roman *Ass* stories and on Lucian (even if most of the discussion will be at the theoretical level).

I am going to call this kind of narrative a fictional autobiography rather than (for example) a first-person, homodiegetic, or ego narrative, because these latter terms imply too much investment in the narratological category of the narrator as discrete from the author, which assumes automatically precisely what I claim to be *sous rature*. The idea of fictional autobiography is a deliberate paradox, since (as Philippe Lejeune has argued) the "autobiographical contract" (whereby author and narrator are assumed to be identical) categorically excludes the "fictional contract" (the prerequisites of which are overt fictivity and nonidentity between the two).[18] The narratives that we are dealing with, or rather the reading conventions that they imagine, precisely blur (I argue) the boundaries between these categories.

There is a serious philosophical and psychological complexity in both composing and reading a story whose narrating "I" is a performance, an ego that is not the author's own. The pronoun *I* marks not a concrete reference—like all pronouns, it is exclusively deictic and hence can be used to denote a potentially infinite number of human beings—but a social and linguistic function: it indicates (a) the person who is speaking (or, by extension, who has written), and (b) that this person is the subject of the utterance.[19] Fictional autobiography breaks the rules of that particular contract. Now it might be argued that the very fact of fictivity suspends the normal rules: after all, we can comfortably read *The Lovely Bones* without assuming that Alice Sebold, the author, is dead like the narrator. But this easy acceptance of fictional conventions is, I think, a peculiarly modern effect of the omnipresence of fiction in our world, which has dulled our sense of the transgressiveness of this kind of speech act.

It is that transgressiveness, the discomforting jolt, that I want to recapture here. Fictional autobiography generalizes the paradox that critics have identified in relation to Apuleius's famous "Quis ille?" (Who is that?) in the prologue to the *Metamorphoses* (1.1): a question, spoken by the narrator but ventroloquized by the addressee, that shifts the narrator from the first to the third person.[20] In first-person fiction, the narrator is an uneasy blend of *ego* and *ille*, authorial identification and distantiation. I want to pursue the implications of taking Augustine's approach to Apuleius as a paradigmatic ancient strategy for dealing with first-person fictions rather than as a failed attempt at a modern one. My hypothesis is that the modern instinct to divide author from narrator does violence to the fictional conventions of the ancient world, foreclosing its complex and unresolved play between the autobiographical and the fictional modes.

18. Lejeune 1982, 203.
19. I borrow here from Lejeune's 1982 reformulation of Émile Benveniste (197–99).
20. Among many discussions, see especially Winkler 1985, 180–203 (especially 194–96); Laird 1990, 155–156; Too 2001.

To offer some psychological contextualization for the phenomenon I am describing, we need to move well beyond literary narrative, into the world of performance. Let us first consider the singing of poetry in early Greece. Rhapsodic performance of Homer seems to have been more than simply the tactical adoption of a Homeric persona; the rhapsode in a sense inhabited the role of Homer for the duration of the performance, albeit without sacrificing his own identity. This is what the rhapsodic rapture described in Plato's *Ion* suggests: Ion is magnetically enthused with Homer's spirit even as he maintains his independent status as Greece's top performer of Homeric poetry (541b2). Similarly, the situational vagueness of Sapphic poetry has been taken as a device to allow reperformance by male singers, allowing them to "be" Sappho more plausibly—although here, of course, gender difference would provide a strong marker of the residual nonidentification.[21]

Gregory Nagy has expanded this model of performative identification into a more radical theory of poetic composition in early Greece, claiming that in many cases authorial identification is no more than a corollary of composing in a particular genre: thus, for example, to write blame poetry is to become Archilochus, to write rustic or theogonic epic is to become Hesiod, and so forth.[22] Although these particular examples are speculative, we can see an indisputable instance in sympotic love poetry, where until Byzantine times poets adopted the identity of Anacreon.[23]

The assumption underlying all of these models is that to say *I* is, in a complex but serious way, to lay claim to the selfhood that one performs. To unpack some of the complexity, let us look sideways to dramatic acting. Actors in performance are not usually confused with authors in the way that we have been describing[24]— which is why I call this a sideways look—but they do occupy a similarly double role in relation to their characters. An actor onstage is at once the flesh-and-blood actor and a character.[25] This is the point of the famous anecdote about Polus the actor, who played the role of Sophocles's Electra using an urn containing the ashes of his own son. Thus the grief of the acted Electra merged with that of the actor: "He filled everywhere not with appearance and imitation but with real grief and living laments."[26] Ismene Lada-Richards aptly cites in this connection

21. Most 1995, 33–34.
22. See, e.g., Nagy 1979, 243–52; 1990, 47–50.
23. Rosenmeyer 1992.
24. The widespread "Euripides says that" phenomenon (when discussing lines attributed to a character) is only a limited exception, since it is not keyed to the challenging ontology of the fictional "I" (and is a function of textuality rather than performance). A more pungent case is that of the Aristophanic parabasis, alluded to below, n. 40.
25. Amply discussed at Lada-Richards 2002, 395–401; see further Easterling 1990.
26. Aul. Gell. 6.5.1–8, at 7. This anecdote is the opening hook for a metatheatrical discussion at Ringer 1998, 1–5; on its reception see Holford-Strevens 2005.

Dicaeopolis's words in Aristophanes's *Acharnians*, which can clearly be taken as a metatheatrical allusion to theatrical acting: "For I must this day seem to be a beggar, be who I am and yet not seem to be" (440–41).[27] The two sides of the acting self, the actor and the role, coexist in the same person, their simultaneity indicated grammatically by the balancing particles *men* and *de*. Both passages create a clear ontological hierarchy between the true, real actor and the fictitious representations that his acting depicts, but both, in their different ways, acknowledge a convergence between the two identities.

Acting is thus conceived of as a form of illusion, a central concept in Greek aesthetics. Gorgias famously commented on tragedy that it is "a deception in which the deceiver is more just than the nondeceiver and the deceived is wiser than the undeceived."[28] The paradoxical nature of the illusion—it fools you that it is real, when you know all along it is a fiction—is a running theme of much ancient rhetorical and literary criticism, particularly that in the orbit of literary vividness (*enargeia*).[29] What illusion does, primarily, is elide textuality while insisting on it.[30] When pseudo-Longinus describes the impact of Orestes's vision of the Furies in Euripides's *Orestes* and *Iphigenia in Tauris*, he claims that "the poet himself saw the Erinyes and has made his audience all but see what he imagined."[31] Audience and poet alike are transported into an imaginative fantasy in which they can see what Orestes can see . . . or, rather, they can *all but* see it, the characteristic ecphrastic "qualification" marking the residual awareness of textuality, of fictionality.[32]

Fictional autobiography is a form of illusionism. In Augustine's response to Apuleius, the authorial "I" slides fictitiously into the (narratorial) alter ego even as the reader retains an awareness of the irreducible fictionality of the process. Viewed from the perspective of ancient aesthetics, this is not a case of mistaken narratological identity but a conventional instance of illusionistic impersonation, a textual mimicking of the performative conventions that cluster around rhapsodes and actors.[33] The idea of impersonation, it seems to me, better captures the fundamentally nonnarratological approach to the fictional "I" that prevailed in the ancient world: like an actor playing a role, the fictional autobiographer created an

---

27. Lada-Richards 2002, 396.

28. DK 82 B23 = Plut., *Quomodo adulescens* 15D. Lada-Richards 2002 cites examples of similar phrases more narrowly focused on acting.

29. On pictorialism, *enargeia*, and *ecphrasis* in ancient literature see in general Webb 2009, especially 87–130.

30. In Ruth Webb's words, "the audience . . . combine a state of imaginative and emotional involvement in the worlds represented with an awareness that these worlds are not real" (Webb 2009, 168–69).

31. *De subl*. 15.2. The Euripidean passages are *Or*. 255–257 and *Iph. Taur*. 291.

32. Webb 2009, 168.

33. Hence no doubt the markers of oral performance that percolate Apuleius's text, on which see most recently Gorman 2008.

illusion of identity with the role he played—an illusion that was ever predicated on universal awareness of its unreality. A model of impersonation highlights two particular features of fictional autobiography that a narratological model represses, or at least deproblematizes:

1. Impersonation is a variety of illusion, whereby the author imitates another figure.
2. This illusion oscillates between success (readers are led to believe in the impersonation) and self-exposure (our attention is drawn to the very artificiality of the illusion).

Narratology, by contrast, sees fictional biography as nothing more than a particular instance of the author/narrator divide that is universal to narrative and hence as both nontransgressive and entirely stable.

The transgressiveness and instability of impersonation manifest themselves as a variety of the figure that Gérard Genette names "metalepsis." Metalepsis, in his account, is the elision of difference between two narrative levels, the traversal of "a shifting but sacred frontier between two worlds."[34] An excellent example comes in the 2006 Hollywood film *Stranger than Fiction* when the protagonist, Harold Crick, begins to hear a voice inside his head; in time he realizes this is the voice of the author who is writing his life story and who plans to kill him off. Of course, a fictional character does not usually meet his or her author; the film is predicated on an elaborate postmodern flouting of conventional narrative realism. But despite the *avant-gardiste* flavor of instances like this, recent discussions have detected instances of metalepsis in older literature, including that of classical antiquity (for example, Homeric apostrophe).[35]

Impersonation of the kind we have described is a subspecies of metalepsis that (as Genette notes) attaches itself particularly to the figure of the author and to fictional writing.[36] Strikingly metaleptic are those moments when the text's impersonated "I" seems to morph transgressively into the identity of the author, such as Lucius's description of himself in Apuleius's *Metamorphoses* as "from Madaura" (9.27; see above). A subtler case is Theocritus's *Idyll* 7, whose first line's "I [*egōn*]" might be thought to be the poet himself (a city dweller walking into the countryside: a suitable image for pastoral composition) until an interlocutor, Lycidas, identifies him as one "Simichidas" in line 21. But the possibility that Simichidas

---

34. Genette 1983, 234–37, at 236; more generally 2004.
35. Fludernik 2003 emphasizes the premodern ancestry of metalepsis, as indeed does Genette 2004. See de Jong 2009 on classical literature (93–97 on apostrophe); Whitmarsh 2011a on the later Greek novels; Whitmarsh, forthcoming b, on tragedy and comedy. Pier and Schaeffer 2005 is an interesting collection of essays.
36. See Genette 2004, 10, for "la métalepse de l'auteur."

might be a cover for Theocritus is continually toyed with, as he and Lycidas compete in bucolic song (36) and possible future competitions with the real poets Asclepiades (himself referred to by a pseudonym) and Philitas are alluded to (40). Simichidas thus "both is and is not Theocritus."[37] Or, in other terms, the text alternately interposes and cancels distance between the two.

In Genette's model, metalepsis consists of isolated, discrete moments when the text can be seen to conflate the narrative levels of the author and the fiction; these are figural precisely because they disturb the narrative homeostasis. The process that I have described as impersonation, by contrast, is dynamic and ongoing. In fictional autobiography, the narrative "I" continually serves as a wormhole connecting the real author and the fictional, and even on those occasions when distance is enforced, when the fictional contract reasserts itself, readers can feel the absence of identification tensed against the contrary force.

Let me take, as a particularly complex and entertaining example of this phenomenon, Lucian's *True Stories*. Lucian is one of antiquity's most metaleptic authors, often manifesting himself in his own works within their fictional texture but under pseudonyms that simultaneously mark nonidentity (Momus, Parrhesiades, Tychiades, and so forth).[38] In the dialogue *Fisherman,* revenant philosophers from the past arraign Parrhesiades for having "written certain slanders in a thick book"[39]—the book in question being Lucian's *Sale of Lives*. This scenario is an impossible fantasy of the dead coming to life, obviously fictional, but into that imaginary world the real Lucian has levered an authorial alter ego to defend his own writing of a different work. (This technique, I think, owes more than has been recognized to the *parabaseis* of Aristophanes's comedies, which similarly slide between identification with and distantiation from the authorial voice—a topic for another occasion.)[40]

Lucian is persistently metaleptic across his works, but nowhere more so, I argue, than in his *True Stories*. This is a different kind of fictional autobiography than Apuleius's or Petronius's: it involves not the impersonation of another human being but the projection into the author's own life of "things that I have neither seen nor experienced nor heard from anyone else—things that do not exist at all and could not exist in the first place."[41] The narrator and protagonist of the story

---

37. Bowie 1985, 67–68, at 68.
38. Whitmarsh 2001, 248–53, and Goldhill 2002b, 63–67, discuss this phenomenon. Whitmarsh 2009a covers other examples of Lucianic metalepsis.
39. *Pisc.* 26.
40. Goldhill 1991, 188–205, at 199: "The parabases of Aristophanic comedy develop and play with the tensions and disjunctions between the roles of the chorus as a character in the drama, as a medium for the words of the *sophos,* as a celebrant of the festival of Dionysus, as the performer of lyric poetry." See further Hubbard 1991.
41. *VH* 1.4.

clearly is (a version of) the author because—unusually in the Lucianic corpus—he is directly named as "Lucian" in the inscription set up on the Isles of the Blessed (2.28). As Karen Ní Mheallaigh has recently argued, this very act of naming reestablishes the link between author and narrator that the prologue denies: it is precisely the name that is normally expected to underwrite the autobiographical guarantee ("I, the undersigned, testify that this happened to me").[42]

We can see this kind of metaleptic play throughout the *True Stories*. Let us briefly consider another example. At one point in book 1, we read of the distinctive eyes of the inhabitants of the moon: "I am reluctant to tell you what sort of eyes they have, for fear that you may think me lying because of the unbelievability of the story."[43] This is of course a "humorous twist"[44] on a historiographical convention, but it is more than just a joke. The historiographical topos aims to establish the plausibility of the account, guaranteeing that the author (the real, flesh-and-blood author) will personally testify to this truth. Yet at the same time, the reference to "unbelievability" reminds us of the prologue's claim that "my readers must not believe" in any of the events described.[45] In fact, we know that the real, flesh-and-blood Lucian has disavowed the entire tale; the metaleptic reappearance of Lucian-the-(prologic-)author here does not guarantee truth but double-dares us to disbelieve.

I have argued not that the critical category of the narrator should not exist or does not make sense but that narratology's automatic compartmentalization of the narrator as discrete from the author discounts much of the metaleptic play on which prenarratological fiction depends. The issue arises primarily because narratology is a theory with pretensions to the objective description of literary form and in no sense a theory of composition or reading, but at the same time, like any critical system, it contains an implicit normativity. "Better" authors or readers, we are encouraged to think, will be aware of narratological categories. But the cases of Augustine and Photius show the limitations of this assumption: both were expert readers in ancient terms, and both formulate their responses in markedly nonnarratological ways.

It is almost certainly true that any narrative in world history could be described in narratological terms. Narratology is, to this extent, universal. But the same could be said of any formal classificatory system, however arbitrary. Imagine, for example, a science of literature that reordered the sentences of a given text by number of phonemes: universal, yes, but it would tell us nothing about how real

---

42. Ní Mheallaigh 2010, 128–30. My formulation here (following Ní Mheallaigh's) leans on Lejeune 1982.
43. *VH* 1.25.
44. Georgiadou and Larmour 1998, 141.
45. *VH* 1.4.

readers in a given culture made sense of their texts. Narratology is certainly not useless in that way, but it does name, reify, and concretize certain categories—prime among them being, I have argued, "the narrator"—and in so doing lends them a false impression of objective value.

Like many readers, I suspect, I have long found the antiseptic formulae of narratologists incompatible with my experience of reading. We read for identifications with characters, whether emotional, psychological, intellectual, or otherwise, not to pinpoint the CF-p or EN1. And it is the bloodless anonymity of "the narrator" that is particularly intolerable. In his theoretical attack on the narrator, Robert Walsh argues that narratology absconds from the implications of speech-act theory, which demands an originating agent who can be held accountable for the truth or fictionality of an utterance.[46] In his view, all "narrators" are in fact characters within the text or the author. This, I think, is true enough: communication, context-specific as it is, requires that someone should own and be responsible for every utterance (even if this normative expectation may often be flouted). Fictional autobiography, however, is a special case, where the character/author divide becomes perpetually unstable, ever susceptible to metaleptic play.

---

46. Walsh 1997.

5

Metamorphoses of the *Ass*

In chapter 4, we briefly met Photius, the formidable ninth-century bishop of Constantinople; to him we owe our knowledge of Lucius of Patrae, one of the now lost authors of a version of the *Ass* story. Let us have a look in more detail at the crucial passage, codex 129 of his enormous *Library* (written for his brother at some point before he—Photius—became patriarch in 858):[1]

> Various books of the *Metamorphoses* of Lucius [*Loukios*] of Patrae were read. It is lucid in its style, pure and prone to sweetness. It avoids neologism, but in the narrative it seeks out flummery excessively. One might say it was another Lucian [*Loukianos*]. The first two books are all but reworkings on Lucius's [*Loukios's*] part of Lucian's [*Loukianos's*] story titled *Loukis or The Ass*—or Lucian [*Loukianos*] has reworked Lucius's [*Loukios's*] story. It seems more likely that Lucian [*Loukianos*] is the rewriter (although that is a guess; which is the prior is impossible to know for sure): Lucian [*Loukianos*] subtilized the ribaldry of Lucius's [*Loukios's*] discourse and cut out the parts that did not seem to him to serve his own purpose. Bringing together the rest into a single story, using the same words and syntax, he named the material he had plagiarized *Loukis or The Ass*. Each's story is full of mythical fictions and disgraceful magic. The difference is that Lucian [*Loukianos*] is aggressively mocking Greek superstition, in this work as in his others. Lucius [*Loukios*], however, is serious and thinks that transformations from humans into animals are credible: he has woven

---

This chapter draws on material first published as Whitmarsh 2011c. I am grateful to Publicacions i Edicions de la Universitat de Barcelona for permission to reuse it.

1. On this passage and its implications see especially Perry 1967, 211–18; Van Thiel 1971, 2–7; Mason 1994. Hägg 1975 argues for Photius's general reliability in meticulous detail.

into his text transformations from beasts into humans and back again, and all the rest of the idle nonsense we find in the ancient myths.

The first point to note is the obvious one, that the *Ass* is a "text network"[2] rather than a text, a cellular organization rather than an incorporated company. The complexity of the *Ass* tradition is increased by the existence not only of Apuleius's *Metamorphoses* but also of an Oxyrhynchus papyrus containing a different version of the episode where the ass penetrates a lusty woman (corresponding to ps.-Luc. 51 and Apul., *Met.* 10.20–22), narrated in the third rather than the first person. There were thus at least four distinct versions of the story current in antiquity; this is one of those traditions like the *Alexander Romance*, the *Life of Aesop*, *Joseph and Aseneth*, and *Apollonius, King of Tyre* that circulated in multiple, apparently non-hierarchical forms.

What is more interesting, however, is the giddying, unsettling nature of the bishop's presentation of the tradition, even in this snapshot, a discombobulation that is effected through the perplexing use of names. To make the point clearer, I have supplied exact transliterations of the Greek forms of these names. Photius claims to have read two versions of the *Ass* narrative: a longer *Metamorphoses* by Lucius (*Loukios*) of Patras (perhaps dealing with multiple different narratives) and a shorter *Loukis or The Ass* by the well-known satirist Lucian (in Greek, *Loukianos*); the latter would appear to be identical with the text transmitted in some manuscripts of Lucian under the title of *Lucius* (in Greek, *Loukios*) *or The Ass*. Now, according to Photius, Loukios plagiarized Loukianos's text called *Loukis* (or vice versa). What is going on with this nomenclature? Why is Lucian's (*Loukianos*'s) text said to be called *Loukis* (there is no evidence for that in our surviving text)? Is *Loukis* a corruption (how?) of an original *Loukios*? And is the text attributed to Lucian genuinely Lucianic or has it become integrated into the manuscript tradition of Lucianic texts thanks to the similarity of names?[3] *Loukios* of Patrae raises problems too: since this name is shared with the protagonist of the story,[4]

---

2. Selden 2010.

3. The idea of Lucianic authorship of our text is unfashionable, in part since it is usually decried as either unliterary or an epitome (or both). More prevalent, among the few who risk an opinion, is the view that the original text from which ours was supposedly epitomized is Lucianic: see especially Perry 1967, 211–35, Holzberg 1984. Whatever the truth of this (unverifiable) hypothesis, it is unlikely in my view that Lucian was the first to come up with the story, for two reasons. First, because the relative dates of Lucian (ca. 125–80?) and Apuleius (ca. 125–70?) give an awkwardly brief, if not impossible, period for a Lucianic text to travel to North Africa. Second, and more significant, the new papyrus fragment demonstrates that multiple versions were in circulation.

4. Apuleius's Lucius is from Corinth. The significance of this shift has been discussed particularly by Mason 1971, stressing Corinth's greater familiarity to Roman readers and centrality as an Isiac cult space, and Graverini 2002, emphasizing the significance of Corinth as a space for thinking through Greco-Roman relations.

Photius (or the tradition he follows) would seem to have mistaken the first-person narrator for the flesh-and-blood author, which is to say he seems to take the *Ass* as a variety of what we have called "fictional autobiography" (see previous chapter).

It is possible that this conflation is caused by some flagging zeal on Photius's part; even he must have tired occasionally. What slender evidence we have, however, suggests that the confusion of Lucius and Lucian, at any rate, affected more readers than just Photius.[5] My working hypothesis in this chapter, indeed, is that Photius responds to features in the *Ass* tradition, features that we can trace in the surviving text attributed to Lucian. We saw in chapter 4 how Apuleius's *Metamorphoses* activates a metaleptic shuttling between author and narrator, particularly in the celebrated passage where Lucius pronounces himself to be from Madaura (also called Madauros), Apuleius's hometown (*Met.* 11.27). We also saw how Augustine was stimulated to read this *Metamorphoses* as fictional autobiography (*Civ.* 18.18). What Photius shows us is that a parallel phenomenon could take place for the Greek *Ass* tradition. Like Augustine, Photius reads first-person narrative metaleptically, as fictional autobiography, rather than narratologically (i.e., by imposing the strict author/narrator separation). But again, as with Augustine, we should attribute this to different reading conventions rather than to a want of sophistication. Certainly Photius differentiates between author and narrator even as he conflates them: in the case of the Lucianic *Ass*, he detects behind the voice of the narrator a Lucianic "hidden author," who has not only toned down the ribaldry and cut out the extraneous material but also introduced a skeptical, satirical edge. By contrast, Photius appears to read Lucius's *Metamorphoses* as naïvely credulous. I take this distinction as programmatic for a reading of the *Ass* tradition as a whole, and even of all first-person narrative (from Odysseus's *apologoi* onward) that demands to be taken (contradictorily) as both personal testimony and artful contrivance, or, to use the terms that we derived from Augustine in chapter 4, as both *indicatio* and *fictio*.[6]

The Greek *Ass* is a short version of the story unfurled at length in Apuleius's *Metamorphoses*. Lucius of Patrae visits a friend of his father's in Thessaly. While there he discovers that the mistress of the house is a magician and can change her form into that of a bird. Lucius seduces the slave Palaestra, who shows him her mistress's room; unfortunately he transforms into a donkey rather than a bird. The remainder of the story is told from the perspective of the donkey, until finally

---

5. The *subscriptio* in a tenth-century Vatican codex (Γ in Macleod's catalogue) refers to our extant *Ass* as "Lucian's epitome of Lucius's *Metamorphoses*."

6. See also Perry 1967, 325–29, on first-person fictions, which argues that there is a generic expectation that such tales will be "wonder stories" (328); the consequence of this observation (which Perry does not draw out) is that the credibility of the narrator is in such cases often under examination.

Lucius manages to come across the roses that he needs to eat in order to restore his human shape.

The instability of narratorial identity is thus built into the narrative itself. As we shall see, this text is centrally about the question of what kind of voice, what kind of consciousness, we can attribute to the asinine Lucius. But let us begin with the issue of naming, which is artfully exploited from the start. The narrative opens with an unidentified speaker stating that "I once went away to Thessaly." There is no context at all in terms of characterization (such as we find in the earlier Greek romances); the reader is left to uncover the narrator's identity hermeneutically. The first clue is that his father has links with a local man. This turns out to be "Hipparchus by name [*tounoma*]" (1); the naming of his contact only emphasizes the concealment of the speaker's identity. When he arrives at Hypata, he asks the inhabitants where Hipparchus lives, saying that he has letters for him. We deduce, then, that the narrator is on a mission from his father, but there is still a mystery about him. On arrival at Hipparchus's house, he is asked, "Who is it who is asking, and what do you want?" (2). The narrator replies that he brings letters from Decrianus the Sophist—but once again subtly declines to reveal his own name. It is not until Hipparchus welcomes him in and feeds him that we learn that his name is Lucius (twenty-nine lines in, in M. D. Macleod's Oxford Classical Text). Like Odysseus, the prototype of all first-person narrators, Lucius strategically delays the revelation of his identity.

As again with Odysseus, we have hints of the narrator's deceptiveness. When asked by Hipparchus what he plans to do next, he replies, "I am leaving for Larissa" (3), to stay for several days. This, we are then told, is a mere pretext (*skēpsis*; 4): actually he wishes to see some magic. Lucius's unreliability as a narrator is an issue for his external readers as well as Hipparchus: his initial statement to us that he was in Thessaly on business was, it transpires, also a pretext. The parallel between his false claims to Hipparchus and to his readers is underlined verbally: "I am leaving for Larissa" (3) responds to the opening of the narrative, "I once left for Thessaly" (1).

These subtle games with the mutability of identity and the unreliability of narration prepare readers for the narrative's central episode, Lucius's metamorphosis into a donkey. The motivations supplied are interestingly different here from those given in Apuleius, where Lucius simply tells Fotis that he wants to know more about that kind of magic ("Sum namque coeam magiae noscendae ardentissimus cupitor," 3.19). The Greek Lucius, however, in explaining to Palaestra, roots his desire in philosophical investigation: "I wished to learn by first-hand experience [*peirai*] if when metamorphosed [*metamorphōtheis*] from a human I would also have the soul of a bird" (13). The transformation is thus framed as an empirical (note *peira*) experiment in the nature of identity.[7]

---

7. Van Thiel 1971, 206, with n. 104.

We should at this point pause to fill in the theoretical background to this kind of question. The issue of animal rationality is readily paralleled across a number of philosophical and related works. Already in the fifth century B.C.E. we find Alcmaeon arguing that the existence of reason is exclusive to humans: "A human differs from other beasts in that it alone has understanding, whereas the others perceive but have no understanding" (fr. 1a DK). Throughout antiquity, ancient philosophers maintained a keen interest in subtle differentiations between human and animal modes of cognition.[8]

The *Ass* does not engage with these issues at the level of highbrow philosophy; the primary reference (although there is no direct verbal echo) is rather Circe's transformations in the *Odyssey*. There Odysseus comments that her victims "had the heads, voices, hair, and bodies of pigs, but their minds remained intact as before."[9] This passage becomes the theme of Plutarch's *Gryllus*, an interview between Odysseus and a talking pig who is unwilling to be turned back into a human because he prefers his new life.[10] The Circe episode is also alluded to briefly in Lucian's *On the Dance*, where the speaker arguing in favor of dancing describes it as like a drug, only "you will not have the head of an ass or the heart of a donkey, but your mind will be intact, although in your pleasure you will not give anyone else even a tiny bit of the potion."[11] It is clear, then, that by the second century C.E. Homer's account of the transformation of Odysseus's crew had become the focus for philosophical speculation, a thought experiment probing the possibility of animal rationality.

Ancient philosophers interested in the theme of animal rationality were particularly exercised by the question of speech. Do animals speak? What does speech consist of? Phonematic utterance or rational content? Aristotelians, Stoics, and Epicureans all debated these issues.[12] In *Lucius or The Ass*, as in Apuleius's *Metamorphoses*,[13] vocalization becomes a central issue. Loss of the capacity for speech is Lucius's first sensation on transformation: "When I looked at myself in the round, I saw myself an ass, and I no longer had the voice to reproach Palaestra" (13).

---

8. Sorabji 1993.

9. *Od.* 10.239–40.

10. Apuleius's Lucius claims descent from Plutarch (*Met.* 1.2, 2.3): these passages are usually connected with the latter's Platonism and *De curiositate*, but the *Gryllus* is an equally relevant intertext.

11. *De salt.* 85. This passage is interesting for broader reasons. There is no doubt that Lucian is alluding to Circe here (he proceeds to refer directly to Hermes's wand, with a quotation from the relevant passage). Why then does he introduce the element of transformation into an ass? Asses do not appear in the list of Circe's animals. That Lucian immediately reaches for this example suggests that he is at least aware of the *Ass* tradition, even if it cannot be said to be direct evidence for his authorship of our text.

12. Sorabji 1993, 20–28, 80–86.

13. Finkelpearl 2006, 213–18.

Speech is one of the primary markers of his loss of human identity. By the time the *Ass* was written, indeed, the word *alogos* had developed from its original meaning of "lacking rationality" or "lacking speech" to also mean "animal."[14]

In a subsequent moment of self-diagnosis, voice is again the key feature of differentiation between human and animal: "I was in other respects an ass, but in my mind and thoughts that human Lucius—except that I had no voice" (15). This passage is notable in that it separates out the dual aspects of the narrator's identity: mind and thoughts still belong to "that," or perhaps "the same old [*ekeinos*]," Lucius,[15] but everything else to the donkey. The capacity for speech havers between the two: the narrator seems to anticipate categorizing it along with rational intelligence, but in fact it turns out to be casualty of the animal metamorphosis. Speech, it would appear, is conceived of ambiguously in this dualistic body-soul model: it is the physical manifestation of mental processes.

On two further occasions, Lucius attempts speech but fails to articulate it:

1. "I wanted again and again to say 'O Caesar!,' but all I did was bray; I cried out the 'O' excellently and in full voice, but the 'Caesar' did not follow." (16)
2. "I was deeply grieved by my transformation and wanted to cry out: 'I have tolerated my sufferings thus far, wretched Zeus!'—however, it was not my voice that emerged from my throat but the ass's. I gave an almighty bray." (38)

The first of these cases is the better known, since it forms part of the basis for politicized readings of the *Ass* as a commentary on Roman imperial power: the attempt to offer a prayer submissively to the emperor in his capacity as protector of his citizens is, it is claimed, subverted by translation into ass speak.[16] To my knowledge, however, scholars of passage (1) have not noted the existence of the second, parallel passage—but the relationship between the two did not escape Apuleius, who reproduced his version of the "O" joke found in (1) at the equivalent point in the narrative represented by (2).[17] The two passages are thematically interconnected by the focus on the voice as the locus of identity confusion, the thematic reduplication (a technique used consistently by the *Ass* author)[18] serving to reinforce the centrality of the motif to the narrative as a whole.

---

14. LSJ, s.v. "alogos" II. See, e.g., ps.-Luc., *Amor.* 27, 33, 36.
15. For this usage see LSJ, s.v. "ekeinos" 2; see however later in the chapter, on the *Ass*'s ch. 54.
16. E. Hall 1995, 52; Finkelpearl 2007, 266–67. The analogous passage in Apuleius is *Met.* 3.29: politically alert interpretations at Graverini 2002, 72; Finkelpearl 2006, 213–15; Finkelpearl 2007, 267.
17. *Met.* 8.29 ("I tried to shout 'Forward, O Romans!,' but in the absence of the other letters and syllables only the 'O' came out").
18. Van Thiel 1971, 207–8.

When Lucius attempts to speak, his self divides. In the earlier passage, the use of first-person forms is telling. Initially, Lucius's "I" is given responsibility for rational deliberation: "I wanted ... to say." Here it is the internal self, the originator of intention, who is identified. But "I" is also the brute animal who cannot fulfill that intention: "I cried out [*eboōn*] the 'O' excellently and in full voice," "all I did was bray [*ōgkōmēn*]." This raises the possibility that Lucius considers his asinine and human forms as unified. In the final phrase quoted from this passage, however, the failure to articulate the word *Caesar* is left strangely unattributed: "the 'Caesar' did not follow." It is as if Lucius identifies with the speaking ass insofar as he articulates the "O" but then withdraws that identification when the intended next word does not follow. The issue of speech thus sets in motion an identity crisis whereby Lucius both is and is not the ass; he is partially alienated from the body he inhabits.

Similar ambiguities surface in the second passage. To Lucius's "I" are ascribed the desire and the intention of a rational human ("I was deeply grieved ... [I] wanted") but also the braying of an ass ("I gave an almighty bray"). Once again, however, there are impersonal aspects. The emerging of the voice is described in the third person and here even more explicitly marked as separate from the speaker's self: "It was not my voice that emerged from my throat but the ass's."

This goes beyond philosophical theory and into the self-reflexivity of the *Ass* as narrative. Language is the medium not only for Lucius's failed attempts to communicate within the story but also for the very communication of the story to us. The form of the retrospective ego narrative—or analeptic homodiegesis, as narratologists would say—gives a particular urgency to this issue, for the narrator is speaking to us now in precisely the way that he could not at the time as an ass. The distinction between *auctor* (author) and *actor* (agent) is one of narratorial epistemology and ontology: although the former can reconstitute the experience of the latter through memory, the two are fundamentally distinct in kind, the latter being mute and incapable of expression. The silencing of the ass can thus be seen as a manifestation within the narrative of a theoretical principle that applies to all retrospective first-person narration: the "I" who is the agent within the text inevitably represents the *post eventum* ventriloquizing of the narrating "I." Yet the first-person singular, the text's *egō*, is also the site of convergence of between the two, and to that extent any distinction between them always threatens to collapse. Like an accordionist's hands, auctor and actor are continually pulling apart and pushing back together. This, I suggest, is why Lucius's "I" oscillates between identification with and distantiation from the ass's corporeal form.

Mute actor and eloquent auctor reunite at the end, when Lucius, while performing in an amphitheater in Thessalonica, eats the antidotal roses and is restored to his human form. This is expressed as the disappearance of "that [*ekeinos*] long-time ass" and the reemergence of "the Lucius himself inside" (54).[19] This passage hierarchically stratifies the true, internal identity of Lucius and the false, external image of the ass; the ass, moreover, is set apart by the distal pronoun *ekeinos* (literally "that one over there").[20] At this juncture in the narrative, then, the ontological questions seem to be answered: Lucius is identified with the psychic self, and the ass is presented as a mere casing that can be shed without harm to the inner being.

Yet lest we assume too quickly that the complexities of identity are now resolved, two notes of caution should be sounded. The first is that this passage picks up the language of chapter 15 (quoted above): "I was in other respects an ass, but in my mind and thoughts that [*ekeinos*] human Lucius." The two passages clearly respond to each other, since each immediately follows the moment of metamorphosis. Yet they are also crucially different in the way that they stratify identities: in the first, *ekeinos* modifies Lucius, in the second the ass, and in the first Lucius identifies part of himself with the ass ("I was in other respects . . .") but in the second he does not. This reminds us that articulations of identity are contingent on circumstance, that although Lucius may cease to identify with the ass now that he has regained human form, it was not always thus.

The second point is, relatedly, that the narrative circumstances matter too. The divestment of the asinine form from Lucius's identity also portends the closure of the narrative, at the point where auctor and actor converge. It is, tellingly, now that Lucius reclaims his voice, not just as a human being but as a literary narrator: his first action is to run to the provincial governor and tell him a story, in fact this story, of how he was transformed into an ass (54).

Lucius also reacquires his name at this point—the very name that, as we saw, he artfully repressed at the start of the narrative. The governor's request for Lucius to identify himself constitutes a prosified, Romanized version of the formula used at analogous points in Homer's *Odyssey*:[21] "Tell me your name and those of your parents and kin (if you can lay claim to any relatives) and your city" (55). This Odyssean echo particularly invokes the episode in book 8 of Homer's text (*Od.* 8.550–56) where Alcinous (a powerful ruler) asks Odysseus (a high-status individual concealed in a lowly guise) to reveal his name (*ounoma*), homeland (*gaian*),

---

19. This is the MSS reading, which seems to me not to warrant the suspicion that has been foisted upon it.

20. See slightly earlier in the same chapter: "That guise [*ekeinē . . . opsis*] of the pack animal fell away from me and was destroyed."

21. "Who are you, where among men are you from, where are your city and parents?" Forms of these phrases appear at *Od.* 1.170, 7.238, 10.325, 14.187, 15.264, 19.105, 24.298; see also *Il.* 21.150. See Webber 1989, with further literature.

people (*dēmon*), and city (*polin*).²² In Homer's text, the request presages Odysseus's celebrated *apologoi*, the model for all subsequent first-person narrative. In the *Ass*, the restoration to human form—and, in particular, the restoration of the human voice and the power to communicate—is the precondition for the telling of the narrative that we have in our hands. In both cases, the reclamation of name and identity initiates the storytelling.

There is, however, a paradoxical irony around Lucius's name. By an interesting quirk of fate, an apparent textual crux undermines his public assertion of his name and identity:

> "'My father,' I replied, '. . . is Lucius, and my brother's is Gaius. We hold our other two names in common. I am the author of histories [*historiai*] and other things; he is an elegiac poet and skilled prophet. Our homeland is Patras, in Achaea.'" (55)

The transmitted text of the first sentence is meaningless, so scholars since Konrad von Gesner (in the sixteenth century) have plausibly suggested that the lacuna has swallowed the paternal name and a phrase like "and my own name is." The resulting reconstructed sentence would mean something like "My father's name is [e.g.] Titus Asinius Pictor; my name is Lucius, my brother's is Gaius, and the remaining two names we hold in common." It is at the very least ironic that a text so preoccupied with identity and naming fails us at the very moment of self-revelation. Lucian, whether or not the text is his, would have enjoyed this.

This passage is playing two other games. The first relates to Roman names: whether the full threefold nomenclature (*tria nomina*) was given in the original text or not, "Lucius" and "Gaius"²³—who hail from the Roman colony of Patrae, founded under Augustus for military veterans—are evidently Roman. As a number of scholars have noted, this is the only Greek fictional text of the period (with the partial exception of Iamblichus's *Babyloniaka*) that acknowledges the Roman present.²⁴ Edith Hall has even argued that the ass becomes a figure for the suffering and complicity enforced by Roman rule.²⁵ But Lucius is playing a strange game with Romanness. On the one hand, as we have seen, he clearly identifies himself as a Roman citizen. Yet even while asserting his Romanness to the governor, he does not actually title himself with his full Roman *tria nomina*, skating over it in passing

---

22. Linguistically, the governor's words are closer to the standard version of the formula cited in the previous note, but that does not impede any allusion to Alcinous's variant version. Lucius's social status is apparently nearly as high in the *Ass* as it is in Apuleius (Mason 1983).

23. Perry 1967, 221, notes that Roman jurists use these two names to denote typical Roman citizens, like the English "Smith" and "Jones"; see also E. Hall 1995, 59 n. 24.

24. In addition to Lucius's cry "O Caesar," discussed above, and the appearance of the provincial governor in the passage under discussion, we have a Roman soldier who beats a gardener for failing to understand his Latin instructions (44).

25. E. Hall 1995; see also Swain 1996, 113 n. 36; Finkelpearl 2007.

("We hold our other two names in common") as he identifies himself after the Greek fashion as *x*, of profession *y*, from place *z*.[26] The politics of naming are extremely difficult to judge at this distance. Is Lucius, perhaps, balancing his desire to appeal to the Roman governor as a fellow Roman with his need to avoid provoking the Greek audience in the amphitheater? Or is it that he partially represses his Romanness for the purposes of his Greek readership? We can say at least that there is more going on than meets the eye. When Lucius gives us his name, he also draws attention to the fact that self-naming, in the Roman period, is a dangerous act of cultural self-positioning.

The other point to which I wish to draw attention is Lucius's assertion that he is a writer of "histories and other things." This is clearly, at one level, self-reflexive: the work that we are reading is a literary composition. This self-reflexivity also operates at the level of truth and fiction: Lucius is playfully asking us, perhaps, to consider whether the present story falls into the category of history or "other." If we reopen the question of Lucianic authorship, moreover, there is still more to be said. Lucian of course is a "writer [*suggrapheus*]," and a composer of fantastical tales that play games with traditional (historical) conceptions of plausibility. This might be a moment not just when the ass reveals himself to be Lucius but also when Lucius reveals himself to be Lucian—except, of course, that we have learned to be extremely cautious before accepting self-identification at face value, in this of all texts.

Whether the *Ass* is Lucianic is not a question that we are in a position to address directly. What we can say, however, is that it engages centrally with questions of the mutability of identity—cultural, literary, and ontological identity. Questions of this sort were current in Lucian's intellectual climate and indeed in his own works. It is true that the *Ass* is unlike anything else in the Lucianic corpus, but we are beginning to realize just what a sophisticated and proficient literary mimic Lucian was. Not only did he learn Attic Greek up to a stellar standard, possibly without a background in the Greek language, but he also mimicked styles effortlessly. This is explicit in the *True Stories*, where he begins by asserting that he is writing through literature rather than experience. *Astrology* and the *On the Syrian Goddess* show him taking on Herodotean Ionic.[27] With *On the Syrian Goddess* there are, of course, questions of authorship that parallel those of the *Ass:* can we really imagine Lucian writing a text that is so eccentric within his corpus? The answer, I think, is in both cases yes: let us not forget the story in the Arabic Galen of Lucian forging the

---

26. A similar dancing around Roman identity appears earlier in the text. Lucius's only named friend, one Decrianus, is referred to as "a sophist of Patras" and "the best of the Greeks" (2)—but again has a Roman name (indeed, a name shared with an architect with an instrumental role in Hadrian's building program: see *SHA Hadrian* 19).

27. Lightfoot 2003, 91–174.

works of Heraclitus.²⁸ This is an author with a real facility for imitation, someone whose entire literary identity is predicated on his ability to take on roles.²⁹

In the *Ass*, the author—whether, ultimately, it is Lucian or not—takes on such a role. To compose a fictitious first-person narrative is already to assume a literary role: one speaks as an "I" that one is not. In the case of the *Ass* narratives, the matter is complicated by the fact that this literary role has a preexistent heritage: much as sympotic poets assumed the identity of Anacreon and spoke through his voice, or elegiac moralists did with Theognis, the author of this text is aware that he is playing the part of Lucius. To write as Lucius was, clearly, to metamorphose oneself into him.

We began by pondering how Photius, or the tradition on which he leaned, ended up with such a metaleptic muddle. We can see now that this confusion is already provoked in the one complete Greek *Ass* that we possess. Metamorphosis is a theme that readily invites reflection on the instability of the self, reflection that ramifies into philosophical, literary, metaliterary, and meta-authorial fields.

---

28. Strohmaier 1976.
29. See, e.g., Whitmarsh 2001, 247–94.

6

Addressing Power

Fictional Letters between Alexander and Darius

How does narrative fiction correspond to (or with) epistolography? The huge surge of critical interest in epistolary fiction (as form, cultural praxis, vehicle for revolutionary ideology, and normative mapping of gender roles) has lent it a central role in modern discussions of the formation of the European novel, particularly as a driver of all that is bourgeois, literate, kinetic, feminine, dialogic, sexual, self-reflexive.[1] The European novel, as is well known, grew up at a time when the materialities of literary practice were evolving rapidly: not just the spread of printing (which Walter Benjamin in particular saw as instrumental in the invention of the novel)[2] but also the emergence of the popular press, leafleting and pamphleting, and—notably—postal services open to private individuals; in other words, a time when new ideas were being aired about the making, addressing, sending, receiving, and interrupting of intimate, self-author(iz)ed or samizdat text. If the hallmarks of the modern novel are intrigue, a transgressive prurience, and the illicit circulation of both discourse and identities, then much of this energy is common to the new technologies of correspondence.

Yet letters are also, from a different perspective, decidedly nonfictional: documentary, often interpersonal rather than designed for publication, "real" or at least mimicries of the real. They occupy a different sociocultural space than literature,

---

This chapter is a version of Whitmarsh, forthcoming c; I am grateful to Brill for permission to reprint.

1. Altman 1982, a formalist approach to epistolarity as literature, initiated the vogue. See also Kauffman 1992; MacArthur 1990; Favret 1993; Watson 1994; Alliston 1996; Cook 1996; Zaczek 1997; Versini 1998; Beebee 1999; Bray 2003.

2. Benjamin 1999, 87.

in that their generic conventions (for writers and readers alike) rest on the presumption of directness and intimacy. "A letter should be very largely an expression of character," writes the author of an ancient literary manual. "Perhaps every one reflects his own soul in writing a letter."[3] This kind of comment, which is widespread both in antiquity and later, should not be confused with naïve realism, embedded as it is in this case within a prescriptive discussion of the proper style that one should adopt in epistolography (style, after all, is designed, taught, habituated, nonnatural). What it points to instead is a sense that the best letter disavows its own literariness: it "mimics the effect of improvisation."[4] This is the "affectation of simplicity which covers the writer's rhetoric" that Derrida detects already in Isocrates's letters and emulates in his pseudepistolographic *The Post Card*.[5] Letters tend to shuttle back and forth over the boundary separating the artful from the ingenuous, the constructed from the sincere.

It is this paradoxical status of the letter, hovering between categories, that has driven much of the recent critical interest in the epistolary novel alluded to above. In romanticism, we read, "the letter ... hints at a correspondence between public and private experience, and that correspondence continually revises—and disrupts—fixed images of narratives."[6] Or again, in terms of gender, the fictional letter represents "the masculine 'posing' as feminine in order to be 'posted/positioned' within a fixed system of public circulation and exchange."[7] Letters both embody the novelistic fiction of access to a hidden world and deconstruct it by exposing its very fictionality.

In antiquity too the letter is there at the very origins of fiction. A number of studies have pointed to the emergence in the Hellenistic period of fictional letter collections relating to Themistocles, Hippocrates, Euripides, and others, to the epistolary *Chion of Heraclea*, and to the central role of epistolarity in the later Greek ideal romance, particularly Chariton.[8] We cannot pinpoint particular Hellenistic transformations in print technology (or the redefinition of the private sphere or revolutionary fervor) to explain these processes, but it is clear (not least from Oxyrhynchus)[9] that the letter assumed a position of centrality at every level of society in the Hellenistic and Roman periods, in a world that was increasingly both literate and subject to remote governance and legislation and in which

---

3. Ps.-Demetrius, *On Style* 227, translated in Russell and Winterbottom 1972.
4. "Mimeitai autoskhediazonta": Ps.-Demetrius, *On Style* 224, translated in Russell and Winterbottom 1972.
5. Derrida 1987, 92.
6. Favret 1993, 9.
7. Ibid., 14.
8. Rosenmeyer 2001 is comprehensive and standard.
9. Thoughtful survey at Hutchinson 2007.

kin, friends, and lovers were increasingly likely to be separated by work or misadventure. I shall return in conclusion to the "textual energy" of the postclassical period.

This chapter considers what may be our very earliest example of a Greek "novel" (however we choose to define that slippery term), the *Alexander Romance*. The misleading singular title *Romance* in fact covers a textual tradition extending into five multilingual manuscript families, each of which contains interwoven material from a variety of dates.[10] To make matters more complex, the text is conventionally taken to have been patched together from several preexisting literary fabrics: a narrative vita detailing Alexander's journey, a collection of letters exchanged between Alexander and Darius (and various other figures), a dialogue with the Brahmans, and various smaller sections.[11] Despite the evident difficulties involved in stratifying a text like this, it seems likely that the earliest elements date to the Ptolemaic period, perhaps even early in that period.[12] This would indeed make it (caveats conceded) our earliest surviving work of prose fiction from Greek antiquity (with the possible exception of Xenophon's *Cyropedia*).

A FLUID TRADITION

The epistolary core of the *Romance* centers on four sets of exchanges: between Alexander and Darius (5–8, 11–12, 14–16), Darius and Porus (18–19), Alexander and Porus (32–34), and Alexander and the Amazons (35–38).[13] Interwoven with this are two other narrative strands: one relating the commanders (both Darius and Alexander) to women and family life (10+24,[14] 13, 20, 26–27, 29–31) and one relating them to other commanders, satraps, and subjugated cities. At the heart of the epistolary sequence lies the exchange between Alexander and Darius (and their various subordinates), the key players in the letters' military and political events.[15] Every single letter bar one (28) involves at least one of these two, and while Darius is alive almost half (ten out of approximately twenty-four)[16] involve both. It is likely, I think, that the "epistolary novel" on which the *Romance* draws

---

10. For a recent account see Stoneman 2007, lxxiii–lxxxiii; also 2003.

11. Stoneman 2007, xliii–xlviii.

12. Stoneman 2007, xxviii–xxxiv, reviews the arguments and defends a Hellenistic date for the earliest stratum.

13. To avoid cluttering the page, I use the *Briefroman* numeration in Merkelbach 1977 (1954) for the letters, which is explained just below in the chapter; table 1 can be used as a concordance.

14. I.e., the single letter in the *Romance* that Merkelbach bisects, discussed later in the chapter.

15. Discussed by Rosenmeyer 2001, 177–84.

16. Absolute certainty is impossible because (as will be discussed presently) the letters do not respect any authoritative external chronology.

focused on these two figures. Certainly it is in their relationship that we see the most sustained and dynamic characterization.[17] What is more, the two epistolary papyri that we have relating to the tradition focus exclusively on Alexander, Darius, and their underlings.

Most of my discussion will be devoted to reading this exchange between the two rulers as a sophisticated and vibrant expression of a culture exuberantly obsessed with dynamic modes of textuality, as well as with the themes of kingship and cultural identity. Before we get there, however, let us briefly consider the nature of these letters and the way in which they have been transmitted. This discussion will serve partly to introduce this recondite material to those unfamiliar with it and partly to foreground some of the attendant text-critical problems, but more importantly, as we shall see in due course, issues of literary interpretation cannot in this case be isolated from issues of textual transmission. Letters always insist on their own materiality and on the practicalities of circulation within both the fictional and the philological world.

Alexander and Darius's epistolary exchange is distributed throughout the *Romance* (see table 1).[18] Scholars since Reinhold Merkelbach have assumed that these letters were imported into the narrative from an original epistolary novel, primarily on the basis of the two fragmentary papyri mentioned above, which seem to be from epistolary collections. The first (*PSI* 1285) contains an exchange between Darius and Alexander (and, in one case, between Polyidus—apparently the fourth-century tragedian—and Darius): five letters in total, the last two of which reappear at *Romance* 2.10. The second (*P.Hamb.* 605) contains six letters, four relating to Alexander, two of which are also found in the *Romance* (1.39, 2.17).[19] On this basis, Merkelbach reconstructed and published a *Briefroman* of thirty-eight letters, some of which are merely hypothesized on the basis of extant letters that seem to be responses.[20]

Merkelbach's *Briefroman* is, at one level, a *Quellenforscher*'s fantasy. For a start, it depends on a hypothesis that the Florence papyrus, or some similar text, is

---

17. This is not to deny that the Porus and Amazon exchanges work as a continuation of the narrative sequence. Porus functions as an afterecho of the now dead Darius, who has primed him to treat Alexander with hostility (letters 18–19). The Amazons are more interesting: they seem as if they too will play the role of aggressive, barbarian other (they refer to themselves as "the most powerful leaders among the Amazons," 38)—but end up being compliant and welcoming Alexander, in pointed contrast to Darius and Porus. These exchanges are however too brief to allow the kind of detailed narrative reading I propose.

18. I do not include in this discussion the "marvel letters" to Alexander's mother (2.24–41, 3.27–29), conventionally assumed to come from a different epistolary tradition.

19. Merkelbach 1947; 1954. The final letter, however, has phrases in common with *Romance* 3.2. The remaining letters are from Hannibal to the Athenians and from Philip to the Spartans.

20. Merkelbach 1977 (1954), 230–52.

TABLE 1. Concordance of Alexander letters

Briefroman	Romance	P.Hamb. 605	PSI 1285	Contents
1	1.39.7			Satraps to Darius
2	1.39.3–5	No. 1*		Darius to satraps
3	2.10.4–5			Satraps to Darius
4	1.39.8–9			Darius to satraps
5	1.36.2–5			Darius to Alexander
6	1.38.2–7			Alexander to Darius
7	1.40.2–5			Darius to Alexander
8		No. 3		Darius to Alexander
9				[Missing] Darius to Alexander
10	2.23 (β)			Alexander to Olympias
11	2.17.2–4*	No. 2		Darius to Alexander
12			No. 1	Darius to Alexander
13			No. 2	Polyidus to Darius
14			No. 3	Alexander to Darius
15	2.10.6–8*		No. 4	Darius to Alexander
16	2.10.9–10		No.5*	Alexander to Darius
17	1.42.1–3			Darius and Alexander to commanders
18	2.19.2–5			Darius to Porus
19	2.12.1–2			Porus to Darius
20	2.12.3–5			Rhodogyne to Darius
21	2.11.2–3			Alexander to satraps
22	2.11.4–5			Satrap to Darius
23	2.11.6–7			Darius to generals
24	2.23 (β)			Alexander to Olympias
25	2.21.3–21			Alexander to Persian cities
26	2.22.2–6			Alexander to Stateira and Rhodogyne
27	2.22.7–10			Stateira and Rhodogyne to Alexander
28	2.22.11			Stateira and Rhodogyne to Persian *ethnos*
29	2.22.12			Alexander to Stateira and Rhodogyne
30	2.22.13			Alexander to Olympias
31	2.22.14–16			Alexander to Roxane
32	3.2.2–5			Porus to Alexander
33	3.2.8–11			Alexander to Porus
34		No. 4		Porus to Alexander
35	3.25.3–4			Alexander to Amazons
36	3.25.5–11			Amazons to Alexander
37	3.26.1–14			Alexander to Amazons
38	3.26.5–7			Amazons to Alexander

* = partial

primary and was inexpertly filleted by the author of the *Romance*. A key prop in this argument is the belief that the "original" epistolary text was consistent with the historical chronology of Alexander's travels: this is clearly a questionable enough assumption in itself (when has fiction ever respected history?), but the theory faces the additional problem that there is no possible explanation, beyond incompetence, for why the author or authors of the *Romance* might have disturbed the sequence so violently. It is true that in the sequence that appears in the *Romance* there is one letter (*Briefroman* 19 = *Alex. Rom.* 2.12.1–2) that looks as if it might respond to a later letter (18 = 2.19.2–5), which would of course imply chronological dislocation, but in fact this is not a necessary conclusion; the letters also make perfect sense in their existing places in the *Romance*. More important, the quest for a chronologically accurate *Briefroman* does serious violence to the transmitted text. The most striking example is letter 10 (*Alex. Rom.* 2.23, only in the β tradition), from Alexander to his mother Olympias: Alexander reports his success at the battle of Issus, his foundation of two cities, and the capture and death of the wounded Darius. Now in the *Romance* chronology this letter is ideally positioned since we have just been told that Darius has died. Merkelbach, however, is vexed by the historical inconvenience that Darius did not die after Issus, so he cuts letter 10 in half. The parts about Issus and the city foundings he inserts at this point in the narrative, but the section about the death of Darius now becomes a new letter, number 24. This is clearly a desperate expedient.

There is one more major problem with the hypothetical *Briefroman*. The Getty Museum houses a relief dating to the early years of Tiberius (*SEG* 33.802). In 1989 Stanley Burnstein published an identification of four fragmentary lines on its reverse: three come from the letter of Darius to Alexander found only in the Hamburg papyrus, and the fourth (which translates as "When this letter arrived . . .") shows that the letter was, or at least could be, embedded in a larger narrative.[21] This, of course, undermines Merkelbach's argument that the author of the *Alexander Romance* was an incompetent writing around 200 C.E. who found a collection of letters and took the decisive step of dropping them into a preexisiting narrative; in the first century, clearly, there was already in existence at least one Alexander epistle set into a narrative framework, a framework, moreover, that was not the *Romance* as we have it. An additional complexity is that the Getty inscription contains the same words as the Hamburg papyrus, but the spaces available in its lacunae are insufficient to house the whole Hamburg papyrus text. In other words, we are dealing with (as, to his credit, Merkelbach conceded in his response to Burnstein)[22] a multimedia matrix of textual variants, a "text

---

21. Burnstein 1989.
22. Merkelbach 1989.

network"[23] rather than an originally pristine *Briefroman* thereafter debased in the *Romance*.

Let me make two points at this stage. The first is just the obvious need for caution. Alexander letters obviously circulated in multiple forms, both in anthologies (as the Hamburg and Florence papyri show) and embedded in narratives (as the *Romance* and the Getty relief show). Any conclusions that we draw about the relationship between these letters and their narrative contexts need, then, to be both provisional and local. The second point, however, is more constructive. That these letters are reshuffled so often, like the cards in a croupier's pack, is surely down to more than the adventures of transmission. This seems to point instead to an intrinsic feature of epistolarity in the Alexander tradition: like real letters, these can be intercepted and rerouted. There is a constant slippage with letters between content and the material form that conveys it, both within the fictional work and—in this case at least—in the very processes of transmission. The fluidity of this epistolary series is another manifestation of the tense and ambiguous relationship between letters and narrative that we saw at the outset of this chapter: the Alexander letters are simultaneously integral to the *Romance* tradition (in that they are fully naturalized in their narrative contexts) and capable of organic independent existence.

I turn now to what may seem an unorthodox reading of the Alexander letters, which will reflect both their seemingly constant process of coupling with and uncoupling from narrative, and the unusually protean nature of the collection. What I propose to do is to read the assemblage of Alexander-Darius letters from a variety of sources as a (stochastic) unity, even though there is no evidence that they were ever gathered in this way in a single text. This is not, however, simply a return to the idea of a single, originary *Briefroman*. The central difference is that the reading pursued here will avoid enforcing an arbitrary concept of structure, emphasizing instead the multiple possibilities for combination and recombination. If epistolarity's cathection of narrative totality—its very own *objet petit a*—is always fantasmatic, that is exceptionally so in this case.

DEFINING THE TERMS

The exchanges between Alexander and Darius center on the attempts of each to capture linguistically and conceptually the relationship between the two. When Alexander first invades Persia, Darius seeks to paint him as an impish child who should submit to his superiors. Let us begin with Darius's letter to his satraps, number 2 in Merkelbach's scheme:

23. Selden 2010.

Arrest him and bring him to me, without doing any physical harm, so that I can strip him of the purple and flog him before sending him back to his homeland, Macedonia, to his mother, Olympias, with a rattle and a die (which is how Macedonian children play). And I shall send with him a pedagogue with a whip to teach him self-control, who will encourage him to have a man's sense before he becomes a man himself. (letter 2)[24]

Particularly notable is Darius's attempt to define the relationship between himself and Alexander in terms of authority. Alexander is infantilized, as he is in another letter (5, earlier in the *Romance* but later in Merkelbach's scheme); Darius by contrast is a teacher, who will give his charge a lesson, albeit by proxy ("pedagogue ... teach"). This is a complex metanarrative moment. The learning of lessons implies a temporal sequence of transgression and restitution, decisively resolved into a clear moral closure. The narrative of Alexander's learning "self-control [*sōphrosynē*]" and "sense [*phronēma*]" suggests that his aggression against Darius betokened the absence of these qualities. Yet there is clearly a deep irony working against Darius's words, since the very framework that he creates can and will be redeployed to evaluate him (an inevitability, given the Herodotean resonances discussed in the final section below). At this relatively early stage in the narrative, then, readers are thus required to judge between competing models (Alexander the conqueror versus Alexander the boy) for anticipating and morally assessing the impending events. Here we see a strong example of the perspectival relativity that epistolary narrative creates.

Indeed, at the same time that they saw the character Darius seeking to control the representation of Alexander, Greek readers will have been aware of a textual strategy defining Darius in relation to a tralatitious image of Persian kingship. Darius's overweening pride, which manifests itself in his threats toward Alexander's person (a repeated feature of these exchanges), links the tradition stretching back to Herodotus of arrogant Persians dismissive of Greek power with the ethics of power (no doubt also reflecting current discussions of the ethics of power within Hellenistic kingship theory). Homonymy underpins intertextuality: the fourth-century Darius III plays the role of Herodotus's Darius I, and (by association) his son Xerxes too.

One of the features of epistolography is that it is an active, energetic, kinetic form of writing: letters do not simply describe a state of affairs but prescribe, or (in cases like this, where the writing character's intention is subverted in the reader's eyes) seek to prescribe, a way of looking at the world. The exchange between Darius and Alexander rests precisely on this idea. Their letters represent competing, and indeed fundamentally conflicting, ways of construing their relationship. Darius begins by lording it over Alexander; we see in Alexander's responses to Darius's

---

24. Translations of the *Romance* letters adapted from Dowden 1989; all others are mine.

self-aggrandizing a group of refusals to adopt the terms set up by Darius, and converse attempts to establish a different modality of relationship. Take Darius's adoption of titulature in letter 5 and Alexander's creative response in the next letter (which follows in the *Romance* and in Merkelbach's scheme):

> [Darius:] King of kings, kinsman of the gods, throne sharer with Mithras, I who rise to heaven with the Sun, a god myself, I Darius to my servant Alexander give these orders . . . (letter 5)
>
> [Alexander:] King Alexander, son of Philip and Olympias, to Darius, king of kings, throne sharer with divine Mithras, descendant of the gods, who rise to heaven with the Sun, great god, king of the Persians: greetings. (letter 6)

Alexander parrots back to his addressee all the titles used in the original letter but subverts them by styling himself only "King Alexander, son of Philip and Olympias." No claims to immortality here; the juxtaposition of grandeur and humility produces an effect of comic bathos. Quotation reframes meaning; recontextualization parodies, in the way that (for example) Aristophanes parodies Euripides through citation. The epistolary exchange depends on a process of negotiation and renegotiation of cognitive contracts.

There are numerous parallels of this process of competitive redefinition. Patricia Rosenmeyer points to one: Darius sends Alexander gifts of a whip, a ball, and some gold, which he intends to symbolize Alexander's punishment, his youthfulness, and his need to pay his troops on their impending retreat; Alexander responds creatively (letter 6), explicitly "reinterpreting" (Rosenmeyer's word) these to refer to the whipping he will give the Persians, his likely conquest of the world (the ball), and the tribute he will exact (the gold).[25] These gifts thus embody the fluctuations of meaning in the epistolary exchange.

A subtler example concerns, once again, names and titles. The word *great* (*megas*) recurs repeatedly in these exchanges. It forms part of Darius's titulature, and most of the time when he writes to people or is written to he is "the great king." Alexander, however, presents greatness as something that can be acquired through competition: "If I beat you," he writes, "I shall become famous and a great [*megas*] king among the barbarians and the Greeks" (letter 6). His success against Darius, indeed, guarantees his inevitable acquisition of the surname the Great, which Darius's subsequent address to him as "my great master [*despotēi*]" (letter 11) affirms. Here we have Darius forced, in defeat, to accept the terms of the relationship initially vied for in the epistolary exchange. There is, however, an additional twist, in that Darius writes to Alexander, after his defeat, warning him not to *megalophronein*: "be arrogant," or literally "think *megas*" (letters 11, 12). Darius seems to be trying to claw

---

25. Rosenmeyer 2001, 177–80, at 179.

back some of the status he has lost in acknowledging Alexander's "greatness" by advising him that being great and thinking great are not the same thing. Or, put differently, he is attempting to reestablish some of the authority he has lost in the competition over the word *megas* by offering a new perspective on it, this time from a psychoethical perspective. Like the whip, the ball, and the gold, the word *megas* is subject to creative redefinition through the medium of the letter.

NEGOTIATING STATUS

The epistolary negotiation between Alexander and Darius is, for readers, overdetermined by the inevitability of the latter's defeat, guaranteed by our awareness of both history and the quasi-Herodotean genre of narratives of Eastern kingship (arrogant Eastern kings must come a cropper). This peripeteia is, once again, enacted through the language and particularly through the shifting discourse of immortality. In the letters before his defeat Darius adopts self-divinizing titles and demeans Alexander: "King of kings, kinsman of the gods, I who rise to heaven with the Sun, throne sharer with Mithras, a god myself, I Darius to my servant Alexander give these orders . . ." (letter 5).[26] Alexander objects vociferously to the self-arrogation of these titles:

> It is a disgrace if Darius, such a king, priding himself on such power, who shares a throne with the gods, should fall into base slavery to a human being, Alexander. The titles of the gods, when they come into the possession of men, do not confer great power or sense upon them, rather they aggravate the gods, since the names of the immortals have taken up residence in destructible bodies. As a result you are in my eyes convicted of having no power; rather, you adorn yourself with the titles of the gods and attribute their powers on earth to yourself. I am waging war on you mortal to mortal; whichever way victory goes depends on Providence above. (letter 6)

This letter flat refuses the contractual relationship of immortal-mortal that Darius proposes in the letter to which (both in the *Romance* and in Merkelbach's scheme) it responds: it promises to engage with Darius not qua god "but mortal to mortal." More than this, however, it refers self-reflexively to the praxis of naming, of *onomasia* (bis). It does more than simply deny Darius's divinity; it denaturalizes it, drawing attention to the transgressive cultural processes involved in describing a human as a god. This letter asks us to think about the illocutionary power of letters, which do not simply relay content but also (seek to) prescribe the relationship between writer and addressee.

---

26. His divinity is a theme in letter 7 too, but in letter 8 I see no need for Merkelbach's supplement "βασιλεὺς βασιλέων θεὸς μέγας."

When Darius accepts defeat, conversely, generic logic suggests that he should concede his mortality. This is indeed what he does, but it is not quite a capitulation; rather, he seeks to renegotiate their relationship. Adopting an authoritative tone (note the imperative and the instructional use of parables), he attempts to turn the tables on Alexander:

> First of all, realize that you are mortal; this should be enough of a reminder that you should avoid arrogance. For Xerxes, who showed me the light, was overweening and held all humanity in contempt, and conceived a great desire to march against Greece, unsatisfied with the gold and silver and the rest of the wealth that he had inherited, but nevertheless he came away without his huge army and tents full of gold, silver, and clothing. (letter 11)

This letter adds another twist: the narrative is not, as we may have been led to believe, straightforwardly resolved when the arrogance of the barbarian king is punished. Having learned from experience the mutability of fortune, Darius now, Croesus-like, applies this very lesson to Alexander. He here suggests a new framework for the narrative to follow, whereby Alexander's failure to return home and to consolidate his empire is to be understood as a function of the same excess and lack of self-awareness that did for Darius. The epistolary mode, however, leaves readers uncertain as to how much authority to grant this framework. Is this the best way to understand Alexander? Has Darius grasped something essential about the impermanence of human power? Certainly the reference to a "reminder [*hypomnēma,* which can also mean 'dissertation' or 'notebook']" seems a self-conscious allusion to literary memory and particularly to Herodotus (the principal source both for the Xerxes narrative and for the theme of the instability of power). But could this not instead be merely a case of a defeated king trying to exert some moral leverage in his position of abjection? Darius, in this reading, would be not simply capitulating but attempting once again to redefine the relationship in his favor, this time by exploiting his experiences in order to construct himself as the wise adviser of a young king (a different version of the pedagogical relationship he claimed earlier). It is impossible to adjudicate securely between these positions. Epistolary relativism, as we have seen, militates against authoritative judgment.

A renegotiation of divine status appears in letter 12, also from Darius to Alexander: "The same god who gave victory to his son [took it away].... As for you: now that the gods have granted you victory, [acknowledge] what I suffered in my arrogance; make sure that [you yourself are] not arrogant. Even [the children of gods] are mortal. We are of the same descent, and [although of the same descent we] are still not immortal." The restoration of the text is highly conjectural, but it seems probable that for the last two sentences, something like Dino Pieraccioni's reconstruction must be right.[27] The letter, then, seems to seek an extraordinarily captious escape from the discourse of divinity. Darius still asserts that he is the descendant of gods, but being god-born is now not the same as immortality; to the contrary, Darius haughtily suggests that mortals should know their place in the scheme of things. Despite the apparent concession that he was wrong in the past (in his arrogance, if the restoration is correct), Darius's primary concern seems to be extricating himself from his earlier, now refuted claims to divinity (as opposed to divine ancestry).

ALEXANDER/DARIUS: MIRRORING POWER

Darius's new tactic is designed to rescue an impossible situation. At the moment when his status is most under threat, he can no longer claim superiority over Alexander, so instead he claims a kind of parity. Alexander and Darius are placed on the same level, in this new category of human but god-born (which, ironically, the *Romance* narrative specifically denies: Alexander's human father, Nectanebo, seduces Olympias by pretending to be a god [1.5–10]). This mirroring inhabits even the formal phrasing of the letter (again, with the caveat that much is restored). The same god can both give and take away; the verb *megalophronein* is used of both Alexander and Darius; they share a divine heritage. Epistolarity in general binds author and recipient into a tight nexus of reciprocity, a model of equally weighted exchange at the material level; here Darius transforms that functional reciprocity into a sense of identity between the two players. Despite these claims to parity, however, once again he can be found seeking to control the situation by constructing an authoritative epistolary identity: the gnomic phrasing and imperative (if the restoration is correct) indicate his claims to greater insight.

For all that this sense of identity between Alexander and Darius is a figment of Darius's conjuring, it also represents an important, recurrent theme of the epistolary exchange, which shuttles between assimilation and differentiation of the two men. In the earlier episodes, Darius insists on difference, emphasizing (as we have seen) the polarization of their statuses, as he sees it, along a number of axes: Persian-Greek, immortal-mortal, king-upstart, adult-child. Alexander, by contrast, works to minimize the differences of status by professing their common humanity and denying Darius's divinity (while implicitly emphasizing the differences between Greek and barbarian). After his defeat, however, it is Darius who stresses how much they have in common: their divine descent (letter 12) and the fact that Alexander, by virtue of his conquests, has become "the great king." Epistolary

---

27. Pieraccioni 1951. Merkelbach proposes "θνητὰ δὲ καὶ [ἀνθρώπινα φρόνει. δι]ογενεῖς ἐσμεν, ὁμό[τιμοί τε θεοῖς, ἀλλ' ο]ὐκ ἀθάνατοι." The words are different, but there is a similar emphasis on common divine ancestry coupled with common human status.

exchanges, with their constant settling on and renegotiation of contracts, seem to demand an emphasis on the play of identity and difference between senders.

This mirroring of Darius and Alexander works along the cultural axis too. When writing to his satraps, Darius refers to his intention to send Alexander a rattle and dice, "with which Macedonian children play" (letter 2): an amusing intrusion of quasi-ethnographic description into an administrative letter. More substantial is Alexander's reference in a letter to Darius to the story of Zethus and Amphion, "whose exploits and stories the philosophers in your court can translate/interpret [*hermēneuousi*] for you" (letter 14). What is interesting about this is its apparent emphasis on translation, with its implication of linguistic and hence cultural difference. Also interesting, in terms of cultural difference, is the mention of court philosophers. I suspect the reference here is to figures like Ctesias, bilingual Greeks who can mediate between the two cultures. In fact, a specific example of such a figure crops up in the Florence papyrus: one Polyidus, a Greek who seems to be intimate with Darius's family and who writes to the king to reassure him that they are all being looked after (letter 13). This Polyidus is usually identified with the dithyrambic poet of the fourth century, known from other sources. And, in fact, his poetic credentials are very much on show in this letter, a pastiche of Homeric quotations and allusions coupled with a quotation from the tragic poet Chaeremon.[28] Polyidus's role seems to be to embody, in a way that is more than a little comic, the point of contact between Darius's court and Greek culture.

But this ethnological emphasis on cultural difference stands in tension with the implicit assimilation between the two discussed above and particularly with Darius's revised strategy after his defeat, which rests on his claim that he and Alexander are "of the same descent [*homogeneis*]" (letter 12, also quoted at the end of the previous section). In a letter preserved in the Hamburg papyrus and the *Romance*, the defeated Darius appeals to a more precise affiliation: he and Alexander, he says, have a "common kinship [*syggeneia*]" from Perseus (letter 11). In mythological terms this just about works: Perseus is the grandfather of Heracles (the ancestor of the Macedonian royal house) and the father of Perses (the eponym of the Persians). But Alexander implicitly contests this family stemma—in part perhaps because it would cede to the Persians genealogical priority—with his reference to descent from Zethus and Amphion (letter 14, quoted in the previous paragraph) and thereby rejects Darius's attempt to affiliate with him and hence to efface their cultural difference. Darius and Alexander, indeed, are engaging in exactly the kind of practice that interstate negotiations often involved in the Hellenistic era, what Christopher Jones calls "kinship diplomacy":[29] the deployment of mythical ancestry to reach political accommodations in the present.

---

28. Pieraccioni 1951, 186–87, gathers the allusions.
29. C. P. Jones 1999.

FAMILY, INTIMACY, EMOTION

Much of Darius's epistolary efforts post-Issus thus go toward reestablishing his status in relation to his new conqueror. That, however, is not all that he wants. Issus is the occasion when Alexander captures Darius's mother (Rhodgyne), wife (Stateira), and children; letters 11, 12, and 15 contain the deposed monarch's pleas for the restitution of his family. This is the broader context for the attempts that we have already considered to define ethical limits and the proper behavior of a human being, a fact that introduces a new aspect to the epistolary exchange, an emotional timbre that is quite out of keeping with the earlier alpha-male power plays. In letter 11, Darius asks for pity (*oikteiron*) and supplicates Alexander ("Hiketas, pros Dios hikesiou"). In 12, in a section of papyrus unfortunately damaged, there seems to be more appeal to pity, combined with a threat ("If I cannot persuade you even in this way, you must reckon that I will not leave off from testing your guts—enough parts of my empire remain intact"). The capture of Darius's family calls for a different set of resources latent in the epistolary tradition: intimacy, emotional appeals, and particularly relationships between the genders.

Darius's plea for the return of his family casts him in a different role: no longer the mighty potentate, but the distraught son, husband, and father. Here too there may be a distant memory of the Xerxes narrative and perhaps more specifically of Aeschylus's *Persians*, the play that tells the story of the Greek victory at Salamis in terms of Persian grief and bereavement. The redefinition of Darius from great king to family man is of course another move in the constant epistolary game of jockeying for power (whether political or moral). But given that his new stance is prima facie less hypocritical and more emotive, it might also prepare the way for readers to view him in a more sympathetic light.

How is Darius's request for the return of his family received? Here the *Alexander Romance* diverges from the Florence papyrus. In the *Romance*, Alexander flat refuses. In the Florence papyrus, by contrast, he offers to meet Darius in Phoenicia and there restore to him "your children, your wife, and everything that is with them, and the cups of Dionysus and the endless gold and the treasure stores, and you will be safely restored to the territories you used to rule over" (letter 14, to which we shall return presently). Then in the Florence papyrus, Darius replies in a letter of which a portion appears in the *Romance* (2.10); in the extended part not in the *Romance*, he refuses to accede to this "haughty [*huperēphanon*]" request to meet in Phoenicia (letter 15). The papyrus, with its offer and refusal of a Phoenicia date, thus takes a different narrative route than the *Romance* at this point, a difference that also impacts the characterization of the two men. In the *Romance*, Darius pathetically asks for pity and the return of his family but is rebuffed by Alexander. In the papyrus, Alexander magnanimously offers to restore to him absolutely everything that he has taken—only to have his offer knocked back by an intemperate Darius

(Alexander accuses him of adhering to his "angry, barbarian mentality" in letter 14). The papyrus, then, seems to work toward fixing the meaning of the incident on the polar axis of Greek and barbarian ethical behavior, while the *Romance* leaves open the possibility that Alexander's cruelty is at fault. The treatment of family hostages, then, is an ethically problematic issue that can be nuanced differently in the tradition, depending on how the particular branch of that tradition wishes to finesse the characterization of the two men.

The *Alexander Romance* is among the earliest of Greek prose fictions, and the exchange between Alexander and Darius possibly the earliest epistolary novel (depending on our view of the *Letters* of Isocrates and Plato). Even at this stage (and despite the complexities of a protean textual tradition) we can clearly see a sophisticated grasp of the potentialities of letters as a fictional narrative form. The paradoxical, liminal quality that (as we noted at the outset) scholars have seen as the driving force behind modern epistolary fiction can already be discerned in the Alexander letters. Identities are negotiated and renegotiated, made and remade; the two protagonists move from assimilation to differentiation, always obsessively locked in a battle for dominance but at the same time mimetically tracking each other's moves.

Letters were not, of course, new to the Hellenistic era. But its expanded Greek world created a greater need for epistolary networks, particularly in political negotiations. The Alexander letters, although occupying a different intellectual niche, are as much a product of the intense textualization of the Hellenistic world as, for example, Callimachus's *Pinakes,* his catalogue of the library at Alexandria: both point to a new fascination with the written word, with the power and limitation of graphic technology. Writing is everywhere in the *Alexander Romance,* the shell that houses the majority of these letters, not just in the letters but also in the many stone inscriptions (1.3, 1.30, 1.32, 1.33, 1.34, 2.31, 2.34, 2.41)[30] and particularly in the riddling use of acrostics: the naming of the sectors of Alexandria after the first five letters of the Greek alphabet signifies "Alexander, king [*basileus*] of the race [*genos*] of Zeus [*Dios*], founded [*ektisen*] the city" (1.32), and the letters of Sarapis's name also have significance (1.33).[31] The Alexander epistles are thus part of a wider celebration of textuality in the *Romance* that, if not without precedent, reflects a new accentuation of material form in the early Hellenistic world. (One useful parallel is the Hellenistic Jewish *Letter of Aristeas,* addressed to one Philocrates and crammed with pseudodocumentary references.) This heightened interest in texts and textuality and in the resources (and limits) of the written word formed the backdrop against which appeared the earliest example of what would become a major literary genre.

30. Not all found in all recensions: Sironen 2003, 297–98, has the details.
31. Stoneman 1995.

7

Philostratus's *Heroicus*

Fictions of Hellenism

The reinvention of imperial Greek literary studies has afforded to Flavius Philostratus arguably the greatest net gain of any writer of the era. Where once he was "inadequate, even injudicious,"[1] a "second- (or third-) rate ... mediocrity,"[2] he is now seen as the towering figure of Greek literary production under the Severans.[3] Nowhere is the Philostratean revolution more evident than with the dialogue *On Heroes*. Until the mid-1990s, it was easily accessible only through the Teubner texts of Ludo de Lannoy (1977) and Carl Ludwig Kayser (1870). Since then, it has been translated with commentary into modern Greek, Spanish, Italian, German (twice), English (twice, although one remains unpublished), and Polish.[4] A text that was once consigned to the footnotes of scholarship on religion (particularly as supposed evidence for a revival of hero cult under Caracalla)[5] and Sophistic

---

This chapter draws on material in Whitmarsh 2009b, reproduced with the permission of Cambridge University Press.

1. Bowersock 1989, 95. Translations are based on Maclean and Aitken 2001, with occasional differences of interpretation.
2. Wardy 1996, 6.
3. See in general the essays in Bowie and Elsner 2009; my survey of Severan literary production in Whitmarsh 2007b.
4. Greek: Mandilaras 1995 (*non vidi*); Spanish: Mestre 1996; Italian: Rossi 1997; German: Beschorner 1999, Grossardt 2006; English: Maclean and Aitken 2001; Polish: Szarmach 2003 (*non vidi*). The (excellent) unpublished English translation is that of Jeffrey Rusten.
5. Mantero 1966 offers a book-length study of the philosophical and religious background; for recent discussions see C. P. Jones 2000; C. P. Jones 2001b; Whitmarsh 2001, 103–5; the collection of essays in Aitken and Maclean 2004; Hodkinson 2011, which reads the text as a self-conscious revision of Plato's *Phaedrus*.

Homerkritik[6] has been reclaimed as a work of intrinsic literary and cultural-historical interest. There is, however, much left to be done in unpacking this brilliant and provocative work. This chapter offers a contribution to its further reclamation and indeed to the merging of cultural-historical and literary approaches to our author. My central argument is that the *Heroicus*'s self-reflexive literary sophistication is inseparable from the issues of identity that are tested throughout it, and vice versa. The first part introduces the interpretative issues, the next two explore questions of identity and literary strategy, and the final part ties the themes together.

MAKING SENSE OF THE *HEROICUS*

How do we read the *Heroicus*? As an expression of religious piety or as a Sophistic *jeu*? Readers in search of the meaning of a text usually try to reconstruct an underlying intention. Few scholars, of course, are comfortable with the romantic idea of literature as an expression of authorial consciousness, but in truth the cognitive process of reading almost always involves hypothesizing some kind of intelligent design supporting the text, a unifying principle or set of principles (whether we attribute these to an author or, in the modish language of much criticism, to "the text"). As Stanley Fish puts it, "The efforts of readers are always efforts to discern and therefore to realize (in the sense of becoming) an author's intention."[7] Like Fish, I take this "intention" not as a presence latent in the text but as a (necessary) confabulation generated by the reading process: "a succession of decisions made by readers about an author's intention."[8]

Like the homodiegetic fictions discussed in chapters 2, 3 and 4, then, the *Heroicus* encourages readers to locate a (necessarily fictitious) authorial surrogate within the text. The major difference, however, is that of form: this is a dialogue between two fictional characters. There is no primary narrator or any frame for the dialogue; as a result, readers are left without a point of narrative authority and forced to reconstruct an implicit meaning from the characterization of the two figures and from the dynamics of their relationship. Dialogue, like drama, derives its traction from the absence of hierarchical authority and from the relativization of perspectives.

The questions of who to believe and what kind of plausibility we can attribute to what kinds of narrative are also indeed thematically central at the level of content. Let us recap the situation. The *Heroicus* reports a discussion set on the Thracian Chersonese between a Phoenician sailor, whose ship has been beached by

---

6. Huhn and Bethe 1917; Anderson 1986, 241–57; Bowersock 1994, 68; Merkle 1994, 193–94; Beschorner 1999, 219–31; Billault 2000, 126–38; Zeitlin 2001, 255–66; Maclean and Aitken 2001, lx–lxxvi; Grossardt 2006, 55–120, especially 99–102; Kim 2010a, 175–215.

7. Fish 1976, 475.

8. Ibid., 476.

lack of wind, and a local vinegrower. During the course of the discussion, the vinegrower reveals that he is in regular discussion with the epiphanically reanimated hero Protesilaus, who in periodic encounters corrects the prevailing (i.e., Homeric) view of the events in the Trojan War. The particular problem, we are told, is that the villainous Odysseus bought off Homer, who repressed the story of the true hero, Palamedes, and his murder by Odysseus.[9] The *Heroicus* thus sits in the line of playful critiques of Homeric versions of mythical events that connects Dio Chrysostom's eleventh oration (arguing that Troy was not captured) and Dictys and Dares right back to Stesichorus and Euripides.[10]

At one level, Philostratus invites us to identify the vinegrower's revelations with narrative truth. It is the Phoenician's transition from initial skepticism to final conviction that expresses this most clearly. "By Athena!," he exclaims near the start, "I do not believe you!" (3.1; similar phrasing at 7.9, 7.11–8.2).[11] By the conclusion, though, he has decided that there is more to the vinegrower's tales than Chersonesian lies: "I believe you [*peithomai soi*]!," he comments in the conspicuous position of the final line of the text (58.6; similarly 16.6, 44.5). The Phoenician's passage from skepticism to belief, then, constructs him, provisionally at least, as one implied reader of the text. The *Heroicus* might thus be taken as a *logos protrepticus*, that is to say a dialogue aiming to exhort the reader by dramatizing the conversion of an interlocutor to the position of the speaker.[12] In this connection, it has been interpreted as proselytizing for the revivalism of hero cult, whether particularly that apparently sponsored by Caracalla (211–17)[13] or the more general movement in the second and third centuries.[14]

There is a perhaps even a general resemblance between the Phoenician's embrace of "belief" in the cult and Christian conversion narrative. It is not impossible that Philostratus may have come into contact with Christianity through figures like Julius Africanus (the author of a secular miscellany and doctrinal works), who successfully served as an ambassador to Severus Alexander—or even that emperor himself, who (we are told, however implausibly) kept effigies of Abraham and Jesus Christ (as well as Apollonius of Tyana) in his lararium.[15] If, as has been

---

9. On the central opposition between these two figures, see Rossi 1997, 28–32.
10. See especially Kim 2010a, 175–211.
11. The reason for the choice of Athena is not obvious; perhaps it suits the Odyssean texture of the dialogue's opening, on a seashore.
12. See Maclean and Aitken 2001, lxxx–lxxxi, for this interpretation; also Beschorner 1999, 167–68.
13. Huhn and Bethe 1917, 613–14; Eitrem 1929, 1–5; Mantero 1966, 13–14; Bowersock 1989, 98; Merkle 1994, 193; Beschorner 1999, 235–40. But cf. Grossardt 2006, 34–46; Whitmarsh 2007b, 35–38.
14. See especially C. P. Jones 2001b, 146–48.
15. *SHA Sev. Alex.* 29.2 = *FGrH* 1064 T5. See Eitrem 1929, 8–9, for *pistis* (belief) as religious faith. For wider discussion of religious themes, see especially Mantero 1966; Massenzio 1997; Nagy 2001.

claimed, the *Heroicus* is a variety of "conversion dialogue,"[16] then we may be entitled to take the Phoenician's "belief" at the end as powerfully normative.

Yet there are reasons to resist such a hieratic reading. The resemblances between discourses of belief in the *Heroicus* and in Christian literature are passing ones: when the Phoenician says, "I believe you," he is not professing religious faith but acknowledging the persuasiveness of his interlocutor ("I believe," *peithomai*, is simply the passive of "I persuade," *peithō*). As we shall see presently, Philostratus draws this language to a much greater extent from historiographical discourse. More importantly, the dialogue form, as noted above, militates against interpretative closure. Whereas for instance an oratorical speech or an Aristotelian tract seeks to create meaning authoritatively by promoting a single, self-consistent voice to the exclusion of others, dialogue puts the emphasis on dissent, on the dynamics between individuals, and this creates space for resistive reading. (Similarly, readers of Plato—a formative influence on Philostratus here, of course[17]— should pay more attention to the dialogue form rather than being bewitched by Socrates's notionally superior argumentation.)[18] In the *Heroicus*, we do not even have the organizing figure of Socrates, with all of his tralatitious reputation for wisdom. How then are readers to judge securely whether to treat the vinegrower's account as a divine revelation or as a parody?

We should question any assumption that the Phoenician's "conversion" to belief provides the only possible model of response to the vinegrower's story. The relational aspect of dialogue invites a plurality of responses and asks each reader to find a place somewhere on the scale between skepticism and acceptance or even to consider more laterally what might be at stake in crediting these extraordinary tales. To take this text as a straightforward expression of religious adherence would be naïve.

What does the Phoenician mean when he proclaims that "I believe you"? We have already mentioned the *Heroicus*'s superficial similarity to Christian conversion narrative. The primary hypotexts, however, lie in the Greek historiographical tradition. The contrast developed between the Phoenician's skepticism and the vinegrower's belief activates a specifically Herodotean play with the value of travel and autopsy. This is most visibly worked out in the passage where the vinegrower convinces his interlocutor of the existence of giants on the basis of bone finds:[19]

---

16. Schäublin 1985.

17. Hodkinson 2011, with 22–24 on the dialogue form; Trapp 1990, 171 (on the Phaedrean setting); Grossardt 2006, 44, 111, 117. See also Whitmarsh 1999, 155–58, on the dialogue *Nero*, which may be by the same Philostratus.

18. For example, Numenius of Apamea finds Euthyphro, as portrayed by Plato, to be "a foolish braggart, and as poor a theologian as you could find" (fr. 23 Des Places).

19. Rusten 2004 discusses Philostratus's possible sources, noting that a generation before Philostratus, Pausanias too shows an interest in giant bones.

Vinegrower: But do not yet regard as credible [*pista*] what I have said, stranger, until you sail to the island of Cos, where the bones of earth-born men are on show, the original Meropes, so they say, and until you see the bones of Hyllus, son of Heracles, in Phrygia. [list of big bone finds] . . . (8.14)

Phoenician: I congratulate you on your research [*historia*], vinegrower. I was ignorant of such great bones, and out of ignorance I disbelieved. (8.18)

In this crucial sequence, where the Phoenician begins to articulate his "conversion" for the first time, what clinches the case for the vinegrower is his to personal experience. In this interchange, the two have played the roles of Herodotus and Thucydides: the Phoenician has assumed a Thucydides-like position of disbelieving "mythology [*muthologian*]" (7.9), on the grounds that it is based on tralatitious rather than experiential knowledge (8.3);[20] the vinegrower, however, advises a Herodotean suspension of disbelief of apparently miraculous phenomena (note *thauma*, "wonder," at 8.13) until a personal judgment can be reached.[21] The Phoenician's congratulation of his new friend on his "research [*historia*]" underscores the latter's victory in the contest for historiographical voices.

The preference for a Herodotean idiom is perhaps unsurprising, given the prominent placement of this very cult site of Protesilaus in the closing chapters of the *Histories* (9.114–22),[22] to which the *Heroicus* later directly alludes (9.5, on which see below). But another passage specifically problematizes the *Histories* as a source for wonders. "Well, if I were mythologically inclined, I would have described the seven-cubit-long corpse of Orestes, which the Spartans found in Tegea," the vinegrower proclaims (8.3), referring to a celebrated Herodotean passage (1.66–68).[23] In this instance, Herodotus has evidently become a less than infallible guide to credible reportage.

The *Heroicus*'s language of *pistis*, then, is not narrowly religious: the account of the epiphanically revealed "truth" of the Trojan War may represent the meat of the vinegrower's case, but it is carefully framed with rationalist, historiographical markers. Nor, indeed, is Heroican belief straightforwardly coercive: the Herodotean case demonstrates precisely the difficulty of placing absolute confidence in

---

20. See Thuc. 1.22.4 for the programmatic rejection of the mythical (*to muthōdes*). Thuc. 7.10's sneering at specifically childish mythology, however, alludes to Plato (*Leg.* 887d; Grossardt 2006, 385). Kim 2010a, 199–203, discusses the rationalist strain in the *Heroicus*.

21. See especially Periander's conduct in the programmatic story of Arion and the dolphin: initial skepticism (*apistiē*) is replaced when he engages in research (*historeesthai*) into the truth of the matter (Hdt. 1.24.7). See further the narrator at 4.96.1: "I do not disbelieve [*apisteō*] or overly believe [*pisteuō ti liēn*] in this." "Herodotus is the prototype of the historian who always marvels" (Momigliano 1975, 25).

22. On this passage, see Boedeker 1988; Nagy 1990, 268–73. Like the *Histories*, the *Heroicus* (53.17–54.1; also 56.6–11) concludes with a hero avenging insults, viz. Achilles (Anderson 1986, 247).

23. For Herodotus as *muthologos* see also Arist., *GA* 756b; Grossardt 2006, 389–90.

one single authority. This in turn problematizes any attempt to read the *Heroicus* as religious propaganda, in that it raises the question of who we are to believe (the vinegrower? Philostratus?), all the more so in view of the long history of ludic or semiludic revisions of Trojan narratives (the so-called Schwindellitteratur tradition) reaching back from Dictys and Dares, Ptolemy Chennus, and Dio's eleventh oration through the Hellenistic authors Iambulus, Hegesianax, Dionysius Scytobrachion, and Euhemerus to the fifth-century Sophists Hippias and Gorgias.[24]

That the *Heroicus* does not embody any coherent belief system—"der Glaube der Hellenen"—does not, however, mean that it is simply Sophistic (as Ulrich von Wilamowitz-Möllendorff and others have claimed).[25] As we have seen, pluralism and relativity are constituent features of dialogue in general. The *Heroicus* is a catacomb of multiple hermeneutic alleys and vaults. This is to claim not that interpretation is infinitely open—on the contrary, it is trammeled in certain fundamental ways—but that the text makes an issue of interpretation. My central contention in this chapter is that this text is not an inert expression of Greek religious piety; rather it fully engages its readers in the play of meaning, challenging them to revise their sense of selfhood. Heroics are "performed" through the act of reading, not megaphonically proclaimed in the act of writing. In the pursuit of such a performative interpretation, I shall focus less on the better-known sections that engage in Homeric revisionism and more on the framing and structure of the text as a whole, considering what sort of demands—intellectual demands but also self-investments and commitments of identity—it makes on its readers.

LANDSCAPE, LANGUAGE, AND IDENTITY

Let us begin our exploration of Heroican identity by thinking about the geographical setting.[26] Within the vast expanse of the Roman empire, geography is always a marked discourse, whether it involves appropriating alien territory and rendering it amenable to imperializing knowledge[27] or idealizing an impossibly primitive countryside as a counterpart to the ambiguous sophistication of modern urban life.[28] The *Heroicus* intersects with a tradition of texts, originating in Hellenistic pastoral, that strategically relocate the centers of Hellenism from the

---

24. See Grossardt 2006, 1.55–74; Kim 2010a, 177–81; more generally above, ch. 1.
25. Wilamowitz-Möllendorff 1956, 2.514; Anderson 1986, 241–57, also plays up the Sophistical aspects.
26. C. P. Jones 2001b discusses *realia*. Martin 2002, 156–58, stresses the cultural importance of physical setting to the *Heroicus*.
27. Momigliano 1975, 65–66; especially Nicolet 1991.
28. Whitmarsh 2001, 100–108, with further references.

traditional grand urban and religious centers to rural backwaters.[29] Dio's seventh oration, the *Euboicus*, is a case in point. This text (discussed in the *Lives of the Sophists* and important for the *Heroicus*, as we shall see) begins by siting the tale "in practically the middle of Greece" (Dio Chr. 7.1), a marker of cultural centrality that underscores the normative, moralizing narrative.[30] The oration's hunters of Euboea are "true" Greeks, preserving their traditions through innocence of city traditions: the "center" has been paradoxically shifted from the usual claimants (Athens, Olympia, Delphi) to rural Euboea. In another passage with important implications for the *Heroicus*, Philostratus himself in the *Lives of the Sophists* discusses a certain Agathion, who decries the corrupted, "barbaric" speech to be found in the center of Athens, whereas "the interior of Attica is pure of barbarians, and hence its language remains uncorrupted and its dialect sounds the purest strain of Atthis" (*VS* 553).[31] Once again, the relocation from mainstream urban center to a rustic context (which in this account is a center of a different kind: the *mesogeia*, or "middle land") is constructed as a search for Hellenic purity.

The Heroican landscape is a place of divinity and eroticized beauty. When the two speakers relocate to another spot to exchange stories (an obvious reworking of the Platonic cliché),[32] the Phoenician comments that the fragrance from the flowers is "sweet" (3.3), a word that powerfully invokes the landscape of Hellenistic pastoral.[33] The vinegrower replies, "What do you mean, sweet? It's divine!" (3.4). This phrasing positions the *Heroicus*, in metaliterary terms, as hyperpastoral, possessed of qualities that exceed mere "sweetness." This hyperbolic description of the cultic landscape is amplified by the heavy use of superlatives: the cult site is, according to the Phoenician, "the part of the land that is sweetest and divine" (5.2–3). The language of divinity is used to describe a site that transcends "normal" description, or, better, it marks the failure of received language, including (self-reflexively) that of the pastoral literary tradition, to represent a space that lies (just) beyond the reader's imagination.

---

29. Mantero 1966, 45–47, on "motivi nazionalistici." I argue later that Philostratus's use of the language of "sweetness" has pastoral resonances.

30. For this point, see Trapp 1995, 164–65; Moles 1995, 177–80.

31. This is a more complex passage, however, than is often assumed: I attempt to unpack it at Whitmarsh 2001, 105–8.

32. *Phaedrus* 227a–30e; see Trapp 1990, 171, with copious contemporary parallels. Grossardt 2006 ad loc. reads the passages discussed in this paragraph in predominantly Platonic terms, neglecting the pastoral effects.

33. Thanks primarily to its programmatic placement at the start of Theocritus 1: see Hunter 1999, 70, on Theocritus; 1983, 92–97, on later theorizations of *hēdonē* and its close ally, *glukutēs*. A significant parallel to Philostratus's usage comes at Ach. Tat. 1.2.3 (another reworking of the *Phaedrus*: Trapp 1990, 171): "This place is altogether sweet [*hēdus*] and appropriate for erotic stories." Martin 2002 compares Achilles's and Philostratus's narrative settings.

In a characteristically Philostratean metatextual gesture, the beauty of topography is connected with the beauty of language and knowledge. The vinegrower's rural labor is cast as a form of philosophy (2.5–6), contrasting with the ruinous urban philosophy that he undertook earlier in his life (4.6). Literary culture and viticulture are metaphorically interlinked. Conversely, the land embodies intellectual values. The fertility of the soil ("there is no stinting [*phthonos oudeis*]," 2.3; "everything on the land teems [*bruei*] for me," 4.10) is matched by the abundance of Protesilaus's wisdom ("he has wisdom to spare too," 4.10). On hearing of the intellectual fertility of this space, the Phoenician responds with a praise of the site, on the grounds that "you do not only cultivate olives and grapes in it, but you also harvest divine and pure wisdom" (4.11). The transferability of metaphors from Protesilaus's landscape to his knowledge signals that his learning partakes of identically fructose qualities.

The land itself also seems to assume the mythical, storied aspect of Protesilaus. A later, ecphrastic description of Protesilaus employs markedly vegetal imagery: "He teems [*bruei*] with luxuriant down, and his fragrance is sweeter than autumn myrtles" (10.2).[34] The verb *bruein* (to teem) has already been used of the vegetal abundance of the cult site (4.10, quoted above), and *sweet* is, as we have seen, a key marker of pastoral landscape. In this divine, superpastoral space, the hero's eroticized presence inhabits the very soil of the land.[35]

There are also human-made features in this landscape. The monumental cult site is described in quasi-periegetic terms, familiar to modern readers from Pausanias:

> You see how little of the sanctuary is left. But back then it was lovely and not small, as can be made out from its foundations, This cult statue stood on a ship, since its base has the shape of a prow, and he is set there as the ship's captain.[36] Time has worn it away, and, by Zeus, those who anoint it and seal their vows here have changed its shape. But this means nothing to me, for I spend time with and see the hero himself, and no statue could be more pleasant than him. (9.6)

As so often in Pausanias, a sanctuary is a *lieu de mémoire* (in this case, a cult site famous from the end of Herodotus) overhung by the fear of forgetting. Experiencing the site is to engage reflexively with a cultural tradition perceived as age-old.

---

34. This is evidence not that Protesilaus was "originally" a vegetal god (so Mantero 1966, 113–19; similarly Boedeker 1988, 37–38) but that there was an ongoing association between the hero and the land (see later in the chapter). Maclean and Aitken 2001's "he has a full, splendid beard" makes too much of an adult of the hero.

35. See 9.1–3 for the miraculous trees on the Chersonese that face Troy (compare the Phoenician's response at 9.4, which seems to mean "Though I might marvel, I do not"—rather than "I am not surprised that I continue to marvel," so Maclean and Aitken 2001).

36. Taking *hidrutai* as passive with most translators, contra Maclean and Aitken 2001 ("the ship's captain dedicated it").

Philostratus employs "sublime" tropes similar to those that James Porter has identified in Pausanias: "Sublimity in its most startling form is to be found in the wondrous and the miraculous, and above all in what lies beyond reach in the present."[37] This ancient cult site, suffused with ancient, indescribable divinity, is awesomely sublime, a decayed relic of a once great past simultaneously reanimated by a living presence. Unlike in Pausanias, however, the frailty of the human-made monument is supplemented, for the vinegrower, by the experience of the epiphanic hero himself. Human art, however venerable, is not the embodiment of Greek culture but a weak substitute for it.

This place of beauty and "sweetness" is also imaged as Hellenic. In literary terms, it is constructed from a series of pastoral elements borrowed from central texts of the Hellenic heritage: in particular the *locus* both *amoenus* and *classicus*, the *Phaedrus*, bulks large.[38] There are, however, more direct markers of Hellenism. The nightingales, the vinegrower claims, "Atticize" here (5.4). It is worth taking some time to draw out the subtleties of this claim. In line with the general emphasis on pastoral pleasure in the *Heroicus*, the song of this typically mournful, elegiac bird is transformed into something sweeter: the Phoenician responds that from what he has heard, they do not "lament" but merely sing here. Yet in drawing attention to the usual expectation that nightingales lament, the Phoenician's words (combined with the reference to Atticism)[39] hint at the tragic narrative of the Athenian Procne, who suffered violent rape at the hands of the Thracian tyrant Tereus (most famously in Sophocles's play of that name). As so often in the Greek tradition, cultured Hellenism—here distilled into Atticism, by synecdoche—is defined by opposition to brutal barbarism.

The subtle allusion to Procne's rape by a Thracian develops a motif found in an earlier episode in the *Heroicus*, where the vinegrower reports the attempts by one of the local potentates (*dunatoi*), the suggestively named Xeinis (Foreigner), to acquire the cult site. Protesilaus, we are told, blinded him (4.2). Although an apparently Greek Chersonesite, Xeinis occupies the negative role in a series of overlapping polarities: urban-rural, wealthy-peasant, outsider-insider. The cult site of Protesilaus is constructed as a space protected from incursion by quasi-tyrannical "foreigners." This theme of the sacred protection of Greek space from barbarian

---

37. Porter 2001, 71–72. Mantero 1966, 153–57, already adverts to the similarities between the literary effects of Protesilean narrative and the Longinian sublime. Philostratus may have read Pausanias (Rusten 2004).

38. See Trapp 1990, 171; Grossardt 2006, especially ad 3.3, 3.4, 5.3, 5.5; Hodkinson 2011.

39. Grossardt 2006, 369, notes additionally both that nightingales are associated with the grove of the Eumenides at Colonus (and, as Ewen Bowie reminds me, the cult site of Protesilaus is set on a *kolōnos*, 9.1) and that women often sing like nightingales in Attic tragedy.

aggression is reactivated near the end of the text, where the Amazons are repulsed from the holy island of Leuce and attacked and then consumed by their own horses (57)—perhaps another "Thracian" echo, of the flesh-eating horses of Diomedes.[40]

Most important of all, the setting alludes to Herodotus's narrative of the Persian Wars, the paradigmatic exploration of relations between Greek and barbarian. At one point, the vinegrower points to the temple where the Mede committed hubris in the time of our fathers, "in response to which they say the salt fish came to life" (9.5). The allusion (signaled by "they say"—a "hyper-Alexandrian" footnote)[41] is to the end of Herodotus's text, where Xerxes's governor Artaüktes deviously gains permission to ransack Protesilaus's temple by describing the latter to his master simply as "a Greek who attacked your territory and justly died for it" (Hdt. 9.116; see also 7.33). The horrible irony is that Artaüktes employs this pretext to effect a transgressive incursion himself, into the sacred space of the temple—and is subjected to divine vengeance, including the salt fish (*tarikhos*) coming to life (a prognostication of the reanimation of the "corpse"—also *tarikhos*—of Protesilaus) as a result. Supernatural powers often protect geographical boundaries in Herodotus.[42] Philostratus's knowing echo of Herodotean narrative, the paradigmatic exploration of the cultural-political-sacral-cosmic ramifications of military invasion, serves once again to reinforce the construction of Protesilaus as the protector of this enclosed, Hellenic space.

These issues also remind us, however, that identity is most insistently defined where it is most at risk; cultural boundaries can be imagined only at the point of their transgression. This space described in the *Heroicus* is not, in fact, unequivocally Greek. For all these themes of barbarians invading Greek space, the Chersonese is where the Greeks themselves began their incursions into the East at the time of the Trojan War. Situated at the juncture between East and West, this space is the meeting point for both a Greek vinegrower and a Phoenician sailor. The difference in cultural background between the two, indeed, is manipulated in the course of the dialogue, as the Phoenician protests that the vinegrower is favoring the Greeks (19.1–2, 19.8) and the latter teases the former for his partiality toward the Trojans (20.1). If this landscape is—or can be constructed as—hyper-Hellenic, it is also a boundary, a site of negotiation and problematization.

---

40. Kurtz 1975 conveniently assembles the older sources that reference Diomedes. Mossman 2006 stresses the central importance of Leuce to the *Heroicus*.

41. "Hyper-Alexandrian" in that "they say" phrases are characteristic of Herodotus himself, used in a different sense (i.e., referring to oral tradition rather than literary text).

42. Romm 1998, 77–93; also Boedeker 1988, 42 and especially 45: "As a hero buried at the entrance to the Hellespont, and one not fated to survive a hostile crossing between the continents, Protesilaus colors Herodotus's logos about the Persian invasion of Europe. His vengeance against Artayktes suggests a broader justice directed against the entire armada."

This sense of liminality is figured in Protesilaus himself, who died just as he alighted on barbarian soil, at the exact point where the Hellenic meets the non-Hellenic; as his name suggests, he was the "first [*prōtos*]" of the Greek "host [*laos*]" to set foot on barbarian land. Indeed, Protesilaus is arguably the in-between figure par excellence. He left just after marriage; Homer refers to the "half-built house" he began with his wife (*Il.* 2.701, imitated at Cat. 68.74–75). Philostratus underlines his liminal status in terms of religion (he is semidivine: 7.3, 16.4) and age (he is an ephebe: 10.2).

The liminality of the Chersonese invokes the interpretative crisis that Dan Selden has named "syllepsis":[43] like the peninsula, the text is equipoised between East and West and can be approached from either side. Indeed, in a sense the reader must approach it as an outsider. The protected space of the cult site and the protected knowledge of Protesilean revelations inevitably construct the reader as an interloper, an invader of this privileged space. Despite the welter of more or less familiar literary reference points, the central revelations of the text are, by definition, anticanonical, predicated as they are on an idiosyncratic, exclusive, and wholly private modality of knowledge gathering: the direct, epiphanic encounter (*xynousia*) with a deity.[44] Many of Philostratus's readers might think of themselves as true Greeks, but when it comes to the anticanonical, protected "truths" of this text they are no better informed than the Phoenician. Although the *Heroicus* parades the culturally iconic status of pastoral landscape, then, it inevitably engages and challenges any reader's sense of cultural self—insider or outsider? resident or invader?—as she or he approaches the text.

If the *Heroicus* is a dialogic or sylleptic text at the level of cultural identity, it raises parallel questions at the level of social class. As is well known, the literature of the period conventionally articulates the distinction between elite and nonelite through the polarity of "the educated [*pepaideumenoi*]" and "the rustic [*agroikoi*]."[45] I turn now to consider how this quasi-pastoral text implicates and interrogates the reader's implied self-construction as an urban sophisticate in its dialogic exploration of identity.

The first sections of the text (1–5) establish the rural setting, at first blush constructed as a golden-age, rural paradise offset against the decadence of the polis (a strong theme in the literature of the time: Dio Chrysostom's *Euboean Oration* is

---

43. Selden 1994.

44. See Mantero 1966, 64–68, interpreting the focus on *xynousia* (straight) as evidence of the text's religious dimension; also Zeitlin 2001, 255–66, a rich demonstration of the central and immediate role of visuality to the communion between man and hero.

45. See in general Swain 1996, 113–41; Whitmarsh 2001, 100–101. This polarity is, of course, central to Longus's *Daphnis and Chloë*: on the self-conscious play between naïveté and knowingness in that text, see especially Hunter 1983, 45, 59; Zeitlin 1990, 430–36.

only the most prominent example).⁴⁶ The Phoenicians represent, paradigmatically, the vices of the city. The vinegrower is quick to note the sailor's extravagant dress, commenting that "Ionic Sybaris has captivated all Phoenicia at once, and there, I imagine, you could be prosecuted for *not* living luxuriously" (1.1—a clever inversion of Solon's prohibition of luxury).⁴⁷ He proceeds to observe that Phoenicians "have earned a negative reputation" for being "nibbling money-grubbers [*philokhrēmatoi te kai trōktai*]" (1.3). This mention of the Phoenicians' "negative reputation" constitutes another Alexandrian footnote: Homer uses the rare word *nibblers* (*trōktai*) of the Phoenicians in the *Odyssey* (15.416; similarly 14.289), while Plato refers to the "money-grubbing [*philokhrēmaton*]" aspect of the Phoenicians in the *Republic* (436a).

Commerce and its absence become the central focus of the ethical polarization of Phoenician and vinegrower. The former, apparently piqued by the charge laid against his people, asks whether the vinegrower is not affected by any commercial pressures or whether instead he buries his wine in the ground like Maron (another Odyssean reference: *Od.* 9.196–211, although Homer has no mention of burying the wine). The vinegrower counters with an equally Homeric riposte: Cyclopes, he says, have no need for money, but farmers do, in order to make a livelihood and to hire labor (1.5–7). Even so, he does not deal with merchants nor "even know what a drachma is" (1.7), an assertion that clearly has more to it than meets the eye (and to which we shall return below). The attack on mercantilism reinforces the paradigmatic status of the two interlocutors, the Phoenician embodying urban commerce and the rural vinegrower the uncomplicated generosity of the land. The Phoenician's response styles the vinegrower's barter economy as belonging to a Hesiodic golden age: "That is a golden marketplace that you are talking of, belonging more to heroes than gods" (2.1).⁴⁸ The countryside is, then, constructed as a place of freedom from mercantile values: indeed, it is even metaphysically defended against commercial appropriation, as Xeinis the now-blind Chersonesite has discovered (4.2, discussed above).

But does the vinegrower really embody rural values? Let us return to his claim that he does not know what a drachma is (3.2), an assertion whose force seems to depend, metaleptically, on the very knowledge it denies. Pastoral innocence conventionally precludes such self-consciousness; the generic contract between author and reader stipulates that characters should be unaware of their innocence. What is more, the vinegrower speaks in sophisticated Attic, brandishing optatives

---

46. Hunter 1983, 119 n. 29.
47. Grossardt 2006, 349.
48. The vinegrower conflates Hesiod's golden race (*Op.* 109–19) with the heroic (156–73). A further allusion to the Hesiodic golden age comes with "there is no stinting" (2.3, discussed earlier): see *Op.* 117–18; Grossardt 2006, 354, 356.

and deictic iotas with a flourish. At one level, this is part of the standard texture of the Roman Greek countryside: the peasants in Dio Chrysostom's *Euboean Oration*, for example, puncture the surface of Lysianic naïveté with such showy words as "hamēgepēi" (somehow or other).[49] Philostratus's vinegrower is, however, on any terms an extreme case: not only is his Greek sharp and faultless, but also, as we have seen, right from the start he trades more or less recondite allusions (particularly Homeric) with the Phoenician sailor.

The *Heroicus* gives the tradition of eloquent peasants a self-conscious spin. In what I take as a knowing play on this topos, Philostratus makes the Phoenician sailor ask the eminently reasonable question "How come your speech is so educated? You do not seem to be uneducated" (4.5). Herodes Atticus asks an almost identical question of Agathion, the autochthon from Marathon, in the *Lives of the Sophists* (*VS* 553).[50] But whereas Agathion responds that the countryside is the best source of education, the vinegrower of the *Heroicus* turns out to be an impersonator of a rustic: he spent the first part of his life "in the city," "being educated and philosophizing" (4.6); eventually, his fortunes sank so low that in desperation he consulted Protesilaus, who advised him to "change your clothes" (4.9). The vinegrower presently understood that this was a suggestion to change his "style [*skhēma*]" of life (4.10). So the vinegrower is in fact a transvestite, whose peasant dress belies his urban background. Despite the metaphorical nature of the hero's command, it is literally the vinegrower's physical aspect that has misled the Phoenician—just as the vinegrower initially mistook him for an Ionian. Appearances can be deceptive—a lesson both for the Phoenician and for the reader, who may have been misled into believing that this is a conventionally unrealistic account of Atticizing peasants.

AESTHETICS

What I hope to have shown so far is that the *Heroicus* engages its readers' investment in urban elite Greek identity dynamically, provoking and teasing them, introducing countercurrents and tensions that enrich the construction of a Hellenic ideal. I turn now to consider in greater detail how Philostratus presents his text to the reader. What is most striking, initially, is the erotic lure of narrative. Pastoral settings, from the *Phaedrus* onward, are imagined as places for exchanging pleasurable narrative, and the *Heroicus* is no exception: the eroticism of the landscape seeps into the Trojan tales told by the vinegrower. Stories, like plots of land, are "sweet [*hēdus*]" (25.18). The Heroican rewriting of the *Iliad* becomes a love story: Protesilaus, whose five lines in the *Iliad* Catullus has already converted into an erotic epyllion (poem 68), represents the beautiful young lover, whose

---

49. Russell 1990a, 116, on this term, "a conspicuous Atticism."
50. Whitmarsh 2001, 106.

tragic, premature death separates him from his new wife, Laodamia. The vinegrower alludes to the reciprocity and heat of their desire: "He desires her and is in turn desired: their relationship is as hot as those of newlyweds" (11.1). If this evokes the "sexual symmetry" of the young lovers of the Greek novels,[51] the match can never be exact. Laodamia and Protesilaus may be "like [*hōsper*]" young lovers, but that telltale word also insists that they are not novelistic characters. An uncanny eroticism: long-dead heroes, ten cubits high, playing the roles of Chaereas and Callirhoe. Given that romances with gods usually end in disaster, the hero's semidivinity adds an element of (pleasurable?) risk, even perversity, to this erotic fantasy.

The issue of the covetability of Protesilaus is important for the reader too. Can we see him? Can we touch him? How real does he become for us? The vinegrower's reaction to seeing him lounging is conspicuously erotic: "If I catch him at leisure—wow, what sexy, lovely eyes!" (10.2). The word here rendered "at leisure" (from *anhiēmi*) perhaps carries undertones of remission of codes of sexual propriety.[52] These seductive invitations to fantasize about the desirable ephebe are presently redoubled. "It is sweetest to encounter him when he is naked: he is compact and light, like herms [*hermōn*] set up at racetracks" (10.4). Once again, the language of "sweetness" is a metapoetical marker: the vinegrower's pleasure at beholding the ephebe's gorgeous body stimulates and figures the reader's pleasurable imaginings of the sight. Now, the comparison of a beautiful body to a statue is reasonably common in erotic discourse,[53] so it is the choice of the word *hermēs* that is most striking about this sentence. The most definitive feature of a herm is the absence of limbs. Compact and light they may be, but they are not obvious *comparanda* for an athletic male body. The second most definitive feature is the erect phallus.[54] There is no reference, here or elsewhere, to Protesilaus's penis. The herm simile, however, invites the reader to fantasize. Indeed, as soon as we have begun thinking about

---

51. Mantero 1966, 212–15. For the novels' construction of sexual reciprocity, Konstan 1994 is still fundamental.

52. LSJ, s.v. "aneimonos" II.8 for *aneimonos* = "dissolute." In principle, *aneimenou* could also mean "undressed," from *anennumi*. But the particular compound of *ennumi* is not otherwise attested to my knowledge, and the vinegrower proceeds to a separate description of the sight of Protesilaus naked (10.4).

53. Jax 1936. As Roland Barthes explains it, beauty is marked by its ineffable qualities that overflow language, indescribable except by reference to other signifiers (art, divinity, or pleonastically to beauty itself). See Barthes 1990, 33–34; also 114.

54. Modern scholars, for sure, refer to the Roman-influenced portraits in the shape of a square bust—which lack the phallus—as portrait herms, but I am unaware of any evidence that Greeks called this kind of statue a herm. What is more, the vinegrower's reference to racetracks suggests the traditional ithyphallic style. Plut., *An seni* 797e shows that imperial writers could still associate the word *herm* with penile erection.

penises, we might wonder what precisely the phrase "compact and light [*eupagēs . . . kai kouphos*]" means. To which part(s) of the anatomy could this phrase refer? Protesilaus's penis is not there in the text, but its invisibility is more than just an absence: it is an invitation to imagine. The penis is *sous rature*, visible in its evanescence, a present absence. This is description as strip tease, the "staging of an appearance-as-disappearance";[55] Philostratus is flirting with his readers' erotically charged desire to visualize.

What of the Phoenician's responses to the vinegrower qua internal narratee? Complementing the vinegrower's eroticized descriptions, he is driven by desire ("I desire to hear," 7.1; "one who desires," 23.1).[56] He is, indeed (as the vinegrower characterizes him), a "lover of listening" (48.2). He takes in every emotional twist and turn: "Tears have come upon me" (20.3); "I am burdened" (40.1). He is entirely rapt. When the vinegrower encourages him to pay attention, he replies: "Pay attention?! The beasts did not even gape at Orpheus as much as I, when I listen to you, prick up my ears, and rouse my mind" (23.2). Later, he compares himself to a consumer of the lotus flower, so transported is he by the account (43.1). Clearly, at one level these reactions exalt the account that the vinegrower—and Philostratus— transmit. Yet they are not unambiguous markers of the way the reader is supposed to respond. As we saw earlier, dialogue characteristically suspends any authoritative judgment over the discourse it represents. Like Cnemon, the equally rapacious listener in Heliodorus's *Charicleia and Theagenes*,[57] as much as the Phoenician hams his role as appetitive listener, he also problematizes it for Philostratus's readers. If we come to the text as sophisticated Greek readers, can we really identify with him?

In particular, we might be troubled by the Phoenician's seemingly naïve approach to narrative as sensual experience. He imagines the sound of battle: "The 'din' of horses and men now 'strikes my ears'" (25.18, with nested quotation from Hom., *Il.* 10.535). In particular, he is lured (again like Cnemon)[58] into imaginary visualization: "I have seen the young man," he replies in response to the description of Protesilaus (10.5). Later, he asks: "May I please see Palamedes too, as I saw

---

55. Barthes 1975, 10.
56. Also "I wish [*boulomai*]" at 2.11, 3.1.
57. For Cnemon's desire to be a "spectator" of the narrative see Hld. 3.1.1, 3.1.2 (building on Thuc. 3.38.4: "You have accustomed yourselves to being spectators of speeches"). For Cnemon as a model for reader response see especially Winkler 1982, 140–46; J. R. Morgan 1989; Whitmarsh 2011a, 170–76; also above, ch. 2. That Heliodorus uses Philostratus has long been accepted; has the Phoenician novelist, then, made his appetitive listener an Athenian in revenge for the Athenian Philostratus's negative depiction of his countryman?
58. Hld. 3.4.7: "I thought I could see them, although they are absent." See Whitmarsh 2002.

Nestor, Diomedes, and Sthenelus?" (33.38). This paradigm of reading-as-visualization (which the Greeks called *phantasia*)—discussed more fully below—rests on the theoretical discourse of rhetorical *enargeia*, whereby vivid language is charged with the task of transcending the gulf between mimesis and reality.[59]

As befits a text that always ups the interpretative stakes, the Phoenician is not content with seeing alone. He also imagines Protesilaus's tangibility: "Do you embrace him when he arrives, or does he elude you in the fashion of smoke, as he does the poets?" (11.2).[60] The vinegrower replies that he can indeed touch Protesilaus: "He likes being embraced, and he allows me to kiss him and have my fill of his neck" (11.2).

Protesilaus, then, even manifests himself to the human touch. Like the Phoenician, however, we readers can only imagine what it is to feel his body. The suggestively imprecise language amplifies the frustration. Although kissing and embracing are compatible with polite greeting, it does sound—particularly given the pervasive air of eroticism—as though the ephebic Protesilaus is playing the passive role in pederastic courtship: the vinegrower seems to initiate the pursuit, while Protesilaus "allows" him to indulge in some minor petting. The final phrase, however, is difficult. The neck is conventionally a sexually privileged part;[61] what does it mean to "have one's fill of" it? Some translators have imagined the vinegrower throwing his arms around the hero's neck—rather like the willing *erōmenos* of an Attic vase painting—but nothing in the Greek suggests that.[62] Rather, the precise nature of the activity has been suppressed, leaving readers once again to fill in the gaps. The particle *ge* also demands comment. At one level, it simply means "yes," in response to the Phoenician's question (although postponed to a strikingly late position in the sentence).[63] It can also, however, imply limited agreement, hence the common translation "at any rate." This interpretation suggests that the vinegrower agrees that

---

59. Now a huge field. See especially Zanker 1981; Webb 1997a, 1997b, 1999, and especially 2009; Elsner 2004, 2007a; Platt 2011; the essays in *Ramus* 31 (2002) and *CPh* 102, no. 1 (2007). For Philostratean *enargeia* see especially Bryson 1994; Elsner 2000; Zeitlin 2001, 255–62, specifically on fantasies of visual presentification in the *Heroicus*.

60. The reference is to *Iliad* 23.100, where Patroclus's ghost eludes Achilles's grasp "like smoke." Other examples of this topos at Lucr., *DRN* 3.456; Verg., *Georg.* 4.499–500; *Aen.* 5.740; compare also the insubstantiality of ghosts at Hom., *Od.* 11. 207–8; *Aen.* 6.702. Normally, we might expect this reference to be "footnoted" with a phrase like *as the poets say*. What the Phoenician actually asks, however, is whether Protesilaus eludes his interlocutor as he eludes the poets. The sentence thus becomes a self-conscious meditation on the difficulty not just of reading but also of representing the hero. Grossardt 2006, 413, detects a coded attack on Euripides's *Protesilaus*.

61. E.g., Hom., *Il.* 3.396; Sappho 94.16 Lobel-Page.

62. Rossi 1997, "getti le braccia al collo"; Maclean and Aitken 2001, "cling to his neck." By contrast Beschorner 1999 and Grossardt 2006 accurately render the sense of "satisfying oneself with."

63. Denniston 1950, 133–34.

Protesilaus likes to be hugged but only lets him go so far. Even the vinegrower, then, yearns for more. For the reader, however, the elliptical, euphemistic language stimulates even more desire, a desire not only to fondle this "light, compact" body but also before that to penetrate the obscure veils of language. In this case, a trap is laid for the reader: we too are invited to imagine, along with the Phoenician, what the hero's body feels like.

In a discussion of Platonic dialogue, David Halperin writes of "the erotics of narrativity," the tempting of the reader's desire to close the gap between text and reality, to see through textual representation to "what really happened."[64] A similar phenomenon arises in the *Heroicus*, except that here we have not so much the erotics of narrativity as the erotics of description. The Phoenician has a mild interest in storytelling but is keener to visualize the actors in luscious detail.

At one point, the Phoenician's preference for description over narrative is thematized explicitly. The vinegrower breaks off and says, "These digressions are thought by some, stranger, to be idle chatter and nonsense, for those who do not lead a life of leisure" (53.2).[65] The model for this episode is the narrative intermezzo at *Odyssey* 11.328–84, with a subtle reversal of roles: Odysseus breaks off from narrating to think about his ship (11.330–32), while the vinegrower encourages the Phoenician to think of his. Like the spellbound Phaeacians (Hom., *Od.* 11.334), however, the Phoenician is not in any mood to give up now: "Who cares about the ship and everything in it? The cargo of the soul is sweeter and more profitable. Let us consider narrative digressions not as nonsense but as the surplus profit derived from this commerce" (53.3). The Phoenician here translates the Odyssean exploration of narrative digressivism into the idiom of seafaring and mercantilism (an idiom he employs frequently in the *Heroicus*).[66] Deviation turns out to be a marked metaphor. Description bears the same relation to narrative as the Chersonese does to a commercial journey: both are detours offering their own pleasures. And as in a comparable passage in Heliodorus's *Charicleia and Theagenes*,[67] the threat to break off is rescinded. The Phoenician's words approach a theorization of erotic reading: counterposed to the teleology of "commercial" reading, the pleasures of divagation and engaged fantasy offer their own rewards and profit. As in Achilles

---

64. Halperin 1992.
65. The Phoenician's propensity toward leading the vinegrower to digressions is also illustrated at 20.1 (see "diversion [*ekbolē*]").
66. Grossardt 2006, 130, discusses the frequent collocations of sailing and narrative, although I am unconvinced by the arguments for an Epicurean underlay. To Grossardt's list of passages (6.3–7, 14.2, 14.4, 23.3, 55.6) add 34.3–4, 58.6.
67. Hld. 3.4.1–3.5.2: see especially P. R. Hardie 1998, with 22 on the Odyssean prototype.

Tatius and Heliodorus, rich and seductive description intersects and arrests linear plot.⁶⁸

The Phoenician is not the only listener in the *Heroicus* seduced by description: Achilles and Helen, we are told, fell for each other after death solely on the basis of report. Normally, the vinegrower observes, desire (*tou eran*) lies in the eyes (54.4).⁶⁹ These lovers, however, were aroused to mutual desire "by discovering their ears as the genesis of physical desire" (54.4). The description hints at an inversion of Candaules's famous words to Gyges in Herodotus 1: the Lydian king tells his servant not to take his word for his wife's great beauty but to see for himself, since the ears are more untrustworthy than the eyes (Hdt. 1.8.2). The apophthegm in Herodotus, the great traveler and researcher (*histōr*), privileges autopsy; Philostratus's character, by contrast, sets visual experience in competition with the seductive power of literary representation. This is clearly a metatextual moment: as we have seen throughout the *Heroicus*, language and description are connected with the stimulation of readerly desire.⁷⁰

This passage also serves as an implicit commentary on the text's *Homerkritik*, where questions over direct testimony and secondary representation are very much in play. Protesilaus offers an account of the Trojan War that bypasses Homer's parti pris version (Odysseus having bought off the poet). Like the pseudodiaries of Dictys and Dares (and their Hellenistic avatars, particularly Hegesianax), the *Heroicus* offers us a (supposedly) more accurate version delivered by one who was there. Unlike Dictys and Dares, however, Protesilaus died before the war began, so his version remains at one remove from the "reality" it purports to describe. As much as Philostratus seeks to cancel the mediating role of the Homeric text by substituting direct experience, he also reminds his readers that his version remains resolutely textual and mimetic. For everyone involved in the long chain of Philostratean transmission—we readers, the Phoenician, the vinegrower, Protesilaus himself—it has indeed been the ears rather than the eyes that have been seduced.

---

68. See Rommel 1923 for the sources of Achilles's and Heliodorus's digressions. Bartsch 1989 argues that digressions are (or are expected to be) relevant to the plot; Morales 2004 sees them as repositories for outré sexual fantasy. On digressivity and relevance see Whitmarsh 2011a, 235–40.

69. The implicit pun on seeing (*horan*) and loving (*eran*) is familiar Philostratean territory: see especially *Ep.* 52, with Walker 1992, 132–33, for further parallels.

70. For parallels see Grossardt 2006, 739. The most suggestive occurs at Achilles Tatius's *Leucippe and Clitophon* 2.13.1: the young profligate Callisthenes is held to have become "a lover by hearsay [*ex akoēs erastēs*]." Achilles's narrator associates this (rather hypocritically) with moral deviancy: "The wantonness of the licentious is so great that even with their ears they wallow in erotic pleasure, and they suffer through mere words the effects that wounded eyes usually administer to the soul" (2.13.1). In associating aural eroticism with wantonness, Achilles playfully stigmatizes any appetitive response on the part of the reader.

This interplay between textual report and autoptic viewing also permeates the vinegrower's descriptions more generally. The physiognomonical descriptions that dominate the text are brilliantly ecphrastic, providing a high level of pictorial detail—reminding us, if we needed reminding, that Philostratus (always assuming the two Philostrati are the same) composed a series of *Imagines,* descriptions of paintings in a Neapolitan gallery.[71] When the Phoenician puts in a request for his heroes, he asks, for example, "Can I see Palamedes?" (33.38) or "Will you show him and sketch in [*anagrapseis*] his appearance?" (48.1). The use of iconic language here (*anagraphein,* translated as "sketch in")[72] redoubles the textualizing play.

As well as painting, statuary is used as a resource for visualization. We have already seen Protesilaus compared to the herms of runners, and there are three other instances of comparisons to statues (10.3, 10.5, 42.3). Art is the paradigm of beauty: Neoptolemus is physically lesser than his father "to the degree that the handsome are lesser than their statues" (52.2). For readers of Lucian, this technique recalls the satirist's *Imagines,* where Lycinus describes the emperor's mistress to Polystratus (who is just as erotically enthralled as the Phoenician here) by comparing her body parts to those of different statues.[73] Philostratus does not dismember his statues as Lucian does, nor does he name any specific artworks. But although loose comparisons with statues are very much part of the package of erotic description in the period (analogies can be found in Aristaenetus and the novels),[74] these are not simply throwaway topoi but part of a complex and provocative thematic that runs through the entire text. At times, statues serve as paradigms for description: on one occasion, *agalma* is even used as a nigh-synonym for "description" (26.13: "I can also give you an *agalma* of Nestor"). On other occasions, it is the inertness of statues that is brought to the fore, their inability to match the animated vitality of real subjects. Hector, for example, is said to be "sweeter [*hēdiō*]"—a key word in the aesthetics of the *Heroicus,* as we have seen— and bigger than his statue (37.5). Unlike humans, who only worship statues and intimations (*huponoias*) of the gods, heroes have open dealings with them (7.3). In a passage that we have already considered, the cult statue of Protesilaus is ruined and delapidated (9.6), but the vinegrower says that he does not care, for he meets with (*xuneimi*) and sees (*blepō*) the hero in person, who is sweeter (*hēdion*) than any statue (9.7).

In these passages, statues are seen as feeble, second-order versions of "the real." At other times they seem to strive after vitality, straining, like the Laocoon group

---

71. Mantero 1966, 69–70; Rossi 1997, 23.
72. *Anagraphein* also in this sense at 27.13, 47.2; also *diagraphein* at 10.1, 48.12.
73. In turn modeled on the celebrated story of Zeuxis's painting of Helen (Dion. Hal., *De imit.* fr. 6), discussed in ch. 8.
74. Jax 1936, 47.

in Gotthold Lessing's celebrated discussion, at the leash of static artwork ("die Grenzen der Malerei").[75] A statue of Hector has peculiarly lifelike properties: it is, the vinegrower tells us, "so lifelike [*empnoun*] that it draws the viewer to touch it" (19.3). The novelists use *empnous* of statues in a deliberately paradoxical way, marking girls who look like "living statues."[76] Hector's statue is equally paradoxical, partaking of both inert matter and the vitality and exuberance of heroic stuff. The boundary between art and life is here threatened but perhaps not yet transgressed. What follows, however, is remarkable. Like the statue of Orpheus in Arrian's account of Alexander's expedition (*Anab.* 1.11.2),[77] this one sweats, particularly when excited by cult worship (19.4), and when a Syrian lad came and mocked it, even claiming that it represented Achilles and not Hector, he came to a horrid, watery end when Hector later drowned him (19.5-7).

Philostratus's treatment of statuary is complex and variegated, but what abides throughout is an intense interest in how lifelike these representations are. This questioning of the power of mimetic arts to approximate, capture, or even create reality links to a characteristically Philostratean metadiscursivity. Plastic and literary description alike are means of making present (in a partial, transitory, and provisional way) what is absent. The issue of the physicality of the objects of description is a concern that pervades the *Heroicus,* and not just in terms of the alluring, attractive notion of touching hermlike heroes: the heroes are also terrible, vengeful figures who can, even now, wreak havoc on those whom they choose to visit. We have already considered Hector's vengeance on the youth who abused his statue; equally tangibly "real" is Achilles's violent response to the Thessalians who did not keep up his cult (53.22). The heroes' physical presence is an ongoing issue.

CONCLUSIONS

One of the many themes of the *Heroicus* is the idea that even now—despite the passing of time, our hypermodern skepticism and sophistication, and multiculturalism—traditional, heroic energies inhabit the landscape.[78] Homeric Greece maintains a physical reality in the present. The mythical heroes of the past are not simply the stuff of tales told to children by their nurses, as the Phoenician puts it in his early, skeptical phase (7.10, 8.2); heroes inhabit, and share potency with, the landscape of their cult sites. The Achaeans, for example, embraced Achilles's tomb "thinking they were embracing Achilles" (51.13). Enormous footprints, traces of Protesilaus's presence, are left in the soil of the cult site (13.2–3). These marks have a semiotic, almost

---

75. Lessing 1962 (1766), subtitle.
76. E.g., Hld. 1.7.2; Aristaenet. 1.1.
77. See Bosworth 1980, 97, with further references; also Mantero 1966, 134–36.
78. Eitrem 1929, 38–42.

graphematic quality, like the "spoors" of her brother that Electra tracks in Aeschylus's *Choephoroe*.[79] The past is legible in the text of the landscape. But it is deeply significant that Protesilaus's footsteps are said to be not always visible: when the hero runs too fast to leave a trace, the ground is *asēmos*, literally "without a sign/signifier" (13.3). If we are right about the self-reflexivity of this text, then this episode can be read as a meditation on the process of reading as reinscribing, reincorporating, the plenitude of the past, even as it evanesces.

Reading, imagining, re-viewing can serve as a (circumscribed, imperfect) traversal of the boundaries that separate past from present. "Whatever the style of viewing," comments Froma Zeitlin, "real or imaginary, the eyes, as no other faculty, give life and credence to vivid recollections of the past and the preoccupations of a shared cultural heritage."[80] When the Phoenician asks, prompted by a passing remark of the vinegrower's, when the heroes "were seen [*ōphthēsan*]" on the plain of Troy, the vinegrower replies by correcting his interlocutor's tense: "They *are* seen [*horōntai*], I said, they *are still* seen by cowherds and shepherds on the plain. They are great and divine, and sometimes their appearance spells trouble for the land" (18.2). The word *still* marks the crucial juncture between traditional narrative and actuality. Philostratus's vinegrower adopts the voice of Herodotean archaeology, as mediated through Hellenistic etiology, recording the visible traces of the past.[81] In Philostratus's account, however, and exceptionally, a mystical power grants the heroes of the past a capacity to transcend the etiolating effects of time, to retain across the ages an existential plenitude. And yet there is a palpable tension here: the past inhabits the present, but only just, and with a certain strain or surprise (*still* carries a concessive force: "even so," "nevertheless").

The *Heroicus* dramatizes not simply the ongoing valency of the Greek cultural tradition but also the pleasures and challenges of re-creating it through the fictional *imaginaire*. It engages its readers in a creative, dynamic, but ultimately impossible task: the construction of identity by reembodying the past, spectral and elusive though it remains. The seductive pleasures of the text are at once its frustrations: the strategy of generating teasing glimpses of the past, behind the veils of both time and narrative representation, is predicated on an unresolved (and irresoluble) play between absence and presence, oblivion and memory, death and vitality. The *Heroicus* can thus be read as a cultural parable, an articulation of the

---

79. Aesch., *Cho.* 228, with Goldhill 1984, 128–29, for the metaliterary interpretation.
80. Zeitlin 2001, 263.
81. Herodotus signals the persistence of cultural tradition with such expressions as "even up to my day [*eti es eme*]" (1.52), which occurs some fifty times (depending on what is counted) in his corpus: there is a quick survey of the issues at Cobet 2002, 397. The more familiar phrase "even now [*eti kai nun*, and similar]"—used by Philostratus at *Her.* 33.28—is not directly paralleled in Herodotus but is common in the periegetic tradition (especially Pausanias: Akujärvi 2005, 69–77).

ambiguous position of third-century Greeks in relation to their cultural traditions. The narrative time of the encounter is the autumn (3.2, 10.2, 11.9),[82] the season serving as a pregnant metaphor for the self-diagnosed posterity of Philostratus's world. In the context of Roman Greek culture, this knowingly "late flowering of eloquence,"[83] the past is sublime, powerfully meaningful and self-present, but at the same time elusive and distant. It is this delicate equipoise that we negotiate every time we read the *Heroicus*.

---

82. Just as Protesilaus smells "sweeter [*hēdion*] than autumn myrtles" (10.2).
83. Rohde 1876, 291.

8

Mimesis and the Gendered Icon in Greek Theory and Fiction

Pictorialism, as we saw in the previous chapter, is a fixture in postclassical literature. Everywhere we look we find texts referencing artworks, particularly in erotic contexts. In this chapter I delve further into this connection between art, textuality, and eroticism, focusing on questions of gender politics. What does it mean to compare a woman to an artwork? Why this preoccupation with looking? How is the male gaze hooked, satisfied, problematized? My test cases are two later romances, Achilles Tatius's *Leucippe and Clitophon* and Heliodorus's *Charicleia and Theagenes*, which I read in dialogue with (what I argue to have been) an influential work of literary criticism, Dionysius of Halicarnassus's *On Imitation*.

"She looked like a picture I had once seen of Selene on a bull." These words of Achilles Tatius (1.4.3) are famous partly for the textual uncertainty (should we read *Selene* or *Europa*?), a philological ambiguity that has provoked an unusually sophisticated response, couched in terms of both cultural and gender politics.[1] But even if we leave aside the critical question of whether (or, better, how) this picture relates to the narrator's earlier ecphrasis of the painting of Europa on a bull (1.1.2–13), it is clear that this passage invites us to reflect on the triangular relationship between beauty, gender, and *mimēsis*. As is now widely recognized, romance beauty is regularly expressed in terms of availability to the dominant, aestheticizing gaze.[2] Leucippe is like a picture in that she exists to be surveyed, contemplated,

---

1. Discussion and further references at Morales 2004, 38–48, which lays the emphasis on voyeurism; see also Selden 1994, which explores the play of cultural perspectives (discussed further at Whitmarsh 2011a, 80–82).
2. See especially Morales 2004; also Haynes 2003, 53–70.

and (particularly in *Leucippe and Clitophon*, with its distinctive homodiegetic narrative form) textually constructed by a male viewer.

Despite the incontrovertible masculinism of the (and particularly this) Greek romance, however, this is not simply a celebration of male subjectivity. The picturelike Leucippe wields enormous power over Clitophon, which is imaged in military terms: "As soon as I saw her, I was destroyed [*apolōlein*], for the wounds [*titrōskei*] of beauty are more piercing than those of a missile [*belos*]" (1.4.4). This impression is reinforced by the inevitable echo[3] of the pictorial ecphrasis near the start of the romance, where (for all that the hypotextual narrative is one of rape)[4] Europa seems strikingly in control: she holds the bull's horn "as a rider would a bridle," and indeed he "is steered in this direction, responding to the pressure from the rider's hand" (1.1.10); she holds her veil as though she were sailing the bull like a ship (1.1.12). The unnamed narrator interprets the painting as a parable for Eros's authority over even the king of the gods (1.1.13, 1.2.1).

Clearly at one level this "power" possessed by the love object is circumscribed by very traditional male ideology, limited as it is to the capacity to impress men and constituted exclusively of "to-be-looked-at-ness."[5] Viewed from this perspective, the woman's apparent force is, as Laura Mulvey would have it, simply a male projection of the fear of castration.[6] Indeed, Achilles's imagery of wounding suggests a troubling vulnerability of the male body to the phallic "missile," a translation into the romance genre of the Homeric "drooping poppy" syndrome,[7] and Europa's firm hand on Zeus's "horn [*keras*]" needs little explication.[8]

At another level, however, this will not do. The eroticized, aestheticized woman is also the blazon of the romance as a genre (a fact, I have argued, that the very titling conventions signal).[9] This tendency becomes explicit in late-antique and Byzantine commentaries, which personify Heliodorus's text in particular in the form of its female protagonist; thus an enthusiast for this romance can be described

---

3. Less direct if we read *Selene* rather than *Europa*, but no less insistent. If we read the two paintings as identical (which would involve an ironic reading of *pote*, "once"), I wonder whether we could take Clitophon to be implicitly "correcting" the unnamed narrator in a second sense (i.e., in addition to identifying the subject as Selene rather than Europa): he supplies the face that is missing from the earlier description.

4. In Moschus's canonical version, Zeus "snatches" her (*Eur.* 110), and she bewails her fate (146–48).

5. Mulvey 1975, 837.

6. Ibid., 840.

7. Hom., *Il.* 8.306–8, with D. P. Fowler 1987 on Latin versions that develop the nexus of wounding, defloration, and castration imagery more explicitly (Cat. 11.21–24; Verg., *Aen.* 9.435–37; Ov., *Met.* 10.190–93).

8. See Henderson 1991, 127, for the slang *keras* = "penis."

9. Whitmarsh 2005b; see also ch. 2, n. 4.

as "the lover [*erastēs*] of Charicleia."[10] But it is already implicit in the romances, where the very pictorial, "graphic" quality of the description of beautiful protagonists presents them as constructed, artifactual: in effect, embodiments of textuality. When Achilles (or Clitophon) compares Leucippe to "a picture I had once seen of Selene on a bull," what he actually says is, more literally (if less elegantly), "I had once seen Selene like that, represented [*gegrammenēn*] on a bull" (1.4.3). The word *represented* exploits the well-known indeterminacy of the Greek *graphein* (encountered in the previous chapter), which can refer either to painting or to writing. If readers think back to the initial ecphrasis of Europa on the bull, the irony doubles, since that was of course a textual transcription of a painting, in other words a *graphē* in both senses simultaneously.

The textualization of Leucippe is underlined presently, as Clitophon describes her cheek: "Her cheek was white, the white reddening toward the center in imitation of purple, such as a Lydian woman uses to die ivory" (1.4.3). The blush of her cheek is said to have "imitated [*emimeito*]" purple; at exactly this moment, Clitophon engages in an ostentatious literary imitation, invoking a famous couplet from Homer (*Iliad* 4.141–42).[11] If the cliché is characteristic of the bombastic Clitophon, readers may wish to ascribe to the author the sophisticatedly self-reflexive manipulation of the language of mimēsis (along with the ingenious evocation of a simile used by Homer to describe wounding, in the context of an egregious beauty that will turn out to "wound" its beholder). But these distinctions are hard to enforce (hidden authors are, after all, well hidden).[12] The crucial point is that Leucippe has become a portmanteau, a woman-text: an irreducibly physical being who has a physical effect on Clitophon[13] but also an imaginary cipher for the power of textual representation.

Put in the simplest of terms, women in the Greek romances should be understood both as passive objects of the gaze and as positive embodiments of the genre's creative power. My point is not the familiar (and clearly true) one that there are examples in the narratives proper of both weak and strong women[14] nor that the romances might be both oppressive and empowering for women readers.[15] The issue here is rather different and relates primarily to aesthetics: in the economy of the romance, women are at once alienated from the text (that is, fixed at the other

10. See, e.g., Philip the Philosopher 12–13 (Hld., *Test.* XIII Colonna).
11. Jax 1936 discusses the many uses of this quotation.
12. On the difficulties of separating author from narrator in Achilles Tatius see Whitmarsh 2003, 2011, 82–9; Marinčič 2007; J. R. Morgan 2007.
13. Note the orgasmic language of Clitophon's response: the *petit mort* of *apolōlein* (I was destroyed), the "outpouring [*katarrhei*]" of beauty into his soul (1.4.4; the Platonic language is echoed in 1.9.4–5, whose allusions Bychkov 1999 traces).
14. Haynes 2003 surveys representations of women; see also Johne 2003.
15. So Egger 1988; 1994.

end of the narrative telescope) and figuratively constitutive of it.[16] Each construction of femininity is in equal measure androcentric and stereotyped, but the second tenses against the first in ways that have not (I think) been well enough appreciated.

In this chapter, I trace this emphasis on female iconicity in rhetorical theory and fiction. My primary focus will be, in the first instance, the *On Imitation* (*Peri mimēseōs*) of Dionysius of Halicarnassus, a treatise on the art of imitating prior literary models.[17] What we shall find in this text is a powerful theorizing of the bifocal gendering of textuality noted above; I then return in conclusion to the romances, arguing both that Dionysius is a direct source for at least one of the later romancers and that the romance's complex treatment of this theme can be better understood if read against a Dionysian backdrop.

On Imitation, originally in three books, survives in the form of a few fragments of book 1 cited by late-antique and Byzantine commentators on the rhetoricians, additional fragments and an extensive epitome of book 2 (again probably late antique or later), and a couple of cross-references elsewhere in Dionysius's work.[18] In addition, chapter 3 of the *Letter to Pompeius Geminus* contains a partial quotation, or perhaps reformulation, of book 2's discussion of historians, which supplies the addressee (one Demetrius) and the contents of the three books (the first is the theory of mimēsis, the second the literary models to be imitated, and the third, unfinished, the methods of mimēsis).[19]

Dionysius is best known for his distinctive combination of cultural classicism with general support for Rome: this comes out in both his rhetorical works (*On the*

---

16. Kenaan 2008 is thought-provoking on the complex relationship between gender and textuality in Greece and Rome.

17. On the distinction between this sense of *mimēsis* and the "philosophical" one of imitating reality see especially Flashar 1978, which however overemphasizes the discreteness of the two meanings ("In Dionysius's opinion linguistic imitation was an aspect of imitation in general," Goudriaan 1989, 688).

18. *Ep. Pomp.* 3.1; *De Thuc.* 1. The fragments are to be found in Usener and Radermacher 1965; Aujac 1992; Battisti 1997. The latter two are less confident than Usener and Radermacher in the attribution of fragments to particular books. In this chapter I refer to Usener-Radermacher (hereafter U-R), for ease of consultation. Radermacher 1940 identifies another possible fragment. On the *De imitatione* see Flashar 1978, 87–88; Russell 1979, especially 5–6; M. Heath 1989; Aujac 1992, 11–22; Cizek 1994, 17–19; Battisti 1997, 9–30; Whitmarsh 2001, 71–75; Hunter 2009, 107–27. More generally on Dionysian mimetic theory see Goudriaan 1989, 1.218–50 (for readers of Dutch; I have used the English summary at 2.688); Hidber 1996, 56–74; Fornaro 1997, 12–14; Halliwell 2002, 292–96 (oddly omitting any mention of *De imit.*). See now Wiater 2011 for an excellent account of the cultural and ideological forces underpinning Dionysius's classicism.

19. *Ep. Pomp.* 3.1, a section that is, however, heavily emended (discussion at Fornaro 1997, 164–66). There are some discrepancies, notably in the apparent weight given to historians: M. Heath 1989 discusses the relationship between the *Letter* and the *Epitome*, reasserting U-R's claim that the *Letter* reflects a draft version of *On Imitation* and the *Epitome* the revised, published version.

Ancient Orators 3.1 credits Roman conquest with stimulating the return to the Attic style)[20] and more directly in his *Roman Antiquities*, which is both an assertion of Rome's providentially ordained imperial destiny and a demonstration that the city was originally ethnically and culturally Greek.[21] What is striking about the surviving portions of *On Imitation*, however, is the emphasis not (as elsewhere) on cultural identity but on sexuality and gender. Mimēsis is repeatedly imaged in terms of heterosexual erotics. This principle is staked out in what looks like a programmatic definition of *mimēsis* and its sibling *zēlos* (emulation) in book 1: "Mimēsis is an activity [*energeia*] of receiving the impression of the model, through theorems. . . . *Zēlos* is an activity [*energeia*] of the soul when it is stirred [*kinoumenē*] to wonder at something that seems beautiful" (*De imit.* fr. 3 U-R).

The second sentence is striking for its phallic imagery: not only does the idea of the soul being "stirred [*kinoumenē*]" into "activity [*energeia*]" suggest tumescence, but the roots of both words can also carry an obscene, sexual sense.[22] The first sentence, by contrast, presents mimēsis in terms of receptivity: still an activity but now one that involves "receiving the impression of [*ekmattomenē*]" the literary original, like wax receiving the imprint of a seal.[23] Both sentences, moreover, describe the imitative activity with a passive, feminine participle. The mimetic process is imagined, then, as hybridized between the genders, a hermaphroditic phenomenon.[24]

The imagery of "receiving an impression" also locates us squarely within the metaphorical field of cultural production, of the artificed manufacture of goods. Dionysius is deeply concerned to identify the position of mimēsis on the spectrum between nature and culture. (This focus may at first sight seem to be a departure from our themes of sexuality and gender; the connection will, however, become clear presently.) But here too matters are intricate, since elsewhere mimēsis seems to be better when it is natural. One fragment from *On Imitation* contains the claim that "the most important part of talent lies in our nature [*phusis*], which it is not in our power to have in the way that we want it."[25] To unpack the implications of this position, let us look to a passage from Dionysius's *Dinarchus* that expands on what seems to be the same point:

---

20. Although Dionysius seems to have only minimal respect for Rome as a producer of culture: Hidber 1996, 75–81, sketches the various critical positions on this point.

21. See inter alia Gabba 1991, 10–22; Hartog 1991; Luraghi 2003.

22. See LSJ, s.v. "energein" III; for the well known *kinein* = *binein*, see LSJ, s.v. "kinein" II.4, and Jeffrey Henderson 1991, 151–52, with index s.v.

23. *Mattein*, again, can have a sexual sense (Jeffrey Henderson 1991, 194).

24. Compare ps.-Longinus's equally gender-bending imagery presenting mimēsis in terms of both insemination (13.2) and militarism (13.4); see further Whitmarsh 2001, 57–60.

25. *De imit.* fr. 3 Aujac = 5 U-R. Dionysius proceeds to oppose "talent" to *prohairesis*, an Aristotelian word denoting the parts of our character that are open to us to develop through training. Compare also fr. 1 U-R: in *politikoi logoi*, you need "a dexterous nature, accurate learning, and rigorous discipline."

Speaking generally, you will find two different types of mimēsis of the ancients. The first is natural [*physikos*] and is acquired from long instruction and nurturing; the second, closely related to the first, proceeds from technical rules [*tōn ek tēs tekhnēs pareggelmatōn*]. About the first, what is there to be said? About the second, it might be said that all models are suffused with a certain natural [*autophuēs*] grace and beauty, whereas in the copies, even if they reach the pinnacle of imitation, there is still an artificial [*epitetēdeumenon*], nonnatural [*ouk ek phuseōs*] quality. (7.5–6)

The "two different types of mimēsis" turn out to be clearly marked: the natural type is better, producing the "grace and beauty" that the cultural type can never quite attain. Dionysius is here intervening in the familiar debate over the relative weighting of nature and nurture, or more specifically innate ability and training, in literary production.[26] What is interesting, however, is that immediately on articulation, the nature/culture distinction deconstructs itself. The superior form is not purely natural: it also develops "from long instruction and nurturing" (even if Dionysius seems to have the education specifically of the child in mind,[27] i.e., the process of acculturation will have been completed by the time that the adult effects his literary imitations). The sharp line between superior, "natural" mimēsis and the inferior, "cultural" form begins to pixelate; the two are indeed "closely related." Mimēsis seems to occupy not the absolute states of the natural and the cultural (or the feminine and the masculine) but the fluid spaces in between.

What is at stake in this emphasis on the ambiguous position of mimēsis between nature and culture? One answer must surely be to do with the kind of cultural capital that Dionysius is hoarding. Insisting that only the "naturally" talented can succeed at the highest level allows him to minimize the socially transformative effects of education, in effect barricading aesthetics so as to prevent undesirables (including Romans?)[28] from accessing elite prestige. At the same time, if nature alone were sufficient, then the pedagogue Dionysius would be out of a job. For Dionysius, mimēsis is about more than just literary reproduction: it's also about social reproduction, the preservation of traditional class hierarchies and cultural exclusivity (in what was, of course, the challenging political context of Augustan Rome).[29]

---

26. Cizek 1994, 69–71, discusses the wider context; see also Goudriaan 1989, 234–40 (in Dutch).

27. *Katēkhēsis* implies the kind of oral training given to the very young (in the Christian Church, *catechism* is prebaptismal instruction); note also *suntrophia*, "joint nurturing."

28. As Ewen Bowie suggests to me, the nature/culture distinction might in certain contexts be taken to distinguish native from nonnative speakers. On imperial Greek strictures on opsimathy see Schmitz 1997, 152–56 (which argues that this accusation is aimed at social parvenus—but Romans might be targeted too?).

29. The classic work on social reproduction is Bourdieu and Passeron 1990. I use the word *reproduction* advisedly, for reasons that will quickly become clear.

But this is not the whole answer, since the discourse of nature and culture does not attach itself exclusively to the faculties of the imitator. If we look back to the *Dinarchus* passage cited above, we can detect a peculiar slippage. At the start of the passage, the "good" type of mimēsis is said to be natural (*physikos*) because it proceeds from the good nature of the imitator. Toward the end, however, this language is cross-applied to the mimetic creations themselves, which possess "natural grace and beauty" or an "artificial, nonnatural quality." Now the ontological status of the artifact is at issue; behind this sentence is a long history of philosophical reflection on the reality of naturalness of the mimetic product.[30] Yet although Dionysius seems to argue here that mimēsis can be natural, this is not an unqualified association: elsewhere he suggests that apparent naturalness in literature in fact springs from cunning artifice (a device he associates particularly with Lysias).[31] As Stephen Halliwell notes, "Dionysius regards mimēsis simultaneously as a kind of stylized fabrication or invention, yet also as a possible means of depicting and conveying truth or nature."[32] Mimetic literature is at once artificial and capable of naturalistic representation.

This is where we rejoin the discussion of sexuality, for the natural production of natural artifacts is, fundamentally, a form of physical reproduction. (The Greek *physis*, "nature," derives from *phuein*, "to beget.") In its ontogenic role, mimēsis is thus closely linked with sexual reproduction. This association is not new with Dionysus (Diotima's talk of "birthing" beautiful and grand logoi in Plato's *Symposium* is an important precursor)[33] and indeed fits into a wider, apparently cross-cultural pattern.[34] Michael Taussig, in his intriguing *Mimesis and Alterity*, describes the womb as "the mimetic organ par excellence," emphasizing "in the submerged and constant body of the mother the dual meaning of reproduction as birthing and reproduction as replication."[35] Reproductive fertility is, perhaps, both the readiest metaphor for and the most primal instantiation of creativity.

An extraordinary story, preserved in the epitome of book 2 of *On Imitation*, underlines this powerful association between mimetic and parturitive creativity.

---

30. Halliwell 2002 offers a rich discussion of philosophical mimēsis, with further bibliography: see especially 37–71, on Plato and the representation of reality (also 138–42, on *Republic* 10); 153–54 (with n. 5), on Aristotle and the naturalness of mimēsis.

31. See, e.g., *De comp.* 20, on the use of appropriate language in mimēsis: "These effects are the work not of Nature improvising but of art trying to represent [*mimēsasthai*] events"; also *Lys.* 3, 8 and *Isae.* 16 for Lysias's skill in dissimulating his artfulness. In general on the dissimulation theme in ancient criticism see Cronje 1993.

32. Halliwell 2002, 292–96, at 295.

33. Pl., *Symp.* 210d 2–6; see Hunter 2009, 115.

34. See, e.g., Friedman 1987.

35. Taussig 1993, 35, more fully explicated at 112–28.

Despite the difficulties presented by the epitome, we can clearly see that the anecdote dramatizes the themes we have traced so far:

> The reader's soul absorbs the likeness of the style [/imprint: *kharaktēros*] thanks to continual observation, rather like the experience of the farmer's wife according to the myth. It is said that a fear arose in a farmer who was ugly to behold that he would become the father of similar children. This fear taught [*edidaxe*] him an artifice [*tekhnēn*] to produce good children. He fashioned [*plasas*] some handsome pictures [*eikonas*] and habituated his wife to look at them. Afterward, he coupled with her and was blessed with the beauty of the paintings. In the same way, in the mimēsis of words too resemblance [*homoiotēs*] is born. (6.1 U-R)

The analogy between reproduction and literary mimēsis is explicit here and underlined by the sharing of imagery: in the last sentence, a resemblance between the emulator and the original author "is born [*tiktetai*]" through the operations of mimēsis. Like the passage on mimēsis and zēlos discussed above, this one plays with the theme of gender hybridity, for the imitator occupies the roles of both husband and wife: the first represents learned (note *edidaxe*, "taught") artistry (*tekhnēn*), the second creative power, both of which are necessary to generate aesthetically pleasing literature. The reference to *tekhnē* also reminds us that the discourse of gender hybridity relates to the nature-culture polarity, here in a way that is as precisely defined as it is cross-culturally familiar:[36] woman stands for nature, man for culture. Despite the depiction of mimēsis as a fusion of female and male qualities, however, the story also reflects a traditional androcentrism: all the decisive actions are taken by the man (the wife is not the subject of any verb), and his cultural intervention transcends the normative expectations of "natural" sexual reproduction.

It is not just the reproductive aspect of mimēsis that is sexualized. For Dionysius, the desire to imitate is stimulated by an erotic desire for beauty. We can see this already in the first quotation above from *On Imitation*, which defines zēlos (emulation) as "an activity of the soul when it is stirred to wonder at something that seems beautiful." Beautiful artifacts are generated when beauty captivates their creator. There is another memorable parable in the epitome of book 2 that illustrates how this erotic mimēsis proceeds:

> Zeuxis was a painter feted among the people of Croton. Now, when he was painting *Helen Naked*, the people sent him the local maidens for him to scrutinize naked—not because they were all beautiful but because it was unlikely that they were all totally ugly. The aspects that were worthy of painting in each of them were united into a

---

36. The classic study of Ortner 1974, especially 71–83, explores this equivalence; its refined conclusion is that women are associated not with nature per se but with the mediation between nature and culture.

single representation of a body. Out of the collage of many parts, artistry [*tekhnē*] composed one complete form. Therefore it is open to you too, as if in a viewing space [*theatrōi*], to inquire into [*exhistorein*] the forms of beautiful bodies and pluck any superior example from their souls, and by bringing together the feast [*eranon*] of polymathy you can shape an image [*eikona*] that will be not destroyed by time, but an immortal beauty formed by art. (6.1 U-R)

The story is well known from Cicero and Pliny, perhaps deriving ultimately from Duris of Samos,[37] but it is here put to a characteristically Dionysian use. The point of the story in other sources is to illustrate the widespread principle that perfection does not exist in any one form.[38] Assuming a reasonable amount of fidelity in the epitomator, we can detect in Dionysius, by contrast, an additional parable about the erotics of art, the omnipotent, fetishizing male gaze, and the power of *tekhnē*: art here works with nature to engender "human" life but also transcends nature, creating out of a collection of flawed bodies a "perfect form [*teleion eidos*]."

This story is all about the authority of the male, who views this pornographic[39] display of female flesh from a detached, dispassionate vantage, as an aesthete rather than a lover. "The story of the painting of Helen casts Zeuxis as Paris, judging the beauty of women and rewarded with the 'naked Helen,'"[40] certainly, and indeed the passage takes its place in a long tradition of prurient accounts of males judging beauty contests (such as the pair of poems by Rufinus where the narrator is asked to serve as a *kritēs* for, respectively, the front and the rear of three women).[41] Compared to other similar accounts, however, Dionysius's story seems pointedly to remove all trace of lustful viewing. In fact, Zeuxis's subjectivity seems entirely erased (if we can trust the epitomator): after the girls arrive, he is never the subject of an active verb. The process of scrutinizing bodies is denoted with one passive verb (the parts "were united [*ēthroisthē*]"); the only agency in

---

37. Cic., *De inv.* 2.1–3; Plin., *NH* 35.64. The attribution to Duris is often repeated but in fact seems to rest on a hypothesis of Jex-Blake and Sellers 1968 (1896), lxi–lxii, which tends to ascribe to him any unattributed story about Greek painters.

38. Cic., *De inv.* 2.3 has a similar sentiment; Xen., *Mem.* 3.10.2 already attributes the point to Parrhasius (noted by Jex-Blake and Sellers 1968, lxii). On the other hand, if the story really does come from Duris, it is not impossible that it was linked to mimēsis there: his interest in the topic is attested in the literary-critical fragments (*FGrH* F 1, p. 89).

39. Literally so, if we define *pornography* as "the reduction of women to fetishized body parts" (see Whitmarsh 2001, 74 with n. 127).

40. Hunter 2009, 117.

41. *AP* 5.35–36, = Rufinus 11–12 Page. We hear of such beauty competitions in Alciphron (4.14.4–6) and Athenaeus (609e–10b, although the women there are clothed); see also Σ Hom., *Il.* 9.28. The reference to a *theatron* (viewing space) in the final sentence of the story quoted above may reinforce this impression of a beauty contest (although I am not aware of any evidence for the space in which such events were held). The male equivalents are better known, thanks to Crowther 1985.

the creation of the picture is granted to *tekhnē*, "art." The narrative is thus transformed from an ethically risky story of a man peering at naked young bodies into a parable about critical judgment. Indeed, the final sentence describes this process of bodily scrutiny as one of "inquiry [*exhistorein*],"[42] a notably intellectualizing word.

At one level, this passage confirms the worst fears about the androcentric psychology underlying ancient aesthetics. Women are reduced to dismembered objects of the male gaze, valued only insofar as one or other part of them may be deemed serviceable to an alien program. They exist for men to consume (a metaphorical association that is expressed in the analogy between the painted Helen and a "feast" of learning). The "perfect form" of woman-as-icon (*eikōn*) is an impossible ideal, realizable only through the medium of (male) art.

This conclusion would not be wrong, but there is more to be said: we also need to integrate the more constructive role given to female (pro)creativity in the alternative (albeit no less androcentric) story of the ugly farmer. The two Dionysian stories present different models of the gendering of mimēsis: in the second, the constructive role is given entirely to male artificing, but the first depends on a cooperation with female reproductivity. This duality is, as we have seen, characteristic of the wider thought of Dionysius, who sees literary creativity as a blend of female and male principles, of nature and art.

Let us return now to the Greek romances: does this reading of Dionysian mimēsis theory help us to understand a case like that of Achilles's Leucippe, the gaze object who also functions as an icon for the aesthetics of the text itself? *Leucippe and Clitophon*, with its scopophiliac ego narrator(s),[43] seems to embody the "Zeuxis" principle, whereby the male eye composes the woman-as-text. The description of the painting of Europa near the start of the text is of course suggestively programmatic in connection with narratives of erotic abduction,[44] but it also acclimatizes readers to a certain "way of seeing" women, both as passive objects of male aesthetic appreciation and as sites of textual dismemberment. The portrait of Europa disaggregates her into a series of eroticized body parts: belly button, stomach, flanks, waist, breasts (1.1.11), all presented in terms of their visibility ("Her body could be seen [*hupephaineto*] through her clothing. . . . Her dress was a mirror of her body," 1.1.10–11), an account that could have come straight from Ovid's *Amores*. This pictorialized, eroticized woman is iconic of the viewing strategies that Clitophon adopts toward Leucippe: a "compelling image, her body is discovered and uncovered, dissected and inspected with increasing ferocity as the

---

42. Hunter 2009, 121, plausibly detects an echo of Herodotean *historia* here (and elsewhere in this passage).
43. Morales 2004.
44. See most recently Möllendorff 2009, with further literature.

narrative progresses."⁴⁵ When he first sees her and (in the passage with which we opened) compares her to a painting, he proceeds to anthologize her physiognomy, this time focusing on her face: her eyes, her brows, her cheeks, her mouth (provocatively compared to a rose "when it begins to part its petal lips," 1.4.3).⁴⁶

Much of the narrative energy of *Leucippe and Clitophon* derives from the ironic tension between Clitophon's attempts to objectify his beloved and her refusal (or inability) to act that role. In the first two of the series of Leucippe's three false deaths, Clitophon thinks he sees her being dismembered (3.15.4–5, 5.7–4), as if the story were transplanting into narrative actuality the metaphoral dissection that his initial description suggests.⁴⁷ Yet she is precisely not dismembered: despite his faulty perception, her body remains intact. Readers of Achilles are aware simultaneously of Clitophon's fetishizing narrative gaze and of the "real" woman who lies behind it, a woman capable of eluding and deceiving his limited vision (as, for example, when she disguises herself as the slave Lacaena in books 5 and 6).

The gender dynamics of Heliodorus are, however, very different. Charicleia is indeed proclaimed beautiful, but she is never anatomized as Leucippe is. When she first appears in the Delphic procession, her description (delivered by the staid priest Calasiris) emphasizes the beauty of her clothing, hair, and accoutrements (3.4.1–6). The account is not unerotic (her breastplate features snakes weaving sinuously under her breasts, for example), but its eroticism is metonymically transferred from her body parts to her clothing,⁴⁸ and, what is more, a similar description of Theagenes parallels her description. In this romance as a whole, the female protagonist is exceptionally strong and energetic,⁴⁹ pointing to a different role not only in the narrative but also in the text's aesthetic structure.

This reappraisal of the female is reflected in the central role that Heliodorus gives to the "ugly farmer" principle, which lies at the narrative heart of *Charicleia and Theagenes*. The impression of the picture of Andromeda on Charicleia's mother at the time of conception creates the extraordinary circumstances of her birth.⁵⁰ It is hard to imagine that Heliodorus did not have Dionysius in mind. In the "recognition" scene, when the crowd wonders "at the accuracy [*akribōmenon*] of the likeness [*homoiotētos*]" that exists between the painting and Charicleia (10.14.7), Heliodorus employs language that not only resonates with art-critical theory (ironically reversed: the girl resembles the picture rather than the other way

---

45. Morales 2004, 156.
46. A comparably florid anatomical portrait comes at 1.19.1. On the eroticization of flower imagery in Achilles see Whitmarsh 2010b, 338 (with n. 57), 340 (with n. 65).
47. Morales 2004, 166–84, thoughtfully discusses the relationship between violence and the gaze.
48. Dubel 2001 explores the general tendency of the romancers to avoid specific physiognomics. See also Keul-Deutscher 1996 on Heliodorus's strategies for depicting or accounting for beauty.
49. Johne 1987.
50. Widely discussed: see, e.g., Reeve 1989; Whitmarsh 1998.

around) but specifically invokes the Dionysian story where "likeness" is also at issue. Dionysius opines that "the reader's soul absorbs the likeness [*homoiotēta*] of the imprint thanks to continual observation" (6.1 U-R); compare Sisimithres's claim that Persinna, Charicleia's mother, "drew in certain images [*eidōla*] and visual forms of resemblance [*phantasias homoiotētōn*] from the picture" (10.14.7).[51]

Of all the romances, *Charicleia and Theagenes* gives the most central role to maternity. In making the royal mother the guardian of a secret, Heliodorus is of course looking to Penelope's role in the *Odyssey*, but the theme is more than tralatitious. Like Dionysius's ugly farmer, Charicleia's father, Hydaspes, shares his paternity with the artwork, a subversive patrilineal minimization. Hydaspes, moreover, is in this respect the dupe of his wife: no wonder she originally feared that he would accuse her of adultery (*moikheian*, 4.8.6), since in a sense an "interloper" has fathered his daughter. Persinna's natural bond with Charicleia is the key to the resolution of the narrative: as Charicleia acknowledges in book 9, "the one undeniable recognition token, Theagenes, is maternal nature [*physis*], thanks to which parents' love for children is affected on first encounter, stirred by some mysterious empathy" (9.24.8).[52] More than this, Persinna presents part of the textual narrative, in the form of the *tainia*, or band, with which Charicleia was exposed and which supplies the missing part of Calasiris's hermeneutic jigsaw (4.8). The tainia is extraordinarily personal, cast in the form of a letter from mother to daughter and metaphorically inscribed with "the tears and blood I have shed for you" (4.8.6). The intimate bond between mother and daughter, their hidden secret, is the central enigma and wondrous conceit of *Charicleia and Theagenes*, and its embodiment in the tainia yields the Heliodorean equivalent of the bed of Odysseus and Penelope.

If the mimetic erotics of *Leucippe and Clitophon* are driven primarily by Clitophon's attempt to anatomize and pictorialize Leucippe, those of Heliodorus rest on the mystification of childbirth. Achilles's inspiration need not have come directly from Dionysius (he had a wealth of poetic erotics on which to draw), but Heliodorus's almost certainly did: *Charicleia and Theagenes* seems to creatively reread *On Imitation* in order to reconceive (as it were) the gendered aesthetics of the romance. As I have emphasized throughout, this is not a question of a warmer embrace of female subjectivity, since the association of women primarily with parturition is an equally masculinist fiction, but it does point to an androcentrism in ancient aesthetics that is much richer and more varied than we might expect.

---

51. The rest of the sentence is unfortunately corrupt.
52. Hydaspes too experiences parental *physis* (10.16.2, 10.16.7).

PART TWO

Poetry and Prose

9

Greek Poets and Roman Patrons in the Late Republic and Early Empire

POETRY AND PATRONAGE

The literary history of Greece under Roman occupation is usually written in terms of the dominance of prose. The reasons for this are many; some of them, indeed, are rooted in antiquity, in later Greeks' own sense of living in a prosaic age (as we shall see in chapter 12). Yet in the first three centuries of our era, poetry was of course still being written, and in remarkable quantities:[1] notably, there are major extant epics by the Oppiani and Quintus of Smyrna,[2] many of the epigrams in the *Greek Anthology*, the numerous poems assembled in Ernst Heitsch's two-volume *Die griechischen Dichterfragmente der römischen Kaiserzeit* (*GDRK*, 1961–64), and Reinhold Merkelbach and Josef Stauber's hefty collection of verse inscriptions, running to five volumes (1998–2004). The inscriptional evidence, indeed, testifies to the continuing prestige of poetry as social currency within Greek poleis, to the wide-ranging influence of performers' guilds, and to the numerous competitions available to singers and performers of song.[3] For the cultural historian, this

---

A version of this chapter was first published as Whitmarsh 2011d; I am grateful to Franz Steiner Verlag for permission to reprint.

1. For some recent discussions of Greek poetry in the imperial era see Bowie 1989a, 1989b, 1990, 2002b; Nisbet 2003; Whitmarsh 2004b and 2005c, reworked as chs. 10 and 12; Höschele 2006, 2010; Baumbach and Bär 2007. Amin Benaissa's edition of Dionysius's fragmentary *Bassarica* is keenly awaited.

2. Quintus's date is not absolutely secure; James and Lee 2000, 5–9, argues for the third century, primarily on the grounds that he may be the father of the poet Dorotheus.

3. A. Hardie 1983, 18–27; Bowie 1990, especially 83–85, 89. For individual poets see Fein 1994, 88–150. In the following chapter we shall consider citharodic poetry and hymns, the performance of which was clearly widespread at this time (Bowie 1990, 83–84; Furley and Bremer 2001, 24–25).

material is often more difficult to deal with than the prose texts of the same era: in many cases we know nothing or next to nothing about the authors and hence about the contexts. Given the generally ahistorical nature of so much poetry, moreover, interpretation has to be oblique and heavily nuanced.

One particular body of poetic texts, however, bears directly on relationships between Greece and Rome and deals substantially with identifiable historical individuals. The *Garland* (*Stephanos*) compiled by Philip of Thessalonica at some point after the accession of Gaius and before the death of Nero was originally an anthology of epigrams from the mid-first century B.C.E. (arranged alphabetically by the first word of each) and was later disaggregated into the *Greek Anthology*. This collection—although now a spectral reconstruction, in many places speculative, of modern scholarship—is our ultimate source for epigrams by such notable figures as Antipater, Bassus, Crinagoras, Euenus, Philodemus, and Philip himself. These poems are on a variety of topics, as one would expect from an epigrammatic florilegium. What interest me in this chapter are the poems addressed to Roman patrons or dealing (directly or allusively) with patronage.[4] Whereas Latin patronal literature has been widely studied, there has been little discussion of the extant Greek authors who were subject to Roman patronage, at least before the second century C.E.[5]

The sponsorship of Greek poets by Roman patrons was widespread from the late Republic onward. A Roman perspective on this phenomenon can be glimpsed in Cicero's *Pro Archia,* (at least a form of) which was delivered before a court in 62 B.C.E.[6] In this speech, Cicero not only defends the claim of Archias, his client, to Roman citizenship but also provides a robust declaration of the complementarity between Greek literature and the Roman hegemonic system. Greek poets, he

---

4. Edition, English translation, and commentary: Gow and Page 1968, from which all texts are cited and to which the numeration of poems refers. Translations are mine, but I acknowledge a debt to Gow and Page. The *Garland* and Rome: Cichorius 1922, 298–362; Bowersock 1965, index, s.vv. "Crinagoras," "Antipater of Thessalonica," "Diodorus of Sardis," et al. The relationship between the *Garland* and the *Greek Anthology* has been much discussed: see in particular Gow and Page 1968, 1.xi–xxviii; Cameron 1968, especially 331–49; Cameron 1993, 33–43, 56–65. Höschele 2010, 76–80, offers a brief but helpful discussion of the wider context of ancient epigram collections. The *Garland* itself is dedicated to a patron, Camillus (Philip 1.5 = *Anth. Pal.* 4.2.5), probably either L. Arruntius Camillus Scribonianus or M. Furius Camillus (Gow and Page 1968, 1.xlix).

5. See especially Gold 1982, 1987, the latter also dealing with earlier Greece; A. Hardie 1983; White 1993; Bowditch 2001; Nauta 2002. On patronage as a wider phenomenon within Roman society see Saller 1982; Wallace-Hadrill 1989. On Trajanic and Hadrianic patronage of Greek literati see Fein 1994. Weber 1993 offers a solid account of patronage in Hellenistic courts.

6. Recent discussion at Dugan 2005, 31–47, which emphasizes Cicero's presentation of the persona of Archias as interdependent with his own, and his preoccupation with self-memorialization through poetry. See also Gold 1982, 87–107, on Cicero and Archias.

avers, satisfy the Roman "lust for glory [*amor gloriae*]," which—he stage-confesses—is in his case "excessively intense [*nimis acri*]" (28). The Greek language, he argues, is the ideal medium for transmitting this glory to the world, since "Greek literature is read in nearly every nation but Latin only within its own boundaries—and those, we must admit, are narrow" (23). In its capacity for mass communication, Greek poetry can be harnessed to the Roman imperial project: "We ought to desire that wherever the missiles from our hands have entered, our glory and fame [*gloriamque famamque*] should also penetrate" (23). Conquest and literary commemoration are imagined as parallel processes, each invading and dominating foreign states.

Cicero's portrait of Greek patronal poetry is not, of course, evidence of a calcified pan-Roman ideology. It is both deeply self-serving and idiosyncratic, aiming as it does to legitimate his self-promotion as a distinctive unifier of traditional Roman virtues with Greek intellectual qualities (what he calls elsewhere in this speech *natura* and *doctrina*, 15). Cicero strives hard throughout to celebrate his achievement in bridging cultural traditions while also defending himself against any accusation that he has diluted his Romanness. What is more, this speech offers (unsurprisingly) a one-sidedly Roman perspective. But it does point to a number of themes that we shall find recurring in the poems: principally, the idea that patronal poetry is a form of exchange between the poet and the patron, a cultural division of labor between practical Roman and educated Greek, and the assumption that the primary function of poetry is to bestow charisma on a patron.

What it does not concede, however, is that there are two parties involved in the exchange. In Cicero's model, Greek literature holds up a mirror to the hegemonic will of the Roman. In practice, of course, language is never like that, especially literary discourse, which is always kinked by genre, resonance, intertextuality, and the ambivalence that inheres in all figurality. One aim of this chapter is to restore the voice of the Greek partner in the dialogue. We cannot, of course, expect this voice to be direct and unmediated, the empire writing back: patronal literature is always deeply implicated in the structures of dominance that it serves. What we will find, however, is that these texts are witty, mobile, proud, and surprising, always keen to escape any categorization as "mere" clientage. These qualities, while in no sense subverting the patronal relationship, encourage ironic distance, play, and at times even a form of resistance.

DOERS OF DEEDS AND SINGERS OF WORDS

The sense of the cultural division of labor that we saw in Cicero's *Pro Archia*, between Roman doers and Greek praisers, is a central theme in the poetry. Let us begin with Antipater of Thessalonica (not to be confused with Antipater of Sidon, who is represented in the earlier *Garland* of Meleager).[7] Antipater's patron was Lucius Calpurnius Piso (whom he simply called Piso), the general whose victorious campaigns in Thrace between 13 and 11 B.C.E. earned him a triumph; his father (Lucius Calpurnius Piso Caesonius) was the patron of Philodemus of Gadara, a father-in-law of Julius Caesar, the recipient of Cicero's *In Pisonem*, and probably the owner of the "Villa of the Papyri" at Herculaneum.

Piso was himself a poet (at a stretch even the author of a poem attributed to "Piso" in the *Greek Anthology*, 11.424) and possibly the dedicatee (along with his sons) of Horace's *Ars Poetica*. Despite the patron's literary credentials, Antipater commemorates him not as a poet but entirely as a man of action. In what looks like a programmatic poem, Antipater appeals for patronage to Piso, the unnamed conqueror of the Bessi (in 11 B.C.E.):

> To you, bearer of the spoils of Thrace, Thessalonica,
>   mother of all Macedonia, has sent me.
> I sing of Bessian Ares subdued beneath you,
>   I who have assembled all that I have learned of this war.
> But pay heed to me, like a god, and listen
>   to my prayer. How can the ear lack the leisure for the Muses?
> Antipater 1 = *AP* 9.428

The division between doers and singers is marked. The text opens (in Greek) with two juxtaposed pronouns, *you* and *me*, signaling the binary division that the entire poem vies to define. Antipater, on the one hand, identifies himself as a singer ("I sing [*aeidō*]," 3), who accesses news of military campaigns through Alexandrian techniques of learning (*edaēn*, 4) and careful assemblage rather than autopsy. Indeed, there is a sense of conflation between poet and poem, as though Antipater were constituted by his words: the *me* of the first couplet is, by epigrammatic convention, the poetic gift couriered to Piso and at the same time the poetic "I," the poet's persona under definition. The recipient, by contrast, is associated exclusively with action: the "lack of leisure [*askholiē*]" in the final line translates the Latin *negotium*, "business," the negation of the cultured *otium* privileged by the Roman neoterics.

This division between war and poetry, between Roman patron and Greek client, has implications for the power status of both. The opening line ("Thessalonica has sent me to you") presents the poem/poet as strikingly disempowered, the object both grammatical and ideological of others' decision making. A subtle undertone assimilates him to a civic ambassador pleading for clemency,

---

7. Although in fact the tradition does confuse the two: see Argentieri 2003, which confirms the attribution to Antipater of Thessalonica of each of the relevant poems discussed in this chapter. Cichorius 1922, 325–32, discusses the historical circumstances of our Antipater.

or even a captive sent to Rome.⁸ In the course of the poem, however, the degree of agency ascribed to the poet changes. In the middle couplet, he is the subject of the self-reflexive verb "I sing": the poem enacts its own performance. In the final two lines, the tone changes again (*alla*, "but," marks the transition), becoming more assertive. Two imperatives ("pay heed," "listen") suggest a more commanding, authoritative figure; indeed, the requests to "pay heed" and to "listen" could be taken—although we shall have to qualify this presently—as a command to submit (Greek often links "listening" and "obeying").⁹ The transition at line 5 is not just one of tone: we are also moving from the sphere of war (embodied in the god Ares, 3), where Piso is dominant, to that of poetry (overseen by the Muses, 6).

From one perspective, then, the poem enacts a movement from war to poetry and from a world where the poet is submissive to one where he is in control. This movement is accompanied by a transition from talk of distant lands to a friendly intimacy, suggested by the appeals to leisure and to "the ear." Yet the poem is not just a *rite de passage* for the returning Piso, a *vademecum* for his reintegration into the world of civilized society. Generically speaking, the final couplet identifies itself as a "prayer." The structure of the penultimate sentence ("But pay heed [*Alla . . . kluthi*] . . ."), indeed, is formulaically prayerlike.¹⁰ As the poet makes his request for patronage, for a literary hearing, he also asks his addressee to imitate mimetically the role of a god in a prayer, to act "like a god." At one level, the ascription of this status to Piso continues the heroization of his military exploits (Homeric warriors are said to be "godlike"; we shall return to the epic context below).¹¹ But there is more to it than that just idealizing flattery: the prayer formula actively casts the relationship between poet and patron as analogous to that between supplicant and deity (a parallel that has its roots in Hellenistic encomium).¹² Similes are always provocations: how, the poem asks us to speculate, is the mortal-immortal hierarchy "like" the poet-patron one? And—conversely—in what respects are the two unlike? For it is an obvious but important point that Piso was not a god: he received no cult in the Greek East, nor (by this date) would one expect anyone other than the emperor to. The "likeness" must have its limits. Note that the reference in the final sentence to the divine Muses picks up the earlier (albeit metonymic) allusion

---

8. For this practice see Millar 1966, 159.
9. LSJ, s.vv. "κατήκοος" II, "κλύω" II.
10. See, e.g., Sappho 1.5 for *alla* + imperative in a prayer context. Antipater adopts a similar prayer formula at 31.3-4.
11. The line-ending formula "godlike [*isotheos*] man" occurs twelve times in the *Iliad* (2.565, 3.310, etc.).
12. See especially Theocr. 17.1-12, with Hunter 2003, 94-96: "'Likeness' and analogy, difference and similarity, are central to the progress of the proem and of the poem as a whole: How is Philadelphus 'like' Zeus? How was his birth like Apollo's?" (94).

to Ares: it is as if the poet were stepping back from deifying Piso by reminding us of the existence of "real" gods.

With its subtle shifts of dynamics, Antipater's poem explores the tense reciprocities that exist between poet and patron.[13] The patron exerts economic and political control over the poet, but the poet (as *Pro Archia* reminds us) has a power of his own, the power to confer glory, to immortalize, to inscribe his subject in an immemorial tradition of heroic verse. This poem doubly images reciprocity, in terms of both gift giving (the poem/poet is "sent" to Piso) and prayer (always imagined as an appeal for a quid pro quo in Greek thought): it is engaged in a seemingly unresolved quest for the right model to capture the precise form that this reciprocity takes.

BESTOWING FAME

Let us consider in more detail the poet's side of the bargain, the immortal fame that he confers. The commemorative function is only implicit in Antipater 1, but it is widespread elsewhere in the genre, for example in the poetry of Crinagoras of Mytilene.[14] Crinagoras was an important figure of mediation between his city and Rome, honored as one of the ambassadors to Julius Caesar in an inscription from the fortress wall of Mytilene dated to 48–47 B.C.E. (*IG* 12.35). He is later found on an embassy to Augustus, in 26 (*IGRR* 4.33), perhaps in Spanish Tarragona.[15] His epigrams contain a number of celebrations of the gens Iulia: of Marcellus, of Antonia, and of the rulers themselves. Crinagoras pays particular attention to commemoration. In his best-known poem, that of the parrot who proclaims, "Hail, Caesar!," he calls Augustus "famous [*kleinos*]" and suggests the immortality of his name (24.3–4); elsewhere, he proclaims that fame [*kleos*] follows Augustus everywhere on his travels (29.3–4). At one level, *kleos* serves as a translation of the Latin *fama* and *gloria*, the terms that are, as we have seen, central to Cicero's conception of the role of patronal poetry in cultivating and enhancing the charisma of the competitive aristocrat. But within the Greek poetic tradition they have a wider function, not only marking social distinction but also anchoring the subject in a heroic tradition stretching back to Homer and Hesiod.

This point is crucial. Patronal poetry in this period is often engaged in a project of fusing Roman subjects to Greek mythic memory. Poetic commemoration is

---

13. Bowditch 2001 excellently explores the representation of and resistance to reciprocity in Horace's patronal poetry.

14. Edition, English translation, and commentary: Gow and Page 1968. On what is known of him and his context see Cichorius 1888, 47–61; 1922, 306–23; more briefly Bowersock 1965, 36–37; also Braund 1984.

15. As is sometimes deduced on the basis of *IGRR* 4.38, which Cichorius 1888, 55, first identified as referring to the same embassy; see however the reservations of Millar 1966, 163 n. 97.

thus an act not only of recording but also of syncrisis: like a Plutarchan parallel life, it compares and perhaps implicitly contrasts the Roman subject with the Greek precedent. Sometimes similes make this process explicit: an excellent example comes a little later, in the second century C.E. Pancrates's poem on the hunt of Hadrian and Antinous compares the lion that attacks the pair to "Typhoeus of yore, confronting Zeus the slayer of giants."[16] This both buttresses the widespread association in Greek literature of Hadrian with cosmic rule[17] and draws to the surface the latent parable of mortal kingship in the Hesiodic depiction of Zeus's coming to power. This double effect is achieved under the sign of *kleos*, "fame," and also of quasi divinization: depending on which supplement we adopt (the papyrus is damaged at this point), Hadrian is described as "the famous god [*theou klutou*]" or Antinous as "god-famed [*theoklutou*]."[18] The process of commemoration is thus directly linked to inscription in the theogonic tradition. Hadrian and Antinous are godlike at numerous levels: because they *are* gods (both received cult; Antinous is also the "son of the slayer of Argus [Hermes]," line 9),[19] because the act of commemorating the hunt gives them godlike luster, and because they are being explicitly assimilated to the Hesiodic Zeus.

This kind of commemoration by analogization is found in the *Garland* too. Let us turn to an epigram by one of the Diodoroi (probably Diodorus of Sardis). This poem compares one of the Neros—probably Tiberius, the future emperor, at some point in the late 20s B.C.E.[20]—to Neoptolemus:

> As in the past Achilles's son, steadfast in war,
>   left the land of goat-pasturing Scyros and sailed to Ilium,
> so among the sons of Aeneas did the leader Nero leader move
>   to the city of Remus, returning to the swift-flowing Tiber,
> a boy with the down still fresh on his chin. The first was vigorous
>   with the spear, this one with both the spear and wisdom.
> Diodorus 1 = *Anth. Pal.* 9.219

---

16. *P.Oxy.* 1085.25 (Page 1941, 516–19 = *GDRK* 1. 51–54, a much better text). See also lines 1–2, where Antinous's horse is said to be swifter than the horses of Adrastus (see *Il.* 23.346–47).

17. On which see further ch. 10.

18. Depending on restoration of the text: "θ[εοῦ] κλυτοῦ' Ἀντι[νόου τε," Hunt; "θ[εο]κλύτου Ἀντι[νόοιο," Heitsch (in *GDRK*). I have translated *theoklutou* as *god-famed*, i.e., whose fame goes up to the heavens (see, e.g., *Od.* 9.20), on the analogy of a formation like *theophilētos* (beloved of the gods). LSJ, however, cites only two appearances of the word: "invoking a god" (Aesch., *Th.* 143) and (a slightly better fit for our passage but still not exact) "listened to by God" (Jos., *Ant.* 1.10.4). But the search for lexical precision is ultimately misguided: if *theoklutou* is the right reading, it associates Antinous with both fame and divinity.

19. In line 31 (legible only in *GDRK*), one of the pair, probably Hadrian, is again called "god [θεοῦ]."

20. Cichorius 1922, 299–300, argues for 20 B.C.E., on Tiberius's return from Armenian campaigns; Gow and Page 1968, 265, argues that a twenty-two-year-old does not have "the down still fresh on his chin," so opts for his first military experience, in Spain in 24 B.C.E.

Once again, the intertextual simile brings to the fore the process of role playing, as the Nero in question is analogized with Neoptolemus (identified only allusively and perhaps hinted at by the paronomastic *meneptolemos*, "steadfast in war") in a poem that contains markedly Ionic dialect and epic diction.[21] Syntax and colometry enact the process of parallelizing: the second line begins, "As in the past Achilles's son ...," responded to in the third line by "so among the sons of Aeneas did the leader Nero ..." This analogy also sets in parallel the two cultural temporalities, "in the past" and "among the sons of Aeneas," thus directly associating Rome with political and military currency and Greece with a distant, mythical world. We shall return to this poem presently.

COSMOS AND *BASILEIA*

Another encomiastic strategy is the alignment of artistic, political, and cosmic order (a well-known feature of Roman poetry and material culture of the Augustan era).[22] We have already briefly considered Pancrates's poem on the hunt of Hadrian and Antinous, with its Hesiodically inflected, elemental conflict between the lion/Typhoeus and Antinous/Zeus. In the more controlled, contained world of epigram, the submission of the natural world occurs in more managed contexts: particularly significant is the space of the Roman arena, a circumscribed site of confrontation between imperial power and the natural order (as it would be later in Martial's *De spectaculis*). This is the setting for an anonymous epigram belonging to the subgenre on animals who willingly submit to a higher power.[23] The "Nasamonian extremities [*eskhatiai*] of Libya," we are told, are freed from "beasts [*thērōn*]" that "the boy Caesar" has trapped and forced to confront spearmen.[24] The taming of the geographically marginal (note *eskhatiai*) space of Libya recalls Pindar's fourth and (particularly) ninth *Pythian* odes and sets the Caesar in question in a line of culture heroes including Heracles and Theseus: "The mountain ridges, where once wild beasts reposed, are now cultivated by men" (8). The confrontation between the gladiators and the

---

21. *Meneptolemos*: Hom., *Il.* 2.740, 749, 4.395, etc.; *ōkurhoēn* (swift-flowing): Ap. Rh., *Arg.* 2.349, 650; *egkhei thuen* (was vigorous with the spear): Hom., *Il.* 11.180, 16.699, 22.272. Diodorus perhaps looked for precedent for the analogization of Neoptolemos to Pindar, *Nemean* 7, on Sogenes of Aegina, a victor in the boys' pentathlon (see also *Paean* 6).

22. See most conveniently Nicolet 1991.

23. See Weinreich 1928, 74–155, in whose view this theme originates in accounts of holy men with power over animals.

24. Anonymous 1 = *Anth. Pal.* 7.626. Cichorius 1922, 332–34, attributes the poem to Antipater of Thessalonica and identifies "the boy Caesar" as Gaius; Gow and Page 1968, 2.419, is rightly circumspect (and Argentieri 2003 does not even mention it).

beasts in the arena is synecdochic of the wider dominance of human over nature and of emperor over empire.

Another poem, perhaps set not in the arena but nevertheless in Rome, brings out these themes even more explicitly. The fourth of the epigrams attributed to Philip (the compiler of the *Garland*) tells of the "phalanx-fighting, immense-tusked elephant" who "no longer, turreted and irresistible, rushes into war"; instead he has submitted to the yoke and pulls the chariot of "heavenly [*ouraniou*] Caesar."[25] This *ouraniou* may be taken to allude to postmortem deification or more loosely to the divinity of the living emperor,[26] but either way it connotes the cosmic power of the emperor in contrast with the monstrous, polemical force of the elephant.

The poem finishes with a couplet that is worth exploring:

> Even a beast has acknowledged his gratitude for peace; he has cast off the instruments
> Of Ares and raises up instead the father of law and order. (5–6)

This couplet thickens the contrast between polemic disorder and "peace" (which for Romans of course means "pacification," the rendering submissive of hostile territory) by introducing the civic virtue of "law and order [*eunomiē*]"—perhaps an allusion, direct or indirect, to the "imperial virtue" of "justice [*iustitia*]," inscribed on the shield that the Senate presented to Augustus in 27 or 26 B.C.E., and in due course associated particularly with Tiberius.[27] What is particularly interesting for our purposes, however, is the acknowledgment of gratitude (*kharis*), which subtly recycles the language of gift exchange. The elephant, a symbol of brutish provincial resistance now rendered compliant by orderly domination, can thus also be seen as a disguised figure for the poet, reciprocating for the gift of empire. This hints at a complex provincial psychology inhabited by the poetic narrator, a psychology that mixes admiration for the imperial project with traces of residual aggression. We might also see the poem, with its narrative of ordered war substituting for brutish militarism, as a metageneric commentary on epigram as translated epic. In this light, the *eunomiē* of the final line might mean, as well as "law and order," "the art of good poetry" (*nomos* also means "tune" and, in later Greek, "poetic composition").[28] If Philip's epigram is indeed committed to an

---

25. Philip 4 = *Anth. Pal.* 9.285. Mart., *De spect.* 17 parallels the theme of the elephant's submission to Caesar; see Weinreich 1928, 74–85, on the *pius elephas* theme.

26. Respectively, Cichorius 1922, 345; Gow and Page 1968, 2.332.

27. Wallace-Hadrill 1981 rightly cautions against any talk of "canons" of virtues, at least as early as the Augustan period. See p. 313 on the distinctive association between Tiberius and *iustitia*.

28. LSJ, s.v. "eunomiē" II. Strikingly similar themes recur in Philip 2 = *Anth. Pal.* 6.236: "The gratitude [*kharis*] for Caesar's law and order [*eunomiēs*] is excellent: he has taught the enemy's arms to nurture the fruits of peace [*eirēnēs*] instead."

aesthetic of *eunomiē*, however, that "order" (both poetic and political) remains predicated on the suppression of a disorder that is implicitly acknowledged.

The resonance between imperial conquest of the world and the poetic articulation of that conquest is widespread in the epigrams of this era. Rome is the "mistress of all the cosmos" (Bassus 6.6 = *Anth. Pal.* 9.236.6); Caesar is "great joy to the western and eastern limits [of the world]" (Thallus 2.1 = *Anth. Pal.* 6.235.1); the empire is "bounded by the Ocean on all sides" (Antipater 47.5 = *Anth. Pal.* 9.297.5); imperial commanders have subdued distant peoples such as Parthians (ibid.), Celts (Crinagoras 26 = *Anth. Pal.* 9.283), Germans and Armenians (Crinagoras 28 = *Anth. Pl.* 61), and the inhabitants of the Pyrenees (Crinagoras 29 = *Anth. Pal.* 9.419); Germans offer no threat (Crinagoras 27 = *Anth. Pal.* 9.291). This sense of balanced control, of imperial equipoise between East and West, is replicated in the epigrammatic form itself. Particularly significant in this connection is Crinagoras 28:

> Risings and settings are the measures of the cosmos, and Nero's deeds too
>   have passed through both boundaries of the earth.
> The rising sun saw Armenia's defeat under his
>   hands, and the descending sun Germany's.
> Let his twofold victory in war be sung; the Araxes knows of it
>   And the Rhine, both drunk by peoples now enslaved.
> Crinagoras 28 = *Anth. Pl.* 61

Here we have political space and cosmic space as coterminous, marked by major military defeats: the closest equivalent we can get (given ancient conceptions of meteorology) to the idea of an empire on which the sun never sets. What is particularly notable, however, is the close association once again between imperial and poetic order. The rising and the setting of the sun constitute the "measures" of the cosmos: *metra* can also refer to poetic meters. In this connection, it is no accident that the "rising [*aniōn*]" sun appears in the third line above (a hexameter) and the "descending [*katerkhomenos*]" sun in the following pentameter. Crinagoras is surely invoking the association in ancient metrics between hexameters and "rising" and between pentameters and "falling."[29] The doubleness that pervades the poem (note "both boundaries" in line 2 and the "twofold victory" in line 5) thus allies with the metrical form of the couplet. And in general, the metrical form of these short epigrams also allies with the imperial project, as the compressed articulation of a world now subdued and ordered.

---

29. See, e.g., Ov., *Am.* 1.1.27 ("Let my work rise [*surgat*] in six feet, and sink [*residat*] in five"), with McKeown 1989, 28, for further (Ovidian) parallels.

DONA FERENTES...

But if these poems are gifts to Roman patrons, they are not straightforward ones. Let us return to Diodorus 1, and consider what it is actually like to read.

> As in the past Achilles's son, steadfast in war,
>   left the land of goat-pasturing Scyros and sailed to Ilium,
> so among the sons of Aeneas did the leader Nero leader move
>   to the city of Remus, returning to the swift-flowing Tiber,
> a boy with the down still fresh on his chin. The first was vigorous
>   with the spear, this one with both the spear and wisdom.
> Diodorus 1 = *Anth. Pal.* 9.219

The syntax is convoluted and initially baffling. The first line stands outside the *hoios* clause to which it properly belongs, misleading the first-time reader. Lines 3–4 also take some disentangling: we struggle to construe Rome and the Tiber as the object of *neitai* and *ameipsamenos* respectively (as A. S. F. Gow and D. L. Page insist, with reason, that we should).[30] We could take this syntactic complexity as a sign of ineptness, but in the context of a poem that is playing with shifting roles, it is surely preferable to see this as a deliberate shimmering, a resistance to neat and tidy mapping of one identity onto another.

Such disconcerting transpositions also occur at the narrative level. It is strange indeed to compare Neoptolemus as he goes to war with Nero (i.e., Tiberius) as he returns to Rome. The traditional association of Rome with Troy (invoked by other epigrams in the *Garland*) underlines this potential hint of aggression toward the city.[31] In what sense is Tiberius's relationship with Rome analogous with Neoptolemus's with Troy? There is also a frisson in the assimilation of Tiberius to Neoptolemus—the lesser son of an egregious father— particularly in light of his later adoption by Augustus, in 4 C.E. As the first four books of Tacitus's *Annals* make clear, the question of how Augustus's successor could match his adoptive father was urgent and problematic. These issues could not have had the same resonance in the 20s B.C.E., but if the poem postdates the death of Marcellus (one of the prime candidates to succeed Augustus) in 23, then issues of succession may well have been in the air. Equally inauspicious for Nero is the fact that Neoptolemus was murdered (at Delphi) on his return to Greece. Also troubling is the implicit commentary on paternal relationships. Neoptolemus had a father he could never match. And again, what are we to do with the odd (and unparalleled in earlier Greek literature) reference to "the city of Remus"? To allude to the victim of the founder's act of fratricide is to invoke

---

30. Gow and Page 1968, 2.266.
31. Bassus 6 = *Anth. Pal.* 9.236; Euenus 2 = *Anth. Pal.* 9.62. Erskine 2001 traces the earlier history of this association, with an emphasis on the variety of its diplomatic uses.

Rome's history of civil strife, in a manner that could never be neutral (particularly in the aftermath of the civil wars).[32]

These uncertainties persist to the end, to the contrast between Neoptolemus and Nero on the grounds that the latter bestrides "both [*amphoterois*]" spheres, warfare and culture. *Both* refers to the dyad that, as we have seen repeatedly, organizes the division of cultural labor between intellectual Greeks and pragmatic Romans. Of course, the prima facie point of the disjunction between Neoptolemos and Nero is to flatter the latter for excelling in the arts too (which is to say, implicitly, that praise is conditional on commissioning Diodorus as a client). But again matters are not straightforward. Following Gow and Page I have translated the verb *thuein* as "to be vigorous," but this is in fact rather too weak: the word really means "to rage" or "to seethe." What does it mean, then, to say that Nero "seethed with wisdom"? The attempt to neatly match up "both" sides of the cultural division of labor, the military and the poetic, results in a palpable grinding of gears.[33] So far from an altruistic gift to Roman patrons, Diodorus's poem seems grudging and barbed.

What do we do with these little troubling hints that disrupt the smooth surface of the client's praise? There are different models that we can adopt. The first would be to see these hints as merely the products of overzealous modern critical practice. According to Elroy Bundy, discussing Pindar and Bacchylides, "There is no passage ... that is not in its primary intent enkomiastic—that is, designed to enhance the glory of a particular patron."[34] This approach, assuming a context that forbids any meaning other than the laudatory, has survived into more recent "optimistic" readings of imperial Latin poetry.[35] A second model, by contrast, emphasizes the ability of such hints to deconstruct the surface-level meaning, through "figured speech."[36] The problem with both of these approaches is that they assume that the poem has a final meaning, whether praise or critique, and that that meaning ultimately defeats any alternatives. How we determine priority rests on which features, textual or contextual, we choose to privilege and thus becomes an exercise primarily in critical self-definition.[37]

On the other hand, it is clearly unsatisfactory to content oneself with infinite ambiguity. It is better, I think, to see the poem's multiple meanings in terms of the psychological and social complexity of gift giving. "Every exchange," writes Pierre

---

32. As Horace's seventh *Epode* testifies ("Remus's innocent blood flowed to the earth / A curse on their descendants," 19–20).

33. We might also recall that there is another *thuein*, meaning "to slaughter," which supplies even more troubling resonances.

34. Bundy 1962, 9.

35. E.g., Galinsky 1994; 1996.

36. E.g., Ahl 1984; Bartsch 1994; Newlands 2002. For a recent example relating to imperial Greek literature see Pernot 2008.

37. See the comments of Kennedy 1992.

Bourdieu, "contains a more or less dissimulated challenge."[38] Gift giving is a cultural technology, an attempt to impose power, or at least to limit the other's, by defining the nature of the relationship. This goes all the more for a gift that is freighted with cultural self-definition, a present from (in effect) Greek culture to Roman power. This poetry cannot afford to give away too much: while praising, it needs to reserve some critical distance, some bite.

Let us emphasize, moreover, that patronal poetry (as Cicero reminds us) is not simply a private gift but the public performance of private gift giving. In other words, the negotiation of status is triangulated between three parties: poet, patron, and public. In this complex, multilateral relationship, the poet must guard against too close an identification with the patron, against giving him exactly what he wants or what might be perceived to be wanted. Greeks of the Roman era knew exactly what to call that phenomenon: *kolakeia,* or (rather weakly) "flattery," the repressed other that haunts the entire discourse of patronal exchange.[39] *Kolakeia* is a gauchely precipitous, undisguised form of reciprocity, a relationship of exchange that embarrassingly denudes the steepling power hierarchies.

The ambiguities of reciprocities, indeed, are worked out in a series of poems by Antipater. Poems 41–45 (in Gow and Page's edition)[40] dramatize a series of episodes of gift giving to Piso: a Macedonian hat "from long ago [*paroithe*]," which "once [*pote*]" routed the Persians, a sword that once belonged to Alexander, a helmet from one Pylaemenes,[41] a set of bowls, and a candle. The first three work by constructing analogies between Greek past (*paroithe, pote*) and Roman present, a technique we have already considered. Gifts that once belonged to others serve as temporal nodes connecting the two: a device found already in Homer (Achilles, for example, has his spear from Chiron via his own father) but here heavily mediated through the Hellenistic epigram tradition.[42] In 41 and 42, the gifts construct Piso as a new Alexander, an identification that—while risky—is productive in the context, since Antipater elsewhere self-identifies as a Macedonian (his hometown of Thessalonica is the "mother of all Macedonia," 1.2 = *Anth. Pal.* 9.428). Macedonian gifts function as emblems of the Macedonian poet's identity as a giver and thus as token of the reciprocal bonds between poet and patron. But as in so many articulations of the patronal relationship, Antipater avoids straightforward encomium. In poem 41, the Macedonian hat appeals to Piso, "But, friend, accept me" (5), a phrase that is clearly a displacement of the poet's appeal for patronage. It is also, however, an

---

38. Bourdieu 1977, 14.
39. Sources in Whitmarsh 2006.
40. *Anth. Pal.* 6.335, 9.552, 6.241, 9.541, 6.249.
41. I prefer the Homeric Paphlagonian (*Il.* 2.851) to the Galatian prince (Cichorius 1922, 329; Gow and Page 1968, 2.54).
42. Hom., *Il.* 16.143–44; compare Posidippus's *Lithica* 4, 8, 9 for gems formerly of famous owners.

allusion to Achilles's words to Lycaon: "But, friend, you too must die" (Hom., *Il.* 21.106), rendered unmistakable by the distinctive form of the vocative *philos*. The poem thus points to an intertextual palimpsest in which a Greek warrior ironically accepts a bond of friendship before slaying his Trojan supplicant. Given the coding of Rome as Troy in the poetry of this era noted above, it is hard not to see this allusion as anything other than disruptive of the encomiastic project. This act of gift giving contains, precisely as Bourdieu would have it, "a dissimulated challenge."

Antipater 2 offers the fullest exploration of the politics of exchange:

> Dew suffices to inebriate cicadas, but drinkers
>   sing louder than swans.
> Just so a singer knows how to give his benefactors in return songs,
>   reciprocating for guest gifts, though he himself has received little.
> So this is our first exchange, but if the Fates
>   wish it, you will often lie in my pages.
> Antipater 2 = *Anth. Pal.* 9.92

The language of friendship and gift giving, reciprocity and euergetism is unmissable. The allusion to drinking in the first two lines, moreover, may suggest a sympotic context. This is traditional for patronal poetry (going back at least to Pindar and Bacchylides and arguably already implied in Homer's Demodocus)[43] and (it seems) also for the performance of epigram since Hellenistic times.[44] The particular significance, for our purposes, is that the symposium appears to permit a certain latitude for playful mockery.[45] Our poem gently teases its addressee for his stinginess: in return for the "little" that the poet has received, the patron gets but a single, short poem; if he gives more, he will get more. The metonymic economy of the symposium measures generosity in liquid terms: the poet asks for copious wine instead of dew. There is a hint of reverse Alexandrianism here too: in aspiring to turn from a dew-drinking cicada into a roaring drunk, Antipater playfully renounces Callimachean principles of subtlety and refinement in favor of material gain.[46] The poem thus unveils itself as a cheeky commentary on the compromise of aesthetic principles that the patronal structure necessitates.

---

43. Carey 2007, 204–5.
44. So Cameron 1995, 76–95, argues, in robust fashion.
45. Ibid., 97–100.
46. Call., *Aet.* fr. 1.29–40 on dew-drinking cicadas, with Crane 1986 on the Tithonus allusion in the closing lines; fr. 178 for the dislike of heavy drinking "in the Thracian style" (11–12). For explicit anti-Callimacheanism in the *Garland* (focusing on pedantry) see Philip 60 (*Anth. Pal.* 11.321) and Antiphanes 9 (*Anth. Pal.* 11.322), which would no doubt have been juxtaposed in the original collection (Cameron 1968, 339).

CONCLUSION

There is, unsurprisingly, relatively little in this body of epigrams that could be taken as an explicit critique of Rome or Romans. The closest we get is a series of poems on the delapidation or devastation of Greek cities—poems that, one would imagine, were composed without patronal commission. Antipater seems to have specialized in these: he focuses particularly on Delos (28 = *Anth. Pal.* 9.421; 94 = *Anth. Pal.* 9.550; 113 = *Anth. Pal.* 9.408), which had been ravaged during the Mithridatic wars. These poems attach no blame to Rome, and indeed most of the depredations were by Mithridates's forces (in 88 B.C.E.) and pirates (in 69 B.C.E.),[47] but even so, the contrast between prosperous past and miserable present on this island, a former hub of Athenian power in the face of a foreign foe, offers itself as paradigmatic of the wider decline of Greece's standing in the world. More directly critical of Rome is Crinagoras 37 (*Anth. Pal.* 9.284), on the plight of Corinth (sacked by Mummius in 146 B.C.E. and refounded by Julius Caesar as a *colonia* in 44): "Alas the great misery of Hellas!" (2), the poet laments, in view of the "resold slaves" now living among the bones of the Bacchiads. The emphasis is, however, primarily on decline and the affront to tradition: horror at Roman brutality, though certainly implicit, has to be inferred.

Yet this is more melancholy reflection than arrant anti-imperialism. Any quest for a literature of resistance among the epigrammatists of our era is, indeed, clearly misguided. Figures like Antipater, Crinagoras, and Philip were deeply implicated in the Roman project. There is no evidence for outright political hostility, nor, indeed, would we expect any, in that they benefited both personally and in terms of civic reconstruction from Roman patronage in the aftermath of the Mithridatic disasters. What we do see, however, is a complex mixture of acceptance of and resistance to the transactional nature of the patronal relationship, where economic and political dependency weigh against the cultural prestige that Greek poetry can offer. In such a situation, the academic cliché that power is to be negotiated seems more resonant. I think it likely that the ambivalent mixture of acceptance and distantiation that this poetry manifests reflects what we would now call a colonial situation: it springs, no doubt, from the "self-division" that accommodation of imperial overlords demands, which can lead to a "massive psychoexistential complex."[48] Yet at the same time we should be wary of assuming that such conflictedness signals a dysfunction in the patronal system. We are once again in the realm of speculation, but it is not implausible that patrons might want a certain amount

---

47. Compare also poem 50 = *Anth. Pal.* 7.705 on the sorry state of Amphipolis, another place captured during the Mithridatic wars. Alpheus 2 = *Anth. Pal.* 9.100 offers a rejoinder to Antipater, praising Delos.

48. Fanon 1967, 17, 12.

of salt in their poetry: after all, patronal reciprocity, at least in the poetic sphere, depends for its respectability on the fiction of a friendly exchange between equals who are entitled to say and do as they please.

Let me finish, however, with surely the most famous poem in the collection, the epigram by Crinagoras (or perhaps Philip: the manuscript attributions are split) on the flattering parrot:

> The parrot, that bird with human voice, left its wicker cage
>   and went to the woods on its florid wing.
> Always it practiced for its greetings the famous name of Caesar
>   and forgot it not even in the hills.
> Every other bird, learning quickly, ran in competition
>   to see which could be the first to say "Hail!" to the deity.
> Orpheus persuaded the beasts in the mountains, but your name, Caesar,
>   every bird now squawks unbidden.
> Crinagoras 24 = *Anth. Pal.* 9.562

The poem's fame rests primarily on its status as the earliest exemplar of what became a topos of imperial literature.[49] For our purposes, it is most interesting as an allegory of patronage.[50] For a start, the poem participates in an encomium of Caesar, as a version of the pancosmic submission theme, which we met in Philip's poem on the elephant: Caesar's magnitude is such that it makes the natural order docile, even humanized ("with human voice," line 1). But the parrot is, much more obviously than the elephant, a figure for specifically poetic clientage.[51] Crinagoras thus offers a Romanized version of the Hellenistic birdcage of the Muses, the "competition" (line 5) now no longer for philological accuracy (as it is in Timon's famous squib *SH* 786) but for adulation. The reference to "greetings" (line 3) further grounds this poem in the hurly-burly of Roman patronage: the clamoring poets are assimilated to the jostling bustle of low-class clients at the morning *salutatio* of a patron.[52] Against this patronal backdrop, the poem bolsters the fiction of

---

49. In particular Mart. 14.73; Stat., *Silv.* 2.4 (especially 29–30); also Plin., *NH* 10.58.117. Weinreich 1928, 113–25, discusses the various sources, including the intriguing complex of stories, presumably earlier than Crinagoras in origin, relating to Hanno or "Psapho the Libyan."

50. On the patronal themes in Statius's parrot poem see Dietrich 2002, 107–8; Newlands 2005, especially 159: "Statius's *Silvae* represent the poet's attempts to work within the Roman system of patronage and yet to make praise meaningful. They are the product of a voice that is divided, aware of the attractions of power . . . and also critically distant from them."

51. For the well-known metapoesis of the parrot, see Ov., *Am.* 2.6, with, e.g., Boyd 1987, Myers 1990; Statius 2.4, with Dietrich 2002, Myers 2002, Newlands 2005, 159–65. P. James 2006 discusses both poems together, with more on ancient psittacology.

52. A point brought out clearly in the Latin versions: "imperatores salutat" (Plin., *NH* 10.58.117), "salutator regum" (Stat., *Silv.* 2.4.29).

voluntarism, that the client really wants to praise the patron:[53] the parrot, after all, is now freed from the cage but still wants to sing of Caesar, and in fact the wild birds do so too, "unbidden," implicitly without the persuasion that Orpheus needs to apply. But the poem's very bathos subverts this portrait of a world of willing poetic submission to the imperial order: the poets in question are imaged as sub-humans, parroting words with phonetic rather than semantic content. The final word (in the Greek) is *squawks:* as so often in the Greek tradition, the assimilation of humans to birds devalues the status of their speech.[54] The poem thus ironically detaches itself from the genre in which it participates, a perfect embodiment of the conflicted approach to the poetic gift dramatized in the patronal poetry of the late Republic and early Empire.

---

53. On this point see especially Bowditch 2001, 161–210, on Horace and "the ideology of voluntarism that the poet exposes as the false consciousness of patronage" and that "becomes a defining component of the more egalitarian *amicitia* ('friendship', in this case) that replaces the patronal relationship" (210).

54. See, e.g., Ar., *Lys.* 506, with Jeffrey Henderson 1987, 133 ad loc.

10

The Cretan Lyre Paradox

Mesomedes, Hadrian, and the Poetics of Patronage

In the previous chapter we saw how epigrams offer a different perspective on relationships between the Greek and Roman worlds in a decisive period when the nature of such relationships was still very much open to negotiation. It is particularly striking that the asymmetries and mechanics of power are, it seems, more visible in the epigrammatists than in the prose writers. The former dramatize hierarchical structures of patronage in a way that we only occasionally glimpse in prose literature, for example in Lucian's *On Salaried Posts* and—implicitly—Athenaeus's *Sophists at Dinner,* set in the house of the superrich Roman Larensis.[1] Prose texts tend to promote the idea of civilized commensality between educated equals rather than tense parleys built around exchange between the empowered and their service providers. Thus Plutarch, for example, mentions numerous Roman friends and even dedicates his *Parallel Lives* to one (Sosius Senecio) without ever explicitly commenting on the nature of these relationships. Perhaps such figures really were friends whose camaraderie was based on intellectual respect. But it is not impossible, either, that they were patrons who offered financial support and/or political protection.

Among the generality of prose texts at the period, the essay *How to Tell a Flatterer from a Friend,* addressed to the plutocratic Philopappus (a descendant of Commagenian kings whose monument still stands on the Hill of the Muses in Athens), comes closest to disclosing an awareness of status differentiation: here

---

A version of this chapter appeared as Whitmarsh 2004b; I am grateful to Verlag Walter de Gruyter for permission to republish.

1. I have discussed patronage in these texts at 2001, 279–93, and 2000 respectively. Larensis is usually identified with the historical *pontifex minor* P. Livius Larensis (see especially Braund 2000).

Plutarch seems to acknowledge that he too is in danger of being taken as a flatterer by his powerful addressee.[2] (Plutarch and Philopappus were, incidentally, both Easterners with Roman citizenship: a reminder that power differentials did not necessarily map directly onto the Greek-Roman axis.) The widespread discourse of flattery is, I believe, a mechanism allowing prose authors to explore such status asymmetries allegorically.

For sure, poetry gives us no less partial a picture of cultural history than does prose. The reason why such asymmetries are more visible in the verse texts lies in the particular shape of the Greek poetic tradition, which from earliest times accommodated the idea of composition in the service of powerful patrons. The patronal epigrams discussed in chapter 9 manipulate tropes that derive from Pindar and Bacchylides and ultimately from Homer and Hesiod. So we must proceed with care, certainly, but the crucial point is that to neglect this material risks acquiescing to an overly "autonomist" view of the literary production of the imperial Greek world, as though writing were unconstrained by material or political pressures. Confident, elite rhetoricians of independent means did not entirely dominate Greek culture of the early Roman period; the idea (fostered by Philostratus's *Lives of the Sophists*) that Herodes Atticus typified the Second Sophistic is to be resisted.[3]

The Greek literary subelite are not easily identified. The case for a few Sophists of low-class origins is not particularly convincing.[4] Among philosophers, the ex-slave Epictetus is extant, but his ideas are transmitted—with what modifications it is impossible to tell—by the elite Arrian. The anonymous *Life of Aesop* is often regarded as "subliterary," but recent criticism has taken it (once again) as mediated by elite discourse.[5] The most significant body of evidence comes from poetry. The specific focus of this chapter is Mesomedes, a Cretan freedman of the emperor Hadrian, whose complex and intriguing poetic output I take to reflect the particularities of his relationship to the emperor.

Mesomedes's writings are not straightforwardly "patronal poetry," in the sense that that term is usually used (as in the previous chapter). This is not a body of texts with named addressees and a stylized language of gift exchange and honorification.[6] In the thirteen extant poems of Mesomedes, not a single mortal is named; there is, moreover, no direct reference to the social context of poetic production. When I write of "patronal" poetry, then, I am invoking not a transparent commitment to encomium but a set of more elusive strategies for the magnification of the subject.

---

2. Engberg-Pedersen 1996; Whitmarsh 2006.

3. On the elite context of much imperial rhetoric see especially Gleason 1995; Schmitz 1997; Whitmarsh 2001, 90–130; Whitmarsh 2005a.

4. Bowie 1982, 54–55.

5. Avlamis 2011.

6. See ch. 9, n. 5.

THE POETRY OF MESOMEDES

Thirteen poems of Mesomedes survive: two in the *Greek Anthology* (12 = *Anth. Pal.* 14.63; 13 = *Anth. Plan.* 323); three, with musical notation, in sixteen manuscripts (1–3);[7] and eight unearthed in a single Vatican manuscript, now known as Ottobonianus (also containing Ariphron's *Hymn to Health*, poems by Michael Akominatos, and Methodius's *Symposium of the Ten Virgins*), in 1903.[8] Poem 1 may well in fact be two separate proemial poems.[9] In addition, the *Suda* refers (s.v. "Mesomedes") to a "Praise of Antinous [*Epainos eis Antinoon*]," now lost (see further below). The poems are written in a variety of meters, with a distinctive preference for the *apokroton* and the paroemiac.[10] The language is mostly uncomplicated,[11] although the mystical poems to Nemesis, Physis, and Isis, in particular, certainly contain a number of bizarre, catachrestic expressions.[12] Mesomedes's poetry achieved sufficient currency to be cited by Synesius, John Lydus, and the *Suda*;[13] the poet himself is reasonably well attested in historiographical sources (on which more presently).

Poems 1–5 are evidently hymnic in form; indeed, (for what it is worth) titles of "Hymn to [*Humnos eis*] . . ." are transmitted with poems 2 and 3 (Helios and Nemesis respectively). Poems 6–8, however, are more difficult to classify. Like poems 1, 4, and 5, these are transmitted with *eis* (to) titles but this time in relation to the Hadriatic sea and to two horologia (one solar, one astrological) respectively. The Hadriatic poem (6) employs hymnic formulation (especially lines 1–2: "From what point shall I begin my hymn [*humnein*] to you?") but also formally resembles an *epibaterion*, or poem of embarkation. The two horologium poems (7, 8) are descriptive, and there is good reason (as we shall see) to consider them alongside poems 9 (the sponge poem, transmitted with the title "Ecphrasis of a Sponge") and 13 (the glass poem), as technological ecphrases. Even so, there are also points of contiguity between the horologium poems and the hymns proper;[14] I suggest below that a choral dance may

---

7. On the musical notation, see Pöhlmann 1970, 22–31.

8. For details, see Heitsch 1959; Pöhlmann 1970, 22–31. I follow the numbering and (except where indicated) text of Heitsch (*GDRK*). For recent discussion see Bélis 2003. The forthcoming commentary by Janna Regenauer is keenly awaited.

9. Pöhlmann 1970, 27–28; followed by Bowie 1990, 85. Pöhlmann (again, followed by Bowie) also argues that lines 1–6 of poem 2 Heitsch (the hymn to Helios) are a separate poem. This is less convincing to my mind: the differences between 1–6 and 7 ff. can be explained by taking 1–6 as a proem attached to the poem. The argument that 1–6 addresses Apollo and 7 ff. Helios is inexplicable (*Phoebos* at 6 is paralleled by *Phoibēidi* at 20).

10. M. L. West 1982, 165, 170, 172–73; see also Husmann 1955.

11. See Wilamowitz-Möllendorff 1921, 600–601; Horna 1928, 17, 31.

12. Wilamowitz-Möllendorff 1921, 607.

13. Synes., *Ep.* 95.9–11 (and *Hymn.* 1[3].72–75 ~ Mes. 2.1–4?); Lydus, *De mensibus*, p. 184 Wünsch; *Suda*, s.v. "Nemesis." N.b. also *Anth. Pal.* 6.65.7 (Paulus Silentarius, of a sponge) ~ Mes. 9.1–6.

14. Horna 1928, 31.

have accompanied poem 8, the longer (astrological) horologium poem, like the hymns. Similarly, it is possible that the now lost "Praise of Antinous"—which also appears to have shared the *eis* titular element—contained quasi-hymnic elements.

The *eis* titles, thus, if they have any ancient authority, forge links between generic idioms that are at first blush separate, particularly the hymn and the ecphrastic description. Indeed, two more Mesomedes poems are transmitted with titles in this form: 10, "To [*Eis*] a Swan," and 11, "To [*Eis*] a Gnat." These pieces, like the sphinx poem (12, transmitted without a title), are riddling fables (*ainigmata*), delivered in simple, sequential narratives; they clearly stand at some distance from the complex, syncretistic hymns to Isis and the rest. It is also, I think, unlikely that these poems would have been performed in the same way (i.e., with choral dance). Even so, there are points of contact, both linguistic and thematic: riddles, fables, and syncretistic hymns, I suggest, share the common aim of stimulating multiple, possibly conflicting, "solutions."

In sum, Mesomedes's poems are generically varied, as they are metrically, but points of contact between the various pieces suggest a common core of concerns, albeit often differently articulated. In particular, we might conclude that the *eis* elements in most of the titles (whether they are authentically Mesomedean or have been superimposed by acute editors) signal a structural feature shared by all the poems. They represent distance between the narrator and the implied community, on the one hand, and the subject of the poem on the other; the former are imagined as looking on, observing, interpreting a particular phenomenon. The significance of this will become clearer.

MESOMEDES'S IMPERIAL POETICS

The above description of the poems will not have given much encouragement that they can be interpreted in the patronal terms I sketched earlier. And yet the biographical information, such as we have, uniformly suggests connections with Hadrian and indeed Antoninus Pius.[15] The *Suda*'s entry (s.v. "Mesomedes") relates that he lived in the time of Hadrian and was "a freedman or one of his particular friends [*ē en tois malista philois*]," a rather confusing formulation; emendation of "or" to "and" is possible.[16] It is in this context that the *Suda* relays the title of the "Praise of Antinous," the Antinous in question being of course Hadrian's lover. Paraphrasing Cassius Dio, the entry continues with the information that "Antoninus" (i.e., Caracalla), who was learning the cithara, constructed a cenotaph for Mesomedes.[17] The

---

15. See especially Fein 1994, 115–18.
16. Heitsch 1960, 144 n. 2.
17. The report is taken verbatim from Cass. Dio 78.13.7 (hence the inference that "Antoninus" is Caracalla).

Historia Augusta implies Antoninus Pius's approval of Mesomedes, claiming that when he withdrew the *salaria* of many, "he even diminished the salary of the lyricist Mesomedes [*etiam Mesomedi lyrico salarium imminuit*]" (*HA Antonin*. 7.8).[18] "Even [*etiam*]" signals the concessive force: Mesomedes's salary was reduced (but—significantly—not withdrawn, as in the case of the others alluded to here) despite some particular factor, which can only have been imperial favor. If the biographical evidence is accepted, it appears that Mesomedes was freed and patronized by Hadrian, who then granted him a salary;[19] Antoninus Pius continued to regard him highly, although he did reduce his salary, a mild gesture within a wider program; and Caracalla later honored the poet with a cenotaph after his death.

The question of imperial content in Mesomedes's poetry, then, poses itself all the more forcefully. What was it that appealed to Hadrian and Antoninus so much? Surely one would expect allusions to these relationships within the texts.[20] It is certainly possible that Hadrian's support derived from a general desire to patronize, and be seen to patronize, citharodic song (he apparently boasted of his skill as a citharode; see *HA Hadr*. 15.9).[21] In what follows, however, I argue that these poems are indeed about power and status, but they express these themes allegorically rather than directly.

PERFORMANCE

A brief consideration of performance contexts for the poems will enrich discussion. Performed they surely were, as the musical notation attached to 1–3 clearly indicates (it is likely too that poems 4–11, transmitted in the Ottobonianus, once had musical notation).[22] There is no reason to assume that Mesomedes's poems honoring deified personifications are "philosophical" and therefore noncultic.[23] The worship of Nemesis (the subject of poem 3) is attested at Rhamnous (where a famous statue by Agoracritus or Phidias stood, the object of much imitation), on Mt. Pagos near Smyrna, and at Patrae.[24] Physis (poem 4) is some-

---

18. On the nature of this *salarium,* see Fein 1994, 116 n. 128.

19. Hadrian's patronage of lyric poetry is also attested elsewhere. Compare the case of Publius Aelius Pompeianus Paeon, epigraphically attested as a "lyric poet and rhapsode of the god Hadrian": Robert 1980, 10–20; Fein 1994, 118–26 (assuming the identity of the two Paeons). Merkelbach and Stauber 1998–2004, 1.329, argues for a further appearance of this Paeon, on an Ephesian statue base.

20. Fein 1994, 117 n. 132, notes that Mesomedes seems to have chosen prose for explicit panegyric.

21. Comotti 1989, 54.

22. Horna 1928, 6, 30–31; Heitsch 1959, 42–43; Pöhlmann 1970, 30–31.

23. So Furley and Bremer 2001, 47: "Since most of these texts are not cult texts in the true sense we omit them," specifically referring to Mesomedes. Wilamowitz-Möllendorff 1921, 606, claims that only the hymn to Isis was cultic.

24. Paus. 1.33.2–8, 7.5.2–3 (worship of the two Nemeses), 7.20.9. For a succinct modern discussion of Nemesis cult, with further references, see C. P. Jones 2001c, 45.

times an aspect of Isis, and it is not impossible that she is so for Mesomedes.[25] We are not, I think, in a position to rule out the idea that the hymns were composed for religious events. There were any number of local competitions where melic poetry might have been performed; imperial cult sites are also a possibility.

Other poems—particularly those on horologia, the sponge, the swan, the gnat, the sphinx, and the glass (7–13)—look more like sympotic pieces. If Mesomedes was as closely connected with Hadrian as the tradition suggests, these may have been performed at the emperor's famous literary symposia,[26] perhaps even on tour with "the restless emperor." Nothing in my argument depends specifically, however, on the hypothesis of imperial presence during performance (although it will be occasionally interesting to speculate); it is enough to accept that his contemporaries would have understood Mesomedes as a poet of Hadrian's circle.

In what form were the poems performed? Cassius Dio, Eusebius, and the *Suda* (following Dio) refer to Mesomedes as the author of "citharodic songs [*kitharōdikoi nomoi*]."[27] Citharodic poetry was usually monodic, performed by a singer accompanying himself on the lyre.[28] In general, the Mesomedean singer refers to himself in the first-person singular (1.1–2, 9; 4.9; 6.1, 16). At 3.16, however, in the hymn to Nemesis, we encounter the first-person plural "we sing [*aidomen*]." This led Ulrich von Wilamowitz-Möllendorff to conclude that a chorus would have taken over from a soloist at this point.[29] Further evidence for choral song might be drawn from 2.17–20: "The chorus [*khoros*] of stars . . . dances [*khoreuei*], singing its unrestrained song." The "chorus of stars" may represent a real chorus miming the roles of the elements (see further below); here they are specifically said to be singing the song. A similar representation of wide-scale melodic unison, this time across the nations, comes at 5.1–3, where "one song" is said to be sung over the entire world. Yet this is not quite conclusive evidence for choral performance. Just as choruses can refer to themselves in the first-person singular, so a monodic singer can represent himself as the representative of a wider community.[30]

The rhetoric of community, however—paralleled also at 2.5–6 ("Phoebus is about to come among us")[31]—is pronounced, particularly in the hymns. Choral

---

25. Thus, e.g., Merkelbach 1962, 332.
26. According to *HA Hadr.* 26.4, theatrical and poetic performances were a regular fixture at Hadrian's symposia.
27. Cass. Dio 78.7; Euseb. 2.2160; *Suda*, s.v. "Mesomedes."
28. Nagy 1990, 86–90, 353–58; Calame 1997, 80–82.
29. Wilamowitz-Möllendorff 1921, 605; dismissed by Bowie 1990, 85 n. 75.
30. Compare Pind., *Pyth.* 1.1–4, *Nem.* 3.1–12, with Nagy 1990, 356: "The Pindaric picture . . . of a prooimion *as if* performed by the chorus is idealized."
31. Heitsch's proposal of the Cretan form *porti* for the transmitted but unmetrical *pros* is ingenious but I think unlikely (there is no parallel in Mesomedes for such obscurantism), but a preposition of this kind is certainly needed.

dance frequently accompanied citharodic *nomoi*, it appears.[32] Mesomedes's poems contain a number of references to choruses (*khoroi*: 2.17-20, 5.17-19, 6.10, 8.25), which will be discussed further below. Much of the language that surrounds these references is attested elsewhere in connection with choruses.[33] But are these choruses to be imagined as singing or simply dancing? Or are they simply tralatitious and/or figurative? These questions cannot be answered with any great confidence.

In sum, there is no strong reason to assume that Mesomedes's poems were performed differently than the generality of other citharodic poems: which is to say, by a monodic singer, probably (in the first instance) the poet himself, accompanying himself. There may, however, have been choral involvement, perhaps in the form of dancing rather than singing. The possibilities for spectacular dancing choruses—particularly in the poems to Helios, Isis, the Hadriatic, and the second horologium—are great (see further below). Choral involvement is likely to have been limited to the hymns (poems 1-5; possibly 6-8 too); certainly, it is difficult to imagine that the seven-line riddle of the gnat, for example, afforded much scope for dancing.

Significant though these issues are, they are not open to resolution. More valuable than speculation over the *realia* of performance (which may in any case have been highly variable) is the point that these poems represent the poet-singer as the spokesperson for a wider community (whether human or pancosmic) addressing itself to a mighty or intractable phenomenon. Whether the interplay between the community and its figurative was, in performance, purely imaginary or whether it received concrete expression in the form of choral performance is less important than the identification of this central dynamic within the text.

HYMNS

This triangular relationship between the poet-singer, the community, and the subject of the poem is enacted most visibly in the hymnic and quasi-hymnic poems. It is to these that I now turn.

The hymn to Helios (poem 2) foregrounds the mighty potency of the sun. The poem opens[34] with a traditional request to the elements to be ritually silent (1-3) in anticipation of a manifestation of Helios. Helios is then addressed. In this invoca-

---

32. Calame 1997, 80-82, with references.
33. *Amplekein*, 2.12; *helissein*, 2.14, 2.25; *tassein*, 8.3, 8.23; *kosmos* (albeit in the sense of "universe"), 2.25, 4.2; the language of circular motion, 2.11, 14, 3.7, 8.3, 8.8. For references and full discussion, I refer to the relevant pages of Calame 1997: *plekein*, 34, 41, 53, 54; *helissein*, 35, 53, 77, 86, 109; *tassein*, 38-40, 72; *kosmos*, 40; circular dancing, 34-38.
34. On the view that the first six lines of poem 2 are separate, see above, n. 9. For Mesomedes's poem in the context of other Helios hymns, see Heitsch 1960.

tion, he is imagined as a charioteer, leading a "rosy chariot of foals" (8). This charioteering imagery is traditional for the sun[35] but nonetheless evocative of its directive power in the universe.[36] It is balanced at lines 21–23 by the description of Selene: "Pale Selene leads seasonal time drawn by white calves." Charioteering imagery is a representation of, precisely, hegemony.

Helios's control of the universe is total: his chariot is driven "around the limitless ridge of heaven [*peri nōton apeiriton ouranou*]" (11); he spins his rays "around the whole earth [*peri gaian hapasan*]" (14).[37] (Note the repeated *peri*, "around," marking the totalizing circularity of the sun's course; this might have been given visual form in the circular choral dance.) In the concluding lines, he is associated with the Stoic cosmic "mind [*noos*]": "The benevolent [*eumenēs*] Mind rejoices in you / as he whirls the multiply-garbed universe" (24–25). The constituent elements of the cosmos, meanwhile, join in reverence of Helios—not just the earth, sea, breezes, mountains, and vales enjoined to silence at the beginning but particularly the star chorus, who sing and dance "for you [*soi*]" (17).[38]

Many of these elements recur in other poems. The metaphor of charioteering, in particular, resurfaces. Isis is a "charioteer" (5.17), who "guides the newborn reins" (5.7–8) of the seasons. In poem 3, Nemesis is said to "steer [*kratousa*] your chariot with your hand" (3.13), where the choice of the verb *kratein* directly signals the imagistic link to power (*kratos*). The transgressive mortals overmastered by Nemesis are figured as the horses of the chariot: "You restrain the airy snortings of mortals with an adamantine bit" (3.3–4); "you bow the haughty [*gauroumenon*] neck" (3.10). In the first poem to the (solar) horologium, the sun is again imagined as the driver of a chariot (7.5).

Like the Helios hymn, other poems present the power of the deity in question as pancosmic. Physis (Nature), in the hymn to her, is the "origin and generator of all" (4.1) and assimilated to Helios, who "torches all the earth" (4.16; similar is 2.14, cited above). Isis is the subject of a single hymn, proclaimed on land and sea (5.1–3). Expressions of pancosmic influence are by no means unusual in late hymns, but it will be clear that Mesomedes places a distinctive emphasis on the theme of universal submission to a single divine potency.

Do Mesomedes's gods, then, provide theological analogies for imperial power? It is certainly possible to see numerous points of contact between the hymns and imperial, and specifically Hadrianic, self-representation. In the hymn to Helios, we might well imagine the emperor as Helios and the empress as Selene (who makes her entry at 2.21–23, discussed above). This identification is facilitated by

---

35. Compare e.g., Hom. *Hymn. Hel.* 14–16; Nonn., *Dion.* 40.371–73.
36. For horse taming as political metaphor, compare, e.g., Atossa's dream at Aesch., *Pers.* 176–214.
37. Similarly "the whole ether," 2.1.
38. Bergk's correction for MS *hoi*; see Heitsch 1960, 148.

potential paronomasia (Hadrianos—Hēlios; Sabina—Selene). Solar imagery recurs in the hymn to Nature (4.15-20, by extravagant syncretism) and in the swan poem (10; see below), and, as we shall see presently, the concept of an ordered cosmos lies at the heart of still more of Mesomedes's work. Hadrian himself was alive to the resonance of solar and cosmic imagery. He had Nero's Colossus reerected and recast as Sol, setting it in the new temple of Roma and Venus that stood in the east precinct of the Forum.[39] The Pantheon, with its eyelike aperture, uses the rotating shafts of the sun to represent its tour of the cosmos.[40] In other contexts, the emperor was addressed in more explicit terms, with globalizing titles such as "savior of the cosmos [*sōsikosmos*]."[41]

Nemesis, again, is subtly linked to the emperor. In her capacity as universal controller of arrogant humans, Nemesis is presented as a judge (*dikaspole*, 3.14; also "daughter of Justice [Dikas]," 3.2; "assessor [*parhedros*, a legal office] of Justice [Dikas]," 3.18); she embodies the absolute judicial authority invested, in the mortal sphere at any rate, in the emperor. She is, moreover, assimilated to "mighty Victory with her broad wings" (3.17). Victory had been a central figure in imperial imagery since Augustan times, and depictions of her were apparently carried before the emperor's busts at celebrations of imperial cult.[42] It is, I think, impossible to imagine that contemporary listeners would have failed to draw connections with imperial iconography.

More evidence for Hadrianism will surface in the course of the discussion, but I want to conclude for now with a brief discussion of poem 6, "To the Hadriatic." The Spanish Hadriani—and indeed the emperor himself, in his now lost autobiography—claimed origins in Hadria ad Picenum, the town that gave its name to the Hadriatic Sea.[43] When Mesomedes addresses the Hadriatic as "master [*despota*]" (6.13)[44] and prays, "Grant it to me ... grant it to me [*Dos ... dos*]" (6.13-14) to see his destination, it is once again difficult to avoid links with the emperor, not

---

39. HA *Hadr.* 19.12-13.
40. Ammianus observes the cosmic aspect of the Pantheon already in antiquity (16.10.14).
41. Birley 1997, 254.
42. Ando 2000, 278-92; especially Hölscher 1967. For the ideological connection between the emperor and Nike, see also *Anth. Pal.* 9.59 (Antipater of Thessalonica). It is possible that the combination of Nemesis and Victory suggests an athletic and gladiatorial contest, since this combination (along with Ares) is found in reliefs at Philippi in such a context: C. P. Jones 2001c, 47, conveniently summarizes the evidence. But there is nothing else in the poem—which focuses rather on cosmic principles—to suggest this.
43. Birley 1997, 133, 299. For the link between Hadrian and the Hadriatic, see also *Or. Sib.* 5.47 Friedlieb. The sea was sometimes known as the *Hadrianum mare* (Cic., *In Pis.* 38, etc.): on the history of the name and shifting geography of the Hadriatic see *RE*[1], s.v. "Adria."
44. It is possible that he turns at this point to address Poseidon rather than the Hadriatic itself, but there is no explicit marker in the text.

because the poem identifies the emperor directly with the Hadriatic but because the former's power over life and death is subtly assimilated to the sea's total control over its passengers.[45] We might note, finally, the imagery of centrality: the Hadriatic is the "center of the sea" (6.2), just as the sun is traditionally the center of the cosmic dance.

But how far do these analogies take us? Can we presume a total identification of the subjects of Mesomedes's hymns with the emperor himself? Surely not. It would be naïve to claim that the masks can be ripped away to reveal "real" faces underneath. There are at least as many ways in which (for example) Isis, Nemesis, and Physis, these female, elemental, abstractions, are not like Hadrian. It is enough that the subjects of these poems have resonances, particularly their potency and benevolence, that at times harmonize with imperial ideology. Mesomedes's theology offers an elaborate but ultimately multiform set of role-playing potentialities.

If there can be no final identification of the figures, does this mean, then, that the poems lack ideological significance? Certainly not. They encourage the audience to perceive themselves as subjects before figures of massive potency, figures that contain aspects that will remind them—albeit fleetingly—of imperial power. They inculcate the habit of submission and prayer. They serve as what Louis Althusser would call ideological state apparatuses, in that they hail or "interpellate" the subject into the symbolic hierarchical order of the political and indeed beyond that, into the cosmic empire of signs.[46]

THE COSMIC DANCE

The process of symbolic interpellation would have been further underlined if we accept my tentative hypothesis above that choral dancing accompanied these poems. The dancing chorus would have enacted the symbolic unity of the community, offsetting the anonymous collective against the egregious singularity of the individual, usually the leader of the chorus.[47] But even if choral dance did not literally take place, Mesomedes's traditional language mobilizes (and, to

---

45. The question of precisely which journey is envisaged is crucial but difficult to answer. The matter turns on the interpretation of the phrase transmitted in the MS as "mētera tēn gēn esidōn polin" (6.15). Wilamowitz-Möllendorff 1921, 599 (followed by Heitsch), emends *gēn* to *gēs* and argues for Rome. Support for this interpretation might be sought from Dion. Perieg. 356 (*GGM* II.124), where Rome is the "mother of all cities." On the other hand Horna 1928, 20, following Lambros, ingeniously reads "mētera tēn gēn esidōn palin," arguing that the poet is envisaging returning home to Crete, his motherland. The phrase *gē mētēr* usually means "mother earth" rather than "motherland" (see *LSJ*, s.v. "mētēr" 2), but there is plausibly a parallel at *SH* 905.24 (a text Horna will not have known): Greeks exhorted to defend their *mētera gēn*?

46. Althusser 1984.

47. Mullen 1982, 46–89; Calame 1997, especially 19–88.

be sure, substantively reconfigures) a paradigm that is deeply rooted in Greek thought.

The image that recurs with most striking regularity in these poems is that of the chorus of stars. In the hymn to Helios, "for you the serene chorus [*khoros*] of stars dances over lord [*anakta*][48] Olympus" (2.17–18). In the hymn to Isis, "all the stars [*astra*][49] dance [*khoreuetai*] to Isis the charioteer through her temples" (5.17–19). In the hymn to the Hadriatic, "The chorus [*khoros*] of stars leans back toward you, and the gleaming spurs of the moon and the well-born stars of the Pleiad" (6.10–12). In the second poem to the (astrological) horologium, the poet refers to the zodiacal inscriptions on the dial as a "chorus [*khoron*]" to match the celestial phenomena (8.25).

The language of star choruses is traditional: it goes back probably as far as Alcman and Sappho.[50] In Archaic poems, the conspicuous luminosity of the stars figures the gloriously exceptional status of those individuals chosen to represent the onlooking, starstruck community in the dance.[51] In the Athenian hymn to Demetrius Poliorcetes, however, we encounter a new development: the star chorus is rotating around a named individual, the political leader of the community. Demetrius "seems something august: his friends are all in a circle, he is in the middle, as though his friends were the stars and he the sun."[52] In this heliocentric conception of the universe, the star chorus is still an elite group of stellar individuals (Demetrius's friends), but they are subordinate to the ruling sun.

All of Mesomedes's star choruses dance for or to the subject of the hymn (apart from that in the astrological horologium, discussed below). There is no strong suggestion that the star chorus danced specifically around a central figure, as in the hymn to Demetrius; indeed, the hymn to Helios looks more like a processional poem (prosodion). Even so, the language of the chorus powerfully represents an idealized

---

48. A number of proposals for *anakta* have been offered, none of them convincing: Bergk had three attempts (*alēkta, nukta,* and *se* for *soi*); Hermann proposed *enanta*. See Heitsch's critical apparatus for details.

49. *Astea*: MS, Powell in *CA*, 198; *aistea*: Horna 1928, 17–18; *astra*: Wilamowitz-Möllendorff 1921, Heitsch.

50. Soph., *Ant.* 1147; Eur., *El.* 467, fr. 593.4–5 N² (similarly *Ion* 1080–81); *Anth. Pal.* 9.270–71; Luc., *Salt.* 7; Men. Rhet. 406.28–29 (p. 148 RW). For Alcman, the matter turns on the identification of the *Peleades* at 1.60 Davies. Opinion is now returning to the view (expressed in the fragmentary scholion ad loc.) that the Pleiads are meant: Gianotti 1978; Segal 1983; Clay 1991, 56–57. Stars are mentioned at Sapph. frs. 34.1–2, 96.6–9, 104(b) LP; none of these fragments is, however, explicitly choral. The χορός at Pind., *Pae.* 3.101 may be a cosmic chorus: see I. Rutherford 2001, 277–79, which draws parallels with Mesomedes's hymn to Helios. Dancing Pleiads also recur at Call. fr. 693 Pfeiffer.

51. See, e.g., *Jos. and Asen.* 2.11, of Aseneth's attendants. Star similes expressing stellar aspects are of course as old as Homer (*Il* 5.5, 22.26).

52. *PLG* 3, *Carm. pop.* 46.9–12 = Duris F 13 *FGrH* = Ath., *Deipn.* 6.253d-f. See also *PLG* 3.47.1.2 = Duris F 10 *FGrH* = Ath., *Deipn.* 12.542e, describing Demetrius as "sun-shaped [*hēliomorphos*]."

community subservient to the greater power. In a text roughly contemporary with Mesomedes's poems, Aelius Aristides describes how "the whole world, more truly than a chorus, sings a single song, praying together that this empire will remain for all time, so well is it organized by this chorus leader" (26.29; similarly 26.32). The powerful imagery of the world as a chorus adoring its *koryphaios* resonates deeply.

This community, however, is not necessarily demographically flat. The hymn to the Hadriatic provides the crucial passage: the reference to the chorus of stars is followed by "the gleaming spurs of the moon" and "the well-born stars of the Pleiad." Two elements appear in addition to the chorus, both of which receive epithets (which the chorus does not). The emphasis on Selene's luminosity is appropriate for a poem about navigation[53] but also suggests that she has a brightness that the chorus lacks. The Pleiad, meanwhile, are *eugeneis*: "elite," perhaps? The poem differentiates between the representatives of the community as a whole and those of the upper classes, and if we are right that the lunar imagery in the hymn to Helios alludes to Sabina (as speculated above), then it is possible that the empress here too figures (whether literally or only in the imagination) as part of the cosmic dance.

This focus on the cosmic dance makes the poems on the horologium, 7–8, all the more interesting. As we have already noted, the second also mentions the zodiacal constellations incised on the bronze as a chorus (8.25). Further musical imagery comes in the references to the "measure [*metron*, which also means 'poetic meter']" of the day that ring the poem (8.2, 29; *metrōn* also at 8.23). The astrological horologium is imagined as a rhythmically ordered cosmic dance. Heavy emphasis is placed on the constructional skill of the creator.[54] The "dance" serves the meaningfully structured order of the cosmos. This order is, implicitly, superimposed on the bestial chaos of the animals of the zodiac, who are described in monstrous terms: particularly notable are Aries, "mighty [*briaron*] with shaggy locks" (8.10), "the identical form of powerful [*kraterōn*] Gemini" (8.12), "powerful [*krateron*], monstrous [*pelōrion*] Leo" (8.14), and "the shameless [*anaidea*] archer Sagittarius [*Kentauron* = Centaur]" (8.18). These terms invoke the cosmic strife of Hesiod's *Theogony*, where monstrous beings vie with Zeus for control of the universe.[55] And, indeed, Mesomedes closes his poem with a reference to the triumph of order over cosmic warfare:

> After the limitless strife [*dērin apeiriton*] of heaven
> the pleasure [*hadona*] of bronze lows
> revealing to mortals the measure of the day. (8.27–29)

---

53. Which may also activate a paronomastic play on *Pleiados* (6.12) and sailing (*plein*), though the latter word does not appear in the poem. For the Pleiades as lights to sail by, see Hes., *Op.* 618–23.

54. "He fashioned . . . with skill [*tekhnēi*]," 8.1; "he arranged [*etaxe*, proposed for unmetrical MS *eteuxe* by Wilamowitz-Möllendorff 1921, 601]," 8.3; *merisas*, 8.5; *horisas*, 8.6; *taxin*, 8.23; *tekhna sopha*, 8.26; *daidaleou . . . tekhnas*, 7.6.

55. Compare especially the hundred-armers, Cottos, Briareus, and Gyges (*Th.* 153).

Cosmological and sonic order coincide: the "bronze" lows, like a domesticated beast rather than a zodiacal monstrosity. Presumably the horologium contained some kind of chiming mechanism;[56] it is possible also that the poem is metapoetically describing its own performance, with a bronze instrument striking a pleasant note to outsound discordant instrumentation. On this interpretation, this poem, like the hymns proper, presents music and dancing as symbolic servants of cosmic harmony.[57]

All emperors since Augustus had understood the valency of astrological prediction,[58] but Hadrian in particular fashioned himself as an astrological adept. According the *Historia Augusta* (*Hadr.* 16.7), every January he used to compose predictions for the following year (a novel twist on the idea of *res gestae* and imperial memoirs).[59] The emperor (whose own horoscope, indeed, survives) had the figures of the zodiac represented in his villa at Tivoli.[60] Further Hadrianic resonances might be detected in the bestial imagery: he was, of course, a celebrated hunter,[61] and a poem of Pancrates's celebrates the emperor and Antinous's victory over a lion in monstrous language that is both explicitly gigantomachic and comparable with that of Mesomedes's zodiacal bestiary.[62] Again, I am not arguing for a direct equivalence between the political sphere and the cosmic: one does not have to reduce these poems to the level of simple allegory to allow that they interpellate the subject into the symbolic hierarchy of the cosmos.

The point needs to be reinforced: these are not the kind of poems that admit of final decoding. They are, for one thing, extremely weird. Elaborate theological syncretism is matched at the linguistic level by the bizarre catachresis throughout. It would be rash in the extreme to assume that a single subtext—political or other—underlies these texts.

Indeed, there is a central ambiguity in the poems' construction of models of leadership. Who is in control here, the patron or the poet? This question is raised from poem 1:[63]

> Sing, Muse dear to me,
> begin my song;

---

56. Horna 1928, 24.
57. What is more, the "limitless strife of heaven" (8.27) echoes the "limitless back of heaven" at 2.11.
58. Barton 1994a, 38–52; Gee 2000.
59. Cassius Dio 69.11.3 also attests to his astrological bent. See further Barton 1994a, 45–46.
60. Le Boeuffle 1989, 110.
61. *HA Hadr.* 20.13, 26.3; Cass. Dio 69.7.3, 10.2–3, 22.2; for his beast hunts as public entertainment, see *HA Hadr.* 19.3, 19.7; Cass. Dio 69.8.2.
62. For the Hesiodic allusion in Pancrates, see *GDRK* 15.2.25 (comparison to Typhoeus); also the previous chapter.
63. I treat these as one poem rather than two: see above, n. 9.

may the breeze from your groves
stir my thoughts.
Wise Calliope,
leader of the pleasant Muses,
and wise mystery giver,
offspring of Leto, Delian Paean,
stand both of you by me in kindness.

When the Muses are envisaged as taking part in choral song (*molpē*), it is usually Apollo who is the choral leader (*khorēgos*)[64] and "begins" the performance;[65] here, however, it is the Muse who is asked to "begin" (*katarkhou*, also implying hierarchy) the song and Calliope who is addressed as "leader [*prokathageti*] of the ... Muses." It is not that there are no parallels for Muses performing this role,[66] and certainly Callimachus's phrase "Calliope began" (albeit narration, though, not song and dance) was known and imitated.[67] But to jam Apollo and Calliope together, as Mesomedes does here, raises an awkward question: which of them is it, then, who will be the ("real"? ultimate?) "leader"? And why (especially in a poem with paeanic features)[68] does Apollo make only a late and unremarkable entrance? Mesomedes's poem trades on the uncertainty in the Greek tradition as to who is the chorus leader of the Muses. The issue, however, is not simply confined to philological archaeology. We have seen above that Mesomedes's poetry consistently forges subtle links between Apollo-Helios and the emperor. We might also note that since Hesiod, Calliope has been imagined as the Muse of poets composing for kings.[69] The question posed by this poem, then, might (I stress *might*) be taken in starker terms: who leads this dance (now), poet or patron?

These issues reappear in the hymn to Helios. As we discussed earlier, the poem constructs Helios as the leader of a cosmic choral dance, representing his power in terms that look notably Hadrianic. At lines 17–20, however, the possibility of a different identification arises:

64. Already implicit at *Hom. Hymn. Ap.* 189–203. For Apollo as leader of the Muses see, e.g., Pind., *Pyth.* 1.1, *Nem.* 5.22–25, frs. 52k, 94c, 140b, 215 Snell-Maehler; *EG* 1025.3; Plut., *De Pyth.* 396c; Ael. Ar. 41.1.

65. See, e.g., hymns 2.5.58–62, 7.5.5–6, 12.4.5–6 in Furley and Bremer 2001.

66. Alcm. fr. 14 (a) Davies; Stes. fr. 278 *PMG*; implicit in *Anth. Pal.* 9.189. Calame 1997, 52–53, attempts to differentiate between Apollo's and the Muses' beginnings; see also Mullen 1982, 10–11.

67. Call. fr. 1.22 Pfeiffer; similarly fr. 759. Ov., *Fast.* 5.80 imitates the first phrase.

68. See especially line 8, addressing Apollo as "Delian Paean." For Delos as a site of performance of paeans, see *Hom. Hymn. Ap.* 157; Eur., *HF* 687–700; I. Rutherford 2001, 29; Furley and Bremer 2001, 142–45. Rutherford 2001, 122 n. 14, refers to Mesomedes 1 as an example of "adaptation of a *paian* to the context of poetics."

69. Hes., *Th.* 79. For a late (fifth century C.E.) parallel, see fr. 36.1–3 *GDRK*; the text is, however, admittedly difficult.

> For you, the serene chorus of stars
> dances over lord Olympus
> ever freely singing its song,
> taking pleasure in the Phoeban lyre.

In this context, Apollo is the leader of the *khoros* but invoked in his citharodic rather than solar aspect. If there is any mortal figure to whom he might be assimilated, it is the poet himself. The use of the phrase "over lord Olympus [*kat' Olumpon anakta*],"[70] indeed, redoubles the impression that Apollo-Helios has been (temporarily) uncoupled from imperial representation. Leaving aside the textual problems here, the phrase would surely have resonated for audiences under the leader who styled himself Olympian.[71] In this passage, then, the game of identifications becomes complex and involved: Apollo as Mesomedes, and Olympus/Zeus as Hadrian. For this brief period, the poet, not the patron, seems to lead the dance.

We should be wary, then, of reducing these complex poems to simple imperial propagandizing. Although they do, as I have argued, interpellate the subjects of the empire into a symbolic dance directed by their cosmic leader, they also flash out alternative interpretative possibilities, of an empire led by a Greek poet rather than a Roman patron. I have argued above that patronal poetry depends necessarily on its ability to generate multiple meanings, to accommodate the needs of its different communities. It is essentially intractable.

ECPHRASIS

I have spent much of this chapter discussing Mesomedes's hymns. I shall be briefer with his ecphrastic poems (this section) and fables (the following one). In fact, we have already considered two of the four ecphrastic poems, those on the horologia, above. In that earlier discussion, we saw that the solar and astrological horologia are presented in terms of the forces of civilized order subjugating monstrous bodies. The poems on the sponge (9) and the glass (13) similarly describe products resulting from humanity's dominance over the natural order. The sponge is "the pierced bloom of the sea's deep rocks" (9.1–2), cut away by a diver, "an intrepid worker [*atromos ergatas*]" (9.12). The glass, meanwhile, is also created by a "workman [*ergatas anēr*]" (13.2), who not only apparently "quarried [*kopsas*]" (13.2, where, however, the text is unsound) the lump (of crystal or soda) but also melted it in a furnace. Fire (*pur*, 13.3; *ekpuroumena*, 13.7) is the vehicle of transition from nature to culture, from the raw to the cooked.

---

70. On the textual problems here see n. 48.
71. On Hadrian *Olumpios*, see especially Birley 1997, 215–34; Boatwright 2000, 150–54.

In terms of cultural context, Mesomedes's ecphrastic poems take their place beside Statius's *Silvae*. With those poems, they share in the discourse of praise of "an Empire at a high level of technological and cultural achievement, delighting in world domination";[72] particularly conspicuous is the implicit awe in the rhetorical question that begins the two horologium poems, "Who made it?"[73] It is significant too that both glass and horologia (although, alas, not sponges) figure prominently in Pliny's *Natural History*.[74] The glass poem, alluding to Hephaestus's forging of Achilles's miraculous shield,[75] describes "a marvel for mortals to behold [*thauma . . . idein brotois*]" (13.8):[76] the poet's audience is invited to join in wonder at the superrefined achievements of humanity at its most advanced. As with the hymns, the subject is once again interpellated into a hierarchical symbolic order: the collective is unified by its awe in the face of the productivity of the imperial system.

Particularly significant, however, is the poet's emphasis on the laborers who manufacture these products. Both the sponge poem and the glass poem, as we have noted, refer to workmen. The worker of the sponge is described as "untrembling [*atromos*]" (9.12), that of the glass "trembling [*tremonta*]" (13.10) lest the glass should break, presumably for fear of spoiling his artifact but perhaps also because he risks the displeasure of his superiors. Though one is fearless and the other fearful, the poet represents the situation in which each labors as perilous, and fear as the anticipated, if not always the realized, response.[77]

The poet's audience, on the other hand, the viewers of the ecphrastic scene, are invited to take pleasure in these products of empire; they are constructed as consumers, not producers. This is particularly striking in the sponge poem, where the diver undertakes the dangerous task

---

72. Newlands 2002, 45.

73. "Who was it who carved . . . ?" (7.1); "Who was it who fashioned . . . ?" (8.1). Compare Stat., *Silv.* 1.1.1–7, 4.3.1–3 (with Coleman 1988, 105); *Anth. Pal.* 6.257.

74. Horologia: Plin., *NH* 2.182, 7.212–15, 36.72, with Healy 1999, 360–68; glass: Plin., *NH* 36.190–99, with Healy 1999, 352–58. There seem to be no precedents for these ecphrases. For late-antique horologium poems see *Anth. Pal.* 9.779–80, 9.806–7. I know of no other ecphrasis specifically of the manufacture of glass, but Ach. Tat. 2.3 makes great play of an elegant dichroic bowl, probably made of rock crystal rather than glass (discussion at Whitmarsh 2010b, 332 with n. 22); see also *Anth. Pal.* 6.33, 12.249.

75. Verbal correspondences: "A workman [*ergatas anēr*] / . . . put [*ethēke*] the lump in the fire [*es . . . pur*]" (Mesomedes 13.2–3) ~ "he turned these toward the fire [*es pur*] and ordered them to work [*ergazesthai*]" (*Il.* 18.469; similarly *ergon, Il.* 18.473; *puragrēn, Il.* 18.477); "he placed [*ethēke*] . . . anvil [*akmas*]" (Mesomedes 13.12–13) ~ "he placed [*thēken*] a great anvil [*megan akmona*] on the anvil block [*en akmothetōi*]" (*Il.* 18.476).

76. This phrase is not used specifically of Achilles's shield, but the similar "wonder to behold [*thauma idesthai*]" is applied to other miraculous divine artifacts: e.g., *Il.* 5.725, 18.377; Hes., *Th.* 575.

77. Opp., *Hal.* 5.612–74, also describes the perils of sponge diving. For commentary on this poem see Hopkinson 1994, 80–82.

> so that it [or you?] might melt from your snowy-white
> limbs, fair lady, the toil
> of ? erotic oglings ? after the night. (9.13–15)

Whatever the true reading of line 15 is,[78] the sense is evident: the diver undertakes his dangerous mission in order to produce a sex accessory for lovers. Elsewhere, the poem again presents the sponge as a luxury toy: Glaucus "takes pleasure in [*terpetai*]" (9.5) it; the Nereids "play with [*paizousin*]" (9.9) it by the waves; it is also used to wash away the spit from Poseidon's foals, his "hobbies [*athurmatōn*]" (9.9). There is a telling clash between the risks accruing to producers and the pleasures accruing to consumers. This poem, then, serves as an aggressive eroticization of productivity: its concept of pleasure is predicated on an explicitation of power differentials between those on the one hand who serve and suffer and those on the other who consume and enjoy. But it concomitantly aestheticizes, transforming others' labor into an attractive symbolic form that minimizes—without altogether effacing—their pain.[79]

Yet in exposing the process of productivity, Mesomedes presents the possibility of an alternative focalization. What does luxury look like from below? This thematic should also be taken as a self-reflexive commentary on the poet's own literary production. Indeed, there are a number of specific suggestions that the sponge, in particular, is to be thought of in poetic terms. The poem begins by referring to "this flower [*anthos tode*]" (9.1), which the reader or audience gradually deduces to be the sponge—but *anthos* can also be used self-reflexively of poetry, hence "garlands" and "anthologies," and the proximal-deictic *tode* might be taken initially as a reference to this very text. The sponge is then compared to a honeycomb from Mt. Hymettus (9.3–4), again an obvious image for poetry.[80] Finally, the self-reflexive tone of the poem is underlined by the reference to the woman's *melē* (9.13): the primary meaning is "limbs," but the word is also used for lyric ("melic") poems in general and for Mesomedes's in particular.[81] A metapoetic reading of the woman's legs is not easy to produce, but the word certainly adds to the poem's general air of self-reflexivity and thereby underlines the analogy between Mesomedes and the diver, two workmen laboring for the pleasure of others.

---

78. "Tōn erōtikōn ommatōn": MS (defended by Baldwin 1993); "ton erōtikon ammatōn": Wilamowitz-Möllendorff 1921; "ton erōtikōn ommatōn": Horna 1928; "ton erōtikon † ommatōn": Heitsch, Hopkinson 1994, discussion at 82; "ton erōtopalaismatōn" is Donald Russell's ingenious suggestion (recorded at Bowie 1990, 89).

79. I borrow here from analyses of pornography: see, e.g., Keuls 1985, 229–66; Kappeler 1986, 5–10.

80. *Smēnos* in line 3 (which is corrupt) is usually taken as a synonym for "Hymettian comb," i.e., "honeycomb": see Hopkinson 1994, 81; further Wilamowitz-Möllendorff 1921, 602; Horna 1928, 25–26. For metapoetic honeycomb, see *Anth. Pal.* 9.190.

81. E.g., at 2.19. *Suda*, s.v. "Mesomedes," says he is a writer of *melē*.

In this context, the question "Who made it?," which begins both the horologium poems (7, 8), is resonant and alive. Who owns productivity, patron or client? To whose glory does it redound? It can be seen quickly the extent to which this central interrogative overlaps with that which we located in the hymns: who leads the dance? Like those texts, the ecphrases pose the fundamental question of the ownership of poetic discourse. This crucial ambiguity, I suggest, springs from the Janus-like identity of the cliental poet, who faces both toward the emperor and his court and toward the wider community, with which he must also communicate. The poet needs—at least—two messages.

FABLES

I have emphasized throughout that Mesomedes's poetry depends on its capacity to accommodate multiple readings. The final poems I want to discuss are 10 ("To a Swan"), 11 ("To a Gnat"), and 12 (transmitted without a title but describing a sphinx or chimera).[82] In ancient terms, 10 and 11 would probably have been called *ainoi*, "fables," that is to say parabolic animal tales (looking back to Hesiod's story of the hawk and the nightingale and finding full expression in Aesop);[83] poem 12, on the other hand, would have been a "riddle [*griphos* or *problēma*]," in other words a playfully opaque description that challenges the reader to guess its identity (there is evidence for sympotic performance of riddles throughout antiquity).[84]

These seem to have been viewed as discrete genres, at least by the time of the redactors of the *Palatine Anthology*, who separated *ainoi* (book 9)[85] from *griphoi* (book 14). They are united, however, in the foregrounding of the hermeneutic act; Mesomedes teases his readers by withholding identification while gesturing toward that tradition. Riddles such as poem 12 are, in this respect, less interesting, since there is a single right answer (or *problēthen*, "thing put forward"). Fables, on the other hand, allow for several readings. "The *ainos*," writes Gregory Nagy, "is a code bearing one message to its intended audience; aside from those exclusive listeners 'who can understand,' it is apt to be misunderstood, garbled."[86] We might

---

82. Sphinx: Wilamowitz-Möllendorff 1921, 605; chimera: Bowie 1990, 88. Musso 1998 points to a similar beast—apparently a sphinx—on a mosaic at Monferrato and argues thence that Mesomedes's sphinx is assimilated to Isis. A similar poem can be found at *Anth. Pal.* 14.63.

83. Hes., *Erg.* 202–11; see Nagy 1979, 238–40, with 239 n. 2 on Aesop. Diogenianus Grammaticus, *Paroemiae* p.1.12–15 defines an *ainos* as "referencing via mythical analogy [*anaplasin*], from dumb beasts or plants, for the exhortation of human beings"; see further the compendious work of Rodríguez Adrados 1999–2003.

84. On *griphoi*, see *OCD*³, s.v. "riddles"; also Ath., *Deipn.* 448b–53c. For the sympotic evidence, see Cameron 1995, 80–81.

85. Notably riddle-like are 1, 2, 83, 86, 87, 95, 99, 233, 240, 264, 267, 273, 339, 370–73, 410.

86. Nagy 1979, 240.

refine this observation by distinguishing between the rhetoric of the *ainos,* which is as Nagy puts it, and the hermeneutic reality that many fables are notoriously difficult to resolve finally. If modern scholars cannot decide what, for example, Hesiod's *ainos* about the hawk and the nightingale is really about, can we expect ancient audiences to have done so?[87] Many *ainoi,* for sure, will have been quickly resolved and thus (as Teresa Morgan argues) will have been used for moral instruction,[88] but we should not automatically assume either that such simple moral decoding exhausted the resonances of any particular fable or that all fables could be resolved in this way.

Let us turn to the gnat poem (11):

> A gnat paused on an elephant's
> ear, beating his wing that was no wing.
> His words were foolish: "I am flying away,
> for you are unable to bear my weight."
> The other said, with a happy laugh,
> "I did not realize when you flew in,
> nor shall I realize when you fly away, gnat."

What is the significance of this story? Where is the "Gnat"'s bite? As it happens, there is approximately contemporary evidence for hermeneutic inference in the context of such fables. In a story similar to Mesomedes's relayed by Babrius (with a bull instead of an elephant), the closing moral states that "it is comical when someone who is a nothing [*ouden*] puffs himself up [*thrasuneth*"] before superior people [*tōn kreittonōn*] as if he were a somebody" (Babr. 84). In book 2 of Achilles Tatius's *Leucippe and Clitophon,* analogously, two slaves exchange Aesopic stories on the theme of big and little animals (2.30–32). In the first, Conops (Gnat) tells Satyrus about the lion's fear of the cock and the elephant's fear of the gnat (*kōnōps*). In the second, Satyrus replies with a story about a gnat boasting to a lion before getting stuck in a spider's web.[89] This jokey[90] exchange barely conceals the threatening subtext; indeed, Satyrus is specifically said to recognize "what was concealed [*to hupoulon*] in the words" (2.31.5).

At stake here are issues of power. Fables, in such instances, exist in order to speak of asymmetries through the safer medium of analogy. Sometimes such asymmetries are explicitly politicized. In Philostratus's *Apollonius,* Damis illustrates his point about the danger posed by Domitian with an Aesopic story about a lion and a fox (7.30). Tyrannical power is easily figured in terms of the

---

87. See most recently Hubbard 1995.
88. T. Morgan 2007, 57–83.
89. Versions of these two fables can be found at Aesop 188, 210 Chambry.
90. "Teased . . . playfully," 2.30.2; "mock," 2.30.3; "laughed," 2.32.7.

power of large beasts over smaller:[91] "These 'speaking animals' play off the law of the jungle against their playing it off, on *our* behalf; they make available to us ways to think with nature as if it were politics; they provide our best arena for catching the manipulative core intrinsic to the nature of politics" (italics in the original).[92]

Does the gnat poem, then, invite readers to ponder the relationship between imperial power and "foolish" attempts to subvert it? For many readers, the answer will be obviously no: nothing in the poem authorizes that kind of reading. But the converse point is that nothing can gainsay it either, and if we accept the principle of interpretative excess, then it becomes inevitable that patronal poetry will generate—or will be expected to generate—a range of responses incorporating metapoetical reflection on its functions.

The final text I wish to discuss is the swan poem (10). Again, the difficulty of interpreting meaning is belied by the effect of simplicity created by the easy meter, the unchallenging lexis, and the straightforwardly sequential narrative:

> A swan was trapped
> in the river by the ice-chained water—
> no need for a snare.
> A rustic goatherd,
> uncultured, saw him
> and resolved to kill,
> harvesting
> his sweet-voiced head
> with his wheat-cutting sickle.
> He was going along
> the frozen path
> with subtle steps,
> when the Titan appeared
> as an ally to the swan
> with his fiery ray.
> The river returned to
> limpid water;
> the herdsman fell;
> the swan surged
> and flew off in joy.

What is this poem about? Wilamowitz-Möllendorff could find in it only two lines' worth of comment, and those on the subject of meter; Ewen Bowie extends

---

91. See, e.g., the famous story of Domitian spearing flies with his pen (Suet., *Dom.* 3.1).
92. John Henderson 2001, 177–93, at 187.

to four.[93] But if we are right that the gnat poem invites identification with figures outside the poem, is this case analogous? The first point to be made is that the swan is traditionally thought of as a poetic bird, sacred to Apollo; here the epithet "sweet-voiced [*liguthroun*]" (line 7 in the Greek, 8 in the English above) brings out this resonance. The rustic,[94] on the other hand, is *amousos*, literally "lacking in the Muse" (line 4 of the Greek, 5 of the English above), and therefore semiotically antithetical to the cultivated bird. The swan thus figures the poet and the rustic a threatening figure with power over him. In this connection, the reference to the frozen river as "ice-chained" (3) is intriguing: the sun's melting of the ice is figured as a liberation from chains. Is this, then, an allegorical narrative of the poet's manumission, when Hadrian (= the sun / Titan) released him from his chained life? In support of this interpretation we could advance the recurrence of solar imagery throughout Mesomedes's poems in contexts that suggest imperial power (see above) and note further that in the hymn to Helios, the chorus specifically sings "freely [*aneton*, literally 'released']" (2.19).

But nothing can guarantee this interpretation. An alternative might be to take the emperor for the uncultured boor who holds the poet in captivity, longing for his freedom. In other contexts, swans sing only when they are threatened with death....[95] This narrative could be substantiated by reference to the hymn to Physis (4), where the poet specifically prays to the god (again addressed as "Titan") for liberation from chains that appear to be holding him in the present: "Pity, Titan, so great / a chain [*desmon*] holding the wretched man" (4.23–24). Of course, in that context (as so often in mystic poetry), the chains are principally those of mortal ignorance, but who can rule out wider allusions? If we focus on the context of reception for this patronal poetry rather than some notionally originary meaning, then the aim of our inquiry should be to track the full range of possible interpretations.

The fundamental point is that concepts such as freedom and constraint are necessarily overdetermined: such contagious concepts have a virulence that overcomes any cozy sequestering. Like his hymns and ecphrases, Mesomedes's fables are—and their communicative strategy rests on their being—necessarily open to multiple interpretations, from the points of view of patron and wider community.

---

93. Wilamowitz-Möllendorff 1921, 602; Bowie 1990, 88. Horna 1928, 27–28, does, it is true, manage two paragraphs, on the meter and the text.

94. The poet seems inconsistent (Bowie 1990, 88): this figure is variously a goatherd, a harvester, and a cowherd.

95. E.g., Aesop 173–74 Chambry.

CONCLUSION

What poetry of Mesomedes's survives is heterogeneous and has been preserved in diverse traditions. What antiquity apparently considered his most famous poem, the "Praise of Antinous," does not survive, and chances are we have lost considerably more of his poems. Notwithstanding that, even the twelve poems that we have manifest an impressive degree of coherence, at the thematic and the linguistic levels. These poems repeatedly recur to questions relating to the ownership of poetic discourse: to the poet's control over his material and his community, to his role in the hierarchy of production, to the degree of freedom he exercises.

I have argued throughout this chapter that it makes sense to supply a Hadrianic context when we interpret these poems: they can profitably be read as energized by the poet's relationship with the emperor on the one hand and a wider Greek community on the other. This bivalence is fundamental to the poet's communicative strategy: to be credible, the poems need to be legible both as imperial ideology, interpellating the community into the political hierarchy of the world (and indeed the cosmos), and as commentary suitably distanced from it, exposing its exploitation and aggression. It is true that there is no unequivocal "proof" for Hadrianic signification in the poems (though the circumstantial evidence is, I think, strong). To this extent, this chapter has been an experiment with possibilities. But if we take a reception-orientated approach, if we accept that a single poem can combine multiple potential meanings, then we can conclude with a stronger, more affirmative point: these poems not only can be interpreted as Hadrianic but also—in terms, at least, of the range of potentialities—cannot not be. To succeed in the tense, energized environment of triangular communication among poet, patron, and audience, this poetry needs to tell us just enough about the imperial figure who looms in the background.

11

Lucianic Paratragedy

In memoriam Michael Foot

I turn in this chapter to a very different kind of poetic text. Lucian of Samosata is one of the acknowledged stars of second-century literature.[1] Born in Syrian Commagene and perhaps not even a native Greek speaker, he became a successful orator first, then turned in later life to writing the satires and parodies for which he is now best known. His influence in the early modern period was immense, particularly in northern Europe, where he came to be seen as the embodiment of a cultivated, intellectually sophisticated skepticism, an icon of wit and learning who could, so it was believed, shine a light on the flummery and ritual of Catholic countries (in the sixteenth century his works had been placed on the papal index of proscribed books).[2]

The vast majority of his works are in prose, but he shows himself well acquainted with Archaic and classical poetry, which he quotes regularly.[3] In particular, as recent studies have shown, Attic tragedy occupies a central role in his writing.[4] Athenian poetry occupied, of course, a high status at this time, and the ability to quote extensively was a marker of social distinction. But Lucian is doing something much more sophisticated than just showing off. For a start, tragedy has

---

1. See inter alia J. Hall 1981; C. P. Jones 1986; Branham 1989; Swain 1996, 298–329; Whitmarsh 2001, 247–94; Goldhill 2002b, 60–107.

2. Initially, in 1559, just *Peregrinus* and *Philopatris*; in 1590, the rest. Lucian's reception has been well studied: see Robinson 1979; Holzberg 1988; Lauvergnat-Gagnière 1988; Baumbach 2002.

3. Householder 1941 catalogues Lucian's quotations. See too Neef 1940, if you can stomach the Nazi insignia.

4. Karavas 2005; Schmitz 2010; see also Seeck 1990.

largely negative connotations: the word itself he associates with bombastic pretension (*tragōidein* means, for him, something close to "bluster"), and he often puts tragic quotation in the mouths of such self-aggrandizers. But it is not a case of simple execration; rather, like Aristophanes (an avowed influence),[5] Lucian cannibalizes tragedy, simultaneously defining his literary production in opposition to it and appropriating it within his radically intertextual mimesis.

Among his many talents were an extraordinary facility for mimicry, which covered genre, style, dialect, and morphology: witness, for example, *On the Syrian Goddess* (if it is his), which tracks the language of Herodotus closely, using the same Ionic dialect.[6] That text—an account of a visit to the cult site of Atargatis in Syrian Hierapolis—has been taken as a variety of what Homi Bhabha would call "colonial mimicry."[7] Lucian apes, closely but uncannily, the language that Herodotus would use to describe a foreign cult, but (as he reveals in the final sentence) this is a cult into which he himself was initiated as a youth. The mimicry of the Herodotean language of othering renders it self-consuming, as the reference points from which self and other are erased.

Lucian's mimic skills extended to tragedy. *Zeus the Tragedian*, as we shall see below, is a brilliant, prosimetric fusion of Platonic dialogue with tragedy. Yet more ambitious, however, and more diverse and sophisticated in its use of tragedy is the poem that forms the central subject of this chapter. At 334 lines of verse, *Podagra* (Gout) represents the only apparently complete tragedy to survive from the vast period between the late fifth century (or fourth, if that is when *Iphigenia at Aulis* and/or *Rhesus* should be dated) and the Lucian-influenced *Ocypus*, perhaps written by the fourth century C.E. orator Libanius. Like Ezekiel's now fragmentary *Exagoge*, discussed in chapter 13, *Podagra* shows (so I shall argue) the capaciousness and suppleness of the tragic genre and, what is more, how Lucian exploits these so as to define, albeit in a manner more allusive and ludic than that of *On the Syrian Goddess*, his literary and cultural identity in relation to the canon.

ZEUS TRAGŌIDOS

Let us start with the prosimetric *Zeus the Tragedian*. This extraordinary dialogue—probably the most religiously controversial work of Lucian's—begins on Olympus

---

5. *Bis acc.* 33; compare *VH* 2.31. Lucian's relationship to Aristophanes is at the heart of in two recent PhD theses, Brusuelas 2008 and Peterson 2010; see especially Camerotto 1998 on Lucian's radical intertextuality, with 133–36 on his mingling of verse and prose. On Aristophanes's complex relationship with tragedy see especially Goldhill 1991, 189–222; Silk 2000, 42–97.

6. Lightfoot 2003, 91–161. Lightfoot also discusses the contested authorship of this text (without committing herself).

7. Elsner 2001; Bhabha 1994, 85–92.

with Zeus, in conversation with Hermes, Athena, and Hera, lamenting the discussions of mortal philosophers that conclude that the "gods do not exist" (4). He proceeds to narrate how the previous day he heard a discussion between the Epicurean Damis and the Stoic Timocles on the question of whether the universe is providentially ordered or not; the Epicurean, arguing against divine involvement, carried favor with the crowd, although resolution of the debate was postponed to the following day (15–18). Momus, the personification of blame, now faults the gods themselves for this eventuality, since they have failed to provide for human beings (19–22). After further discussion about how they can prevent the spread of this atheistic view, the gods eavesdrop on the human debate, in which the skeptic Damis easily prevails (34–53). There is much that could be said about this captivating and complex dialogue, which is both a highly sophisticated work of literature (with a framing device, a reported dialogue, and two "Lucianic" analogues, the divine Momus and the mortal Damis) and a valuable window onto ancient debates around religious skepticism.[8] But it is the reception of tragedy that commands our attention here.

Why is Zeus described as a tragedian? Principally because the opening section, featuring his initial laments, is heavily paratragic (1–2). Hermes opens with four lines of iambic trimeters: "What is in your mind, Zeus, that you speak alone to yourself, / Walking around pale, with the hue of a philosopher? / Confide in me, take me as counselor of your pain; / Do not contemn the blather of a slave" (1). The source of these lines (as Lucianic scholars have not, to my knowledge, recognized) is a comic poet, perhaps Menander (fr. adesp. 1027 *PCG*): a slave counsels his master to take his advice. But Lucian has not only added additional bathos by dropping in the joke about philosophers' proverbial pastiness (line 2)[9] and substituting "blather [*phluarias*]" for "advice [*sumboulias*]" in the final line; he has also given the quotation a tragic "feel" by excising the original comic elements and playing to the generic expectations generated by the title of his dialogue. But even so, the heavy use of a particular metrical feature (i.e., "resolution," the substitution of two short syllables for a long one) is a telltale sign of the verses' origin in comedy.[10] The effect is thus immediately disorienting, with the text havering as it does between quotation and appropriation, between tragedy, comedy, and satire, between classic verse and parodic prose.

---

8. See Van Nuffelen 2011, 194–98.

9. In fact Lucian's second line is entirely new, although it preserves the spirit of the original ("you seem to present the appearance of one grieving"). Note that the joke about the philosopher develops the allusion to peripatetic philosophy in Zeus "walking around [*peripatōn*]."

10. There are six resolutions in four lines. Even Euripides's most resolution-heavy play, *Orestes*, shows this feature in only approximately one line in three (34.7 percent, to be precise: R. B. Rutherford 2012, 41).

The second person to speak is Athena, who also imprecates Zeus to reveal his concerns; she, however, uses Homeric-style hexameters, incorporating one genuinely Homeric line ("Speak out! Do not conceal it in your mind; let us both know it" = *Il.* 1.363, *Od.* 1.45) and one and a half adapted lines ("Yes, father of ours, son of Cronus, highest of rulers," ~ *Il.* 8.31; "Why . . . has pallor seized your cheeks?," ~ *Il.* 3.35). The change to hexameters and epic diction perhaps marks Athena's distinctively Homeric identity, but more than anything it contributes to a sense of radical heterogeneity of meter and genre. Poetry is treated not as a unitary generic marker but as a style that can be mimed, cited, and subverted at will, before being cast off.

Now Zeus himself speaks:

> "There is no word [*epos*] so awful [*deinon*] to speak,
> No suffering, no tragic [*tragōidikē*] calamity,
> That I do not surpass in ten iambics."

This passage pastiches the opening of Euripides's *Orestes*, again with significant changes, which this time provide explicit metaliterary commentary. In the second line, "tragic" replaces Euripides's "heaven-sent," while the third line, with its reference to iambics (the meter in which Zeus is speaking) is entirely new. This changes the meaning of the entire sentence: rather than a banally tralatitious observation about the inevitability of human suffering (which would be in any case inappropriate in a god's mouth), it becomes a metaliterary comment on tragedy's propensity toward bombastic excess. This explicit self-reflexivity activates the secondary meaning of *epos* in line 1, which can also mean "epic poetry." Following on immediately from Athena's Homeric farago, the Euripidean line, thus recontextualized, becomes a playful acknowledgment of the "awful *epos*" that we have just heard.

Athena now replies in iambics, quoting exactly from Euripides's *The Madness of Hercules* (538): "Apollo! With what prelude you begin your speech!" We are confronted immediately with an amusing paradox: Athena ends up incongruously swearing by a different god, Apollo. What is more, although these are Heracles's exact words, they take on a new significance in the Lucianic text: for the word *prelude* (*phrooimion*, sometimes *prooimion*: hence the English *proem*) has become, by this stage, a technical term in rhetoric for the opening salvo of an oration. This resonance is disclosed by the fact that Lucian has taken a passage from the middle of Euripides's text and moved it so that it refers to Zeus's opening words and indeed (intertextually) to the opening of the *Orestes*—so that Athena is now commenting quite literally on a *phrooimion*. This is thus at one level a playful correction of Euripides, ironing out what Lucian would have seen as a misapplication of a technical term. But it is also a brilliantly metaleptic moment, when two characters in the text adopt the perspectives of author and reader.[11] The words belong simultaneously to

11. For metalepsis see ch. 4.

the characters and to Lucian himself (while still being palimpsestically Euripidean). The text brilliantly shuffles these different identities.

Zeus now replies with what seems to be an exact quotation from Euripides: "O vilest chthonic nurslings of the earth / —and you, O Prometheus, what you have done to me!" The first line is known as a fragment (fr. 939 *TGrF*); it is likely, I think, that Lucian's second line completes the Euripidean quotation, otherwise why introduce the name of Prometheus here? Prometheus, however, becomes relevant as a symbol of rebellion against the Olympian order; once again the quotation is resignified in its new context. Athena now replies, "What is it? You will be speaking to a chorus [*khoron*] of family members," another Euripidean quotation (fr. 940 *TGrF*), and again note the self-reflexive word *chorus* (used here not by a chorus but by a principal character). Zeus responds with a line heavy with tragic *ogkhos* (weight) and apparently of Lucian's invention: "Thundering stroke of my whizzing bolt [*megalosmaragou steropas rhoizēma*], what will you do to me?" The noisy alliteration and bold compounding suggest the lofty style of Aeschylus, and the thunderbolt is always a metapoetic symbol of poetic grandeur.[12] After this giddying expostulation, however, Hera's reaction—in prose—bathetically unveils the role playing and pretension in the adoption of poetic models: "Put your anger to sleep, Zeus, if I can't act out comedy [*kōmōidian ... hupokrinesthai*] or play the rhapsode [*rhapsōidein*] as these do, since I haven't drunk down Euripides whole so as to play a supporting tragic role to you [*hupotragōidein*]. Do you suppose we don't know the reason for your grief?"

Hera's reaction acknowledges the generic hodgepodge of the preceding verse (comedy, epic, tragedy),[13] but it is defiantly prosaic, and in two senses: her insinuation (as will become clear in her following intervention) is that Zeus's love for a mortal woman is the cause of his anguish. This prosiness is accompanied by an abrogation of the fictive power of poetry, which is suggested to be a means of artificially exaggerating the truth, and by a concern with the quotidian, in the form of sexual content and a sympotic metaphor ("I haven't drunk down Euripides"). The effect is similar to that of the ripostes of Critylla to Euripides and Mnesilochus in Aristophanes's *Thesmophoriazusae* (904–57). Zeus responds with one final tragic quotation—"You do not know, or else you would shriek mightily" (fr. *adesp.* 293 *TGrF*)—before we revert to prose for most of the rest of the dialogue (which, however, repeatedly invokes poetry as a cipher for bombast and deceit).[14]

---

12. See ch. 14.

13. It is thus not quite that "Hera finds the generic signals bewildering" (Branham 1989, 168); in fact, she has identified the sources of each of the quotations accurately, and in order.

14. There is another Euripidean quotation at 3 (alluding to *Phoen.* 117). At 6, Zeus orders Hermes to call the gods to assembly, bidding him "dignify [*aposemnune*] your proclamation with meter and poetic sublimity [*megalophōniai poiētikēi*]"; Hermes replies that he is not much of a poet ("*hēkista poiētikos*")

Zeus the Tragedian thus plays tragedy as pretentious, stylized discourse adopted for tactical purposes, antinomic to the deflating, bathetic voices represented in the passage above by Hera and later on by Momus and Damis. Yet Lucianic satire is not about defining and founding stable positions so much as edges, transitions, passages. The comedy emerges from the moments of rupture between one style and another, from the incongruity or incompatibility between such different worldviews. It would thus be wrong to define tragedy as in opposition to satire; rather, satire emerges from the very discursive conflict itself. Poetry, though always marked as alien and intrusive in this prose text, is nevertheless central to the Lucianic project here. The text's metrical and generic heterogeneity is both a showcase of the author's versatility and talent and (more important) programmatic for the implicit definition of satire as open, multiple, transient.

Two more points to underline. The first is the metaleptic effect noted above. The alien, artificial quality of tragic discourse prompts a self-reflexivity, to the extent that paratragedy always seems to be signaling its status as a literary construct. When they adopt tragic language, Lucian's characters in *Zeus the Tragedian* seem to speak as much about the process of tragic composition as about the situation they find themselves in: hence the references to "preludes [*phrooimia*]" and the "chorus [*khoros*]." This in turn draws attention to the hidden hand of the author, always an absent presence in Lucian's writing.[15] Here more than anywhere, Lucian's characters threaten to unveil themselves as figments or, better, allegories, or the writer's creative processes.

Second, let us not forget that the theme of the dialogue is the relationship between human and immortal. Or, better, about the relationship between human constructions of the divine and the gods themselves, for Lucian's gods repeatedly slide into representation and figurality, to the extent that they often seem to have no possibility of existence independent of cultural manufacture, whether by poets or sculptors.[16] Poetic language is thus the precondition for divinity. Tragedy is very much the language of the gods, its elevated tone bespeaking the loftiness of Olympus, its segregation from the world of mortals. The fictitiousness and pretense that are recurrently associated with tragedy (even Zeus, in the end, tells Hermes, "Stop

---

but when pressed by Zeus to "mix in lots of the Homeric epic lines [*tōn Homērou epōn egkatamignue ta polla*]" does come up with six lines of hexameters. Zeus quotes Homer at 14. Apollo, who has already been mocked for his poetic style at 6, comes up with a prophecy at 31 that is poetic in style and rhythmically full of dactyls and spondees but only partially hexametrical. Another Euripidean parody comes at 33. At 39–40 the Stoic Timocles cites Homer as a witness to divine providence; Damis replies that he is a poet of fiction. Timocles now appeals to Euripides, and Damis counters that Euripides also represents nontheist positions. Homer is cited at 45 (bis) and Menander at 53.

15. On Lucian's reticence with his name see Whitmarsh 2001, 248–53; Goldhill 2002b, 60–67.

16. See Branham 1989, 168–71, noting that the gods when they are summoned are said to be made of marble, bronze, and gold (7–8; 10).

tragifying," 33) are thus implicitly pressed into the service of the critique of the gods' existence. This line of attack particularly targets Apollo's oracular language, the paradigmatic medium of divine communication between gods and humans: after Apollo's quasi-hexametric nonsense oracle at 31, Momus breaks into laughter, opining that "the prophecy plainly [*diarrhēdēn*] says that this man is a fraud [*goēta*] and that you who believe in [*pisteuontas*] him are pack asses and mules, without so much sense as grasshoppers." Attacks on prophecy's ambiguous language are common in Lucian and indeed in the wider literature of the era,[17] but in this context the mockery is doubly pointed. Momus's comment that no one should "believe in" Apollo refers primarily to the confidence that one places in another's utterances (*pisteuein* classically means "put one's trust in," especially in connection with the gods), but there is also a strong hint that Momus is casting doubt on the very existence of the god, perhaps even echoing the emergent Christian conception of *pisteuein* as religious "faith."

GOUTY POETICS

So to *Podagra*. The action begins with a prologue featuring an unnamed individual announcing his terrible torments in iambics. Then comes the *parodos*, or choral entry, in anacreontics: the chorus (whose gender remains unclear) reveal themselves to be initiates of the goddess Gout (Podagra). The protagonist recognizes the symptoms and guesses that he too is an "initiate." The chorus sings a hymn in praise of the goddess, a virtuoso lyric in the manner of Mesomedes (i.e., built around paroemiacs and *apokrota*); it is likely, I think, that Lucian's "hymn to gout" is an adoxographic parody of Mesomedes's extravagant hymns to personifications (e.g., Nemesis and Physis).[18] Now Podagra herself appears, vaunting her powers in iambics. After a brief choral interlude praising her with a series of flamboyant compound adjectives, a messenger enters, speaking of malefactors who have devised cures for gout. Despite his difficult journey (he too, naturally, is gouty), he has managed to drag the criminals here for Podagra to try. Podagra has punished them already, having sent the Ponoi (Pains) after them in the manner of tragic furies. The doctors repent, and Podagra pardons them. The play finishes with a choral ode in another cutting-edge, nonclassical meter, namely the "myuric" hexameter (in which an iambus substitutes for the final foot of the usual hexameter); the ode lists those who in myth have denied or sought to rival the gods and counsels sufferers to endure with fortitude. Whether or not we choose to divide

---

17. Bendlin 2006.
18. See the previous chapter. On adoxography, the (typically rhetorical) praise of worthless objects, see Billerbeck and Zubler 2000.

the play into three "scenes," Graham Anderson's judgment is unimpeachable: "The writer has been content to display the inevitable trappings of Tragedy, rather than re-create a tragic plot as such."[19]

In overall thematic direction, *Podagra* mimics Euripidean tragedies such as *Hippolytus* and *Bacchae,* plays where (as Lucian's Timocles puts it in *Zeus the Tragedian*) the poet "brings the gods themselves on to the stage and shows them saving heroes and destroying criminals" (41). In terms of the overlapping of the divine and the tragic, the poem can be seen as an inversion of *Zeus the Tragedian:* here the uniformly tragic setting accompanies a general validation of the divine, figured by the closing song of the chorus (ever the voice of normative collectivity)—even if the divinity in question is a comic invention. Although it is (as noted above) metrically highly inventive, and to that extent heterogeneous, there is none of the other text's incessant puncturing of tragic discourse.

Yet this work has its own complexity, partly in the adoption of a theist form for the purpose of hymning a made-up deity, but more significantly in the metaleptic intimations of the author within his tragic fiction. Not that Lucian has any one particular analogue within the text (and I am certainly not making a biographical argument that the real Lucian had gout); rather, Lucianic authorship announces itself repeatedly and prompts readers to fancy that they have gotten a glimpse of the creator's poetic manifesto behind the veils of representation.[20]

Let us consider a passage from Podagra's first speech:

> All these [i.e., who attempt to cure themselves], I tell them to wail [*oimōzein*],
> And those who use them [i.e., spells and cures] and those who test me
> I am wont to confront with more fury.
> But those who do not set themselves against me
> I treat with kindliness, and I am friendly toward them.
> Whoever has a share in my mysteries
> Is taught [*didasketai*] first and at once to keep reverend silence [*eustomein*]
> Delighting all by speaking witty [*eutrapelous*] words. (175–82)

What is striking about this passage is the emphasis on instruction in the proper use of language. Amid a culture devoted to book learning, Podagra's claim that her initiates are "taught" to speak well is highly resonant. *Eustomein* (literally "mouthing well") refers primarily to the care with language (usually extending to silence) enjoined on ritual devotees, but there is an implication too of the articulacy

---

19. Anderson 1979, 153. Anderson's article offers a useful analysis of Lucianic themes in the poem. Karavas 2005 discusses Lucian's manipulation in *Podagra* of his tragic heritage.

20. Readers receive a cue to think of the Lucianic creator figure behind the text when, e.g., the doctors reveal themselves to be "Syrians" (265).

of rhetorical performance so prized at the time. This fine speech consisting of "witty words"—hinting at the salty humor of Lucianic satire—contrasts with the "wailing" of those who resist her: the word, referring to the traditional Greek expression of dismay (*oimoi*—ah me!), recursively evokes tragic discourse. Tragic lamentation, in Podagra's distinctive world, is the consequence of gout's physical impact on the body. Gout seems to be a metaphor for all that is diseased and amiss in the world, and tragedy is opposed to satire just as high-minded contempt for that sickness is to urbane acceptance of it.

Indeed, one of the dominant themes of the poem is a self-reflexive concern with aesthetic deformation. There is also an intergeneric dimension to this. Slow, gouty hobblers function as inversions of Homer's speedy heroes, especially "swift-footed [*podas ōkus*] Achilles." The messenger, though afflicted, has tried to come quickly: "How speedy [*kraipnos*] you have flown," opines Podagra, "messenger of mine most swift [*ōkiste*]" (218–20). The messenger, having referred twice in his entrance speech to feet (*podi*, 204; *poda*, 216), speaks of his laborious journey with the emphasis on his feet:

> A five-runged ladder first of all I left
> Whose loosely-fitted wooden limbs did shake
> And next a beaten floor awaited me,
> A pavement hard and firm that hurt my feet.
> O'er this I sped in haste with painful steps,
> And then I came upon a gravel path
> With sharp and pointed stones most hard to cross.
> Then next a smooth and slippery road I met;
> Forward I pressed though mud clung to my steps
> Making my strengthless ankles drag and trail.
> In crossing this my limbs did drench my feet
> With sweat and drained away my ebbing strength.
> Then wearied in each limb I found myself
> Where was a highway broad but dangerous;
> For carriages to right and left of me
> Did force me on and make me run in haste.
> And I did nimbly lift my sluggish feet [*nōthron . . . poda*]
> To dart aside and seek the wayside strait,
> To let a cart rush by with flying wheel.
> For, mystic thine, I could not run with speed [*takhu trekhein*].
> 221–40, translated by Matthew Macleod (1967)

This antiepic, limping mode is of course already seeded in Homer: in the lame god Hephaestus, who provides the gods with comic relief in the *Iliad* (1.571–600) and whose apprehension of Ares in Demodocus's famous song ("See how the slow catches the quick," *Od.* 8.329) figures Odysseus's supplanting of swift-footed

Achilles as epic hero,[21] and in the figure of the chiding Thersites, "unmeasured in speech [*ametroepēs*]" (*Il.* 2.212), who is "lame in one foot [*khōlos heteron poda*]" (*Il.* 2.217).[22] These episodes seem to hint at the intrusion of an alien genre into the texture of epic, a subheroic species of aggressive,[23] comic verse (note that each Homeric episode mentioned above involves laughter: *Il.* 1.599 = *Od.* 8.326, *Il.* 2.215). It is thus no surprise that the meter of Hipponax's lampoons was styled choliambic, or "having limping iambs."[24] Relatedly, let us recall that a *pous* is a metrical as well as a physical "foot," an association that is at the root of many puns in (particularly) Roman poetics.[25]

The metapoetic idea of gouty poetics as inverted epic is further developed in Podagra's response to the messenger, where she lists figures of myth who suffered from the disease: Zeus had it (249); Priam was called Podarces because he was gouty (*podagros*, 252); Achilles died of gout (253); Bellerophon, Oedipus, Pleisthenes, Philoctetes, Podarces, and Odysseus too were gouty (252–62). These exempla are not merely appropriations into Podagra's world of any mythical figure who has any kind of foot connection (whether in name or in myth); they also offer a cunning parody of the rationalizing style of Palaephatus, Dionysius Scytobrachion, and particularly Ptolemy Chennus, that compiler of parapoetic weirdness (such as the claim that Odysseus's nickname was Otis, "Big ears," reported by Photius, *Bibl.* cod. 190). Thus Podagra denies the version, probably narrated in the lost cyclical *Telegony*, of Odysseus's death by the sting of a ray.[26] "The king of Ithaca, Laertes's son, / was slain by me and not by the barb of a ray" (261–62): a more "realistic," quotidian debunking of epic mythicizing.[27]

Lucian the author is, thus, visible throughout *Podagra*. Lucianic paratragedy is not simply the provisional adoption of another literary form but an exploration of the incompatibility between high poetics and low satire; the poem as a whole explores the incongruous transience between the two. Note particularly the final lines: "Let each sufferer / Learn to bear mockery [*empaizomenos*] and taunts [*skōptomenos*], / For this thing is of such a kind" (332–34): the drama decodes itself as an allegory of Lucianic satire, an apologia for his disfigurement of lofty aesthetics.

---

21. Odysseus claims to be good at all sports except footracing (*Od.* 8.230–31). On the connections between Demodocus's song of Ares and Aphrodite and the wider plot see especially Braswell 1982; Newton 1987. See further Detienne and Vernant 1974, 244–60, on the links between lameness and cunning.
22. Praised by the philosopher Demonax as an ideal cynic at *Dem.* 61.
23. Nagy 1979, 258–64, has Thersites as the embodiment of "blame poetry."
24. Excellent discussion at L. Morgan 2010, 115–30.
25. Ovid, notably, presents elegiacs as "limping": *Am.* 3.1.8, *Tr.* 3.1.11–12.
26. *Argumentum ap.* Procl. *Chrest.*; however, Apoll., *Bibl.* epit. 7.34–37 supplies the detail.
27. Similar is the tactic at 185, where she associates herself with Homer's Ate, or Madness.

12

Quickening the Classics

The Politics of Prose in Roman Greece

The "age demanded" chiefly a mould in plaster,
Made with no loss of time,
A prose kinema, not, not assuredly, alabaster
Or the "sculpture" of rhyme.

EZRA POUND, "HUGH SELWYN MAUBERLEY" II.5–8

"The 'age demanded' . . . a prose kinema," writes Ezra Pound in his (self-)parodic tribute to a bloodless writer. A resonant phrase; a cliché perhaps, meriting the arm's-length inverted commas. But why is it that some ages characteristically demand prose? Why is a cultural shift toward prose so often figured as a decline from an earlier state of plenitude, the inauguration of a new aesthetic delinquency? In Pound's panorama, the new literature is to be industrially produced ("made with no loss of time"), populist (*kinema* suggests the spectacular new medium of film), and deficient ("not, not assuredly" poetical). In the course of the poem, Pound explicitly derives the shape of this narrative from the history of classical, particularly Greek, literature. "The pianola 'replaces' / Sappho's barbitos. / Christ follows Dionysus / . . . A tawdry cheapness / Shall outlast our days. / Even the Christian beauty / Defects" (III.3–14). In this miniature literary-historical narrative—a narrative, to be sure, shelled by the explosive irony of the surrounding stanzas—prose is conceived of principally as a late, lapsarian pathology. Classicism is inherently bound up with the question of poetics—and, hence, of prosaics.

Pound's primary concern is mischievously to mimic (and hence disrupt) the received romantic narrative of the history of literature in terms of a lamentable decline, from the lofty peaks of The Classical to the sterile, industrially repetitious imitation of later centuries. This story was central not just to literary history but also to the wider self-positioning of postindustrial, imperial Europe. In Victorian Britain, to take but one conspicuous example, jeremiads concerning the nonexistence of contemporary epic poetry constituted transfigurations of laments over the supposed weakness of contemporary nationalism and the infiltration of society by the new middle classes.¹ Romantic poetics intermeshed with national-aristocratic politics: the lack of "inspiration" in the contemporary world indicated the passing of a golden age of social order and poetic fecundity. The period of British classicism invoked in Victorian aesthetics signified in both literary and sociopolitical terms.

To take another example, Friedrich Nietzsche's *Birth of Tragedy*—like *Hugh Selwyn Mauberley* mimicking romanticism in spite of its own radicalism²—attributes the death of all poetry to the "Apolline spirit [*das Apollinische*]" that emerged in the late fifth century B.C.E. and in particular to Euripides. Nietzsche uses the term *poetry* in an extended sense, defining it with reference not to metrical language but to Dionysiac inspiration: he is quite aware that metrical verse continues to be written although "tragedy is dead! Poetry itself died with it!"³ But it is the Apolline spirit of rationalism and self-consciousness that does for true poetry, the spirit embodied particularly by Euripides ("Euripides the thinker, not the poet")⁴ and Socrates (that "despotic logician").⁵ Furthermore, all artistic forms from the death of Sophocles until the projected rebirth of tragedy through Wagnerian opera partake of this prosaic frigidity, which Nietzsche sees as crystallized particularly in the "Alexandrian" sensibility.⁶ The presence of Dionysiac poetry in a given historical period indicates not only a high concentration of inspirational effluence, however, but also a vigorous nationalism: the miring of tragedy in prosaic forms results from the "senescent phase of Hellenism,"⁷ just as its rebirth in the contemporary world marks the rejuvenation of the "German spirit."⁸

For Nietzsche, again, literary-historical narrativization purports to serve a self-consciously ideological and protreptic purpose.⁹ This knowing interlinking of poetics and nationalism is at once foregrounded in its clarity and chilling in its implications. Yet he is not alone: the most enduring feature of postromantic constructions of "the classical," particularly but not exclusively in relation to Greece, is the focus on the defining role of poetic inspiration. From "the Homeric world" through "the lyric age of Greece" and its subsequent "golden age" to "the Second

---

A version of this chapter first appeared as Whitmarsh 2005c; I am grateful to Princeton University Press for permission to reprint.

1. Jenkyns 1980, 21–38, especially 22–24.
2. See Silk and Stern 1981, 4, on the romantic background to *The Birth of Tragedy*. For my reading of Nietzsche here I am greatly indebted to Porter 2000a; 2000b.
3. Nietzsche 1993 (1872), 54.
4. Ibid., 58.
5. Ibid., 70.
6. Ibid., 86, 93.
7. Ibid., 56.
8. Ibid., 94–98, 110–13.
9. He refers to his discussion of tragedy as a "historical example" (ibid., 75); see also Silk and Stern 1981, 38, on the "supra-historical" aspect of the Apollonian-Dionysiac polarity.

Sophistic," the history of Greece has repeatedly been taxonomized in terms of its relationship, or lack thereof, with poetry.

Such narratives, however, need reconsideration. In the first place, the opposition between poetry and prose is not as secure as "separatist"[10] theorists might claim.[11] As Aristotle already recognized, the definitional criterion of poetry cannot be meter alone.[12] For sure, Aristotle resisted erasing the boundary, but some thinkers, ancient and modern alike, have indeed averred that the distinction is a matter more of negotiable emphasis than of essence.[13] If we take a more relativizing, pragmatist view of the dichotomy, then it follows that what we say about prosaic and poetical periods is less a pellucid transcription of self-evident historical fact and more a judgmental story—a story, moreover, that quickly betrays its cultural and historical agenda.

In this chapter, I focus particularly on the Greek literature of the first to third centuries C.E., the period now called the Second Sophistic, an infelicitous[14] term that carries a false implication that rhetoric's dominance was uncontested. Writers of this period, as we have seen in the immediately preceding chapters, continued to compose rich, multifaceted poetry, but prose writers—this is my principal argument in this chapter—represented their age, to borrow Pound's self-consciously hackneyed phrase, as "demanding" prose. Again, as with the romantic mythology of decline traced above, the form in which these demands presented themselves was committedly ideological and political. Like Pound, however, the writers we shall discuss also drew, as we shall see, on a rich set of resources to interrogate and destabilize the myth of poetic decline that demeaned their own status as latecomers.

Scholarship throughout much of the nineteenth and twentieth centuries has (in line with the romantic myth of decline) been too quick to fall into complicity with the most superficial reading of the prose kinematics of imperial Greek literature. The enervation of Hellenism is (we have often been told) implicated in the uninspired, prosaic literature of the period. The lack of political self-determination of Greeks under Roman rule has been held to explain the lack of "power" of their

---

10. For this term see Turner 1990, 257.

11. E.g., Jakobson 1987, 114: "Poetry is characterized by metaphor/combination, prose by metonymy/contiguity." See also ibid., 301.

12. "A historian is not distinguished from a poet by whether he composes metrically or not" (*Poet.* 1450a–b).

13. Especially Sartre 1967, 24–25 nn. 4–5 (despite the apparent contradiction on 10: "There is nothing in common between these two acts of writing except the movement of the hand which traces the letters"). For antiquity, see the views of Heracleodorus as denounced by Philodem., *Poet.* 1.199–204, with Janko 2000, 155–65.

14. See introduction.

literature.[15] The prose texts of this period also sprang from a dissolution of the Hellenic tradition: Lucian's status as a Semitic interloper is a notorious theme of nineteenth-century German writing,[16] and the Greek novel, according to Erwin Rohde (an enthusiastic acolyte of Nietzsche's, at least in their early days),[17] risks embodying "something altogether un-Greek [*das ganz Ungriechische*]."[18] For Rohde (who revived the use of the term) the Second Sophistic was an autumnal and ultimately doomed flowering of Hellenism (*Griechentums*) in response to the incursion of Oriental forms.[19] In particular, the Atticizing revival was prompted by the advent of Asianism, the "more weakly and effeminate daughter of the ancient, glorious, Attic art of oratory";[20] it was overly concerned with ornamentation and display and was not "manly [*männlich*]."[21]

Postmodernism has its own mythologies: in our antifoundationalist, millennial age, such broad-brush categorizations of literary *Geist* are routinely viewed as the follies of a less astute era. Classical scholarship is coming to terms with the provisional, strategic relativism of all classicizations, its own and antiquity's. "Belatedness," "posterity," and "secondariness" are taken as rhetorical effects rather than as historically descriptive.[22] The entire history of Greco-Roman literature (perhaps even including "father" Homer) is "late," in the sense of nonoriginary.[23] The idea that a prosaic period might symptomatize a decline from the classical is uncongenial, even quaint, in this context of hypertrophic discursive self-reflexivity.

I do not wish to take issue with this critical orthodoxy, which seems both intellectually responsible and politically serviceable. But I do want to observe that, for all that scholarship in the early twenty-first century may (properly) wish to distance itself from the overweening ideological and nationalist fervor of earlier generations, these nineteenth-century classicizations were not concocted ex nihilo. Nietzsche, Rohde, and the rest took the association between literary form and identity (manliness, sociocultural integrity, political power) from ancient authors, and although for sure they inflected it with their political preoccupations, that does not mean that such associations were innocent of ideology in the ancient

---

15. Rohde 1914, 323, on the lack of *Kraft*; elsewhere Rohde tells us that Greek oratory sank "along with freedom" (310).
16. See Holzberg 1988; Baumbach 2002, 201–43; Goldhill 2002a, 93–99.
17. See Silk and Stern 1981, 90–131, for Rohde's responses to *The Birth of Tragedy*.
18. Rohde 1914, 3.
19. Ibid., 313.
20. Ibid., 310.
21. Ibid., 311–12.
22. See especially Hinds 1998, 52–98; Feeney 1998, 57–63.
23. Bloom 1975, 33–34, already espouses the notion of universal epigonality, though it does insists on the exceptional, originary status of Homer.

sources. Literary-historical narratives such as the decline from poetry into prose are never simply wrong: they always reflect deeply, meaningfully, on the state of the world. This chapter, then, seeks to read antiquity's version of the aesthetic and political demands of a prosaic culture.

DIACHRONIES: THE POLITICS OF THE PAST

I am going to begin by coining a term, *prosography*, by which I mean the marked, stylized use of prose (and hence also the polemical renunciation of poetry). The remainder of this chapter will be devoted to this alone. Unlike prose, which is properly the subject of stylistics in the narrowest, most formalist sense, prosography is a matter of cultural and political significance: it comports a reflexiveness about the authoritative, embedded status of language and about the codification of the history of knowledge. To prosify is to proclaim the value of the archive, the accumulated weight of culturally sanctioned (and necessarily written) learning. In *The Order of Things*, his genealogy of modern thought, Michel Foucault argues (in the course of a chapter titled "The Prose of the World") for the junctural importance of the sixteenth century as a time when the supposedly natural relationship between words and things was questioned. Language was no longer a reflection or representation of the world but now a second-order form, enfolded on itself: "Knowledge ... consisted in relating one form of language to another form of language; in restoring the great, unbroken plain of words and things; in making everything speak."[24] Prose became a self-conscious marker of a historically new systematicity in the perception and construction of the world.

The composition and redaction of vast tracts of prosaic text are also hallmarks of Roman Greece, a self-consciously posterior literary culture[25] in which language was empowered in its ability to plot received knowledge.[26] The entire experiential world could be transcribed into text: landscape (Pausanias), seascape (Arrian in *Circumnavigation of the Black Sea*), dreams (Artemidorus), physiognomy (Polemo and Adimantus), the human body (Galen), the animal kingdom (Aelian), Roman history (Dionysius, Cassius Dio, and Herodian). Polymathy reigned as a form of supreme intellectual achievement (for example, the *Varied Histories* of Favorinus and Aelian; the *Sophists at Supper* of Athenaeus). It is important to remain aware of the complexity of the tessellation that constitutes this picture (to avoid the rhetoric of "cultural totality" that inhabits *The Order of Things*):[27] the Oppianic treatises

---

24. Foucault 1989a, 40.
25. Whitmarsh 2001, 41–47, with further references.
26. See Barton 1994b for a Foucauldian approach to science and power in Roman Greece.
27. Foucault 1989b, 16: "In *The Order of Things*, the absence of methodological signposting may have given the impression that my analyses were being conducted in terms of cultural totality."

on hunting and fishing, for example, are composed in verse. But the exceptional status of those texts, self-conscious innovations within this prosaic culture, serves to prove the rule, and anyhow, as an encyclopedic writer, Oppian invests no less in prosaic values for all that he employs the epic form.

Prosography is born of the rhetoric of institutionalized knowledge: it insistently narrates a diachronic transition from poetry to prose, a fundamentally self-aware articulation of (among other things) the passage of Greek culture from orality to the world of the text. Let us begin by considering Strabo's critique of Eratosthenes (third–second century B.C.E.) in the *Geography* (1.2.12–15), a work of massive erudition composed in the late first century B.C.E. Strabo, a "remarkably pro-Roman author,"[28] not only is a product of Augustan Rome's imperialist drive toward global mapping[29] but also directly synthesizes the increased geographical knowledge brought by large-scale Roman conquest.[30] Imperial conquest, underpinned by the rhetoric of civilizing humanism, invites a teleological view of history, and Strabo's work, eclipsing and rendering obsolete all his predecessors, is a massive monument to the triumph of historical progress.

But Strabo's self-positioning is more complex. His critique of his predecessor Eratosthenes does not simply mark the latter as primitive; it also accuses him of myopically progressivist vanity.[31] Eratosthenes's polemical approach to the Homeric texts was to chastise them for their "lies," decrying with the supercilious confidence of a more "scientific" age the supposed substitution of imaginative guesswork for hard facts. "You will find the location for the wanderings of Odysseus," he declared, "when you find the cobbler who stitched up [*surrhapsanta*] the bag of winds" (fr. a 16 Berger = Strab. 1.2.15). This bon mot subtly alludes to the figure of the rhapsode, or "stitcher of [epic] songs": implicitly, it correlates Homer the creator with a banausic functionary. More important to our purposes, however, is Eratosthenes's argument that poetry is necessarily naïve, inviting supplantation by the intellectual superiority of posterity. It is against this claim, not any obsolescent methodology or data, that Strabo most vigorously positions himself. With his compromised, bipartisan status as a Greek intellectual in Augustan Rome, Strabo wishes to maintain both the intellectual dominance of the Roman present over the past and the deeply enshrined sanctity of ancient Greek tradition.

We shall return presently to Strabo's critique of Eratosthenes, dramatizing as it does the central cultural and political tensions of the emergent Second Sophistic. But let us for now trace the beginnings of self-conscious prosography, in the

---

28. Swain 1996, 313.
29. Nicolet 1991.
30. In particular, he extensively used Posidonius, who was deeply implicated in the imperialist projects of the early to mid-first century B.C.E.; see Momigliano 1975, 32–33.
31. For the background to these debates see Romm 1992, 172–214; Clarke 1999, 262–64.

classical period. Geoffrey Lloyd has convincingly identified in the writings of the Greek scientists of the fifth century a self-consciously new cast of mind, an increasingly intense, agonistic self-positioning in opposition to mythical thought.[32] If the supposed passage from mythicism to rationality ("from *muthos* to *logos*," in Jean-Pierre Vernant's famous phrase)[33] does not have in practice the historical authority of an absolute rupture, it is nevertheless grounded in a series of insistently articulated discursive moves that troped prose writing as postmythical: lucid, contemporary, ingenuous.[34] The shadowy chroniclers Hecataeus of Miletus, Acousilaus of Argos, Hellanicus of Lesbos, and others adopted prose, we can guess, as a polemical marker of their modernity. Thucydides famously stakes a claim for a text that may be less pleasurable owing to its lack of mythical qualities ("to muthōdes") but is nonetheless "useful" (1.22.4). Plato's Socrates, even more famously, bans poets from his ideal city on the grounds that they possess only an ontologically inferior inkling of reality (*Rep.* 607b).[35]

Contemporary stylistics, moreover, increasingly associated poetic language with obfuscation. The distinction between poetry and prose was vigorously contested but always significant. Modern critics usually attribute the instigation of a formal taxonomy of their differences to Aristotle in the fourth century:[36] in his *Rhetoric*, he avers that poetical lexis emerged in order to conceal the foolishness of the thoughts of the earliest composers (1404a). But the parameters are clearly visible already in the fifth century. When Gorgias (in the fifth century) assimilates his prose to poetry, he is making a polemical point: his discourse partakes of both the hypermodernity of Sophistry and the overwhelming power conventionally attributed to poetry.[37] As Aristotle later recognizes disapprovingly, Gorgias also imports a substantial amount of poetic lexis into his rhetorical discourse, a further attempt at integrating the two registers (*Rhet.* 1404a24–29). This does not mean, however, that Gorgias or his contemporaries fail to distinguish adequately

---

32. Lloyd 1987, 56–70.

33. Vernant 1980, 186–207.

34. See especially Thomas 2000, which stresses the eclectic aspect of Herodotus's "rationalistic" drive.

35. For the ontological argument see Pl., *Rep.* 602d–3e, 605a–c.

36. Arist., *Rhet.* 1404a–b; *Poet.* 1447b13–20, 1451a36–b5. See, e.g., Too 1995, 32: "Prior to Aristotle, the majority of fifth- and fourth-century writers ... are so relaxed about generic differences that they even play down the gap between poetry and prose."

37. The assimilation is conventionally argued for (e.g., Bers 1984, 1; Too 1995, 32) from *Encomium to Helen* 11.9 DK ("I consider and define all poetry as prose [*logos*] with meter [*metron*]"). This is best interpreted as meaning that all language is equally powerful and that the presence or absence of meter is not intrinsically important: Gorgias is arguing from the well-known case of the impact of epic poetry on its audience to the likely effect of Paris's persuasive (prosaic) speech on Helen. The definition recurs at Pl., *Gorg.* 502c but here cleverly turned back on the Sophists: Socrates proposes to Callicles that rhetoric is no less than tragedy a form of flattery.

between poetry and prose but that epideictic (as opposed to forensic or public) oratory was definitively hybrid, generically constituted as poetic prose.[38]

Fourth-century Athens does, however, indeed mark an important new phase in the history of prosography. This was a culture increasingly conscious of the burden of the (intellectual, artistic, military, and political) past, a culture in which (for example) the focus of tragic performance shifted (from 386) from new works to reperformed classics and a new breed of politician emerged (most notably Demosthenes) whose expertise lay not so much in military action as in political theory.[39] As the self-definition of Athens shifted from hyperinnovative democracy to historically reflexive city of the classics, prose became increasingly associated with the self-conscious posterity of an archival culture.

The central figure here is Isocrates (an important model, as we shall see presently, for later writers), in the fourth century.[40] For Isocrates, "philosophy" (the term he uses to cover his own discourse, primarily ethical and political rhetoric) is a form of poetry, both stylistically and in terms of its effect. As he asserts in the *Antidosis*, philosophers compose *logoi* "very similar to musical, rhythmic compositions" (46); they use "particularly poetical and variegated lexis" and "particularly weighty and innovative ideas" (47); their speeches are listened to with no less pleasure than "compositions in meter" (47). In this respect, Isocrates is simply extending the epideictic ideals of the fifth-century Gorgias. But the *Evagoras* offers a different spin on this topos, constructing itself as an innovation, a prose encomium whereas (purportedly) previous encomiasts used poetry (8).[41] The difficulty of the challenge, Isocrates writes, lies in the number of "adornments [*kosmoi*]" (8) granted to poets: lexical, figural, and metrical tricks help them as they "entertain [*psukhagōgousi*]" audiences (10). But these are merely superficial devices: "If one were to leave the words and thoughts of the most respected poets and take away the meter, they would be revealed as much lesser than the respect in which they are currently held" (11).

These two works of Isocrates elucidate a crucial point. "Poetic prose" is not the result of a lack of clarity in the contemporary taxonomization of literature and certainly does not manifest the vestiges of an Archaic sensibility; it is, rather, a deliberate and artful attempt to forge a new genre, in the agonistic struggle for

---

38. Denniston 1950, 17–18, is good on the technical aspects but tends to overstate the threat of "contagion" to nonepideictic genres (especially on 16).

39. On tragedy see Easterling 1997, 212–13; testament to this shift is the inscription commemorating Astydamas, which laments that he was born later than his competitors and cannot catch up (*FGE* pp. 33–34 = Astydamas fr. 60 T 2a *TGrF*). For Demosthenes and the new politicians see Harding 1987.

40. Too 1995, 32–34.

41. Ibid., 33–34, notes the conventional and rhetorical nature of such appeals to innovation in Isocrates.

literary identity in the present, from existing literary taxonomies. If Isocrates is inconsistent in his approach (sometimes appropriating, sometimes distancing himself from the power of poetry), this marks the flexibility of his methods and the malleability of his material, not the impotence of the contemporary critical vocabulary.

Isocrates's struggle with his "anxiety of influence"[42] rhetorically appropriates his representation of the relationship between poetry and prose. The addition of prose to a preexistent genre (encomium) constitutes his attempt to innovate within a tradition already freighted with (and overdetermined by) the classics.[43] Prose is necessarily the discourse of posterity, but it also, at least in Isocrates's hopes, offers the possibility of a rebirth, the (re)invention of an origin. Even the apologetic defense of prose as a suitable medium, however, marks the provocative (and no doubt ludic) tendentiousness of the claim.

To Isocrates (and to the intense literary culture that spawned him) can be attributed, therefore, the invention of a seminal discursive move: the self-reflexive meditation on prose writing's always-already-inscribed historical posterity. It is hard to plot the immediate impact of this decisive phase in the history of prosography, owing to the limited amount of extant Hellenistic prose. Although the category of Hellenistic literature is sometimes limited to poetry (partly the legacy of its reception among the neoteric poets of first-century B.C.E. Rome), the increased codification and institutionalization of learning in the Library and Museum of Alexandria also ascribed a new set of values to prose writing.[44] The most significant loss (more significant, perhaps, than even the works of Eratosthenes) is Callimachus's *Pinakes* (or *Tables of All Those Who Were Eminent in Every Kind of Education [Paideia] and of Their Writings, in 120 Books*), a massive prose work to mirror the cosmic rhetoric of the Ptolemies and the global literary appropriation symbolized by the library (for which it served as a critical inventory).[45] But prosaic voices are also discernible in the poetry of the period: the well-known self-consciousness of that verse derives from its importing of prose concerns (textual and literary criticism but also geography, history, astronomy, medicine, animal lore, and so forth). Prose jags into the mellifluous serenity of poetry, insistently reminding readers of the distance between the inspired classics of the past and their scholarly re-creations in the present, between mainland Greece and Alexandria, between Helicon and the librarian's desk.

42. Bloom 1997.

43. Poetry expresses anxiety about this as early as the classical period: see Choerilus of Samos *SH* 317; above, n. 39, on Astydamas.

44. E.g., Neil Hopkinson's *Hellenistic Anthology* (1988) contains only poetic works. On the Library and the Museum, see especially Pfeiffer 1968, 98–104; Fraser 1972, 1.312–35; Too 2010.

45. The only extant fragments are snippets (frs. 429–53 Pfeiffer). See further Blum 1991, 182–88; for Callimachus's other prose works, Pfeiffer 1968, 134–36.

Hellenistic Alexandria, for all that writers of the Roman Greek period often neglected its literature, was a crucial staging post in the history of prosography, because it forged a now indissociable link between prose writing and institutions (a process that had already begun in the fourth century with Aristotle's Lyceum but was elevated to a different level in Alexandria). But let us return (or, rather, once again propel forward) to Strabo. In this context, where the colonial masters patronize learning, where wealthy Romans now largely appropriate and patronize libraries,[46] the teleological historical narrative that prosography implies is also implicated in the politics of cultural definition. Greeks who write prose position themselves in a complex relationship with both the imperial, archive-controlling present and the traditional, verse-dominated Greek past.

We recall that Strabo criticizes his predecessor for a too brief dismissal of the intellectual value of poetry and contends that there is indeed a case for Homer's rationality (or "rhetoric," as he puts it, defining this as "rationality [*phronēsis*] expressed through language [*logoi*]," 1.2.5). In the course of this argument, Strabo claims there is an essential continuity, along the diachronic axis, between poetry and prose:

> Prose (or at least artful prose) is, so to speak, an imitation [*mimēma*] of poetic discourse. For the art of poetry was the first to emerge into public prominence and regard. Then Cadmus, Pherecydes, Hecataeus, and the like wrote, imitating it but abandoning the meter while retaining the other features of poetry. Then later generations successively stripped away some of these and brought poetry down to the present state, as though from a great height. Similarly one might say that comedy took its structure from tragedy but descended from tragedy's height into the state that is currently called prosaic [*logoeidēs*]. (1.2.6)

This passage, with its narrative of cultural decline, positions Strabo in a double relationship with the past: condemned by history to posterity but sensitive (unlike Eratosthenes) to the meaning and values of the classics. I shall have more to say in the next section about the vertical imagery of this passage; for now I wish to concentrate on the temporal pattern it maps out. In one sense, Strabo merely makes explicit what Isocrates implies in his narrative of the emergence of "artful" prose subsequent to poetry. But genealogy also has a specific rhetoric, and it is important

---

46. See Diod. Sic. 1.4.2–3; Plut., *Aem. Paul.* 28; Ath., *Deipn.* 2b–3d; further Whitmarsh 2001, especially 9–16. The history of Roman libraries is the subject of a forthcoming study by Matthew Nicholls and a collection of essays edited by Jason König and Greg Woolf (see for now Fantham 1996, 34–36). The multiple forms of (symbolic, economic, political) connection between libraries and Roman patronage are striking. T. Flavius Pantaenus, for example, dedicated his library at Athens to Trajan, Athena Polias, and the city of Athens (Merritt 1946, 233; Oliver 1979 for discussion), thus placing it under the signs of both Athens and Rome.

to consider precisely what values are being attached to poetry and prose. Strabo contrasts oral and written literature: Cadmus and so forth "wrote," while the phrase used of the work of the early epicists, "parēlthen es to meson" (translated here as "emerge into public prominence"), implies coming forward to address the assembled people. The posterior, graphematic literature is, moreover, presented as an "imitation," a second-order, derivative, atrophied echo of the plenitude of poetry.

The representations of poetry as the primal form of "artful" writing and as an originally public-performative genre are interrelated: both mark (in Strabo's idealization) the undefiled immediacy of poetry as the product of a community. To borrow Jacques Derrida's conceptualization in *Of Grammatology* of the relationship (according to traditional metaphysics) between speech and writing, Strabo presents prose as "supplementary" to originary poetry.[47] This status is ambiguous: the supplement marks both the fruition and the erasure of the origin. Prose yields the rigorous argumentative resources that allow Strabo to prove Eratosthenes wrong and to appreciate the "rhetorical" qualities of Homeric poetry, but it is simultaneously an abasement and a destructive "stripping away" of true literature.

So Strabo's narrativization entails a concomitant "classicization" of the poetical past in a manner unparallelled in Isocrates. For the latter, prose is a resource to facilitate the escape from the tyranny of poetic tradition: his claims to priority in his venture ("no one else before has attempted . . . ," *Evag.* 8) may be overstated, but they articulate the urgency of the contemporary choice between the two forms. Strabo, on the other hand, presents himself as irredeemably consigned by an unrelenting historical teleology to a culture of prose. For this Augustan Greek, as we have noted, prose is the defining marker of a historically determined double bind: the massive resources of Roman imperialism make the archival project possible but also enforce the distance between the Greco-Roman present and the (imagined) presence of the autonomous Greek past.

As the sense of the discrete secondariness of Roman Greek literary culture gradually coalesces in later writers, they amplify this self-imposed historiographical schema in interesting new ways. There are manifold strategies for approaching the problem of literary posterity,[48] one of which may be simply to assert cultural continuity between the classical period and the later one. Thus Maximus of Tyre, retracing but simplifying Strabo's position, claims that Homer was a philosopher

---

47. Derrida 1976, especially 141–64. The various references to the inventors of prose also imply that poetic discourse was an earlier, more natural phenomenon, in contrast to supervening prose: Pherecydes is widely cited as having composed the first prose narrative and Cadmus or Hecataeus the first prose history. See Plin., *NH* 7.205; *Suda*, s.vv. "Hecataeus son of Hegesander," "Pherecydes" (with Schibli 1990 on the biographical tradition).

48. Whitmarsh 2001, 41–89.

(i.e., a rationalist like "us") in every significant sense (*Orations* 4, 26) and that his adoption of poetry was merely a superficial formal technique designed to please his unsophisticated contemporaries (see especially 4.3). Other writers, however, take richer and more nuanced approaches to the question of cultural definition through prose. I turn now to the second century C.E. and in particular to two texts, Plutarch's *On the Pythian Oracles* and Aelius Aristides's *Hymn to Sarapis*. The first is a dialogue, set in Delphi, in which the interlocutors treat primarily of the question of why the Delphic oracle has ceased to prophecy in verse.[49] The second is a prose hymn to the Greco-Egyptian god, including an important, programmatic section on the reasons why hymnists traditionally adopt verse.

The significant part of Plutarch's dialogue, for our purposes, is Theon's long, concluding speech (403a–9c). This is not the place for a detailed treatment of the many theological and philosophical issues this work raises about the nature of prophecy and inspiration.[50] What interests me in particular is Theon's (and Plutarch's) attempt to rescue prose as a medium from the opprobrium it has inherited and to counter simultaneously the perceived preeminent status given to poetry. The butt of Theon's mild-mannered attack is Boethus the Epicurean, who (according to another speaker, Sarapion) is the only post-Empedoclean philosopher to write in verse (402e): as Theon comments with teasing irony, "through you, poetry once more returns from its exile to upright, noble philosophy, castigating the young" (402f). Boethus has already been rebuked for his atheistic beliefs (396e–97e) and has mocked Diogenianus, the impressive young visitor (398d): Theon's speech, while containing a series of important programmatic passages, also constitutes an ad hominem put-down of this outmoded exponent of verse philosophy.

Theon's central argument is that it is not the god but his human agents who make the choice of poetry or prose (404b–5a). The general[51] "change [*metabolē*]" between poetry and prose results not from any change in divine favor but from a change "for the better" in the practice of humans (406b). Theon consistently represents poetry as an accretion that is necessary only in certain circumstances. Prose offers "intelligibility and plausibility" (406f), "persuasion with clarity" (407a), and "simplicity" (409c); poetry "shrouds" (407e, 408c) the simple truth in mystifying obscurity (407a–b). This "change," moreover, is linked to the developing sociopolitical conditions of Greece. The "men of the past [*hoi palaioi*]" needed to disguise the oracle's meaning in verse for fear of the "mighty cities, kings, and tyrants" who approached Delphi for advice on weighty issues (407d). Theon

49. Detailed commentary in Schröder 1990.
50. For discussion and further literature see ibid., 25–59 (particularly on sources and arguing for Plutarch's eclecticism).
51. Theon stresses that prose oracles were also given in the past and that verse oracles are also given in the present (403f, 405e).

continues, "As for the present circumstances about which the god is consulted, I welcome and approve them: there is a profound peace and tranquillity, war has ceased, and there are no longer cases of exile, civic strife, and tyranny nor indeed any other of the sicknesses and woes afflicting Greece that called for, as it were, hypersophisticated [*polupharmakōn*] and superfluous [*perittōn*] powers" (408b).

In stark contrast to Strabo, Plutarch represents poetry as supplementary, in the sense that the need for poetical responses symptomatizes a deviation from Greece's proper state of calm.[52] Indeed, he figures poetry as a form of deviant excess in language. *Pharmakon* (at the root of *polupharmakōn*, here translated as "hypersophisticated") usually refers to drugs, dyes, or poisons: in general, to artificial confections. It is, moreover, the word Plato employs to stigmatize writing in the *Phaedrus* (and a central term for Derrida's discussion of Plato's logocentrism).[53] *Perittos* is an equally eloquent term, tracing a complex semantic arc that includes notions of extravagance, conspicuousness, prodigiousness, and excess. Earlier in his speech, Theon similarly refers to oracular practice, consequent on "the change," as having jettisoned "the superfluous [*to perittōn*]" (406d). In that case, he develops a striking metaphor to elucidate this return to the natural: "it [oracular practice] took off its golden hairnets and doffed its soft frocks; moreover, I imagine, it cut off its hair so luxuriant and untied its tragic buskin" (406d). Superfluity is imaged as barbarian and effeminate, a deviation from the manliness of received Hellenism.

Theon's speech might be interpreted as a manifesto for a prosaic culture. Delphi is synecdochic of Greece,[54] and the failure of the Pythia to prophecy in verse is paradigmatic of the state of Hellenic culture. The common interpretation (as Diogenianus reports) explains this phenomenon by recourse to a narrative of decline: "Either the Pythia does not approach the place in which the sanctuary is located or the spirit [*pneuma*] of the place is absolutely quenched and its power has departed" (402b). This is a Strabonic reading of the politics of prose in terms of dissolution and decline. Theon's sparkling corrective to this common belief, however, presents both a challenge to the received privileging of poetic truth and a powerful assertion of the vigor of contemporary literary culture. Yet this should not be taken as anything as straightforward as Plutarch's "belief." Embedded in a dialogue, with no authorial judgment (indeed, with no subsequent reaction—the dialogue just stops), this speech constitutes one of a number of voices vying in the competitive intellectual climate that Plutarch dramatizes. Though it is striking and appealing (in that it is uplifting, celebratory, and genealogically self-aware) and effectively

---

52. I am unconvinced that the focus on (specifically) Greece's return to a state of tranquillity demonstrates that this passage is "definitely not focused on Rome" (Swain 1996, 180): there is surely an echo of the *pax Romana*.

53. Pl., *Phdr.* 274e; Derrida 1981.

54. See, e.g., ps.-Luc., *Nero* 10, with Whitmarsh 1999, 154–55.

trounces the irritant Boethus, it is nevertheless a partial and carefully circumscribed response to the issue of literary posterity.

The most robust response to the traditional prioritizing of poetry comes in the course of Aelius Aristides's *Hymn to Sarapis*, especially in its programmatic prologue, where the orator defends the project of prosographic hymns. This text is arguably influenced by Plutarch's dialogue[55] and certainly displays a continuity of preoccupations. In literary terms, however, its primary model is Isocrates's *Evagoras*, discussed above: the opening *makarismos*, expressing staged envy at the liberty of poets, builds visibly on the fourth-century orator's account of the indulgence traditionally granted to these figures (*Evag.* 8–11).[56] Isocrates provides Aristides with a model, legitimated by its canonical status, for the self-conscious employment of prose as an innovative affront to tradition. The ironical apologia becomes (as so often) an advertisement of idiosyncratic excellence. In that respect, Aristides articulates a claim precisely analogous to that of Isocrates but, as we shall see, subtly adapts the topos to mark a different genealogical positionality.

At one crucial point, Aristides argues that prose predates poetry:

> But what is more, it is more natural for a human being to employ prose [*pezos logos*], just as it is more natural, I suppose, to walk than to be carried on a chariot. For it is not the case that verse appeared first and then prose and dialectic were discovered, nor did poets appear first and set down the words that should be used for things; rather, the words existed, as did prose, and then for the sake of pleasure and entertainment the art of poetry (the fabricator of these things) came on the scene later. So if we honor nature we should also be honoring the command and will of the gods, and if, as even the poets assert, that which is former and older is better, we should be doing the gods more honor if we addressed them with this style of language—after all, it was they who laid all these things down. (8)

Aristides's argument from nature depends on a pun on the standard Greek phrase for *prose* in this period. *Logos pezos* literally means "pedestrian language" (I shall discuss this further in the subsequent section): in matters of literature and transport alike, pedestrianism is always the more natural option. This ingenious, sophistical appeal to "nature" seeks to inscribe prose at the origin of language, countering the traditional ascription of primacy to poetry. If we place this passage next to Strabo's account discussed earlier, the perspective subtly reorients: Strabo qualifies his discussion as referring specifically to "artful prose," which postdates

---

55. At line 7, Aristides refers to prophecy, noting that most contemporary oracles are given without meter. The argument that speakers should praise the god in accordance with their "powers [*dunameis*]" suggests an allusion to *On the Pythian Oracles* 404b, where Theon proposes that the form of poetry is a function of the capacity of the god's "instrument [*organon*]," not of the power of the god.

56. Russell 1990b, 201.

poetry in Greece's literary genealogy, whereas Aristides refers to prose tout court, the "natural language" of communication. By shifting the parameters in this way, Aristides (like Plutarch) narrativizes the phase of the dominance of poetry as an excrescent deviation from the "naturalness" of prose. But as ever, the appeal to "the natural" is conducted from an eminently sophisticated position.

Both Plutarch and Aristides testify to the second century's increasingly coalescent self-diagnosis as a discrete historical period, characterized by prosography. It is notable that this self-diagnosis is articulated in literary terms. Recent scholarship has tended to treat this period with regard to its political conditions, especially the advent of Roman domination, but this does not always chime exactly with contemporary narratives. This is not to deny that there is a political aspect to these narratives. Prosography, as we have seen, is institutionalized in and mediated through the archive of knowledge, now policed, in part at least, by Rome (through libraries and patronage), and at the same time it comments (knowingly, ironically, and from a distance but also engagedly, sympathetically, and passionately) on the Greek cultural past. Prose is the literary space where the accumulated knowledge of a tradition folds back on itself, the medium for a self-reflexive meditation on Greek identity. With a certain knowing wit, Plutarch and Aristides engage in revisionist history, militating against conventional accounts of the declining vigor of Greek culture. Both are, of course, learned and sympathetic "classicists," in that they are (and expect their readers to be) saturated in the literature of the privileged past, but what is particularly significant is their urgent, ongoing *questioning* of the self-evidence of the relationship between past and present, of the contours that classicizing should adopt.

SYNCHRONIES: THE POSITIONALITY OF PROSE

The narrativization of Greek literary history is, as we have seen, political, in the sense in which all historiography tells an ideologically invested story. But I want to suggest in this section that there are more political prizes at stake here and that these become apparent if we analyze matters on the synchronic plane. What issues of contemporary currency in the second century C.E. did the debates over poetry and prose transvalue?

Let us begin at the borders between poetry and prose, since borders are always sites of political tension. What is at risk when transgression threatens? I focus here primarily on poetic prose rather than prosaic poetry (a category that is of less central importance to the present project).[57] The former is often constructed as a

---

57. See the discussion of the Augustan Dionysius of Halicarnassus in *On the Arrangement of Words*: most people regard the prosaic as a fault in poetry, although a certain form of "elaborate and artistic" prosiness should be distinguished (26). It is sometimes argued (e.g., Freudenburg 1993, 183–84) that

monstrous transgression and (significantly) often imaged in political and ideological terms. As early as the fourth century, in a canonical discussion, Aristotle argues that the importing of poetic style into prose gives it a "foreign/exotic [*xenos/xenikos*]" inflection (*Rhet.* 1404b).[58] The comparison between literary and political identities is explicit: "People have the same response to style as they do when comparing foreigners [*xenoi*] with fellow citizens" (1404b). This response is not universal rejection; indeed this exoticism can generate "wondrousness [*to thaumaston*]." But such techniques must be used only subtly and in moderation. In general, the primary virtue of prose lies for Aristotle in its "clarity [*saphēneia*]," which the use of "proper [*kurios*]" or "familiar [*oikeios*]" words best serves. The last two terms further enrich the subjacent seam that transvalues literary self and other into civic terms. Genres are construed as geopolitical territories, and any intermingling constitutes an act of invasion.

In second-century theory, prose poetry is acceptable for erotic discourse[59] but castigated in more "serious," "proper" genres. Particularly relevant here is Lucian's *How to Write History*, composed (in 165 C.E.?) in the wake of the Parthian campaigns of Lucius Verus. The particular butts of Lucian's attack are the historians who commemorated these campaigns in (to his eyes) an inappropriately "poetical" form:

> Moreover, people of this kind seem ignorant of the fact that there are different aims and special rules for poetry and poems on the one hand and history on the other. For poetry has unalloyed[60] freedom and only one law: whatever the poet wants. For he is inspired and possessed by the Muses, and if he wants to yoke a chariot of winged horses or if he makes others go running over water or the tops of corn, no one cavils. When the poets' Zeus drags up and suspends earth and sea on a single cord, no one fears that the cord might snap and that everything might fall down in a heap. And if he wants to praise Agamemnon, there is no one to stop the latter from being like Zeus in his head and eyes, and like Zeus's brother Poseidon in his chest, like Ares in his girdle: the son of Atreus and Ares has to be entirely a compound of all the gods, for Zeus, Poseidon, or Ares alone would not be enough to do justice to his beauty. If history, on the other hand, takes on board such flattery, what does it become other than prose poetry? It is stripped of the latter's majestic sonority but displays all the other mumbo jumbo unclothed in metrical form, and all the more conspicuously for that. So it is a great—no, an *enormous*—wickedness if one cannot distinguish between the territory of [*khōrizein*] history and that of poetry but imports

---

Horace's *Satires* construct themselves as prose poetry (see especially the "pedestrian Muse," 2.6.17), but a case can be made that satire and iambic are "pedestrian" in a different sense: see my discussion later in the chapter of Callimachus, *Aetia* fr. 112.

58. Isocrates also mentions poetry's description of its subject matter with words "now foreign [*xenois*], now new, now metaphorical" (*Evag.* 9).

59. See Hermog., *Id.* pp. 336–38 Rabe.

60. Reading *akratos* with Du Soul ("*Fort. recte*," comments Macleod).

[*epeisagein*] into history the embellishments of the other: myth, encomium, and exaggeration in these matters. It is as though one were to take one of those mighty, oaken athletes and dress him in purple and all the apparel of a courtesan and rub red and white makeup into his face. By Heracles, how ridiculous [*katagelastos*] one would make him by besmirching him with that adornment! (8)

This discussion of prose poetry meaningfully activates the territorial metaphor I proposed above ("borders"): the great ("no, . . . *enormous*") wickedness lies in a confusion of spatially demarcated properties. It is necessary to "distinguish between the territory of" the two genres and not to "import" from one into the other. Lucian polices the boundaries with self-righteous certainty, not least because so many core cultural values are implicated. In particular, prose is here constructed as a manly form, correlated with the vigor of an athlete. Poetry, on the other hand, is repeatedly linked with (deceptive, and female) clothing and adornment and in the concluding metaphor equates with the garb and makeup of a hetaera. To conflate these two would be "ridiculous," as Lucian tells us in the next sentence: an index not only of the cultural importance of the barrier between poetry and prose but also of the central role of the "ridiculing" satirist in maintaining it. (The author's vigorous maintenance of generic boundaries here does not, however, prevent him from crossing them in other literary works.)[61]

Despite its femininity, however, poetry has a certain power, which is imaged in markedly political terms. It has "unalloyed freedom [*akratos eleutheria*]" and the quasi-autocratic "one law," namely the will of the poet. These phrases evoke the canonical definition of monarchy, namely "rule without accountability."[62] The poet's high-handed approach to the manipulation of plausibility and truth is linked with political authoritarianism. It is notable in this connection that Lucian also accuses writers of prose poetry of toadying to emperors, of producing autocratic texts in the service of autocrats.

This association between poetry and elite sociopolitical station ramifies into a series of puns on the Greek phrase *pezos logos*, "pedestrian speech," the standard expression from the late second century B.C.E. for prose writing. The earliest uses of *pezos* apparently mean "poetry unaccompanied by music," and the reference to

---

61. Notably in *Zeus the Tragedian*: see previous chapter. On Lucian's hybrid "poetic prose" see further Camerotto 1998, 130–36, 213–18.

62. Hdt. 3.80; Pl., *Leg.* 761e; [Pl.,] *Def.* 415b; Arist., *Pol.* 1295a20; Diod. Sic. 1.70.1; *SVF* 3.267 (65), 3.617 (158); Dio Chr. 3.5, 56.5, 56.11 (in this last passage, as Murray 1971, 502–3, points out, Dio overturns the accepted definition by pointing out that Agamemnon is accountable—to Nestor). "Rule without accountability" is "the accepted definition of kingship by Hellenistic times" (Murray 1971, 300; see also Schofield 1991, 138–39 n. 4).

prose is seemingly extrapolated from there.[63] But *pezos* is a neon metaphor signaling its openness to interpretation. This image tantalizes (not least with its proximity to the heavily overwrought puns on metrical "feet" found in the Roman elegists—but that may be another matter).

Even in the sources that use the word *pezos* in a literary sense and predate its specific reference to prose, the metaphor invites detailed unpacking. In the so-called epilogue to the *Aetia*, Callimachus writes (in the early third century B.C.E.), "I shall approach the pedestrian [*pezos*] pasturage of the Muses."[64] Older scholars took this as a reference to a supposed decision to write prose, but there is nothing to suggest that Callimachus gave up poetry (and this would constitute the earliest use of *pezos* in this sense by two centuries): more recent opinion has inclined toward a foreshadowing of the *Iambi*.[65] The central point here is the pronounced imagery of social differentiation in this statement of poetic choice. *Pezos* is a military metaphor, suggesting the infantry as opposed to the cavalry: Homeric discourse, notably, repeatedly polarizes the low-status *pezoi* and the high-status *hippēes*.[66] By marking himself out as a foot soldier rather than a cavalryman, Callimachus is emphasizing his turn toward the "low" and away from the "lofty" (in contrast with, for example, the charioteering verse of Sappho, Parmenides, and indeed what we call the prologue to the *Aetia*).[67] But the word *pezos* also deviously recaptures, as it were, the high ground: a poet is by definition a "pedestrian" traveler, whose paths are mapped out by metrical "feet."

So for the Alexandrian poet ironically abasing his forthcoming poetic project, *pezos* constitutes a cleverly allusive means of proclaiming (and hence revaluing) low status. By the time of Strabo, this metaphorical field polarizing charioteers and foot soldiers has been mapped securely onto the poetry-prose opposition.[68] Let us return to the passage of Strabo cited above. Using the phrase *pezos logos*, Strabo images the decline of literary prose from its origins as an imitation of poetry as a

---

63. For discussion and references see Cameron 1995, 144; Asper 1997, 60. In other contexts, traveling "on foot" might even imply the deployment of verse (i.e., metrical "feet"): see Asper 1997, 33 n. 50, on Pind. fr. 206 Snell-Maehler. The earliest (though Demetr., *De eloc.* 167 may be earlier) use of *pezos* to mean "prose" of which I am aware comes in the course of the recently edited verse inscription from Salmacis, which describes Herodotus as "the prose Homer of history [*ton pezon en historiaisin Omēron*]" (43). See Isager 1998 for editio princeps; also Lloyd-Jones 1999a; Lloyd-Jones 1999b. The inscription is dated to the second century B.C.E., probably to the later part.

64. Fr. 112.9 Pfeiffer, playing of course on *nomos* = "pasturage"/"tune."

65. Compare Horace's "pedestrian Muse" (*Serm.* 2.6.17), cited above, n. 57; see Pfeiffer 1949, 1.125; more recently Cameron 1995, 154–56; Asper 1997, 58–62; Harder 2012, 2.866–70.

66. *Il.* 5.13, 8.59, 11.150; *Od.* 9.50, 17.436.

67. Sapph. fr. 1.7–12; Parm. fr. 1.1–10; Call., *Aet.* fr. 1.27.

68. For this pervasive image, see Plut., *De aud.* 16c; Luc., *Bis acc.* 33 (a prose form—Platonic dialogue—as "charioteering"), *Pro imag.* 18, *Menipp.* 1; further Norden 1898, 1.33–35 n. 3.

descent "as though from a great height," just as "comedy took its structure from tragedy but descended from tragedy's height [*hupsos*] into the state that is currently called prosaic." The discussion ends with a sentence not cited in the earlier section: "And the fact that language without meter is called pedestrian [*pezos*] indicates that it has descended from some great height [*hupsos*] or chariot to the ground" (1.2.6).

The dominant metaphor in Strabo's assessment of the relative merits of poetry and prose is one of height. Prose is a lesser form, according to him, because of its "low" status. Poetry, by contrast, is associated with height or "sublimity [*hupsos*]," a term that can bespeak (for example in the pseudo-Longinian text *On the Sublime*) either literary or social grandeur.[69] No doubt mindful of this duality, Strabo proceeds to distance poetry from social elitism by linking it with democracy and prose with oligarchy: the former is more "useful to the people [*dēmōphelēs*]" and "capable of filling theaters," whereas philosophy (the subset of prosography on which he concentrates) speaks "to the few [*oligoi*]" (1.2.8). Poetry is, for Strabo, a "high" form—but not in the sense that tyrants and oligarchs are "high."

Yet as we have seen with Lucian, the association between poetry and monarchy does not disappear, particularly as we approach the prosaic self-celebration of the second century C.E. In Plutarch's dialogue *On the Pythian Oracles*, Theon reinterprets the imagery of descent from a chariot as an expunging of luxuriant excess: just as prophecy "took off its golden hairnets and doffed its soft frocks," opting for "simplicity" instead of "richness [*poluteleia*]," so "history climbed down from its meters as though from a chariot, and truth was distinguished from the mythical especially by pedestrian language [*pezos*]" (406d–e). In this case, the "height" of poetry closely correlates with its soft, and (in the Greek imagination) implicitly tyrannical, excesses.

The specific accusations of tyranny recur in Aristides's *Hymn to Sarapis*. Aristides too, as we have seen, reclaims the metaphorical polarity of "the pedestrian" and "the charioteer": walking (i.e., writing prose) is "more natural," less presumptuous than riding (8). Poets, on the other hand, are "tyrants [*turannoi*] of ideas" (1), "emperors [*autokratores*] of whatever they wish to say" (13). The dominant force of his critique of poetry centers on the arbitrary power that society concedes to poets: "They are permitted to set up every time whatever themes (false, and sometimes unconvincing) they like" (1); "we have yielded to them" the power to address the gods, as though they were priests (4); the right to compose hymns has been "yielded" to poets alone (13). Prose, however, is for Aristides more subject to the requirements of civic solidarity: "It is not permitted to tell the poets' riddles or anything of that kind, nor to embolden ourselves

---

69. See Innes 1995 on this equivocation.

to add in material irrelevant to the matter in hand; rather, we must remain truly in a state of moderation [*metron*] and always remember ourselves, as though keeping to our station in a military campaign" (13). The image of the prosographer as a nontyrannical, responsible citizen-soldier is here underlined by the pun on *metron*. This is the conventional word for "meter," a definitive feature of poetry, but, Aristides tells us, it "truly" means "measure" or "moderation," the idealized quality of a proper Greek citizen, and is hence more appropriate to prose.[70]

At issue in these debates over the respective political affiliations of prose and poetry is the question of the civic utility of literature. Literature "should" be Hellenic, manly, and "democratic" (a term that calls for carefully nuanced interpretation in this age of Roman-dominated oligarchy).[71] These appeals to tradition are not, however, simply inert, "theoretical" statements reclaiming prose from centuries of prejudice: they are also cultural performatives, strategic attempts to erect concrete definitional boundaries in the fluidity of coeval literary culture. That is to say, the targets of this antipoetic prejudice are not straightforwardly Homer and the tragedians (who are, in general literary culture, as widely appreciated as ever) but (also) contemporary rivals whose profiles can be tainted with accusations of exoticism, effeminacy, and tyranny. Rhetoric is a zero-sum game, and the opportunity to impugn others to one's own advantage is never passed up.

I have argued in this section that second-century writers exploited the poetry-prose polarity in order to map out contemporary cultural, sexual, and political identities. This matrix of ideologies depends on an underlying sense of the dangerous contagiousness of alternative identities: men can be infected with femininity, Greeks with Oriental barbarism, citizens with tyrannical fervor. Analogously, the frontier between prose and verse is not intraversible: certain types of text put this boundary at risk, importing from the one into the other. Such shrill, dogmatic moralizing explains why prose-poeticism is rarely defended. Like "Asianism"[72]

---

70. This pun is first developed in section 11 of the hymn, a passage with numerous difficulties of interpretation. See especially Russell 1990b, 204–5, on the pun here.

71. See, e.g., Starr 1952 for the appropriation of the language of democracy to describe the Roman principate.

72. A problematic concept: although Cicero apparently alludes to the idea (Swain 1996, 24), the term as such does not appear in extant Latin literature until the late first century C.E. (Quint., *Inst. or.* 12.10.12, 14; Tac., *Dial.* 18.4). See most recently Hidber 1996, 30–44, and Swain 1996, 22–24, both with bibliography. In extant Greek, the only direct evidence is Dionysius's reference to the emergence of bad rhetoric from "an Asian pit" (*On the Ancient Orators* 1.7); a pair of titles attributed to Dionysius's contemporary Caecilius, however, are strongly suggestive (*How Attic Emulation Differs from Asian* and *Against the Phrygians*, frs. 6, 11 Ofenloch). This Atticism-Asianism contrast appears to be more generally cultural than the narrowly linguistic focus of the earlier Romans. In the nineteenth century,

and (to a lesser extent) "Sophistry,"[73] "poetic prose" serves principally as an evanescent scare image, a bogey that allows the speaker to plot a rhetorical position by contrast in the reassuringly familiar locus of traditionally regulated identities.

It would be overly simplistic, however, to claim that the prosaic culture of the second century was straightforwardly antipoetic. For a start, poetry remained the primary medium of childhood education, and even such committed prosophiles as Plutarch prescribed it as such (against Plato's advice). Poetry was also the object of educated interest, with varying degrees of philosophical commitment: from Heraclitus's *Homeric Questions* through Dio Chrysostom's eleventh oration (*That Troy Was Not Captured*) and Philostratus's *Heroicus* (see ch. 7) to Porphyry's *On the Cave of the Nymphs*, prosographers explored the vagaries of the poetical canon. Moreover, despite the apparent vehemence of the strictures against poetry, numerous prose texts from this period are highly "poetical" in lexis and rhythms. This is perhaps unsurprising in the case of erotic texts such as Longus's *Daphnis and Chloe:* the risqué subject matter is matched by a venture into "improper" stylistics.[74] Yet even in the prima facie more normative genre of oratory, poeticisms abound.[75] What the best writers know is that the thrill of literature comes from an ability to transgress the rules and get away with it. Such writers are what Pierre Bourdieu would call virtuosi: "Only a virtuoso with a perfect command of his 'art of living' can play on all the resources inherent in the ambiguities and uncertainties of behaviour and situation in order to produce the actions appropriate to each case, to do that of which people will say 'There was nothing else to be done', and do it the right way."[76] Virtuoso masters of the "art of writing" play a dangerous game, introducing poetic words and rhythms, neologisms, and exoticisms into the manly austerity of Greek prose. But the more dangerous the game, the higher the stakes: the agonistic, status-dominated context of epideictic oratory was particularly susceptible to such high-risk experimentation, because sailing close to the wind makes for a more thrilling journey.

---

overstated theories abounded concerning the supposed role of the latter in spurring the archaizing revolution in the Greek literature of the Roman empire (beginning with Rohde 1886 and culminating in the maximum opus of Schmid 1887–96). Wilamowitz-Möllendorff accepted the inviting opportunity to deflate this presupposition while scoring points against his opponents (Wilamowitz-Möllendorff 1900). For saner approaches, see now Horrocks 1997, 81, which argues that Atticism and Asianism represent ever overlapping and interlaced stylistic proclivities rather than absolute states; especially Kim 2010b.

73. See Stanton 1973 on the confusions between *Sophist* and *philosopher*; see especially Hesk 2000, 212–17 (focusing on democratic Athens), on the plasticity of *Sophist* as a term of abuse.

74. See Hunter 1983, 84–98, for detailed discussion of the definitively poetical, "sweet" style of *Daphnis and Chloe*.

75. Norden 1898, 1.367–79.

76. Bourdieu 1977, 8.

Although the prosifying culture of Roman Greece repeatedly marked the relationship between classical and contemporary Greece in terms of the polarity of poetry and prose, it did so with a view not to repressing or expunging poetry but rather to reterritorializing it.[77] In the elite culture of the second century C.E., the poetic was the locus for a complex web of concerns with ideology and identity, and that was precisely why it was needed. I hope to have shown how the diachronic narrative describing the descent of a "high," "classical" culture of poetry into the abyss of prose also encodes synchronic preoccupations with cultural, sexual, and political identity. The creation of a "classical" period is the function of a dynamic and ever unresolved struggle within contemporary culture: to inveigh against the tyranny, barbarism, or effeminacy of poetry was to seek not to replace it with prose but to re-place it as prose's spectral but potent "other." To codify poetry as a powerful, exotic, and/or whorish phenomenon is simultaneously to stigmatize it and to mark it as an object of enduring fascination, of desire even. We do not need to be thoroughgoing Lacanians to observe the centrality of this objectified, dis-placed "other" to the ego of Roman Greek culture: it is through this dialectical interplay between repulsion and attraction that the identity of the prosaic "I" is constituted.

This chapter has analyzed the symbolic associations of the poetry-prose dyad (each element as crystallized into iconic form) on two planes, the diachronic and the synchronic. I want to stress in conclusion, however, that although the two planes can be treated as separate for heuristic purposes, they are inseparable at the symbolic level: any stratification of contemporary society is informed by a reading of history, and any reading of history is simultaneously a retrojection of contemporary cultural concerns. That is to say, Roman Greece's ambiguous relationship to its poetical, "classical" past (the subject of the previous section) is isomorphous with its ambiguous relationship to "poetical" elements (the tyrannical, the female, the barbaric, the "other") in the present. The synchronic and the diachronic replacements of poetry are differently inflected articulations of the same lust (never fully consummated) for identity.

"The past" is not—cannot ever be—simply a historical descriptive but is (also) a function of desire, a desire that disavows even as it lusts. For second-century Greeks, prose writing is not in any sense a simple, natural, self-evident choice: it is, rather, a self-conscious marker of the processual closing and reopening of the temporal chasm that unites and separates the Roman-dominated present from the (idealized) Greek past. Prosography is the discourse of the archive, of language marking its attainment of the second order of representation (where imitation,

---

77. I take this term from Stallybrass and White 1986, 104, on elite responses to eighteenth-century carnival.

allusivity, commentary, and self-reflexivity are the dominant tropes), of a tradition folding back on itself. But Roman Greek prosography did not simply repeat earlier precedents. Or if it was repetitious, then we must acknowledge with Peter Brooks that "repetition is . . . a complex phenomenon": "Is repetition sameness or difference? To repeat evidently implies resemblance, yet can we speak of resemblance unless there is difference? Without difference, repetition would be identity, which would not usually appear to be the case."[78]

Roman Greek literature confesses difference even as it advertises continuity. The advent of Roman patronal resources at once creates the political, cultural, and economic conditions for the reclaiming of the classical past and opens up the gulf that distantiates it. The prosifying trajectory of this culture, as I have emphasized throughout, does not simply "reflect" a historical rupture with the classical past; rather, it constructs (provisionally, strategically, multifariously, ad hoc) an imaginary model of such a rupture. The polarity of prose and poetry, through which the classicizing narrative is so often articulated, is the site of a variety of competing voices, all self-interested, all charged with sociopolitical and cultural tensions. What I have sought to do here is map out these various tensions in both their diachronic and their synchronic functions.

78. Brooks 1984, 124.

PART THREE

Beyond the Greek Sophistic

13

Politics and Identity in Ezekiel's *Exagoge*

For Froma Zeitlin

BEYOND THE GREEK SOPHISTIC

One of the many reasons why we need to travel "beyond the Second Sophistic" lies, as we saw in the introduction, in the excessive Hellenocentrism underpinning it—a Hellenocentrism that, for sure, goes back to certain Greek sources in antiquity but was both magnified and generalized in the nineteenth century by postromantic nationalism. Let us not mistake the rhetorical projections of certain ancients for historical reality. Greek cultural production in the Roman imperial era was not driven, as so many modern accounts (both conservative and progressive) suggest, by an obsessive urge to define the boundaries of Hellenism. We can certainly find expressions that correlate with such a view, but we can also find much more preoccupation with (for example) ethical virtue, beauty, or good style. Of course, such qualities might in certain contexts be associated with Hellenism, but to reduce them to the status of mere metaphors for an underlying cultural imperative is far too simplistic.

For most in antiquity, identity was almost always less determinate, and indeed determinant, than it is for us. The ancient world in general, lacking the apparatus of nationalism that might have allowed communities to imagine themselves in terms of discrete ethnopolitical bodies (distinct "national" currencies, unified educational systems, regular media, and so forth), was a space of fluid, shifting self-perceptions: sometimes one of these might acquire a particular salience, whether for an individual, a community, or a still wider agglomeration; at other times it might recede into the shadows. But most people lived their lives as they did because a combination of biological, geophysical, and economic necessities pressed them to; they followed received traditions where these were available or, where they were not, improvised with whatever cultural resources came to hand. We should always distinguish, heuristically, etic projections of identity—those diagnostics that tell us outsiders that a particular cultural group is at work (e.g., a particular alphabet or pottery type)—from emic ones, a given group's deliberately articulated markers of its own individuation. Because cultural and ethnic identity were generally not superelevated to the same heights in antiquity as in modern nation-states, such emic expressions tend to be less common, and confined to moments of contestation.

The Second Sophistic has been constructed since the nineteenth century as the product of such a contestation, a time when (it is supposed) Greeks were asserting their identity in the face of Roman imperial domination—and, in the nineteenth-century version, far less palatable to modern sensitivities, also in response to the equally aggressive spread of "Eastern" cultures.[1] Yet although the superrich literary elite testify to such anxieties, they were not—I think—universal or even necessarily the primary drivers of literary production. The Second Sophistic was not a cultural constant that enveloped all Greek writers, let alone all Greek people, of the early imperial period; it was rather a localized projection of a very specific phenomenon, relating to a group whose self-proclaimed status as guardians of Greek identity often conflicted directly with their complicity in the Roman imperial project (sometimes mediating between the capital and their native cities through, e.g., embassies, and sometimes directly participating as, e.g., imperial secretaries).

The world of the Hellenized Mediterranean was not one of passports. Greekness itself was not subject to one single, stable definition: thus, for example, while the elite rhetors of Philostratus's *Lives of the Sophists* describe themselves and their students as "the Hellenes"—suggesting that oratorical education is the determinant—Hadrian's Panhellenion seems to have insisted that a "Greek" city should have been founded by Greeks, while in Egypt the tax system differentiated Greeks from others, but within this category fell not only ethnic Greeks but also some Egyptians who worked within the Ptolemaic hierarchy and also some Jews. *Greek* was thus a label that, while always maintaining a strong contiguous connection to mainland culture, was extraordinarily flexible and adaptable to local contexts.[2]

Cultural conflict was epichoric, context-specific, and both complex and variable in its blend of resistance and subordination. What is more, Greek identity was riven with all sorts of class divisions: it is far from clear, for example, that elite

---

This chapter draws on material first published as Whitmarsh 2011c; I am grateful to the Institut Català d'Arqueologia Clàssica for permission to reuse it.

1. See introduction.
2. See in general McCoskey 2012.

Greeks of the imperial era would have identified more with working Greeks than they would have with their Roman peers. We should not be drawing hasty analogies with postcolonial articulations of subaltern identity (such as Rastafarianism, pan-Arabism, or Kurdish nationalism), which both seek, at least in principle, to embrace entire, defined bodies of people within their quasi-nationalist scope and rest on technologies of communication and dissemination (television, radio, social media) that were not available in antiquity.

THE "JEWISH SOPHISTIC"?

There was, however, one people for whom unification remained an ambition and for whom literature represented a medium that might effect it. Jews were certainly not culturally or even religiously homogeneous across the entire Mediterranean, but until its destruction by Vespasian's soldiers in 70 C.E., the Temple remained a symbolic hub for the international Jewish community—and for many pilgrims a literal one too. The Bible, now translated into Greek, rendered the numinous luster of the Temple into portable form, so that each practitioner could partake of Jerusalem's special sanctity.[3] More than anything else, however, the covenant between the one god and his chosen people expressed a permanent bond not just between Yahweh and the Jews but also among the Jews themselves. Even if syncretism, sectarianism, intermarriage, and the lapsing of tradition perpetually confused realities, Jews of the Second Temple era could always invoke the ideal of a united people bound umbilically to Jerusalem and thereby to their god.

Hellenistic Judaism thus offers a much better expression of what many critics seek in the Greek Second Sophistic, namely a coherent articulation of subaltern resistance through literature. What is intriguing about such literature, however, in contrast to that of imperial Greece, is that it is composed in the language, and indeed often the genres, of the colonizer—which is all the more troublesome given that Yahweh's language is always held to be Hebrew. Hellenistic Jews were, to paraphrase Frantz Fanon, trying to dismantle the master's house by using his own tools. Let us exemplify with a brief case study, from the gnomic collection known to Western Christianity as Ecclesiasticus, more properly titled the Book (or Wisdom, or Proverbs) of Jesus Ben Sirach, or (in Greek) Sirachides. This survives in its entirety only in Greek, and an informative preface tells us much about the translator, the grandson of Ben Sirach himself, who came to Egypt in "the thirty-eighth year of the reign of Euergetes," a reference to the second Ptolemy of that title, Ptolemy VII Physkon Euergetes II, who

---

3. See especially Rajak 2009.

came to the throne in 170 B.C.E.; the translation will thus have been achieved some time later than 132.[4]

What is immediately striking is that the grandson is keen to represent himself as highly assimilated. When he came to Egypt, he says, "I discovered no small opportunity for education [*paideias*]";[5] he therefore took upon himself the "devotion [*spoudēn*] and love of toil [*philoponian*]"[6] required for the task of translation, which gave him much "sleeplessness [*agrupnian*]." *Paideia*—that central Greek idea of not just the act of instruction but also the state of being civilized—is one of the primary means of marking elite identity: the translator is proclaiming his erudition in much the same way that a Callimachus or a Theocritus would. And indeed the parallels go further: the emphasis on devoted labor (*spoudē* and *ponos*) might even be taken to blazon a commitment to Alexandrian aesthetics. We can productively compare the prologue to Longus's *Daphnis and Chloe*, where an unnamed narrator claims to have labored (*exeponēsamēn*) to refigure (translate?) a painting into words (*Praef.* 3). In both cases there is an emphasis on interpretation of the original artifact (Longus's narrator has sought out an "exegete" to explain the painting), and both are engaged in a kind of rivalry with the original. Longus seeks to "write in response to the painting [*antigrapsai tēi graphēi*]" (*Praef.* 3), while the translator of Ben Sirach more humbly solicits forgiveness (or is it a knowingly rhetorical *captatio benevolentiae*?) for any perceived inadequacies in his rendition: "What was originally expressed in Hebrew," he observes, "does not have the same force [*ou . . . isodunamei*] when translated into another language." In other words, the translator of Ben Sirach seems aware that he is doing more than simply converting words from one language to the other: he is also packaging his text to meet the expectations of a sophisticated Alexandrian audience reared on elegantly crafted literature. Indeed, one of the most striking features of this prologue is the implicit insistence on a parallel between Jewish and Greek learning: twice the translator refers to the Tanach as *paideia* (along with "wisdom," *sophia*, also a key word in Ben Sirach proper), the same word that he uses of his Greek studies.[7]

For whom, then, was Ben Sirach's translator translating? The prologue finishes with a claim that the work is "also [*kai*] for those abroad [*en tēi paroikiai*] who wish to love learning [*philomathein*], by preparing themselves for living according to the law."

---

4. Euergetes II reigned with his brother Philometor from 170 and alone from 145 to 116 (the other Euergetes, Ptolemy III Euergetes I, is ruled out of consideration by the short span of his reign, viz. twenty-five years). Generally on the date of Ben Sirach see Williams 1994, although any argument for precise dating will be a house of cards.

5. The line is textually complex, but the variant readings do not affect my point.

6. He earlier refers to "my loving efforts [*pephiloponēmenōn*]" in respect to the translation.

7. Analogously, the *Letter of Aristeas* says the translators of the Septuagint are "egregious in *paideia*," with expertise in both Jewish and Greek education (121).

A text written in Greek is seen to reach out to "those abroad ['in the *paroikia*,' the 'substitute home']," who are implicitly contrasted with the Jews of Jerusalem (the grandson here hints at the psychology of the exile, deracinated from the place that he still considers home). But this statement raises numerous questions. Why *also*—in addition to whom? And are "those abroad" to be imagined solely as Egyptian Jews[8] or as gentiles worthy of conversion too? Particularly notable in this connection is the use of *philomathein*, which seems to retain a calculated ambiguity: it could allude to the piety of devoted Jews (as indeed it does twice elsewhere in the prologue), but it could equally well appeal to the self-definition of elite Greeks as intellectually curious.

EZEKIEL, THE *EXAGOGE*, AND BIBLICAL ALLEGORY

Ben Sirach shows how fraught a practice translation could be. Anxieties over the disclosure of a sacred text in a *koinē*, indeed, are relatively widespread in antiquity. In the eyes of some Egyptocentric mystics of the imperial era, when a text entered Greek it lost its sacred "energy," its capacity to store "reality [*erga*]."[9] Not unrelatedly, Lucretius complains of the "poverty [*egestas*]" of the Latin language when expressing Epicurean concepts (*De rerum natura* 1.139), for there was something paradoxically divine about Epicurus's words, in spite of his resistance to organized religion. For this chapter and the following one, however, I shall focus on a more radical and potentially disruptive form of assimilation: the composition of Jewish literature on biblical themes in recognizably Greek poetic genres. This chapter focuses on tragedy; the following will treat epic. In either case, I argue, we can see a highly sophisticated negotiation between Greek and Jewish, between the culturally dominant and the subaltern, and, what is more, a self-reflexivity about this process whereby the texts comment on their bicultural status.

Ezekiel's *Exagoge*, an episodic Greek tragedy (albeit with no chorus) covering the story of the biblical Exodus under Moses, survives in 269 lines of iambic trimeters. It is the only extant example of what must have been a very niche genre, Jewish tragedy.[10] This makes it (another point of interest) by some distance our

---

8. As in 2 Maccabees, cast in the form of an open letter from the Jerusalemites to their "brother Jews in Alexandria" (1.1); see further later in the chapter.

9. *The Definitions of Asclepius to King Ammon* 2, in the *Corpus Hermeticum*; similarly Iambl., *De myst.* 7.5. The paradox is that these texts are written in Greek and there is no evidence that their claims to be translations from Egyptian originals is anything more than pseudoauthentication. By contrast, the hermetic *The Common Mind, to Tat* claims that language is universal and "found to be the same in Egypt and Persia and Greece" (13). Wide-ranging discussions of ancient translation theory can be found at Brock 1979; Vermeer 1992; and Van der Louw 2007, 25–55.

10. The *Letter of Aristeas* refers to one Theodectus, who was apparently blinded by the god of the Jews for using biblical material in his tragedies (316). Theodectus is otherwise unknown; is the name a garbled reminiscence of the fourth-century Athenian Theodectes?

longest surviving piece of Hellenistic tragedy, unless one counts Lycophron's *Alexandra*. Eusebius and Clement preserved its seventeen fragments, apparently on the basis of a selection by the first century B.C.E. Roman polymath Alexander Polyhistor.[11] The narrative as we have it begins with a prologue, in which Moses narrates the story of his birth and upbringing; it then goes through various stages of the Moses story, including his meeting with his wife-to-be Sepphora, a dream in which he witnesses heaven, God's epiphany in the burning bush and prediction of the plague and Passover regulations, the escape through the Red Sea (described in a messenger speech), and an extraordinary ecphrastic scene in which a scout reports to Moses about the oasis at Elim and a sighting of the phoenix bird. Other than this work, we know little that is certain of Ezekiel or his context. The date of the text is not known, although Polyhistor provides a clear *terminus ante quem*. That Ezekiel was an Alexandrian is a speculation, but not an unreasonable one, and accepted by most commentators.[12] It is unclear whether the play was written for performance or for reading;[13] in what follows I make no assumptions either way, although I do in places experiment with possibilities.

If we provisionally assume that the *Exagoge* was composed in and for Hellenistic Alexandria, then questions of context pose themselves. How Alexandrian is this text? What kind of worldview does it embody? What kind of commentary on contemporary affairs? Although there is abundant evidence for a prosperous and vibrant community of Jews in Hellenistic Alexandria,[14] it is hard to know how, phenomenologically speaking, they experienced their surroundings. According to Josephus, the earliest rulers of Alexandria gave Jews equal standing to Macedonians (but probably not "equal rights").[15] Ptolemy IV rehoused refugees from the persecutions of Antiochus Epiphanes. The author of the *Letter of Aristeas* presents what is on any reading a fulsome portrait of life under the benevolent rule of the Ptolemies. Yet more discordant notes are sounded too. The Jews of Jerusalem seem

---

11. A papyrus fragment from Oxyrhynchus (unfortunately with no new material) testifies to the circulation in southern Egypt of either Ezekiel or Polyhistor. The fragment is unpublished at time of writing but was trailed by Dirk Obbink at the Twenty-Sixth International Congress of Papyrology in Geneva, August 2010.

12. Discussion at Lanfranchi 2006, 11–13, which settles on Alexandria as Ezekiel's likeliest location.

13. Ibid., 35–38, argues for performance; see also 39–56, on the evidence for a diverse range of Jewish attitudes toward drama. As so often with this play, however, certainty will never be reached.

14. See, e.g., the rich collection of inscriptions (some Hellenistic, some Roman) in Horbury and Noy 1992. No Jewish papyri survive from Alexandria (damp as the site is).

15. Jos., *Ap*. 2.35 credits the move to Alexander; see however *Ant*. 12.8, which names Ptolemy Soter. For the limited interpretation of *isonomia* (equality before the law) here see Kasher 1985, 35 n. 27. More generally on the Jews of Hellenistic Alexandria see Tcherikover 1999 (1959); Smallwood 1981, 220–35; Kasher 1985; Barclay 1996, especially 27–47; Collins 2000, especially 64–73; Gruen 2002, 54–83. Feldman 2006 tends to focus on Palestine.

to have feared an Alexandrian slide into assimilation. Ben Sirach's grandson, as we have seen, implies that those "in the province [*paroikia*]" stand in need of theological succor and exhortation to cleave to ancestral traditions. This suggests a profound uneasiness about life in Alexandria, with the risks of "assimilation" (for want of a better word) foregrounded. It is possible too that there was direct anti-Jewish agitation; even if we dismiss as a fiction 3 Maccabees and its lurid description of the persecution by Ptolemy IV,[16] it is still possible that the openly anti-Jewish aggression of the Roman era was simmering in the Hellenistic period.[17]

In the culturally and affectively complex environment of pre-Roman Alexandria, Jews will have responded to their Greco-Macedonian masters with a mixture of pragmatism, affiliation, resistance, and fear. These ambivalences can only have been heightened by the distinct symbolic role that Egypt played in the biblical narrative as the paradigmatic locus of oppression and idolatry, from which the Exodus marked an escape into freedom and the light of revealed truth. As Jan Assmann in particular has argued, Judaism's distinctive sense of identity rested on its status as a "counter-religion" defined in opposition to Egypt, which "came to represent the rejected, the religiously false, the 'pagan.'"[18] The representation of Pharaonic Egypt within Alexandrian Judaism was of course heavily filtered through this biblical tradition of antinomy but so too must have been the perception of the Ptolemaic present.

In this chapter, I read Ezekiel's *Exagoge* as one such allegorical commentary on contemporary Alexandria.[19] There was of course no Pharaonic Alexandria, the city having been founded some eleven years after the death, in 342 B.C.E, of the last pharaoh, Nectanebo II. For many of the Ptolemaic city's numerous Jewish inhabitants, however, biblical narratives of oppression under the pharaohs continued to resonate loudly; indeed, as I shall argue in this chapter, the Egyptian episodes of Genesis and Exodus provided them with a crucial repertoire of narratives that allowed them to process their contemporary situation allegorically, without the need to comment directly on their overlords.

---

16. 3 Maccabees 2:39–30. Many see the "persecution" by Ptolemy VIII Philometor (Jos., *Ap.* 2.53–55) as equally fictitious and moreover derived from 3 Maccabees.

17. Notorious pogroms in 38, 41, and 66 C.E. preceded the Jewish War and the Bar-Kochba revolt (see, e.g., Schäfer 1997, 136–38). The *Acta Alexandrinorum* offers ample testimony of anti-Jewish feeling in the early Roman era.

18. Assmann 1996, 50; see more fully 1998; 2009. Greifenhagen 2002 argues that the Pentateuch displays a tension between the normative, overlain Mesopotamian ethnogenesis and an older tradition locating the origins of the Jewish people in Egypt.

19. For edition, translation, and commentary see Jacobson 1983; especially the wide-ranging critical edition Lanfranchi 2006, to which, for convenience, I refer the reader frequently for up-to-date discussion of technical issues (Lanfranchi is in general better on the biblical background and the Jewish context than on classical Greek intertexts, on which Jacobson has perceptive remarks). I have used the text at *TGrF* 1.288–301 and adapted Jacobson's translations.

WHY TRAGEDY?

At the formal level, the most immediate question posed by the *Exagoge* has to do with the choice of genre. What is tragic in a story about the release of the Israelites from slavery and their return to the promised land?[20] There is little that is *tragikos*, in the Aristotelian sense, about the *Exagoge*'s narrative: no cohesion of action (it presents at least five different locales and times) and no negative peripeteia. While there were of course Euripidean "escape tragedies" with dynamic plots and happy endings,[21] the primary reference points for the *Exagoge* are Aeschylus's *Persae* and *Suppliant Women* and to a lesser extent Euripides's *Bacchae* and Sophocles's *Oedipus at Colonus*.[22] There are, it seems, three principal reasons why Ezekiel has chosen tragedy as his vehicle. The first and perhaps most obvious is that Athenian tragedy already models religious revelation and the narration of events that are foundational for an entire community. When Ezekiel's God appears in the form of the burning bush (90–95 and environs), the poet seems to borrow subtly from the "miracles" of Euripides's *Bacchae*: the fire that appears around Semele's tomb (596–99) and the slightly earlier scene where Dionysus's voice is heard but he is apparently not seen (576–84).[23] When God predicts the Egyptian plague and decrees the passover regulations, the model is the kind of ex machina appearance in which Euripides specializes, featuring analeptic predictions of retribution and cult etiology.[24]

The second reason is that tragedy offered him a rich repertoire of meditations on otherness, which (as we shall see in more detail below) is one of the central themes of the *Exagoge*. Aeschylus's *Suppliant Women* demonizes Egyptians as aggressive and sexually predatory in a way that is consonant with biblical constructions.[25] The allusions to Aeschylus's *Persae* are particularly concentrated in the messenger speech, which implicitly assimilates the closing of the Red Sea to the destruction of the Persian fleet at Salamis. The locus classicus of Greek binary self-definition is thus appropriated for Jewish identity, which generates a powerful

---

20. Lanfranchi 2006, 15–25, answers this question by stressing the range of types of tragedy and the genre's evolution in the Hellenistic period. As will become clear, I read Ezekiel as experimenting confidently and innovatively with the template of classical Athenian tragedy.

21. Wright 2005.

22. Jacobson 1983, 237, emphasizes particularly the Aeschylean connection; otherwise, *Bacchae* and *Oedipus at Colonus* are the plays most represented in his index locorum. Broadly the same distribution reappears in Lanfranchi 2006's more comprehensive index, but Euripides's *Phoenissae* (a perhaps surprisingly popular play in postclassical culture) also makes a surge.

23. Jacobson 1983, 99; Lanfranchi 2006, 37.

24. For example at the end of Euripides's *Hippolytus*, where Artemis predicts that she will assail a devotee of Aphrodite's in revenge (1420–22) and that Hippolytus will receive cult on the Athenian acropolis (1425–30).

25. Greifenhagen 2002 explores the dominant, negative portrayal of Egypt in the Pentateuch, arguing that it functions to displace a more positive tradition that can still be glimpsed.

irony, given that the *Exagoge*'s Egyptians are (I suggest) implicitly correlated with the Macedonian-Greek Ptolemies and their agents. The *Bacchae*, mentioned in the previous paragraph, is a particularly interesting hypotext in that it describes the incorporation of an Eastern cult into a Greek context dominated by an aggressively resistant monarchy, a narrative that no doubt had a particular piquancy for Ptolemaic and Seleucid Greeks. More generally, we can locate the *Exagoge* within a wider tradition of creative receptions of the *Bacchae* that lay a particular emphasis on mediation between East and West.[26]

My third and final explanation for the choice of tragedy as a medium is that the play is centrally concerned with suffering, albeit of a kind that is unfamiliar in Attic tragedy. Egypt is constructed as the site of relentless misery for the Israelites, right from the prologue:[27]

> Moses: When Jacob left Canaan he came to Egypt with seventy souls and fathered a great people that has suffered and been oppressed. Right up until these times we have been ill treated by evil men and a powerful regime. For King Pharaoh, when he saw our people increasing in number, devised many plans against us. He afflicted us with brickwork and the hard labor of construction, and he had turreted cities built by our ill-fated men.

This passage is certainly suffused with tragic motifs, particularly the threefold repetition of the *kak-* (bad, ill-) root and the use of the übertragic *dusmoros* (ill-fated). What is less tragic, or at least less Attic tragic, is the focus on common rather than individual suffering. Despite the absence of a choral voice, then, Ezekiel activates a sense of the collective. It is likely that, as so often in Greek literature, the language of pain and suffering is designed to engender a sense of empathic pity in audience members or readers and so to align them affectively with the Israelites. This assimilation is subtly compounded: "Right up until these times [*esakhri toutōn tōn khronōn*] we have been ill treated by evil men and a powerful regime." The phrase "right up until these times" alludes to the well-known Herodotean tag *eti es eme* (even up to my own day) and its periegetic and etiological successor *eti kai nun* (even now), used to highlight the remarkable survival of an ancient tradition, saying, or monument. But this is more than a neat, "Alexandrian" appropriation of a familiar phrase for a new use. It also constitutes a vivid example of what Christiane Sourvinou-Inwood calls the "zooming device":[28] the strategic telescoping, at

---

26. Hunter 2006, 42–80.
27. I do not see the use of the particle *de* in the first sentence as a decisive argument against this being the opening of the play: Ezekiel's linguistic eccentricities are numerous; see Lanfranchi 2006, 115–16, on this point. The passage has obvious similarities to the recapitulatory solo prologue of many an Attic tragedy.
28. Sourvinou-Inwood 1989.

particular junctures, of spaces and times. This process is facilitated by the use of the deictic *toutōn*, "these," which can be taken as indexed either to the time of the biblical Moses or, metaleptically, to that of the audience—or, in fact, to both at once. In other words, the text invites us to identify a continuum of suffering from Pharaonic past to Ptolemaic present.[29]

The representation of Pharaonic Egypt, then, can be seen as a coded political critique of Ptolemaic Alexandria. The Israelites' sufferings in Egypt are brought about not by divine vengeance (as they are sometimes in the Midrashim) but directly by the brutality of the king, jealous as he is of their fecundity.[30] This savagery means that as in the Bible, Egypt is imaged as a kind of underworld, a place that one "goes down" to.[31] There is a satisfying symmetry, then, to a narrative that finally rebounds the sufferings of the Israelites onto the Egyptians. In the conventional interpretation,[32] the pharaoh is said to suffer (*paskhein*) during the divinely wrought plagues, a compensation for the earlier ills inflicted on the Israelites. We can observe a similar boomerang effect in the messenger's speech about the parting of the Red Sea: the initial distress of the Israelites on watching the Egyptian army making for them ("they yelled on seeing [*ēlalaxan idontes*] . . . ," 211) is replicated by the suffering of one of the Egyptians at the sight of the impending tsunami ("he yelled on seeing [*ēlalax' idōn*] . . . ," 238). The narrative of suffering, then, is both conventionally tragic, in that it solicits empathy from external audience (or readers) for internal characters, and unconventional, in that its reversal adopts the structure more of a comedy of release, whereby the initially pathetic suffering transfers to the agents of oppression.

BIRTH, EDUCATION, IDENTITY

The *Exagoge* is simultaneously conventional and unconventional, both like and unlike a classical Greek tragedy. I want to move on now, away from the narrower issues of tragedy as genre, and press harder the related question of cultural affiliation. If I am right that Pharaonic Egypt stands as a cipher for Ptolemaic Alexandria and both are equally execrated, then fresh questions emerge: Why has Ezekiel chosen an archetypically Greek literary medium? Why does he show himself so

---

29. Moses's "account continues the suffering right in a direct line until the Tragedian himself" (J. Cohen 1993, 33). Lanfranchi's counterargument ("The prologue is pronounced not by the author but by Moses . . .") fails to credit Ezekiel with any sophistication (2006, 133).

30. There seems to be here an echo of the *Cypria*'s famous claim that Zeus brought about the Trojan War out of fear of overpopulation (fr. 1.15 *EGF*).

31. Lanfranchi 2006, 117.

32. "Φαραὼ δὲ βασιλεὺς πείσετ' οὐδὲν ὧν λέγω . . ." (149). I concur with Lanfranchi, however, contra Jacobson, that *peiset'* is likelier to be from *peithein* than from *paskhein*: "Pharaoh, the king, will be persuaded of none of my words."

intimate and artful an exponent of tragic intertextuality? Surely these tactics are signs of affiliation with Greeks and hence complicity with the very system he affects to critique. The complex play between traditions is actually thematically seeded in the text itself. For this is not simply a story of straightforward binary opposition between Israelite and Egyptian but a testing site for different models of cultural interaction. Chief among them is acculturation. As in the Bible, Moses is nursed by his mother, Mariam (and, crucially for what follows, told about his "ancestral race [*genos patrōion*] and God's gifts," 35), but brought up in the Egyptian court: "Accordingly, for the period of my youth, during my royal nurturing and education the princess promised me everything as if I were her own son. But when I grew to be an adult, I went forth from the royal palace at my spirit's urging, to see the deeds and devices wrought by the king" (36–41).

Particularly striking here is the emphasis on the "education [*paideumasin*]" he receives, as if he were a blood relation of the royal dynasty. This detail is extrabiblical; predictably so, for the centrality of education to cultural definition is of course definitively Greek and definitively postclassical: *paideia* is a primary marker of civilized Hellenism. The claim that the princess reared Moses as she would her own son indicates clearly that the education in question is Gentile, and contemporary Alexandrian readers or viewers would (I feel sure) have associated this immediately with the sophisticated literary culture of the Library/Museum complex, which could also be seen as a royal palace (built as it was in the Brucheion).[33] We might even see in Moses a reflection of Ezekiel's poetic identity as an ethnic Jew who is nevertheless deeply immersed in Greek learning (was he perhaps a member of the Museum?).

This emphasis on Moses's education is highly significant not only because of anxieties, mentioned near the start of this chapter, over the Hellenization of Alexandrian Jews and its implied threat to their Jewishness but also because his partial "assimilation" picks up on the theme of Mosaic hybridity that can already be detected in the Bible. Biblical scholars emphasize Abraham and Moses as two alternative founders of Israelite identity: if "Abraham is presented in the Hebrew Bible as the genealogical ancestor of the biblical Israel, Moses is cast as its 'vocational' ancestor."[34] The tension between them might be resolved by distinguishing an older tradition, promoting the Egyptian origins of the Jews, which was later (during the Persian period) incorporated within the alternative, and now dominant, Abrahamic narrative of ethnic origins in Mesopotamia.[35] But even if the

---

33. We could also take the *trophaisi basilikaisi* (royal nourishings) as a subtle allusion to the victuals provided for the scholars of the Museum. Barclay 1996, 138, similarly interprets Moses's *paideia* as a sign of "accommodation" between Jewish and Gentile, but as will be clear I disagree with his assessment that this negotiation is smooth and unproblematic.

34. Stavrakopoulou 2010, 55.

35. Greifenhagen 2002, especially 257–58.

normative biblical account seeks to minimize Israel's genetic links to Egypt, the specter of Moses's Egyptianness continues to haunt all subsequent accounts. Jan Assmann famously explained this phenomenon in Freudian terms, as "the return of the repressed."[36] We can alternately detect the processes of return and rerepression in the Hellenistic stories found in Hecataeus and Manetho that make the Jews Egyptian outcasts, and in Artapanus's counterclaim that Moses, while ethnically Jewish, in fact gave the Egyptians their laws and civilization (an argument that seeks at once to explain the Egyptian connection, to avoid assimilating Jew and Egyptian, and to make Egyptians dependent on Jewish beneficence).[37]

Ezekiel's intervention into this discourse is notable for two reasons. The first is that, as we have seen, what appears to be at stake in the education theme is not simply Israel's primordial relationship with Pharaonic Egypt but also contemporary Jews' relationship with the Greco-Egyptian Ptolemies. The second is that education provides a distinctively nonessentialist way of construing the problem of "Moses the Greco-Egyptian," for it is linked both to culture rather than nature and to the liminal phase of youth (the first two lines of the passage punningly localize Moses's *paideia* in the time when he was a *pais*, a youth). Gentile learning is thus a skill acquired and retained but also a childish pursuit that can be left behind when mature vigor awakens: note how Moses's "spirit [*thumos*]" compels him to go off in search of action (*erga*). The palace represents not just Greco-Egyptian culture as distilled into intellectual tradition but also an enclosed, maternal space for nourishing the immature. Alongside the education (*paideumasin*) with which he is provided, Moses receives "nurturing [*trophaisi*]" from the princess as though he had been born from her loins: palace education is thus assimilated to breast feeding (even identified with it, if we take "trophaisi . . . kai paideumasin" as a hendiadys).

The passage raises still deeper questions about the metaphysics of identity. That the princess raises Moses "as if [*hōs*] I were from her own loins" is suggestive: *hōs* asks us to consider just how much like a Gentile he has become and raises the troubling question of whether upbringing can transcend birth, ethics can transcend ethnics. These themes resurface in the romance *Joseph and Aseneth*, where the intermarriage between the biblical patriarch and his Egyptian wife is legitimized by a series of similes comparing Aseneth to an Israelite (1.4–5 Burchard), and indeed Joseph claims to love her like a sister (7.8). Such passages raise, albeit fleetingly, the disturbing possibility that ancestral blood's claim to determine identity may be displaced, that identity can be, to an unspecified degree, remade when a child passes to a new parent. Clearly, these themes will have had considerable

---

36. Assmann 1998, 23–54. Assmann is particularly struck by the possibility that cultural memory linked Jewish monotheism with the celebrated religious reforms of Akhenaton in the fourteenth century B.C.E.

37. Hecataeus: *FGrH* 264 F 6; Manetho: *FGrH* 609 F 10; Artapanus: fr. 3.4–6 *FHJA*.

traction in an environment where the issue of Jewish assimilation into Greek culture was, as we have seen, a key concern.

Yet if the possibility is fleetingly raised here of integration into the Pharaoh's family through education, it is dashed in what follows, where Moses powerfully reasserts his Israelite identity. Immediately after he leaves the palace, at line 41, we encounter the scene, familiar from the Bible, where Moses meets an Egyptian and a "Hebrew" (Ezekiel's standard term for *Israelite*) fighting. Only the "Hebrew" is said to be Hebrew "by race [*genos*]." It would be open to us to take this phrase as a pleonastic addition for the sake of meter alone[38]—but for the fact that the palace narrative has centered precisely on questions of family, ethnicity, and ethnic definition. The combat between Israelite and Egyptian, moreover, condenses the complexity of cultural relationships into a brutally simply polarity and imposes on Moses a stark choice as to which side he will choose. The tough ontological and epistemological questions about belonging, kinship, and acculturation are pared away here; identity politics are distilled into a simple choice, between Israelite *genos* and Egyptian homeland. Moses of course sides with the Israelite, a moment not only of reconnection but also of cultural performativity: when he narrates his choice, saying that "I defended my brother [*adelphon*]" (45), he both retrospectively acknowledges and prospectively designates (using a deep-rooted familial metaphor) his kinship with the Jewish people.

HYBRIDITY AND INTERMARRIAGE

Yet for all Moses's (and Ezekiel's) attempts to disambiguate identity, for all the teleology of the return to the promised land, there is always a constant, shadowing awareness of the possibility of sliding from genetic Israelite into hybrid identities. In the next fragment, which may follow on from the prologue, Moses meets Sepphora, his wife-to-be. Even more than in *Joseph and Aseneth,* here the theme of miscegenation is powerful and unmissable. Moses has declared, in the prologue, that the space in which he now wanders is "a foreign [*allotermona*] land" (58; a claim that, we should note in passing, interestingly identifies Egypt, by antinomy, as his homeland). When the daughters of Raguel approach,[39] we learn that this "foreign land" is identified not (or at least not in the transmitted fragments) as the Bible's Midian (normally understood to be on the Arabian Peninsula) but as Libya, said to be "inhabited by the tribes of all sorts of races [*pantoiōn genōn*], black Ethiopian men" (61–62). Now why Ezekiel has relocated this meeting is as unclear as the exact geographical area he understands by the name *Libya*.[40] But two things

---

38. Thus Jacobson's translation, for example, omits it.
39. Like Nausicaa and her maids, as Jacobson ad loc. observes acutely.
40. Lanfranchi 2006, 151–56, addresses the geographical difficulties this passage raises.

are notable. The first is that he has elected to make Moses intermarry with an African rather than an Arabian—perhaps because he wants the drama to resonate with Alexandrians. The second is that he has chosen a toponym that is associated, in Greek, with alterity, marking an uncivilized space that was seen to demand subjugation, a phenomenon imaged mythically in the defeat of the monstrous giant Antaeus by the civilizing hero Heracles and in the rape and domestication of the wild nymph Cyrene.

We have moved, then, from the fight that seemed to affirm Moses's commitment to one race, one *genos,* that of the Israelites, to a situation where he is choosing intermarriage with a stranger (Moses is called a *xenos* at 67, 83), whose land represents not just ethnic difference (note the marked emphasis on pigmentation, the "black Ethiopian men") but also cultural pluralism ("all sorts of races"). This last phrase, moreover, cannot but evoke the familiar perception of Alexandria as the multicultural city par excellence. The exogamous marriage with Sepphora returns us to the repressed image: not quite of Moses the Egyptian but of Moses the hybrid, fusing Israelite ancestry with (Greco-)Egyptian culture and social mores. Intermarriage, indeed, is one of the primary tropes of cultural fusion in Hellenistic literature, in particular among Jews who vigorously debated biblical prohibitions at this time.[41]

POETICS

I have been arguing that the questions around Moses's affiliation also self-reflexively explore the difficult cultural negotiations of Ezekiel and his diasporic audience or readership. I turn finally to two episodes that make this self-reflexivity more explicit and richer. I shall be briefer with the first. Ezekiel presents, in the burning bush scene, the story of God's mountaintop transformation of Moses's staff (*rhabdos*) into a magic device that will wreak the plagues on the Egyptians. Let's just note in passing that for Greek readers, this cannot but recall Hesiod's bardic initiation by the Muses on Mount Helicon (*Theog.* 22–34), where the gift of a rod marks his investiture. Hesiod's word is not *rhabdos* but *skēptron,* but it is likely, I think, that Ezekiel's peers understood the Hesiodic implement as a *rhabdos,* the iconic symbol of the Archaic rhapsode (ancient pseudoetymology linked the two words).[42] Callimachus, of course, also exploited the metapoetic significance of this scene, in the *Aetia:* another token, perhaps, of Ezekiel's affiliations

---

41. See S. J. D. Cohen 2001, 241–62, which argues that the Bible (Deuteronomy 7:34; Exodus 34:14–16; 1 Kings 11:48; Ezra 9–10) forbids intermarriage only in specific instances (e.g., with Canaanites), whereas Philo, Josephus, and particularly the rabbinical tradition transform this into a generally applied regulation.

42. Graziosi 2002, 23–24.

with his Gentile peers in the world of Alexandrian poetry. The *Exagoge* has, admittedly, no close verbal parallels that I can detect with either the *Aetia* or the *Theogony*. The Hesiodic intertext, however, lends an interesting resonance to the following exchange, where Moses (like his biblical counterpart) frets about his lack of eloquence. Whereas the Muses of the *Theogony* bestow eloquence on Hesiod for him to use in the service of kings, Ezekiel's God diverts the rhetorical ability from Moses to his brother Aaron, to use in a confrontation with Pharaoh. This appropriation marks a reorientation from Hesiod's vision of the ideological complicity of the poet in the royal enterprise toward a new, agonistic poetics.

I want to finish, however, by looking at the extraordinary final fragment, the description of the phoenix (254–69). The question of why Ezekiel should have included this has caused much scratching of heads. Was he perhaps aware of the tradition that a phoenix landed at the temple in Heliopolis? Did Hellenistic Jews, like later Christian writers, use phoenix arrivals historiographically to segment epochs at crucial junctures?[43] Multiple explanations are possible. But neither of these excludes a third possibility, namely that Ezekiel's phoenix serves as a metapoetic figure for the poet's identity (and indeed I shall offer further possible explanations presently).

The phoenix description is, clearly, a flamboyant set piece, an assertion of extraordinary literary sophistication; as Jane Heath has observed,[44] it is, formally speaking, an ecphrasis, a subgenre of Hellenistic and imperial Greek literature that places a high premium on vividness and self-reflexive visuality. Indeed, in imperial times avian ecphrases were commonplace, thanks in part to the familiar assimilation of Sophists to preening birds, particularly peacocks; such descriptions thus become mises en abyme of Sophistic skill.[45] Ezekiel thus offers the earliest extant example of a bird ecphrasis, another sign of his poetic ingenuity. And his is equally self-reflexive.

> We saw something else too, a strange and remarkable creature such as no man has ever seen before. He was about twice the size of an eagle and had multicolored wings. His breast was purplish and his legs scarlet-colored. From his neck, saffron tresses hung beautifully. He head was like that of a domestic cock. He gazed all around with his yellow eye, which looked like a seed. He had the most egregious voice. Indeed, it seemed that he was the king of all the birds, as far as it was possible to judge. For all of them followed behind in fear. He strode in front, like an exultant bull, lifting his foot in swift step. (254–69)

---

43. Lanfranchi 2006, 290–96, surveys the possibilities; see especially 292–93 for these two explanations.
44. J. Heath 2006. Ch. 7, n. 59 cites the bibliography on ecphrasis.
45. Dio Chr. 12.5; see further Morales 2004, 185.

The languages of wonder (*thaumaston*), of variegation (*poikiloisin*) and colors (*khrōmasin*, also used of rhetorical figures) are all, clearly, shared between the thing described and the description itself: this is a blazon of lush, descriptive skill. The words at this point become ambitious, exotic, compounded (see, e.g., the *hapax miltokhrōta*, "scarlet-colored," at 259), and heavily alliterative: note particularly "krokōtinois . . . kara . . . kottois . . . korēi . . . kuklōi . . . korē . . . kokkos." In this context, the emphasis on sound and vision is highly significant, highlighting as it does the visual and auditory field of theatrical performance (whether literally in performance or by association in a *Lesedrama*). The colors (purple, red, saffron, yellow) point ecphrastically to the sight that the messenger's speech represents mimetically (whether at one remove in performance or at two on the page) but cannot reproduce. The messenger's acknowledgment that he has interpreted the visual manifestation underlines the irreducibly mediated nature of this viewing experience: "looked like [*ephaineto*]" (263), "seemed [*ephaineto*]" (265), "as far as it was possible to judge" (266). At the same time, however, the bird is also a viewer, peering out with its "seedlike" eye.[46] The bird is thus simultaneously object and subject of vision. The same goes for language: the marvelous display of descriptive prowess that we are witnessing is mirrored in the phoenix's possession of a "most egregious voice [*phōnēn . . . ekprepestatēn*]" (264). The phoenix thus seems to embody at once the signifier and the signified of dramatic representation.

This self-reflexivity also has cultural and political dimensions. The phoenix is a "strange" or even "alien creature [*zōion xenon*]" such as no one has yet seen (254–55), a description that picks up the earlier emphasis on Moses's "foreignness" in the eyes of the Libyans. It is attractive, then, to also take the phoenix as a cipher for Ezekiel's alterity within the Greek literary tradition, as a rare bird whose colorful exoticism makes him an object of wonder. The phoenix, we are told, is in fact "king of all the birds," leaving the rest following in his train (265–67): a clever figuration, no doubt, of Ezekiel's poetic aims, not just to partake of the tragic tradition but also to dominate it, elevating it to the highest possible state of sanctity and sophistication. The description of the phoenix as "the king of all the birds," moreover, seems to underline the theme of politically antagonistic poetics, offering Ezekiel as an alternative to or even opponent of the oppressive kings of Egypt.

There is more that can be said about the "strangeness" of the phoenix. First, *xenon* gears us up for a puzzle, and indeed the description has something of a riddle about it, with the itemized body parts listed in sequence. The bird is never named: we need to deploy our interpretative skills and our literary know-how (specifically with Herodotus) to identify it.[47] The clue to its identity, moreover, lies

---

46. Just as Achilles Tatius's peacock does, with the "eye" emblazoned on its fan (1.16.3): see Morales 2004, 141.

47. J. R. Morgan 1994.

in the immediately preceding description of Elim (251). Ezekiel presents Elim as a canonical *locus amoenus*,[48] significantly expanding on but also incorporating the sole detail that the Bible gives about it, namely the presence of palm trees. The Greek word for "palm" is of course *phoinix*. Elim thus cleverly provides not only a disguised hint as to the bird's identity but also an artful explication, in the form of a calque, for the poet's striking decision to stage a manifestation of the phoenix there: when Hebrew *bennu* becomes Greek *phoinix*, the pun is activated.[49]

Despite the absence of a first-person, "authorial" persona in the *Exagoge*, then, and despite setting his drama in the distant past, Ezekiel tells us a good deal about life in contemporary Egypt. The caveat that his Alexandrian origin is uncertain bears repeating, but we have at least amassed a certain amount of circumstantial evidence that the play would have gained additional resonance in a setting in Egypt. A sense of the interpenetration of past and present was no doubt widely felt among all communities in Egypt, but Alexandrian Jews must often have experienced a distinctive cultural and religious tension between the pragmatic accommodations they made in the present and their particular investment in sacred narratives of categorical hostility to this space. Dense, sophisticated poetry like Ezekiel's dramatizes not just the story that is literally played out but also the story of contemporary Jewish urban life: from the oppositional discourse of Pharaoh's cruelty and punishment to the phoenix scene at the end of our fragments, which points toward a more exuberant celebration of the poet's identity as an outsider within the Greek literary tradition. We also find Ezekiel exploring different models of hybrid identity: the conjuncture of (Greco-)Egyptian education and Jewish family (*genos*), aggressive confrontation between the two, and multicultural intermarriage. In all, the *Exagoge* reads like a crystalline prism that brilliantly refracts the multiple and sometimes contradictory concerns of urban Jews.

---

48. Discussion at Lanfranchi 2006, 279.
49. Collins 2000, 228; see Lanfranchi 2006, 293, on the history of this interpretation.

14

Adventures of the Solymoi

Tragedy was big business in the Hellenistic era. Although Ezekiel's *Exagoge* (see previous chapter) is the only substantially extant representative of the genre between the latest plays attributed to Euripides and Lucian's *Podagra* (unless we count Lycophron's *Alexandra*, in iambic trimeters but a monologue; see chapter 11 for *Podagra*), we know of many tragedians operating particularly in Alexandria; indeed, grammarians referred to a "pleiad" of tragic poets, an allusion to the bright stars that make up the constellation of that name.[1] More culturally central still, however, was epic, which lay at the very heart of Greek culture at every level. Schoolchildren cut their teeth on Homer. The Homereion (Shrine to Homer) at Alexandria suggests a cultlike role for the poet. In the Pergamon frieze, he sits symbolically at the apex of the Greek literary and cultural tradition. He was the ultimate reference point for literature, and not just in the reams of epic (now largely lost) that were produced throughout the Hellenistic and imperial periods: the Halicarnassus inscription, notably, commemorates Herodotus as the "prose Homer."[2]

In this chapter, however, I am interested less in the Greeks' huge investment in the idea of Homer as the originator of the canon than in the dialogue between Homeric mythology and neighboring cultures, in particular Jews. In the postclassical, epic became a space for cultural negotiation, a flexible and capacious system

---

1. On the postclassical reception of tragedy see Gildenhard and Revermann 2010. There are five lineups transmitted for the "pleiad," not all of which, however, are exclusively tragic: see discussion at Fraser 1972, 1.619–20, 2.871–73.

2. Lloyd-Jones 1999a; 1999b.

for organizing, ranking, and contesting the relationships between different peoples. In one sense this process was older even than Homer himself: Irad Malkin and Robin Lane Fox, in particular, have shown how mythology was developed and adapted in first-wave colonial situations from at least the eighth century B.C.E.[3] In the Hellenistic era, however, epic took on a new, literarily self-conscious vitality, when the challenge was not just to reinvent myth but to read against the template of Homeric and Hesiodic text.

The best-known example of this phenomenon is the Romans' adoption of Aeneas, who had a rich and varied life in Greek local traditions, particularly (although this is contested) in the Troad, long before he pitched up in Rome. The *Aeneid* that we know now is the culmination of a series of appropriations and counterappropriations by different peoples (including, but not limited to, early Romans and Italians).[4] All of these were rooted in creative readings of the prompts and indeterminacies of Homer's text, which already speaks of a significant afterlife of Aeneas beyond the Trojan War (as does the *Homeric Hymn to Aphrodite*).[5] Aeneas's identity as the founder of the Roman people (or, at least, one candidate for the title) was in no way a fait accompli, for all that Vergil might present it as such; the *Aeneid* is a late intervention (decisive to be sure) in a long, circuitous process of debating what that afterlife actually meant.

Another example is Memnon, whose various peregrinations are less well known and deserve to be more fully explored. In the Epic Cycle, Memnon is Ethiopian (hence the name of the epic attached to him, Arctinus's *Aethiopis*).[6] But what does *Ethiopian* mean? Homer famously[7] distinguishes between "eastern" and "western" Ethiopians in the *Odyssey* (1.20–21), which seems to have legitimized a split tradition relating to Memnon's provenance. By the fifth century, he can clearly be thought of as "eastern" and specifically Persian or Mesopotamian. Aeschylus and Herodotus already refer to a Memnoneia at Susa.[8] Ctesias's *Persica*

---

3. Malkin 1998; Lane Fox 2008.

4. Erskine 2001, with 93–112 on the evidence for Greek cities claiming descent from Aeneas; 143–46, 151–52 on the Western tradition. Faulkner 2008, 3–10, surveys the doubts about the existence of the Aeneidae of the Troad and is nevertheless cautiously affirmative.

5. *Il.* 20.307–8; Hom. Hymn. Aphr. 196–97, on which see Faulkner 2008. Nagy 1979, 265–66, suggests (partly on the basis of *Iliad* 13.461) that a lost Aeneas epic lies behind both passages.

6. *EGF* pp. 45–48. Snowden 1970, 151–53, surveys the peregrinations of the Memnon myth.

7. See, e.g., Kim 2010a, 53–54, which explores ancient geographers' responses to this passage.

8. Strab. 15.3.2 (fr. 405 *TGrF*): "Aeschylus too says that Memnon's mother is Cissian" (an authentically Aeschylean word: see *Pers.* 17, 119; *Cho.* 423); Hdt. 5.53–54, 7.151. For the Susan Memnoneia see also Ael., *DNA* 5.1. Memnon is shown with black pigmentation in a painting from around 540 B.C.E., an innovation perhaps introduced by Exekias, but by the mid-fifth century we also find him in "Asiatic" guise (*LIMC*, s.v. "Memnon," 460–61; on the artistic depiction of Memnon in general see Gruen 2011, 213–16).

tells us (via Diodorus's summary), "Memnon the son of Tithonus was sent by Teutamus, the Assyrian king, with twenty thousand men and two hundred chariots to aid Priam (a client king of Teutamus)." Memnon "stood out for his bravery and his brilliance of character" and had a palace on the citadel and a road named after him, still called Memnoneia "to this day" (whether that means Ctesias's or Diodorus's day; *FGrH* 688 F 1b, p. 442). These appeals to physical monuments are not innocent: blocks of stone are ontologically nonnegotiable, concrete symbols of a claimed solidity in the relationship between past and present. Memnon's identity seems thus to have been, like Aeneas's destination, the subject of much contest. Indeed Ctesias (or Diodorus)[9] reports, in Herodotean fashion, that this Persian narrative was challenged by the Ethiopians, who claim their own ancient palace that is called "to this day [*mekhri tou nun*]" the Memnoneia. What is particularly interesting is just how reflexive this process of contestation was: each participant seems aware of and concerned to neutralize rival traditions. Thus Ctesias makes Memnon the commander of an Ethiopian contingent, as if to explain why the Homeric tradition "erroneously" makes him Ethiopian. Contrariwise, Pausanias tells us that Memnon was an Ethiopian but came to Troy via Susa;[10] this tradition seems designed to combat its Susan equivalent. In other sources we find clear attempts to reconcile the two conflicting versions: sometimes there are said to be two Memnons (but one Ethiopian and one Trojan).[11]

Nor apparently was the Memnon tradition confined to literature. Like so many of the dead at Troy, he seems to have received cult at his grave, for which there were numerous locations claimed. According to a tradition that seems to go back at least to Simonides, Memnon's body was brought to Syria and buried there.[12] Pseudo-Oppian writes that the "Assyrians" (i.e., the Syrians) lament (*kōkuousi*) him by the banks of the Orontes (*Cyn.* 2.150–55). But a different tradition had his tomb by the Asepus in the Troad, to which the Hellespontians are said to have made pilgrimage; there was a town there called Memnon.[13] According to Philostratus, he also received cult in Meroë and Memphis.[14] By imperial times, of course, the famous colossus of Amenophis III came to be associated, thanks to the near homonymy, with Memnon, but already in the Hellenistic era we find references to Memnoneia in Egypt.[15]

---

9. As Jacoby believed: see *FGrH* 688 F 1b, p. 442.

10. Paus. 10.31.7.

11. Philostr., *Her.* 26.17; perhaps implicit at *VA* 6.4.1 (thus apparently Grossardt 2006, 526).

12. Strab. 15.3.2.

13. Hes. fr. 353 Merkelbach-West; Strab. 13.1.11; Quint. Smyrn. 2.585–87; see Paus. 10.31.6 for the pilgrimage. See also Erskine 2001, 109.

14. Philostr., *Her.* 26.16–17.

15. Diod. Sic. 2.22.3; Strab. 17.1.46; *UPZ* II no. 189 (p. 191), late second century B.C.E., cited by Gardiner 1961, 91–92, which has a full discussion of the phenomenon of Egyptian Memnoneia and the link to Amenophis III.

We shall return to Memnon in due course, but let us for now reflect on the question of how to conceptualize these creative rereadings of epic mythology. Were they the result of Greek attempts to universalize their culture or non-Greek attempts to write themselves into a Greek narrative cosmos? We need, to be sure, a subtle and capacious model to capture the complex blend of Hellenocentric push and indigenous pull. There is certainly an expansionist strain visible from the earliest writers of Greek epic onward, an attempt to turn Greek myth into a universal cultural system: thus, for example, the end of the *Theogony* (whether or not it is authentically Hesiodic) can already be found rolling out eponyms like *Medeios* and *Latinus*, genealogically connected to the centrally Greek mythological trunk.[16] But there is creative engagement on the non-Greek side too: one prominent example is the Sidonian use of the figure of Europa, who appears prominently on the city's coinage early on, possibly even assimilated to the Phoenician goddess Astarte.[17] We should not, therefore, automatically assume that the intercultural aspects of Greek mythology were straightforwardly the result of either Greeks' attempts to appropriate others into their mythological world or non-Greeks' attempts to write themselves into a "higher" cultural system. Mythology, rather, was a contested space.

In this context, let us revisit an intriguing detail from Ctesias's account of Memnon's deeds. These, we read, were preserved in a "record [*anagraphē*]" (Diod. Sic. 2.22.1 = Ctesias, *FGrH* 688 F 1b, p. 442). Could this be a genuine Persian tradition claiming Memnon as an ancestor? Was the idea of a Memnoneion at Susa something more than a Hellenocentric fantasy? Ctesias claims elsewhere to base his history on actual Persian archives, "royal parchments [*basilikai diphtherai*]"—a claim that more recent scholars have been reluctant to dismiss as a mere authenticating device.[18] Is it possible, then, that Ctesias—who lived and worked at the Persian court and surely knew the language—did see authentic Persian traditions claiming Mesopotamian participation in the Trojan War? The word *authentic* is, of course, the trap, for in this interstitial economy there is no form of cultural truth that is pure, nonhybridized. Wherever Ctesias got his Memnon story—whether it was gleaned from others or dredged from the recesses of his imagination—it must have been already Janus-faced, for Greek mythology no longer belonged to the Greeks alone: it had already become a fluid space in which Hellenized peoples explored their complex mixture of absorption of and resistance to Hellenism.

16. Hes., *Th.* 1001, 1013.
17. Lightfoot 2003, 297–98.
18. Diod. Sic. 2.32.4 = *FGrH* 688 T3, F 5; also Diod. Sic. 2.22.5 = *FGrH* F 1b. Stronk 2010, 15–25, is confident that they existed and indeed that Ctesias could read the Persian language.

JEWISH MYTHOLOGY

More of Memnon presently. My primary focus in this chapter, however, is not Romans, Persians, Egyptians, or Ethiopians but the more complex case of Jews' creative interventions into the mythological script. This complexity relates partly to the intractability of much of the evidence, for the surviving literature of Hellenistic Judaism is primarily that which late-antique Christians saw fit to preserve, and they were not much interested in Greek mythology. But even taking this into account, Hellenistic Jews were, by common consent, strikingly uninterested in connecting their myth-history to that of the Greeks.[19] Cases of the interweaving of biblical and Homeric narrative are remarkably rare. I have been able to find only one passage linking biblical with Greek epic mythology, an intriguing excerpt in John of Antioch (seventh century C.E.): "Letters were brought from Priam to Tautanes, king of the Assyrians, and to David, king of Jerusalem, asking for help [in resisting the Greek force]. David refused [*ou prosieto*], but Tautanes sent Tithonus and Memnon with a large force" (*FGrH* 49 F 6).

This passage is often thought to be based (even directly)[20] on the Greek version of Dictys of Crete's *Journal*. Whether that is true or not, it is surely responding primarily to Ctesias's account of the Memnon story, mentioned above. As in the Ctesian version, Priam reacts to the skirmishing of the Greeks by sending out a distress call to "Tautanes [Ctesias has Teutamus], king of the Assyrians," who mandates Memnon and (in this version) his father, Tithonus. What is distinctive here, however, is that he also asks "David, king of Jerusalem." But David refuses. Where this detail about David came into the tradition is hard to determine (in fact, John of Antioch is himself preserved in a later source, John of Sicily). But whatever the date at which the David detail entered the Ctesian story, what the passage as a whole demonstrates most clearly is the magnetic repulsion of the two mythical systems, the Greek and the Jewish. Whereas Memnon can be used as a hinge between Mesopotamian (or Egyptian) and Greek culture, David cannot and so cannot come to Troy. I take the refusal (*ou prosieto*), then, as metamythical commentary: the biblical tradition simply will not play ball with Greek epic, presumably partly because that would be too much of an outrage to established narrative tradition and partly because participation with the Trojans would place David uncomfortably on the losing side.

So pickings seem to be forbiddingly slim: we have one late, contested passage, which is in any case Christian rather than Jewish. Yet there are reasons to persist. I shall come presently to the intriguing Jewish poets who composed Greek hexameter verse and whose deep learning in the Greek epic tradition is just as impressive

---

19. Gruen 2011, 253–65.
20. N. E. Griffin 1908, 333–34.

as Ezekiel's grasp of tragedy. But let me turn first to this chapter's title. Who were the Solymoi?

The regular Greek for *Jerusalem*, from at least the third century B.C.E. (I shall argue presently for pushing the date back), is *Hierosoluma*. The reason for this choice of transliteration is clearly that it can be easily disaggregated into two pseudetymological Greek elements so as to become "holy [*hiera*]" Solyma.[21] Now the *Iliad* mentions a people called the Solymoi twice, in the Bellerophon story of book 6, where they are identified as doughty fighters localized in Lycia (that is, in southern Turkey).[22] Ancient commentators associated these Solymoi with the Termessians, and indeed there was by the Hellenistic period a cult of Solymus son of Zeus on the mountain that was now called Solyma (Strab. 14.3.9; also Σ Hom., *Od.* 5.283). But while the *Iliad*'s Solymoi are uncontroversially Lycian, the *Odyssey* offers more options, with its solitary reference to the "Solyman mountains" from which Poseidon, on his return from Ethiopia, spies Odysseus back out to sea (5.283). Although the scholia identify this once more with Lycian Termessus,[23] there is no specification of location in the text (other than it being somewhere en route between that elusive place "Ethiopia" and the Mediterranean).

Martin West has argued that the *Odyssey* passage should be emended to read "Elyman mountains" and so refer to Mount Eryx on Sicily.[24] That may or may not be right for Homer's "original text" (itself a problematic concept), but it is conclusively demonstrable that "Solyman mountains" was what later readers encountered in Homer as early as the fifth century B.C.E. Josephus's *Against Apion*, his detailed defense against anti-Semitic propaganda, preserves an ingenious reading of a passage from Choerilus of Samus, the epic poet of the Persian wars who wrote at the turn of the fifth to the fourth century B.C.E.:

> Choerilus, an older poet, makes mention of our race, specifying that they joined the expedition of Xerxes, the Persian king, against Greece. Having enumerated all the races, he drew up ours last of all, saying that:
>
>> They emitted a Phoenician language from their mouths,
>> They lived in the Solyman mountains by the broad lake,
>> Squalid of hair, tonsured [*trokhokourades*], and above themselves
>> They bore the flayed skin of horses' heads, smoke-dried.

---

21. Brenk 2011 discusses the history of the name *Hierosolyma. Solyma* could also derive from *Solomon*: see, e.g., Eupolemos *FHJA* 2b (p. 128).

22. *Il.* 6.184, 6.204.

23. Σ Hom., *Il.* 6.184; *Od.* 5.283. According to Σ Hom., *Od.* 1.23 (see also Σ *Il.* 6.184; *Od.* 5.282), Aristarchus concluded on the basis of this Lycian stop-off that Poseidon had been visiting the eastern rather than the western Ethiopians.

24. M. L. West 2011.

It is obvious to anyone, I think, that he is making reference to us, from the fact that the Solyman mountains are in our territory, which we inhabit, as is the so-called asphalt lake [the Dead Sea], for the latter is broader and larger than the other ones in Syria.[25]

Let us focus for now on the poetic quotation embedded in the midst. Note, first of all, that the poet has opted for the geographically indeterminate Odyssean toponym "the Solyman mountains" rather than the *Iliad*'s ethnic Solymoi. Choerilus's phrase "in the Solyman mountains [*en Solumois oresi*]" occupies, moreover, the same metrical position as the *Odyssey*'s "from the Solyman mountains [*ek Solumōn oreōn*]"—another clear indicator that we should be thinking of the geographically vague *Odyssey* passage rather than the specifically Lycian figures of the *Iliad*. So it seems clear that Choerilus had "Solyman mountains" in his text of Homer.

But where did he place them? Let us zoom outward and consider Josephus's argument. Josephus, apparently, takes the reference to a "Phoenician" (i.e., Semitic) language as an indication that this people originates in Syro-Palestine (note "in Syria" in the last line). Might he be right? Might Choerilus, in other words, have thought that Jews, however dimly he perceived and understood them as a people, joined Xerxes's invasionary force? It is usually argued[26] that Choerilus cannot have been writing of Jews, since Jewish law forbids tonsuring.[27] But a moment's reflection shows how weak this objection is. Choerilus did not witness the invasion himself; his description is based on an amalgam of various Herodotean Eastern peoples, principally the Arabians who wear their hair "cut in a circle [*keirontai . . . peritrokhala*]" (3.8.3) and the eastern Ethiopians whose headdresses are made from horses' scalps (7.70.2). Whoever Choerilus thought he was writing about, he drew the details from literature rather than observation. And of course he did not know the Bible, so any affront to Levitical protocol (even assuming that it was adhered to in practice) would have meant nothing to him. The fact that Choerilus's description of the inhabitants of the Solyman mountains doesn't look like what we assume to be the "truth" about ancient Jews tells us nothing about what he thought he was describing.

What is the positive argument for accepting the construction Josephus places on the passage? First, book 7 of Herodotus's *Histories*—Choerilus's source for the enumeration of Xerxes's forces—refers to "Palestinian Syrians" among Xerxes's troops.[28] Herodotus speaks at one other point of "Palestinian Syrians," in book 2, where he describes them (along with the Phoenicians and others) as practitioners of circumcision (2.104.2–3); there is thus a circumstantial case that Choerilus's

---

25. Jos., *Ap.* 1.172–74; Choerilus, *SH* 320 = *FGrH* 696 F 34e and fr. 4 Kinkel (p. 268).
26. Lloyd-Jones and Parsons in *SH*, 150.
27. Lev. 19:27.
28. Hdt. 7.89.

source, at any rate, thought there was a Jewish presence in the army.[29] Second and more substantially, Paola Radici Colace (1976) shows convincingly that the Greeks used the word *broad* of watery expanses to mean "salty"; this increases the likelihood that "the broad lake" refers to the Dead Sea. Finally, "a Phoenician language" seems to point to Semitic people. It is hard to imagine that any Greek would have thought of the Iliadic Lycians as speaking a language related to Phoenician.[30] Whatever people, ultimately, Choerilus is thinking of, this does apparently locate them in Syro-Palestine and—pointedly—not in the Lycia of the Iliadic Solymoi. Additionally, we might speculate further on whether *trokhokourades*—a hapax legomenon derived from *trokhos* (wheel or circle) and *keirō* (cut)—means something more than "tonsured." If we imagine a conceptual break after "squalid of hair [*aukhmaleoi koruphas*]," could we perhaps take it to refer instead to circumcision, a poetic periphrasis for the usual derivatives from *peritamnein* (cut around)?[31] On balance, I find this less likely, because of the allusion to Herodotus 3.8.3 (Arabians wear their hair "cut in a circle [*keirontai . . . peritrokhala*]"). But reception can activate alternative potential meanings: it is not impossible, that is to say, that Josephus read Choerilus as referring to circumcision.

The wider point, however, is that to ask "Are Choerilus's Solymoi Jews or not?" is to impose too solid and restrictive a framework on an early poetic text. Choerilus did not divide the world into Jews and Gentiles with the same binary zeal that Josephus did or indeed modern scholars tend to. Jan Assmann has pointed to the revolutionary polarization that Jewish monotheism created and its distinctiveness in the context of the wider ancient world, a binarism that encompassed both religious absolutism and ethnic definition.[32] It is a mode of ethnic identification with which Josephus was fully familiar: the idea of "Jew or not" was straightforward to him (hence his comment, in the passage cited above, that "it is obvious to anyone")—even if he himself, Hellenized and politically compromised as he was, was a living embodiment of its unworkability. But a Samian of the fifth century B.C.E. would not have worked with absolutist distinctions of this kind: for Choerilus, Phoenicians, Syrians, Palestinians, Arabs, and "eastern Ethiopians" will have formed a continuum.

Let us return to "the Solyman mountains." If the reconstruction above is right and Choerilus is referring to Herodotus's "Palestinian Syrians," this seems to be evidence for an identification, as early as the fifth century, of Jerusalem with Homer's Solyma—and that would, in the conventional interpretation, be a surprise; scholars have usually assumed that this identification must date to the

---

29. So, e.g., Feldman 1993, 5.
30. For the assumption that Choerilus refers to the Lycian Solymoi see, e.g., Gonzales 2005, 269–70.
31. Hdt. 2.104.2–3.
32. E.g., Assmann 2009, 8–56.

Hellenistic period, when Jews were (it is supposed) attempting to integrate into the Greek world.[33] The name *Hierosolymoi* itself is not otherwise thought to be older than that. What is more, there is no unproblematic connection with Homer's Solyman mountains or Solymi attested before the Flavian era.[34] Yet Choerilus seems to be linking the two already at the end of the fifth century. So either I am misreading Choerilus, his identification is a one-off, or—my preferred hypothesis—the identification existed earlier than we think but has been submerged by history.

ENTER THE SOLYMOI

I am arguing, then, that the Jews were associated early on with the territory of the *Odyssey*'s Solyma mountains, in a tradition visible to us only in the Choerilus fragment. The link with the *Iliad*'s (Lycian) Solymoi, it seems, followed later. Indeed, we can put a provisional date on the latter. After the sack of Jerusalem and the destruction of the Temple in 70 C.E., the identification with the Iliadic Solymoi seems to have spread with remarkable speed: we find it not only in Josephus but also in Tacitus, Valerius Flaccus, Martial, and Statius.[35] In a famous passage from book 5 of his *Histories*, for example, Tacitus offers six accounts of the origins of the Jews, the fifth of which directly references their "famous [*clara*]" origins as the Solymoi, a "people celebrated in Homer's poems [*carminibus Homeri celebratam gentem*]," and avers that the name *Hierosolyma* derives from them (5.2).

This apparently sudden rebranding of the Jews as the Iliadic Solymoi in the Flavian period, as I have suggested (and this is not controversial), must be related to their increased visibility in light of the Jewish revolt and the subjugation of Jerusalem in 70 C.E. Given that the Romans were presenting the Jewish war as a magnificent return to military form, the Iliadic connection can be seen as part of a wider attempt to magnify the Jews' military threat so as to glorify all the more the Romans' defeat of them; after all, the Iliadic Solymoi offer Bellerophon the

---

33. Brenk 2011, 16–19, however, tentatively floats the idea that Ionian Greek traders in the Archaic period may have already named Jerusalem *Hierosolyma* and that Hecataeus of Miletus may have used the term at the turn of the sixth to the fifth century.

34. A difficult passage attributed to Manetho (*FGrH* 609 F 10, p. 95) speaks of the inhabitants of Jerusalem as "Solymites," but this may in fact be a gloss on the part of Josephus, who transmits him at this point (*Ap*. 1.248). Jacoby places the word in double square brackets in *FGrH*; see further Barclay 2007, 140. The second-century Eupolemus also seems to use the name *Hierosolyma* (*FGrH* 732 F 2, p. 675), but again this may be the transmitter (Clement) speaking.

35. See Brenk 1999, 226–35; Jos., *Ant*. 1.180 (which identifies Jerusalem with Salem), 7.67; Jos., *Bell*. 6.438–39; Tac., *Hist*. 5.2; Flacc. 1.13; Mart. 7.55.7, 11.94; Stat., *Silv*. 5.2.138; Juv. 6.544; later, Paus. 8.16.4–5; Philostr., *VA* 6.29.

"fiercest battle [*kartistēn makhēn*]" fought between men (6.185), and Tacitus's "famous [*clara*]" and "celebrated [*celebratam*]" arguably allude directly to the *Iliad*'s description of them as "glorious [*kudalimoisi*]" (6.184, 6.204).

More interesting is the fact that Jews too seem to have bought into this identification, while reversing its implications. The fourth *Sibylline Oracle*, probably a Judaean text of the late first century,[36] describes the Roman destruction of 70 C.E. as an attack on the land of the Solymoi:

> The wicked squall of war will come on the Solymoi too
> From Italy, and will sack god's great temple,
> Whensoever trusting in their folly they shall cast off
> Piety and fulfill their hateful murders in front of the temple.
> ...
> Rome's chief will come to Syria, and will burn with fire
> The temple of the Solymoi, killing many men at the same time,
> And will destroy the great land, with its wide streets, of the Jews. (115–18, 125–27)[37]

What is interesting here is that the passage weaves in a second level of Iliadic reminiscence, intertextually assimilating the sack of Jerusalem with that of Troy. This is a passage crammed full of Iliadic motifs. The "wicked squall of war [*kakē polemoio thuella*]" of line 115 looks to the "wicked squall of wind [*kakē anemoio thuella*]" (in the same metrical position) that Helen, in her self-recrimination in the *Iliad*, book 6, wishes had swept her up before she was born (6.346) and more generally to the central role of wind and storm imagery in the Homeric poems.[38] The word here used for "sack," *exalapazein*, is, perhaps unsurprisingly, used in the *Iliad* primarily of the prospective sack of Troy. The most striking pointer is the epithet "with wide streets [*euruaguian*]" (127), which the *Iliad* applies prominently to Troy. Talk of murders in front of temples also evokes, more indirectly, the atrocities committed (e.g., against Polyxena) by the Greeks after the sack. The Hellenized Jewish author of the fourth *Sibylline* thus seems to have taken over the Romans' Iliadic designation of the Jews as Solymoi and inverted it so it becomes a condemnation of Roman war crimes.

Finally in this section, it is time to rejoin Memnon and to explore a twist in the tale of the Jewish Solymoi. Quintus of Smyrna's *Posthomerica* is a rich hexameter poem, composed in the third or fourth century C.E., completing the story of the capture of Troy from where Homer left off. Book 2 sees the arrival of Memnon to the great acclaim of the Trojans. Welcomed by Priam, he is said to have recounted many stories of his travels and adventures from the edge of the ocean (*ap' Okeanoio*) to Troy. But the narrator elaborates on only one of these:

---

36. K. Jones 2011, 178–81.
37. A briefer mention of the destruction of the "Solyman land" comes at 12.103.
38. Purves 2010.

And he told of how with his strong hands he subdued
The holy army of the vexatious Solymoi [*argaleōn Solumōn hieron straton*], who detained him
On his way—which brought grief and intolerable woe on them. (2.121–23)

The first point to make here is about the use of the adjective *hieron* (holy) to describe the Solymoi's army. There is, to my knowledge, only one other "holy army" in Greek literature: in book 24 of the *Odyssey*, the *hieros stratos* of the Argive spearmen pile up a tomb for Achilles and Patroclus (24.81). Alfred Heubeck comments that "in connection with στρατός [army] the word ἱερός [holy] has lost some of its original, religious meaning, but not all the religious connotations: 'filled with unusual inner strength.'"[39] It may be as Heubeck says, that *hieros* is an appropriate adjective for an army performing ritual duties, as is the case in the *Odyssey*, but the epithet seems jarring in the context of the "vexatious" Solymoi, whose actions bring grievous woe on themselves. I cannot see that *hieros* can serve any function in this line other than to suggest an identification between the Solymoi and the Hierosolymoi, which is to say the Jerusalemites.[40] If that is right, then Memnon's sacking of their city—unattested in any other tradition—is surely supposed to serve as a prequel to Vespasian's, with the "grief and intolerable woe [*pēma kai askheton . . . potmon*]" resonating against the latter's notoriously brutal treatment of the Jews. Similarly, Memnon's glorious entry into Troy may recall Vespasian's (and Titus's) triumph in 71.

So Quintus seems to telescope time, using the reference to the Solymoi as a narrative wormhole connecting two very different events, one from myth and the other from relatively recent history. But why is it Memnon who is said to sack the city of the Solymoi? The crucial point is that Memnon's journey from Ethiopia to the Mediterranean via the land of the Solymoi is surely designed to retrace the steps and make sense of Poseidon's journey in the *Odyssey*.[41] One can see that a plausible route from Ethiopia to Troy might have gone overland through Palestine. So this may be simply a philological tidying up, on Quintus's part, of a longstanding geographical ambiguity in Homer's text. But I wonder if there is more to it than this. Josephus in his *Jewish War* speaks of yet another Memnoneion ("Memnonos mnēmeion"—a pleasing play on words), near Ptolemais, the city in Galilee (2.189). Was there therefore a hero cult of Memnon in Galilee? And was there therefore a tradition that Memnon was in fact claimed by Galileans or at least had some benign connection with territory that could be thought of (however

---

39. In Russo, Fernández-Galiano, and Heubeck 1992, 369.

40. Ingo Gildenhard and Calum Maciver have each pointed out to me different aspects of the distinctive syntactical arrangement of the phrase *argaleōn Solumōn hieron straton*, which functions as a double hypallage with a reversal of the anticipated order *hiera Solyma*.

41. As implied by A. James 2007, 277.

inaccurately) as Jewish? If this is right, then perhaps Quintus is interpreting the Galilean Memnoneion as a victory monument—and one moreover that foreshadows the later destruction of (relatively) nearby Jerusalem.

JEWISH EPIC

Let me turn, finally, to what seems to have been a brief but significant flowering of creativity in the intellectual contact zone between Greek and Jewish traditions probably at some point in the third and second centuries B.C.E. Like those of Ezekiel the Tragedian, the fragments of Theodotus and Philo ("the elder," not the better-known Alexandrian Platonist) are preserved in Eusebius's *Preparation for the Gospel*. Eusebius in turn found them extracted in Alexander Polyhistor's *On the Jews*, a seemingly remarkable work (now lost) of the late republic that is indirectly responsible for most of our sources on Hellenistic Judaism. Early medieval sources attest to a third writer of Hellenistic Jewish epic, one Sosates—said to have been known as "the Jewish Homer."[42]

This material is very difficult to deal with.[43] The problems begin with the highly selective nature of the (double) excerption. Theodotus's work seems to have been called *On the Jews* (*Peri Ioudaion*), but the eight preserved fragments (ranging from two to fifteen lines long) deal exclusively with the city of Shechem, which was in the territory of the "northern kingdom" of the Samaritans, historically antagonistic to Judah in the south. Does this mean, as some have claimed, that Theodotus in fact confined himself to Samaritan history? Was he a Samaritan writing a pro-Samaritan text?[44] As I shall argue presently, that seems to misread the tenor of the poem. Of Philo's work, apparently called *On Jerusalem*, we have even less. Of at least fourteen books (if the text of Eusebius is right at the point in question)[45] we have only six fragments, totaling nineteen lines. These are, what is more, arguably the most difficult and rebarbative lines in all of Greek poetry. Recondite vocabulary

---

42. S. J. D. Cohen 1981. One place where epic and biblical significantly converge is exegetical scholarship: see the excellent study of Niehoff 2011.

43. I cite from *FHJA*. Kuhn 2012 came to my attention only after I had submitted my manuscript; as a result, I engage with this valuable text only minimally.

44. Freudenthal 1874–75, 99–100, bases its argument principally on the centrality of Shechem in the fragments and its description as a "holy city." Pummer 1982, 177 nn. 2–3, gives a full list of supporters and opponents of the theory to that date. Collins 1980 (but compare 2000, 57–60) musters the most powerful arguments against, noting inter alia that (i) we cannot be certain that our selection is representative, (ii) the inhabitants of Shechem are represented in a negative light (a point I shall develop in more detail later), and (iii) there is no mention of Mt. Gerizim. Mendels 1987, 109–16, reasserts the position of Freudenthal and others, but I remain convinced that Shechem is ultimately constructed as Jerusalem's other in this text.

45. Euseb., *Praep.* 9.24.1 = Philo fr. 3 *FHJA*.

is showcased in obscure morphology and opaque syntax, to the extent that sometimes even the gist of the sentence is entirely mysterious. Take, for example, the first word of the first transmitted fragment, which is *ekluon*: does this come from *ekluō* (release) or *kluō* (hear)? Is it first-person singular or third-person plural? These questions bear on the interpretation of the passage as a whole, which most commentators believe to be about circumcision: thus Carl R. Holladay's *Fragments from Hellenistic Jewish Authors* translates, "They unloosed the loins for our ancestors just as once (they were commanded) by the (divine) ordinances." Hugh Lloyd-Jones and Peter Parsons in *Supplementum Hellenisticum*, by contrast, paraphrase as "I heard, Abraham, that you of old acquired the highest glory, from the sacrifice of Isaac"—nothing to do with circumcision here.[46]

The central point here, however, is not the correct reading of the passage (although I have views on this)[47] but the extreme difficulty of the Greek: why did Philo opt for this obscure, challenging mode of expression? The most recent discussion plausibly links it to an oracular poetics, comparing texts such as Lycophron's *Alexandra* and the *Sibylline Oracles*.[48] It is a reasonable hypothesis (as with Ezekiel), however, that he was an Alexandrian and influenced by the complex allusivity of that particular poetic tradition. But it seems unlikely that passive influence alone could explain such an extraordinary linguistic register: not even Lycophron writes with such gnarled compression. A better hypothesis is that Philo aims at a sublimity that seeks to express the matchless grandeur of his subject matter. Time and again, he writes in terms of excess, of transgression, of superabundance. In fragment 1, Abraham is addressed as "famous-sounding [*klutoēkhes*],"[49] "all-shining [*pamphaes*]", and "cascading" (if this is what *plēmmure* means), with "great-shouting calculations [*megaukhētoisi logismois*]."[50] Note

---

46. *SH* 681, p. 328. Kuhn 2012, 22–23, follows Lloyd-Jones and Parsons by assuming a missing second line and thus avoids circumcision.

47. "Ἔκλυον ἀρχεγόνοισι τὸ μυρίον ὥς ποτε θεσμοῖς / Ἀβραὰμ κλυτοηχὲς ὑπέρτερον ἄμματι δεσμῶν / Παμφαὲς, πλήμμυρε μεγαυχητοῖσι λογισμοῖς / θεοφιλῆ θέλητρα." In my view, ὥς in the first line is critical, and suggests indirect statement; that implies that Ἔκλυον means "I heard," with apostrophe to the vocative *Abraham* in line 2. The problem, then, is that we have no verb for the subordinate clause, so I wonder whether we should not read ὑπέρτεμον for ὑπέρτερον in line 2, i.e., "they cut at the top." Ὑπερτέμνω is not otherwise attested in ancient Greek, but Philo seems unconstrained by such concerns. I would then take an emended μηρίον (for μυρίον) as object, i.e., "I heard, famous Abraham—luminous, overflowing with glorious thoughts [πλήμμυρε μεγαυχητοῖσι λογισμοῖς]—how once with ancient rites [ἀρχεγόνοισι... θεσμοῖς] they cut above the penis [μηρίον—not an obvious word to use], divinely pleasing gestures [θεοφιλῆ θέλητρα]." So in this reading it is about circumcision and in particular the *kleos* that attaches to circumcision via the link to the sacrifice of Isaac.

48. Kuhn 2012, 68–71.

49. The parallel with Philo's frequent description of Abraham as "elect father of sound [*ēkhous*]" has been noted: see Holladay in *FHJA*, 2.249, with literature.

50. Kuhn 2012, 65, notes the prevalence of water and light imagery.

particularly the emphasis on his voice: "great-shouting" not only evokes the *Iliad*'s yelling heroes but also points self-reflexively to the vocal power arrogated to Philo's epic. Similarly, the Jewish god is described as *briēpuos*, "loud-shouting" (8), an Iliadic epithet of Ares (13.521), and grants Abraham an immortal voice ("athanaton ... phatin"):

> When he [Abraham] left the glorious enclosure
> Of the dread-born ones (?), the revered heavy-caller, checking the burnt offering,
> Made his voice immortal. (fr. 1.4–6)

Briēpuos literally means "heavy-calling," the first part deriving from *brithos*, "weight"; this epithet certainly offers support to James Porter's thesis that sublimity in ancient discourse is rooted in ideas about the materiality of language.[51] It appears there is also a hint of Yahweh the thunderer here, an association facilitated by both the "weight" of his voice and the proximity of *briēpuos* to other Greek words for thunder (*brontē, bromos*),[52] and although Philo at this point seems (seems!) to be alluding to the sacrifice of Isaac, when there is no thunder (Genesis 22:1–19), Yahweh thunders at other points of intervention in the Hebrew Bible—most notably when the Israelites reach Mt. Sinai (Exodus 19:16). Thunder is a complex, multivalent image. Thunder is certainly associated with the biblical god, but the iconographic link with the Zeus of Greek epic is closer and more pervasive. What is more, thunder becomes a self-reflexive marker of sublime poetry: arguably already in the sonically extraordinary Titanomachy of Hesiod's *Theogony* (689–712), in Aristophanes's *Frogs* (814, of Aeschylus),[53] and most canonically in Callimachus, who rejects such poetics in his *Aetia* with the comment that "the thunderbolt [*brontē*] is Zeus's, not mine" (fr. 1.20 Pfeiffer). Philo thus seems deliberately to reject the delicate poetics of Alexandria: to paraphrase Callimachus, he claims the thunderbolt both for his god and for himself.

This emphasis on refractory, excessive speech continues into fragment 3, which mentions Joseph as "the *thespistēs* of dreams" (8–9), where the noun, meaning "prophet," etymologically indicates the possession of divine language. Joseph, Philo expands, would whirl (*dineusas*) time's secrets in the flow (*plēmmuridi*) of fate: the image is that of a vortex, which seems to point to the sublime cosmic imaginings of the pre-Socratics.[54] Notable too is the language of flux, which not

---

51. Porter 2010.
52. Holladay at *FHJA*, 2.257 (again, with literature) intuits this interpretation: "It [*briēpuos*] could easily be taken with αἰνετός and rendered as 'praiseworthy thunderer.'"
53. Scharffenberger 2007 interestingly discusses Aristophanes's presentation of Aeschylus in terms of aural effect.
54. Sources listed at *TEGP*, vol. 2, index, s.v. "vortex." On the sublimity of the pre-Socratics see Porter 2010, 151–73.

only picks up the description in fragment 1 of Abraham as "cascading [*plēmmure*]" with thoughts but also looks forward to a dominant theme in the remaining fragments. These focus ecphrastically on the wonders (note "thambēestaton" in line 1 of fragment 4) of the plumbing in Jerusalem, and one particularly opaque sentence in fragment 4 alludes to the "deep flow [*bathun rhoon*]" of the water in question. In fragment 5, the water again causes wonder (*thambos*, 4) but this time is also associated with the qualities of luminosity and visibility we saw in fragment 1. It is "high-gleaming [*hupsiphaennon*, a *hapax*]" (1), "visible from far off [*tēlephaē*, an extremely rare word]" (4): these epithets capture the range, magnitude, and sublimity (note the *hupsi-* root) of the discourse itself. This language of the wondrous coursing of water, shared between metaphor and literal description of plumbing, seems to point and respond to the programmatic metaliterary water imagery familiar from Callimachus's epigrams and *Hymn to Apollo* 105–13 (and from Pindar before him),[55] yet as with the imagery of the thunderbolt, it engages primarily in order to mark distance from mainstream Hellenistic aesthetics, celebrating the torrent instead of the fountain.

The excess of linguistic signification, then, the irreducibility of this poetry to simple meaning, can be seen as part of a deliberate strategy to represent sublime divinity in poetic discourse. It is worth remembering that, as more recent scholarship has been at pains to insist, stylistics were a central concern to translators of the Septuagint too: the extraordinary syntax and vocabulary adopted for Biblical Greek was the product not of an inadequate grasp of classical Greek or of passive interference between Greek and Hebrew in the minds of bilinguals but of a concerted attempt to create a new hierolect as a vehicle for the sacred word.[56] The language of the Septuagint, that is to say, seems to have been deliberately turned so as to be unsettling; its translators employed the strategy that Lawrence Venuti names "foreignizing" as a "form of resistance against ethnocentrism and racism, cultural narcissism and imperialism."[57] Even many Jews who composed in Greek thereafter employed "foreignizing" tactics and thus ended up producing "pseudo-translations" that mimicked the dislocating effect of the Septuagint translation, such as 3 and 4 Maccabees, Baruch, and the Wisdom of Solomon.[58] As a result, where we have no Hebrew or Aramaic original, it is often impossible to tell whether the "Semiticisms" in a Greek text are absorbed from a genuinely Semitic original or are knowingly engineered in the Greek original.[59] The linguistic contortions of Philo are of course different, in that they hint not at translation from a Semitic

---

55. Widely discussed: see especially Poliakoff 1980; Knox 1985.
56. Van der Louw 2007; Rajak 2009, 125–75, with further literature.
57. Venuti 1995, 16.
58. Davila 2005, 34 n. 82; Van der Louw 2007, 21.
59. Davila 2005.

original but at a primally sublime epic theology, but both comparably use obscurity to defamiliarize conventional language and thereby to betoken a higher, divine language.[60]

Let me turn finally to Theodotus, an easier poet both stylistically and in narrative terms: his eight fragments, as we have seen, deal with events in the history of the city of Shechem, and they do so relatively straightforwardly. In contrast to Philo, Theodotus aims to "domesticate" Jewish history as he translates it into an epic idiom that is largely tralatitious. "The most striking literary feature of Theodotus's work is its thoroughly epic complexion. . . . The work is characterized by numerous distinctively Homeric . . . terms."[61] Why then did Theodotus choose epic instead of, for instance, prose history, like Artapanus, Eupolemus, and Josephus? The answer, I think, is that he set himself the task of writing a poem that—like the *Iliad* and the *Odyssey*—would offer a map of identity in terms of hospitality and its rejection and in terms of the restoration of proper sexual behavior. His poem does not simply use the Greek epic tradition as a rich palette with which to paint, although it does do that; it aims, rather, to refine and accentuate the theme of cultural differentiation already latent in Homer. Theodotus is a receiver of Homer in the full, dynamic, sense: he aims not only to become (like Sosates) a "Jewish Homer" but also to appropriate Homer as a proto-Jewish writer.

In particular, intertextual echoes help us to decode the representation of Shechem in the surviving fragments. Fragment 1 offers a description of the city that is saturated in specifically Odyssean language:

> Now thus the land was indeed fertile, goat-rearing and well-watered,
> Neither was it a long road to enter the city
> From the country. Nor were there ever dense thickets for laborers.
> And out of it very near two mountains appear steep,
> Full of grass and trees. And between them
> Is cut a path, a narrow hollow, and on the other side
> The living [city] of Shechem appears, a holy city,
> Built below at the base [of the mountain], and around it a smooth
> Wall, running under the foot of the mountain, a lofty bulwark.
> (translation adapted from Holladay)

---

60. Note too that the one explicit reference to Jewish scripture in (probably) pre-late-antique polytheistic Greek literature, ps.-Long., *De subl.* 9.9, refers directly to sublimity of language (with respect to Gen. 1:1). On this celebrated passage see now Usher 2007, which does not, however, quite convince (me, at any rate) that (ps.-)Longinus engages with the context of the biblical source.

61. Holladay in *FJHA*, 2.72. See also Pummer and Roussel 1982; Kuhn 2012 observes that Theodotus's vocabulary stretches beyond Homer into tragedy and *Kunstprosa* (53–55) and tends to avoid the language of the Septuagint (29–31).

The language is borrowed fairly promiscuously from the topography of the *Odyssey*:[62] Shechem is being associated predominantly with Ithaca but also with various other idealized locations. The city is described as "goat-rearing [*aiginomos*]" and "well-watered [*hudrēlē*]" (1); this points to Athena's description of Ithaca at *Odyssey* 13.246–47: "good for goat-feeding [*aigibotos*] and oxen-feeding; there is every kind of forest, and abundant waterings [*ardmoi*]."[63] The word *hudrēlos* (well-watered) is an ingenious twist: if "goat-rearing" necessarily links Shechem to Ithaca, this epithet in fact looks rather to *Odyssey* 9.133, where it describes the meadows on the island near the Cyclopes' own, which, of course, is characterized by its abundance of goats (9.124). Theodotus has identified the two distinctively goaty places in the *Odyssey* and forged allusive links between them. The narrator then proceeds to describe the journey (*hodos*) from the fields (*agrothen*) into the city (*polin*, 2–3), which echoes Odysseus's journey (*hodos*, *Od.* 17.204) with Eumaeus to the polis of Ithaca (*Od.* 17.201).[64] Theodotus's path (*atrapitos*) leads between two mountains (4–6); similarly, Odysseus's "path [*atarpitou*, by metathesis]" (*Od.* 17.234) is "steepling" or "rugged [*paipaloessan*]" (*Od.* 17.204).[65]

These allusions do more, I think, than simply add intertextual color to the description. First, they mark Shechem out as an especially significant place in the poem's value system; the city occupies, Theodotus suggests, a role analogous to that of Ithaca in the *Odyssey*. In this connection we should note the much-discussed reference to Shechem as a "holy city [*hieron astu*]," the interpretation of which is critical for the question of Theodotus's origin in Samaria or elsewhere.[66] It is true enough that the epithet *hieros* is applied apparently blandly to a number of cities in the *Iliad* without any implication of distinctive sacredness, but when used in the context of a biblical epic, it can hardly be dismissed as simply a topos.[67] The crucial point, in my view, is that the phrase marks Shechem as a potential competitor to Jerusalem, a city not only canonically holy but also, as we have seen, with *hieros* in the Hellenized form of its name. Used of Shechem, then, the phrase is provocative and ironic. Note too that *Sikimōn* in the same line hints at the metri-

---

62. Holladay in *FJHA*, 2.136–45, and Kuhn 2012, 56, list many of the allusions.

63. Holladay in *FJHA*, 2.136, points by contrast to *Od.* 15.405–6, where Syria is described as *agathē men, euboτos, eumēlos*; compare Theodotus's *agathē te kai aiginomos*. While Theodotus is certainly looking to that passage with *agathē*, the reference to goat rearing is distinctively Ithacan.

64. *Agrothen* is used twice in the Cretan lies (*Od.* 13.268, 15.428; see *FHJA*, 2.137). The road that is "not long [*oude . . . dolikhē*]" picks up and inverts Eidothea's prediction to Menelaus that he will have a "long [*dolikhēn*] and grievous road [*hodon*]" home (*Od.* 4.393); see Holladay in *FJHA*, 2.137.

65. Other Odyssean echoes: thickets (*dria*; similarly *Od.* 6.106, 14.353); the "narrow [*araiē*]" path (*Od.* 10.90).

66. Holladay in *FJHA*, 2.143–44.

67. So Kuhn 2012, 56.

cally identical *Solumōn*—reinforcing the suggestion that Shechem serves as a Doppelstadt of the "holy city of the Solymoi."[68]

From a different perspective, the intertextual density of the description makes Shechem a space for poetic self-reflexivity. All *loci amoeni* are, in a sense, compressed poetological manifestos. In this case, the larding of Homeric referentiality on to a biblical space encourages us to read that space as paradigmatic of the interstitial poetics embodied by Theodotus. In this connection, the reference to the "path" becomes highly suggestive, since imagery of paths and journeys is, of course, central to the Greek tradition, from the Homeric "ways [*oimoi*] of song" onward. Theodotus's path passes between two mountains; does this express the poet's position between two cultural systems?

Let us return to firmer ground. The most important role that the Odyssean texture plays is to create the expectation of an episode in which the values of civilized behavior and the etiquette of reciprocity are tested. Presently we are told of Jacob's arrival in the city (fr. 2, alluding to Gen. 33:18–34): he has left the "broad flow [*euru rheithron*] of the Euphrates, a thundering river [*potamou keladontos*]" (fr. 3.1–2). This description suggests the landscape of the Trojan plain[69] and serves to reinforce the analogy between Jacob and the Odysseus who returns from Troy. Yet the analogy discloses points of difference as well as similarity, for Shechem is no homely Ithaca for Jacob. The Shechemites turn out to be disastrous hosts. We have already been warned in fragment 2 that the king, Hamor, and his son, the eponymous Shechem (in Greek *Sukhem*—which slightly conceals the eponymy with *Sikima*) are a "mad [*ateiree*, whose root is *atē*, that violent, destructive force that predominates in Attic tragedy]" pair (fr. 2.6). Theodotus, as we shall see, assimilate the Shechemites to the *Odyssey*'s transgressive hosts: the Laestrygonians, the Cyclops, the suitors.

The sense of foreboding is consolidated in fragment 3, where we move apparently analeptically away from Shechem to hear how Jacob married Rachel (Gen. 29:10–28). There is, however, a strong thematic correlation with the episodes set in Shechem, which also focus on hospitality and sexual impropriety. Jacob's father-in-law Laban is said to have "received him graciously [*prophrōn hupedekto*]" (fr. 3.8), a phrase that recurs in both the *Odyssey* and the *Iliad*;[70] we may thus feel we have been conditioned to expect Phaeacian-style hospitality, particularly

---

68. The exact construal of the first half of this line (and hence the syntactical role of *Sikimōn*) is unclear: see Holladay in *FJHA*, 2.142–43. The best reading would no doubt be to take *Sikimōn* as possessive genitive after *hieron astu*, but this would require a fresh emendation for the (far from certain) first two words of the line, *hē dierē*.

69. Hom., *Il.* 21.304, etc. (*euru rheontos*), 18.576 (*potamon keladonta*, on Achilles's shield); Holladay in *FJHA*, 2.163.

70. Hom., *Il.* 9.480, 23.647; *Od.* 2.387, 14.54, 20.372, 23.314; see Holladay in *FJHA*, 2.164–65.

when Laban offers his daughter to Jacob (as Alcinous does to Odysseus). Yet Laban attempts to trick Jacob by sending his elder daughter, Leah; the biblical narrative deviates from the Odyssean template, as the Alcinous figure turns out to be deceptive.

The Laban episode paves the way for the worst case of sexual transgression in the transmitted fragments. In fragment 4 (~ Gen. 34:1–2), back in Shechem, Shechem (the king's son) rapes Dinah (the daughter of Jacob and Rachel) at a festival. As if he were in a New Comedy, Shechem then turns up with his father to ask Jacob's permission to marry her (whereas in Gen. 34:3 he simply tells his father of his desire for marriage). But this is not comedy; Jacob refuses on the grounds of the interdiction of intermarriage: "For indeed it is not proper [*ou themiton*] for Hebrews to bring home sons-in-law and daughters-in-law from another place [*allothen*], but only one who boasts of being of the same race [*geneēs . . . homoiēs*]" (fr. 4.20–21). There is a firm, unbreakable boundary between Jew and non-Jew. The following fragment (5) deals with circumcision—the marker of Jews' distinctness from other peoples—and in the final transmitted episode (frs. 6–8) Simeon and Levi exact fearsome revenge, slaughtering the Shechemites for their violation of the laws of hospitality ("for they did not honor [*etion*] / whoever came to them," fr. 7.4–5) and their injustice ("nor did they dispense justice [*dikas edikazon*] throughout the city, or laws [*themistas*]," fr. 7.6). The Shechemites are thus implicitly assimilated to the Odyssey's Cyclopes, who also shun "justice" and "laws": the same words (*dikas, themistas*) are used in the *Odyssey* (9.216), in the same case (and in the case of *themistas* the same metrical position).[71] The slaughter of the Shechemites is crammed with Iliadic martial motifs[72] and thus implicitly cast as Homeric retribution for adultery, both Paris's and the Odyssean suitors'. Like the *Odyssey*, Theodotus's poem is built around a journey, episodes of hospitality and its rejection, and the violent reestablishment of proper sexual order in the aftermath of transgression. In both poems, what is more, the story encodes a narrative of identity making; the difference is that Theodotus welds the story to a powerful moral of ethnic differentiation, in effect rereading the *Odyssey* and the *Iliad* as parables treating of the disastrous effects of intermarriage. Reading the Homeric poems through a distinctively Jewish lens, Theodotus takes them as stories fundamentally about the dangers of allowing one's women to marry exogamously.

Theodotus and Philo thus offer two very different examples of highly sophisticated play with the epic repertoire: each exploits a deep familiarity with canonical Greek epic but to express a distinctively Jewish vision. One can only wonder what the

---

71. For the absence of *themis* among the Cyclopes see also *Od.* 9.106, 9.112, 9.114.
72. Holladay in *FJHA*, 2.198–204; Pummer and Roussel 1982; Kuhn 2012, 61.

entire poems looked like or what Sosates, "the Jewish Homer," came up with. When this material is set alongside the evidence for creative readings of the Homeric "Solyman mountains" and "Solymoi," it becomes evident, I think, just how deeply immersed some Hellenistic Jews were in Homeric epic. Certainly such material was not central, and the individuals capable of such dynamic mediation between traditions are likely to have been rare. Yet we should also, conversely, remember just how little Hellenistic Jewish material we have and (again) how dependent we are on the filtering of Roman and early Christian redactors (who necessarily have their own distorting agenda). We have seen enough to conclude that any picture of Jews as systematically resistant to Greek literary culture is entirely misguided. In the prerabbinical period, Hellenized Jews, like other Near Eastern peoples, responded to the top-down pressure of Greek cultural influence in a variety of ways: these undoubtedly included the kind of hostility we find in the Maccabees but also ranged at the other end to intricate hybridization.

It is tempting to explain this spectrum in geopolitical terms: whereas Palestine, particularly in the Hasmonaean era, was separatist, Alexandria and other cities under Greek or Roman control nurtured intercultural literary experimentation. Yet this is probably a simplification, not only because the Alexandrian origin of Ezekiel, Theodotus, Philo, and others is just guesswork but also because even "separatist" texts like the Maccabees have hybridized features (especially, but not exclusively, the highly rhetorical 4 Maccabees). The point bears repeating: before the destruction of the Temple in 70 C.E. and the subsequent turn toward Hebrew and Aramaic as the vehicles of Mediterranean Judaism, Jews were fully, creatively engaged in negotiating an identity simultaneously within and against the Greek tradition. In this extraordinarily fertile window of cultural exchange, it makes sense to speak of a "Jewish Sophistic," practitioners of which used literary composition cunningly and self-consciously to fashion for themselves and their people a distinctive voice in the midst of the raucous, Hellenistic babble.

REFERENCES

Agapitos, P. A. 1998. "Narrative, Rhetoric and 'Drama' Rediscovered: Scholars and Poets in Byzantium Interpret Heliodorus." In *Studies in Heliodorus*, edited by R. Hunter, 125–56. Cambridge, U.K.
Ahl, F. 1984. "The Art of Safe Criticism in Greece and Rome." *AJPh* 105: 174–208.
Aitken, E. B., and Maclean, J. K. B., eds. 2004. *Philostratus's Heroikos: Religion and Cultural Identity in the Third Century* C.E. Atlanta.
Akujärvi, J. 2005. *Researcher, Traveller, Narrator: Studies in Pausanias' Periegesis*. Stockholm.
Alcock, S. E., Cherry, J., and Elsner, J., eds. 2001. *Pausanias: Travel and Memory in Roman Greece*. New York.
Alliston, A. 1996. *Virtue's Faults: Correspondences in Eighteenth-Century British and French Women's Fiction*. Stanford.
Althusser, L. 1984. "Ideology and Ideological State Apparatuses." In *Essays on Ideology*, 1–60. London.
Altman, J. G. 1982. *Epistolarity: Approaches to a Form*. Athens, OH.
Anderson, G. 1979. "Themes and Composition in Lucian's *Podagra*." *RhM* 122: 149–154.
———. 1984. *Ancient Fiction: The Novel in the Graeco-Roman World*. London.
———. 1986. *Philostratus: Biography and Belles-Lettres in the Third Century* AD. London.
Ando, C. 2000. *Imperial Ideology and Provincial Loyalty*. Berkeley.
Argentieri, L. 2003. *Gli epigrammi degli Antipatri*. Bari.
Asheri, D., Lloyd, A. B., Corcella, A., Murray, O., and Moreno, A. 2007. *A Commentary on Herodotus Books I-IV*. Trans. Barbara Graziosi. Oxford.
Asper, M. 1997. *Onomata allotria: zur Genese, Struktur und Funktion poetologischer Metaphern bei Kallimachos*. Stuttgart.
Assmann, J. 1996. "The Mosaic Distinction: Israel, Egypt, and the Invention of Paganism." *Representations* 56: 48–67.

———. 1998. *Moses the Egyptian: The Memory of Egypt in Western Monotheism.* Cambridge, MA.
———. 2009. *The Price of Monotheism.* Trans. Robert Savage. Palo Alto.
Aujac, G. 1992. *Denys d'Halicarnasse: opuscules rhétoriques.* Vol. 5. Paris.
Avlamis, P. 2011. "Isis and the People in the Life of Aesop." In *Revelation, Literature and Community in Late Antiquity,* edited by P. Townshend and M. Vidas, 65–101. Tübingen.
Bakhtin, M. M. 1986. "The Problem of Speech Genres." In *Speech Genres and Other Late Essays,* translated by V. W. McGee, edited by C. Emerson and M. Holquist, 60–102. Austin.
Bal, M. 1997. *Narratology.* 2nd ed. Toronto.
Baldwin, B. 1993. "What Comes Out in the Wash? Mesomedes 9.15." *LCM* 18.9: 141–2.
Barclay, J. 1996. *Jews in the Mediterranean Diaspora: From Alexander to Trajan (323 BCE to 117 CE).* Edinburgh.
———. 2007. *Flavius Josephus: Translation and Commentary.* Vol. 10, *Against Apion.* Leiden.
Barns, J. W. B. 1956. "Egypt and the Greek Romance." *Mitteilungen aus der Papyrussammlung der Nationalbibliothek in Wien* 5: 29–34.
Barthes, R. 1975. *The Pleasure of the Text.* Trans. R. Miller. New York.
———. 1990. *S/Z.* Trans. R. Miller. Oxford.
Barton, T. 1994a. *Ancient Astrology.* London.
———. 1994b. *Power and Knowledge: Astrology, Physiognomics, and Medicine under the Roman Empire.* Ann Arbor.
Bartsch, S. 1989. *Decoding the Ancient Novel: The Reader and the Role of Description in Heliodorus and Achilles Tatius.* Princeton.
———. 1994. *Actors in the Audience: Theatricality and Double-Speak from Nero to Hadrian.* Cambridge, MA.
Barwick, K. 1928. "Die Gliederung der Narratio in der rhetorischen Theorie und ihre Bedeutung für die Geschichte des antiken Romans." *Hermes* 68: 261–87.
Battisti, D. G. 1997. *Dionigi d'Alicarnasso, sull'imitazione. Edizione critica, traduzione e commento.* Pisa and Rome.
Baumbach, M. 2002. *Lukian in Deutschland: eine Forschungs- und Rezeptionsgeschichtliche Analyse vom Humanismus bis zur Gegenwart.* Munich.
Baumbach, M., and Bär, S., eds. 2007. *Quintus Smyrnaeus: Transforming Homer in Second Sophistic Epic.* Berlin.
Beebee, T. O. 1999. *Epistolary Fiction in Europe 1500–1850.* Cambridge, U.K.
Bélis, A. 2003. "Un lyrikos de l'époque des Antonins: Mésomède de Crète." In *Colloque La poésie grecque antique: actes,* edited by J. Jouanna and J. Leclant, 223–35. Paris.
Bendlin, A. 2006. "Vom Nutzen und Nachteil der Mantik: Orakel im Medium von Handlung und Literatur in der Zeit der Zweiten Sophistik." In *Religions Orientales—Culti Misterici: Neue Perspektiven, Nouvelles Perspectives, Prospettive nuove,* edited by C. Bonnet, J. Rüpke, and P. Scarpi, 159–207. Stuttgart.
Benjamin, W. 1999. *Illuminations.* With an introduction by Hannah Arendt. London.
Bers, V. 1984. *Syntax in the Classical Age.* New Haven.
Beschorner, A. 1999. *Helden und Heroen, Homer und Caracalla: Übersetzung, Kommentar und Interpretationen zum Heroikos des Flavios Philostratos.* Bari.
Bhabha, H. 1994. *The Location of Culture.* London.
Billault, A. 2000. *L'univers de Philostrate.* Brussels.

———. 2004. "Histoire et roman dans les fragments du *Roman de Ninos.*" *Ktema* 29: 215–21.
Billerbeck, M., and Zubler, C. 2000. *Das Lob der Fliege von Lukian bis L. B. Alberti.* Bern.
Birley, A. 1997. *Hadrian, the Restless Emperor.* London.
Bloom, H. 1975. *A Map of Misreading.* New York.
———. 1997. *The Anxiety of Influence: A Theory of Poetry.* 2nd ed. New York.
Blum, R. 1991. *Kallimachos: The Alexandrian Library and the Origins of Bibliography.* Trans. H. Wellisch. Madison.
Boatwright, M. 2000. *Hadrian and the Cities of the Roman Empire.* Princeton.
Boedeker, D. 1988. "Protesilaos and the End of Herodotus' *Histories.*" *ClAnt* 7: 30–48.
Bohak, G. 1996. *Joseph and Aseneth and the Jewish Temple in Heliopolis.* Atlanta.
Bosworth, A. B. 1980. *A Historical Commentary on Arrian's History of Alexander.* Vol. 1, *Commentary on Books 1–3.* Oxford.
Bourdieu, P. 1977. *Outline of a Theory of Practice.* Trans. R. Nice. Cambridge, U.K.
Bourdieu, P., and Passeron, J. C. 1990. *Reproduction in Education, Society and Culture.* 2nd ed. London.
Bowditch, P. L. 2001. *Horace and the Gift Economy of Patronage.* Berkeley.
Bowersock, G. W. 1965. *Augustus and the Greek World.* Oxford.
———. 1969. *Greek Sophists in the Roman Empire.* Oxford.
———. 1989. "Philostratus and the Second Sophistic." In *The Cambridge History of Classical Literature* 1.4, edited by P. E. Easterling et al., 95–98. Cambridge, U.K.
———. 1994. *Fiction as History: Nero to Julian.* Berkeley.
Bowie, E. L. 1982. "The Importance of Sophists." *YCS* 27: 29–59.
———. 1985. "Theocritus' Seventh *Idyll*, Philetas, and Longus." *CQ* 35: 67–91.
———. 1989a. "Greek Sophists and Greek Poetry in the Second Sophistic." *ANRW* 2.33.1: 209–58.
———. 1989b. "Poetry and Poets in Asia and Achaea." In *The Greek Renaissance in the Roman Empire: Papers from the Tenth British Museum Classical Colloqium, BICS* supplement 55, edited by S. Walker and A. Cameron, 198–205. London.
———. 1990. "Greek Poetry in the Antonine Age." In *Antonine Literature,* edited by D. A. Russell, 53–90. Oxford.
———. 1993. "Lies, Fiction and Slander in Early Greek Poetry." In *Lies and Fiction in the Ancient World,* edited by C. Gill and T. P. Wiseman, 1–37. Exeter.
———. 1994. "The Readership of the Greek Novel in the Ancient World." In *The Search for the Ancient Novel,* edited by J. Tatum, 435–59. Baltimore.
———. 2002a. "The Chronology of the Earlier Greek Novels since B. E. Perry: Revisions and Precisions." *Ancient Narrative* 2: 47–63.
———. 2002b. "Hadrian and Greek Poetry." In *Greek Romans and Roman Greeks: Studies in Cultural Interaction,* edited by E. N. Ostenfeld, 172–97. Aarhus.
———. 2003. "The Ancient Readers of the Greek Novels." In *The Novel in the Ancient World,* edited by G. Schmeling, 87–106. 2nd ed. Leiden.
———. Forthcoming. "Milesian Tales." In *The Romance between Greece and the East,* edited by T. Whitmarsh and S. Thomson. Cambridge, U.K.
Bowie, E., and Elsner, J., eds. 2009. *Philostratus.* Cambridge, U.K.

Boyd, B. W. 1987. "The Death of Corinna's Parrot Reconsidered: Poetry and Ovid's *Amores*," *CJ* 82: 199–207. Repr. in *Oxford Readings in Classical Studies: Ovid*, edited by P. Knox, 205–16. Oxford.

Branham, R. B. 1989. *Unruly Eloquence: Lucian and the Comedy of Traditions*. Cambridge, MA.

Braswell, B. K. 1982. "The Song of Ares and Aphrodite: Theme and Relevance to *Odyssey* 8." *Hermes* 110: 129–37.

Braun, M. 1934. *Griechischer Roman und hellenistische Geschichtschriebung*. Frankfurt-am-Main.

Braund, D. C. 1984. "*Anth. Pal.* 9.235: Juba II, Cleopatra Selene, and the Course of the Nile." *CQ* 34: 175–78.

———. 2000. "Learning, Luxury and Empire: Athenaeus' Roman Patron." In *Athenaeus and His World: Reading Greek Culture in the Roman Empire*, edited by Braund and J. Wilkins, 3–22. Exeter.

Braund, D. C., and Wilkins, J., eds. 2000. *Athenaeus and His World: Reading Greek Culture in the Roman Empire*. Exeter.

Bray, J. 2003. *The Epistolary Novel: Representation of Consciousness*. London and New York.

Brenk, F. E. 1999. *Clothed in Purple Light: Studies in Vergil and in Latin Literature, Including Aspects of Philosophy, Religion, Magic, Judaism, and the New Testament Background*. Stuttgart.

———. 2011. "*Hierosolyma*. The Greek Name of Jerusalem." *Glotta* 87: 1–22.

Brock, S. 1979. "Aspects of Translation Technique in Antiquity." *GRBS* 20: 69–87.

Brooks, P. 1984. *Reading for the Plot: Design and Intention in Narrative*. Cambridge, MA.

Brown, M. K. 2002. *The Narratives of Konon: Text, Translation and Commentary on the Diegeseis*. Munich.

Brusuelas, J. 2008. "Comic Liaisons: Lucian and Aristophanes." Diss., University of California, Irvine.

Bryson, N. 1994. "Philostratus and the Imaginary Museum." In *Art and Text in Ancient Greek Culture*, edited by S. Goldhill and R. Osborne, 255–83. Cambridge, U.K.

Bundy, E. L. 1962. *Studia Pindarica*. Berkeley.

Burnstein, S. M. 1989. "*SEG* 33.802 and the *Alexander Romance*." *ZPE* 77: 275–76.

Bychkov, O. 1999. "ἡ τοῦ κάλλους ἀπορροή: A Note on Achilles Tatius 1.9.4–5, 5.13.4." *CQ* 49: 339–41.

Calame, C. 1997. *Choruses of Young Women in Ancient Greece: Their Morphology, Religious Role, and Social Function*. Trans. D. Collins and J. Orion. Lanham.

Cameron, A. 1968. "The Garlands of Meleager and Philip." *GRBS* 9: 323–49.

———. 1993. *The Greek Anthology, from Meleager to Planudes*. Oxford.

———. 1995. *Callimachus and His Critics*. Princeton.

Camerotto, A. 1998. *Le metamorfosi della parola: studi sulla parodia in Luciano di Samosata*. Pisa.

Carey, C. 2007. "Pindar, Place and Performance." In *Pindar's Poetry, Patrons, and Festivals: From Archaic Greece to the Roman Empire*, edited by S. Hornblower and C. Morgan, 199–211. Oxford.

Carver, R. 2007. *The Protean Ass: The Metamorphoses of Apuleius from Antiquity to the Renaissance*. Oxford.

Chatman, S. 1978. *Story and Discourse: Narrative Structure in Fiction and Film*. Ithaca.

Cichorius, K. 1888. *Rom und Mytilene*. Leipzig.

———. 1922. *Römische Studien: Historisches, Epigraphisches, Literaturgeschichtliches aus vier Jahrhunderten Roms*. 2nd ed. Stuttgart. Repr., 1961.

Cizek, A. N. 1994. *Imitatio et tractatio: die literarisch-rhetorischen Grundlagen der Nachahmung in Antike und Mittelalter*. Tübingen.

Clarke, K. 1999. *Between Geography and History: Hellenistic Constructions of the Roman World*. Oxford.

Clauss, J., and Cuypers, M., eds. 2010. *A Companion to Hellenistic Literature*. Oxford.

Clay, D. 1991. "Alcman's *Partheneion*." *QUCC* 37: 47–67.

Cobet, J. 2002. "The Organization of Time in the *Histories*." In *Brill's Companion to Herodotus*, edited by Egbert J. Bakker, Irene J. F. de Jong, and Hans van Wees, 387–412. Leiden.

Cohen, J. 1993. *The Origins and Evolution of the Moses Nativity Story*. Leiden.

Cohen, S. J. D. 1981. "Sosates the Jewish Homer." *HThR* 74: 391–96.

———. 2001. *The Beginnings of Jewishness: Boundaries, Varieties, Uncertainties*. Berkeley.

Coleman, K. 1988. *Statius, Silvae 4*. Oxford.

Collins J. J. 1980. "The Epic of Theodotus and the Hellenism of the Hasmoneans." *HThR* 73: 91–104.

———. 2000. *Between Athens and Jerusalem: Jewish Identity in the Hellenistic Age*. 2nd ed. Grand Rapids.

Colpe, C. 1995. "Utopie und Atheismus in der Euhemeros-Tradition." In *Panchaia. Festschrift für Klaus Thraede*, edited by M. Wacht, 32–44. Münster.

Comotti, G. 1989. *Music in Greek and Roman Culture*. Trans. R. V. Munson. Baltimore.

Conte, G. B. 1996. *The Hidden Author: An Interpretation of Petronius's "Satyricon."* Trans. Elaine Fantham. Berkeley.

Cook, E. H. 1996. *Epistolary Bodies: Gender and Genre in the Eighteenth-Century Republic of Letters*. Stanford.

Crane, G. 1986. "Tithonus and the Prologue to Callimachus' *Aetia*." *ZPE* 66: 269–78.

Cronje, J. V. 1993. "The Principle of Concealment (*TO ΛΑΘΕΙΝ*) in Greek Literary Theory." *AClass* 36: 55–64.

Crowther, N. B. 1985. "Male 'Beauty' Contests in Greece: The *Euandria* and *Euexia*." *AC* 54: 285–91.

Culler, J. 1975. *Structuralist Poetics: Structuralism, Linguistics and the Study of Literature*. London.

Currie, G. 1990. *The Nature of Fiction*. Cambridge, U.K.

Davila, J. 2005. "(How) Can We Tell If a Greek Apocryphon or Pseudepigraphon Has Been Translated from the Greek?" Journal for the Study of the Pseudepigrapha 15: 3–61.

Dawson, D. 1992. *Cities of the Gods: Communist Utopias in Ancient Thought*. New York.

De Angelis, F., and Garstad, B. 2006. "Euhemerus in Context." *ClAnt* 25: 211–42.

de Jong, I. J. F. 2001. "The Prologue as Pseudo-dialogue and the Identity of Its (Main) Speaker." In *A Companion to the Prologue of Apuleius' Metamorphoses*, edited by A. Kahane and A. Laird, 201–12. Oxford.

———. 2009. "Metalepsis in Ancient Greek Literature." In *Narratology and Interpretation: The Content of Narrative Form in Ancient Literature*, edited by J. Grethlein and A. Rengakos, 87–115. Berlin and New York.

Denniston, J. 1950. *The Greek Particles*. 2nd ed. Oxford. Repr., London, 1996.

Derrida, J. 1976. *Of Grammatology.* Trans. G. Spivak. Baltimore.
———. 1981. "Plato's Pharmacy." In *Dissemination,* translated by B. Johnson, 65–171. London.
———. 1987. *The Post Card: From Socrates to Freud and Beyond.* Trans. A. Bass. Chicago.
Detienne, M., and Vernant, J.-P. 1974. *Les ruses de l'intelligence: la métis des grecs.* Paris.
Dietrich, J. S. 2002. "Dead Parrots' Society." *AJPh* 123: 95–110.
Dochhorn, J. 2000. "Ein 'Inschriftenfund' aus Panchaia: Zur Ἱερὰ Ἀναγραφή des Euhemeros von Messene." In *Internationales Josephus-Kolloquium Aarhus 1999,* edited by J. U. Kalms, 265–97. Munster.
Doulamis, K. 2002. "The Rhetoric of *Eros* in Xenophon of Ephesus and Chariton: A Stylistic and Interpretative Study." Diss., University of Exeter.
Dowden, K. 1989. "The *Alexander Romance.*" In *Collected Ancient Greek Novels,* edited by B. P. Reardon, 650–735. Berkeley. Repr., 2008.
Dubel, S. 2001. "La beauté romanesque ou le refus du portrait dans le roman grec de l'époque impériale." In *Les personnages du roman grec,* edited by B. Pouderon et al., 29–58. Paris.
Dugan, J. 2005. *Making a New Man: Ciceronian Self-Fashioning in the Rhetorical Works.* Oxford.
Easterling, P. E. 1990. "Constructing Character in Greek Tragedy." In *Characterization and Individuality in Greek Literature,* edited by C. Pelling, 83–99. Oxford.
———. 1997. "From Repertoire to Canon." In *The Cambridge Companion to Greek Tragedy,* edited by Easterling, 211–27. Cambridge, U.K.
Egger, B. 1988. "Zu den Frauenrollen im griechischen Roman: die Frau als Heldin und Leserin." *Groningen Colloquia on the Novel* 1: 33–66. Repr. as "The Role of Women in the Greek Novel: Woman as Heroine and Reader," in *Oxford Readings in the Greek Novel,* edited by S. C. R. Swain, 108–36. Oxford, 1999.
———. 1994. "Women and Marriage in the Greek Novels: The Boundaries of Romance." In *The Search for the Ancient Novel,* edited by J. Tatum, 260–80. Baltimore.
Eitrem, S. 1929. "Zu Philostrats *Heroikos.*" *SO* 8: 1–56.
Elsner, J. 2000. "Making Myth Visual: The Horae of Philostratus and the Dance of the Text." *Mitteilungen des deutschen archäologischen Instituts* 107: 253–76.
———. 2001. "Describing Self in the Language of the Other: Pseudo (?) Lucian at the Temple of Hierapolis." In *Being Greek under Rome: Cultural Identity, the Second Sophistic and the Development of Empire,* edited by S. Goldhill, 123–53. Cambridge, U.K.
———. 2004. "Seeing and Saying: A Psychoanalytic Account of Ekphrasis." *Helios* 31: 157–86.
———. 2007a. "Viewing Ariadne: From Ekphrasis to Wall Painting in the Roman World." *CPh* 102: 20–44.
———. 2007b. *Roman Eyes: Visuality and Subjectivity in Art and Text.* Princeton.
Engberg-Pedersen, T. 1996. "Plutarch to Prince Philopappus on How to Tell a Flatterer from a Friend." In *Friendship, Flattery and Frankness of Speech: Studies on Friendship in the New Testament World,* edited by J. T. Fitzgerald, 61–79. Leiden.
Erskine, A. 2001. *Troy between Greece and Rome: Local Tradition and Imperial Power.* Oxford.
Eshleman, K. 2012. *The Social World of Intellectuals in the Roman Empire: Sophists, Philosophers and Christians.* Cambridge, U.K.
Fanon, F. 1967. *Black Skin, White Masks.* Trans. C. L. Markmann. New York.
Fantham, E. 1996. *Roman Literary Culture: From Cicero to Apuleius.* Baltimore.

Faulkner, A. 2008. *The Homeric Hymn to Aphrodite: Introduction, Text, and Commentary.* Oxford.
Favret, M. 1993. *Romantic Correspondence: Women, Politics and the Fiction of Letters.* Cambridge, U.K.
Feeney, D. C. 1991. *The Gods in Epic: Poets and Critics of the Classical Tradition.* Oxford.
———. 1998. *Literature and Religion in Ancient Rome: Cultures, Contexts and Beliefs.* Cambridge, U.K.
Fehling, D. 1989. *Herodotus and His "Sources": Citation, Invention and Narrative Art.* Trans. J. G. Howie. Leeds.
Fein, S. 1994. *Die Beziehungen der Kaiser Trajan und Hadrian zu den Litterati.* Stuttgart and Leipzig.
Feldman, L. H. 1993. *Jew and Gentile in the Ancient World.* Princeton.
———. 2006. *Judaism and Hellenism Reconsidered.* Leiden.
Finkelberg, M. 1998. *The Birth of Literary Fiction in Ancient Greece.* Oxford.
Finkelpearl, E. 2006. "The Language of Animals and the Text of Apuleius' *Metamorphoses*." In *Lectiones Scrupulosae: Essays on the Text and Interpretation of Apuleius' Metamorphoses in Honour of Maaike Zimmerman,* edited by W. Keulen, R. R. Nauta, and S. Panayotakis, 203–21. Groningen.
———. 2007. "Apuleius, the *Onos,* and Rome." In *The Greek and Roman Novel: Parallel Readings,* edited by M. Paschalis, S. Frangoulidis, S. J. Harrison, and M. Zimmermann, 263–76. Groningen.
Fish, S. 1976. "Interpreting the *Variorum*." *Critical Inquiry* 2: 465–85. Repr. in *Is There a Text in This Class? The Authority of Interpretive Communities,* 147–73, Cambridge, MA, 2010; and in *Reader-Response Criticism: From Formalism to Post-structuralism,* edited by J. P. Tompkins, 164–84, Baltimore and London, 1980.
Flashar, H. 1978. "Die klassizistische Theorie der *Mimesis*." In *Le "Classicisme" à Rome au Ier siècle avant et après J.-C,* edited by Flashar, 79–96. Fondation Hardt, Entretiens 25. Vandoeuvres.
Fludernik, M. 2003. "Scene Shift, Metalepsis, and the Metaleptic Mode." *Style* 37: 382–402. Repr. as "Changement de scène et mode métaleptique," in *Métalepses: entorses au pacte de la representation,* edited by J. Pier and J.-M. Schaeffer, 73–94. Paris, 2005.
Fornaro, S. 1997. *Dionisio di Alicarnasso, epistola a Pompeo Gemino. Introduzione e commento.* Stuttgart and Leipzig.
Foucault, M. 1989a. *The Order of Things: An Archaeology of the Human Sciences.* London.
———. 1989b. *The Archaeology of Knowledge.* London.
Fowler, A. 1982. *Kinds of Literature: An Introduction to the Theory of Genres and Modes.* Cambridge, MA.
Fowler, D. P. 1987. "Vergil on Killing Virgins." In *Homo Viator: Classical Essays for John Bramble,* edited by M. Whitby et al., 185–98. Bristol.
Fraser, P. M. 1972. *Ptolemaic Alexandria.* 2 vols. Oxford.
Freudenburg, K. 1993. *The Walking Muse: Horace on the Theory of Satire.* Princeton.
Freudenthal, J. 1874–75. *Hellenistische Studien. Heft 1 und 2. Alexander Polyhistor und die von ihm erhaltenen Reste judäischer und samaritanischer Geschichtswerke.* Breslau.
Friedman, S. S. 1987. "Creativity and the Childbirth Metaphor: Gender Difference in Literary Discourse." *Feminist Studies* 13: 49–82.

Furley, W., and Bremer, J. 2001. *Greek Hymns: Selected Cult Songs from the Archaic to the Hellenistic Period.* 2 vols. Tübingen.

Fusillo, M. 1989. *Il romanzo greco: polifonia ed eros.* Venice.

Gabba, E. 1991. *Dionysius and the Early History of Rome.* Berkeley.

Gaisser, J. H. 2008. *The Fortunes of Apuleius and the "Golden Ass": A Study in Transmission and Reception.* Princeton.

Galinsky, K. 1994. "Roman Poetry in the 1990s." *CJ* 89: 297–309.

———. 1996. *Augustan Culture: An Interpretive Introduction.* Princeton.

Gardiner, A. 1961. "The Egyptian Memnon." Journal of Egyptian Archaeology 47: 91–99.

Garin, F. 1909. "Su i romanzi greci." *SIFC* 17: 423–60.

Gärtner, H. 1967. "Xenophon von Ephesos." *RE* IX A2: 2055–89.

Garvie, A. F. 1994. *Homer, Odyssey, Books VI–VIII.* Cambridge, U.K.

Gee, E. 2000. *Ovid, Aratus and Augustus: Astronomy in Ovid's Fasti.* Cambridge, U.K.

Genette, G. 1983. *Narrative Discourse: An Essay in Method.* Trans. J. E. Lewin. Ithaca.

———. 2004. *Métalepse: de la figure à la fiction.* Paris.

Georgiadou, A., and Larmour, D. 1998. *Lucian's Science Fiction Novel "True Histories": Interpretation and Commentary.* Leiden.

Giangrande, G. 1962. "On the Origins of the Greek Romance: The Birth of a Literary Form." *Eranos* 60: 132–59. Repr. in *Beiträge zum griechischen Liebesroman,* edited by H. Gärtner, 125–52. Hildesheim, 1984.

———. 1976–77. "Les utopies grecques." *REA* 78–79: 120–28.

Gianotti, G. F. 1978. "Le Pleiadi di Alcmane (Alcm. fr. 1, 60–63 P.)." *RFIC* 106: 257–71.

Gildenhard, I., and Revermann, M., eds. 2010. *Beyond the Fifth Century: Interactions with Greek Tragedy from the Fourth Century BCE to the Middle Ages.* Berlin.

Gill, C. 1973. "The Genre of the Atlantis Story." *CQ* 23: 287–304.

———. 1979. "Plato's Atlantis Story and the Birth of Fiction." *Philosophy and Literature* 3: 64–78.

———. 1993. "Plato on Falsehood—not Fiction." In *Lies and Fiction in the Ancient World,* edited by Gill and T. P. Wiseman, 38–87. Exeter.

Gill, C., Whitmarsh, T., and Wilkins, J., eds. 2009. *Galen and the World of Knowledge.* Cambridge, U.K.

Gill, C., and Wiseman, T. P., eds. 1993. *Lies and Fiction in the Ancient World.* Exeter.

Gleason, M. 1995. *Making Men: Sophists and Self-Presentation in Ancient Rome.* Princeton.

Gold, B. K., ed. 1982. *Literary and Artistic Patronage in Ancient Rome.* Austin.

———. 1987. *Literary Patronage in Greece and Rome.* Chapel Hill and London.

Goldhill, S. 1984. *Language, Sexuality and Narrative: The Oresteia.* Cambridge, U.K.

———. 1991. *The Poet's Voice: Essays in Poetics and Greek Literature.* Cambridge, U.K.

———, ed. 2001a. *Being Greek under Rome: Cultural Identity, the Second Sophistic and the Development of Empire.* Cambridge, U.K.

———. 2001b. "The Erotic Eye: Visual Stimulation and Cultural Conflict." In *Being Greek under Rome: Cultural Identity, the Second Sophistic and the Development of Empire,* edited by Goldhill, 154–94. Cambridge, U.K.

———. 2002a. *The Invention of Prose.* Oxford.

———. 2002b. *Who Needs Greek? Conflicts in the Cultural History of Hellenism.* Cambridge, U.K.

———. 2008. "Genre." In *The Cambridge Companion to the Greek and Roman Novel*, edited by T. Whitmarsh, 185–200. Cambridge, U.K.
Gonzales, M. 2005. "The Oracle and Cult of Ares in Asia Minor." *GRBS* 45: 261–83.
Gorman, S. 2008. "When the Text Becomes the Teller: Apuleius and the *Metamorphoses*." *Oral Tradition* 23: 71–86.
Goudriaan, K. 1989. "Over classicisme: Dionysius van Halicarnassus en zijn program van welsprekendheid, cultuur en politiek." 2 vols. Diss., Vrije Universiteit van Amsterdam.
Gow, A. S. F., and Page, D. L. 1968. *The Greek Anthology: The Garland of Philip and Some Contemporary Epigrams*. 2 vols. Cambridge, U.K.
Graverini, L. 2002. "Corinth, Rome, and Africa: A Cultural Background for the Tale of the Ass." In *Space in the Ancient Novel*, edited by M. Paschalis and S. Frangoulidis, 58–77. Groningen.
Graziosi, B. 2002. *Inventing Homer: The Early Reception of Epic*. Cambridge, U.K.
Green, S. J. 2004. *Ovid, Fasti 1: A Commentary*. Leiden.
Greifenhagen, F. V. 2002. *Egypt on the Pentateuch's Ideological Map: Constructing Biblical Israel's Identity*. Sheffield.
Griffin, J. 1995. *Homer, Iliad IX. Edited with an Introduction and Commentary*. Oxford.
Griffin, N. E. 1908. "The Greek Dictys." *AJPh* 29: 329–35.
Grossardt, P. 2006. *Übersetzung und Kommentar zum* Heroikos *von Flavius Philostrat*. 2 vols. Basel.
Gruen, E. S. 2002. *Heritage and Hellenism: The Reinvention of Jewish Tradition*. Berkeley.
———. 2011. *Rethinking the Other in Antiquity*. Princeton.
Hägg, T. 1975. *Photios als Vermittler antiker Litteratur: Untersuchungen zur Technik des Referiens und Exzerpierens in der Bibliotheke*. Uppsala.
———. 1983. *The Novel in Antiquity*. Oxford.
Hall, E. 1995. "The Ass with Double Vision: Politicising an Ancient Greek Novel." In *Heart of a Heartless World: Essays in Cultural Resistance in Honour of Margot Heinemann*, edited by D. Margolies and M. Jouannou, 47–59. London.
Hall, J. 1981. *Lucian's Satire*. New York.
Halliwell, S. 2002. *The Aesthetics of Mimesis: Ancient Texts and Modern Problems*. Princeton.
Halperin, D. M. 1992. "Plato and the Erotics of Narrativity." In *Innovations of Antiquity*, edited by R. Hexter and D. Selden, 95–126. New York.
Hansen, W. 2003. "Strategies of Authentication in Ancient Popular Literature." In *The Ancient Novel and Beyond*, edited by S. Panayotakis, M. Zimmerman, and W. Keulen, 301–14. Groningen.
Harder, A. 2012. *Callimachus, Aetia*. 2 vols. Oxford.
Hardie, A. 1983. *Statius and the Silvae: Poets, Patrons and Epideixis in the Graeco-Roman World*. Liverpool.
Hardie, P. R. 1998. "A Reading of Heliodorus, *Aithiopika* 3.4.1–5.2." In *Studies in Heliodorus*, edited by R. Hunter, 19–39. Cambridge, U.K.
Harding, P. 1987. "Rhetoric and Politics in Fourth-Century Athens." *Phoenix* 41: 25–39.
Harrison, S. J. 1990. "The Speaking Book: The Prologue to Apuleius' *Metamorphoses*." *CQ* 40: 507–13.
Hartog, F. 1991. "Rome et la Grèce: les choix de Dénys d'Halicarnasse." In ἙΛΛΗΝΙΣΜΟΣ: *quelques jalons pour une histoire de l'identité grec*, edited by S. Saïd, 160–67. Leiden.

Haynes, K. 2003. *Fashioning the Feminine in the Greek Novel.* London and New York.
Healy, J. 1999. *Pliny the Elder on Science and Technology.* Oxford.
Heath, J. 2006. "Ezekiel Tragicus and Hellenistic Visuality: The Phoenix at Elim." *JTS* 56: 23–41.
Heath, M. 1989. "Dionysius of Halicarnassus *On Imitation.*" *Hermes* 117: 370–73.
Heath, S. 2004. "The Politics of Genre." In *Debating World Literature,* edited by C. Prendergast, 163–74. London and New York.
Heitsch, E. 1959. "Die Mesomedes-Überlieferung." *Nachrichten von der Akademie der Wissenschaften in Göttingen. Philologisch-Historische Klasse* 1959: 35–45.
———. 1960. "Drei Helioshymnen." *Hermes* 88: 139–58. Repr. in *Gesammelte Schriften III,* 125–46. Munich and Leipzig, 2003.
Henderson, Jeffrey. 1987. *Aristophanes, Lysistrata: Edited with Introduction and Commentary.* Oxford.
———. 1991. *The Maculate Muse: Obscene Language in Attic Comedy.* 2nd ed. New York.
———. 2009. *Longus, Daphnis and Chloe; Xenophon of Ephesus, Anthia and Habrocomes.* Cambridge, MA.
Henderson, John. 2001. *Telling Tales on Caesar: Roman Stories from Phaedrus.* Oxford.
Henrichs, A. 1975. "Two Doxographical Notes: Democritus and Prodicus on Religion." *HSCPh* 79: 93–123.
———. 1984. "The Sophists and Hellenistic Religion: Prodicus as the Spiritual Father of the Isis Aretalogies." *HSCPh* 88: 148–52.
———. 2011. "Missing Pages: Papyrology, Genre, and the Greek Novel." In *Culture in Pieces: Essays on Ancient Texts in Honour of Peter Parsons,* edited by D. Obbink and R. Rutherford, 302–22. Oxford.
Hesk, J. P. 2000. *Deception and Democracy in Classical Athens.* Cambridge, U.K.
Hidber, T. 1996. *Das klassizistische Manifest des Dionys von Halikarnass: die praefatio zu De oratoribus veteribus.* Stuttgart and Leipzig.
Hinds, S. 1998. *Allusion and Intertext: Dynamics of Appropriation in Roman Poetry.* Cambridge, U.K.
Hodkinson, O. 2011. *Authority and Tradition in Philostratus' Heroikos.* Lecce.
Holford-Strevens, L. 2005. "Polus and His Urn: A Case Study in the Theory of Acting, c. 300 B.C.–c. 2000 A.D." *IJCT* 11: 499–523.
Hölscher, T. 1967. *Victoria Romana.* Mainz.
Holzberg, N. 1984. "Apuleius und der Verfasser des griechischen Eselsroman." *WJA* 10: 161–78.
———. 1988. "Lucian and the Germans." In *The Uses of Greek and Latin: Historical Essays,* edited by A. C. Dionisotti et al., 199–209. London.
———. 1993. "Ktesias von Knidos und der griechische Roman." *WJA* 19: 79–84.
———. 1995. *The Ancient Novel: An Introduction.* London.
———. 2003. "Utopias and Fantastic Travel." In *The Novel in the Ancient World,* edited by G. Schmeling, 621–32. 2nd ed. Leiden.
Honigman, S. 2009. "Euhemerus of Messene and Plato's Atlantis." *Historia* 58: 1–35.
Hopkinson, N. 1984. "Callimachus' *Hymn to Zeus.*" *CQ* 34: 139–48.
———. 1988. *A Hellenistic Anthology.* Cambridge, U.K.
———. 1994. *Greek Poetry of the Imperial Period: An Anthology.* Cambridge, U.K.
Horbury, W., and Noy, D. 1992. *Jewish Inscriptions of Graeco-Roman Egypt: With an Index of the Jewish Inscriptions of Egypt and Cyrenaica.* Cambridge, U.K.

Horna, K. 1928. "Die Hymnen des Mesomedes." *Sitzungsberichte der Akademie der Wissenschaft in Wien, Philosophisch-historische Klasse* 207.1: 1–40.
Horrocks, G. 1997. *Greek: A History of the Language and Its Speakers*. London.
Höschele, R. 2006. *Verrückt nach Frauen: der Epigrammatiker Rufin*. Tübingen.
———. 2010. *Die blutenlesende Muse: Poetik und Textualität antiker Epigrammsammlungen*. Munich.
Householder, F. W. 1941. *Literary Quotation and Allusion in Lucian*. New York.
Hubbard, T. 1991. *The Mask of Comedy: Aristophanes and the Intertextual Parabasis*. Ithaca.
———. 1995. "Hesiod's Fable of the Hawk and the Nightingale." *GRBS* 36: 161–75.
Huhn, F., and Bethe, E. 1917. "Philostrats *Heroikos* und Dictys." *Hermes* 52: 613–24.
Hunink, J. V. C. 2003. "'Apuleius, qui nobis Afris Afer est notior': Augustine's Polemic against Apuleius in *De civitate dei*." *Scholia* 12: 82–95.
Hunter, R. 1983. *A Study of Daphnis and Chloë*. Cambridge, U.K.
———. 1994. "History and Historicity in the Romance of Chariton." *ANRW* 2.34.2: 1056–86.
———, ed. 1998. *Studies in Heliodorus*. Cambridge, U.K.
———. 1999. *Theocritus: A Selection*. Cambridge, U.K.
———. 2003. *Theocritus, Encomium of Ptolemy Philadelphus: Text and Translation with Introduction and Commentary*. Berkeley.
———. 2006. *The Shadow of Callimachus: Studies in the Reception of Hellenistic Poetry at Rome*. Cambridge, U.K.
———. 2009. *Critical Moments in Classical Literature: Studies in the Ancient View of Literature and Its Uses*. Cambridge, U.K.
Husmann, H. 1955. "Zu Metrik und Rhythmik des Mesomedes." *Hermes* 83: 231–36.
Hutchinson, G. 2007. "Down among the Documents: Criticism and Papyrus Letters." In *Ancient Letters: Classical and Late Antique Epistolography*, edited by R. Morello and A. D. Morrison, 17–36. Oxford.
Innes, D. 1995. "Longinus, Sublimity, and Low Emotions." In *Ethics and Rhetoric: Classical Essays for Donald Russell on His Seventy-Fifth Birthday*, edited by Innes, H. Hine, and C. Pelling, 323–33. Oxford.
Innes, D., Hine, H., and Pelling, C., eds. 1995. *Ethics and Rhetoric: Classical Essays for Donald Russell on His Seventy-Fifth Birthday*. Oxford.
Isager, S. 1998. "The Pride of Halikarnassos: *Editio princeps* of an Inscription from Salmakis." *ZPE* 123: 1–23.
Jacobson, H. 1983. *The Exagoge of Ezekiel*. Cambridge, U.K.
Jaffee, M. S. 2001. *Torah in the Mouth—Writing and Oral Tradition in Palestinian Judaism, 200 BCE—400 CE*. New York and Oxford.
Jakobson, R. 1987. *Language in Literature*. Eds. K. Pomorska and S. Rudy. Cambridge, MA.
James, A. 2007. *Quintus of Smyrna: The Trojan Epic (Posthomerica)*. Baltimore.
James, A., and Lee, K. 2000. *A Commentary on Quintus of Smyrna Posthomerica V*. Leiden.
James, P. 2006. "Two Poetic and Parodic Parrots in Latin Literature." In *The Role of the Parrot in Selected Texts from Ovid to Jean Rhys: Telling a Story from an Alternative Viewpoint*, edited by J. Courtney and P. James, 1–32. Lewiston, NY, and Lampeter, Wales.
Janko, R. 2000. *Philodemus: On Poems, Book 1*. Oxford.
Jax, K. 1936. "τόποι." *WS* 54: 43–51.
Jenkyns, R. 1980. *The Victorians and Ancient Greece*. Oxford.

Jex-Blake, K., and Sellers, E. 1968 (1896). *The Elder Pliny's Chapters on the History of Art*. Chicago. First published London.

Johansen, T. K. 2004. *Plato's Natural Philosophy: A Study of the Timaeus-Critias*. Cambridge, U.K.

Johne, R. 1987. "Dido und Charikleia: Zur Gestaltung der Frau bei Vergil und im griechischen Liebesroman." *Eirene* 24: 21–33.

———. 2003. "Women in the Ancient Novel." In *The Novel in the Ancient World*, edited by G. Schmeling, 151–207. 2nd ed. Leiden.

Jones, C. P. 1986. *Culture and Society in Lucian*. Cambridge, MA.

———. 1999. *Kinship Diplomacy in the Ancient World*. Cambridge, MA.

———. 2000. "The Emperor and the Giant." *CPh* 95: 476–81.

———. 2001a. "Pausanias and His Guides." In *Pausanias: Travel and Memory in Roman Greece*, edited by S. E. Alcock, J. Cherry, and J. Elsner, 33–39. New York.

———. 2001b. "Philostratus' *Heroikos* and Its Setting in Reality." *JHS* 121: 141–49.

———. 2001c. "A Statuette of Nemesis." *EA* 33: 45–47.

Jones, K. 2011. *Jewish Reactions to the Destruction of the Temple in A.D. 70*. Leiden.

Kahane, A., and Laird, A., eds. 2001. *A Companion to the Prologue of Apuleius' Metamorphoses*. Oxford.

Kappeler, S. 1986. *The Pornography of Representation*. Minneapolis.

Karavas, O. 2005. *Lucien et la tragédie*. Berlin.

Karla, G., ed. 2009. *Fiction on the Fringe: Novelistic Writing in the Post-classical Age*. Leiden.

Kasher, A. 1985. *The Jews in Hellenistic and Roman Egypt: The Struggle for Equal Rights*. Tübingen.

Kauffman, L. S. 1986. *Discourses of Desire: Gender, Genre and Epistolary Fiction*. Ithaca.

———. 1992. *Special Delivery: Epistolary Modes in Modern Fiction*. Chicago and London.

Kearns, E. 1982. "The Return of Odysseus: A Homeric Theoxeny." *CQ* 32: 2–8.

Kekkos, K. 1890. "Χαρίτων μιμητὴς Ξενοφῶντος καὶ Ἡλιοδώρου." Diss., Friedrich-Alexander-University, Erlangen-Nuremberg.

Kenaan, V. L. 2009. *Pandora's Senses: The Feminine Character of the Text in the Ancient World*. Madison.

Kennedy, D. F. 1992. "'Augustan' and 'Anti-Augustan': Reflections on Terms of Reference." In *Roman Poetry and Propaganda in the Age of Augustus*, edited by A. Powell, 26–58. Bristol.

Kerkhecker, A. 1999. *Callimachus' Book of "Iambi."* Oxford.

Keul-Deutscher, M. 1996. "Heliodorstudien 1: Die Schönheit in den *Aethiopica*." *RhM* 139: 319–33.

Keuls, E. 1985. *The Reign of the Phallus: Sexual Politics in Ancient Athens*. Berkeley.

Kim, L. 2010a. *Homer between History and Fiction in Imperial Greek Literature*. Cambridge, U.K.

———. 2010b. "The Literary Heritage as Language: Atticism and the Second Sophistic." In *A Companion to the Ancient Greek Language*, edited by E. J. Bakker, 468–82. Chichester.

Kissel, W. 1990. *Persius, Satiren; herausgegeben, übersetzt und kommentiert*. Heidelberg.

Knox, P. E. 1985. "Wine, Water, and Callimachean Polemics." *HSCPh* 89: 107–19.

König, J. 2009. *Greek Literature in the Roman Empire*. London.

König, J., and Whitmarsh, T., eds. 2007. *Ordering Knowledge in the Roman Empire*. Cambridge, U.K.

Konstan, D. 1994. *Sexual Symmetry: Love in the Ancient Novel and Related Genres.* Princeton.

———. 2009. "Reunion and Regeneration: Narrative Patterns in Ancient Greek Novels and Christian Acts." In *Fiction on the Fringe: Novelistic Writing in the Post-classical Age,* edited by G. Karla, 105–20. Leiden.

Konstan, D., and Saïd, S., eds. 2006. *Greeks on Greekness: Viewing the Greek Past under the Roman Empire.* Cambridge, U.K.

Kost, K. 1971. *Hero und Leander: Einleitung, Text, Übersetzung und Kommentar.* Bonn.

Kraemer, R. S. 1998. *When Aseneth Met Joseph: A Late Antique Tale of the Biblical Patriarch and His Egyptian Wife, Reconsidered.* New York.

Kroll, W. 1926. *Historia Alexandri Magni.* Vol. 1. Berlin.

Kuhn, T. 2012. *Die jüdisch-hellenistischen Epiker Theodot und Philon: literarische Untersuchungen, kritische Edition und Übersetzung der Fragmente.* Göttingen.

Kurke, L. 2010. *Aesopic Conversations: Popular Tradition, Cultural Dialogue, and the Invention of Greek Prose.* Princeton.

Kurtz, D. C. 1975. "The Man-Eating Horses of Diomedes in Poetry and Painting." *JHS* 95: 171–72.

Kytzler, B. 1988. "Der utopische Roman in der klassischen Antike." In *Groningen Colloquia on the Novel* 1: 7–16.

Lada-Richards, I. 2002. "The Subjectivity of Greek Performance." In *Greek and Roman Actors: Aspects of a Profession,* edited by P. Easterling and E. Hall, 395–418. Cambridge, U.K.

Laird, A. 1990. "Person, 'Persona' and Representation in Apuleius' *Metamorphoses.*" *MD* 25: 129–64.

Lalanne, S. 2006. *Une éducation grecque: rites de passage et construction des genres dans le roman grec ancien.* Paris.

Lane Fox, R. 2008. *Travelling Heroes: Greeks and Their Myths in the Epic Age of Homer.* London.

Lanfranchi, P. 2006. *L'Exagoge d'Ezéchiel le tragique.* Leiden.

Lauvergnat-Gagnière, C. 1988. *Lucien de Samosate et le lucianisme en France au XVIe siècle: athéisme et polémique.* Geneva.

Lavagnini, B. 1921. "Le origini del romanzo greco." *ASNP* 28: 9–104. Repr. in *Beiträge zum griechischen Liebesroman,* edited by H. Gärtner, 41–101. Hildesheim, 1984.

Le Boeuffle, A. 1989. *Le ciel des romains.* Paris.

Lefkowitz, M. 1991. *First-Person Fictions: Pindar's Poetic "I."* Oxford.

Lehmann, W. 1910. "De Achillis Tatii aetate, accedit corrolarium de Achillis Tatii studiis Lucianeis." Diss., Universität Viadrina, Breslau.

Lejeune, P. 1982. "The Autobiographical Contract." In *French Literary Theory Today: A Reader,* edited by T. Todorov, 192–222. Trans. R. Carter. Cambridge, U.K.

Lenfant, D. 2004. *Ctésias de Cnide: La Perse, l'Inde, autres fragments.* Paris.

Lessing, G. 1962 (1766). *Laokoon, oder über die Grenzen der Malerei und Poesie.* Paderborn.

Létoublon, F. 1993. *Les lieux communs du roman: stéréotypes grecs d'aventure et d'amour.* Leiden.

Lieu, J. 2004. *Christian Identity in the Jewish and Graeco-Roman World.* Oxford.

Lightfoot, J. L. 1999. *Parthenius of Nicaea: The Poetical Fragments and the Erotica Pathemata.* Oxford.

———. 2003. *Lucian: On the Syrian Goddess. Edited with Introduction, Translation and Commentary.* Oxford.
Llewellyn-Jones, L. 2010. Introduction to *Ctesias' History of Persia: Tales of the Orient,* edited by Llewellyn-Jones and J. Robson, 1–87. London.
Lloyd, G. E. R. 1987. *The Revolutions of Wisdom: Studies in the Claims and Practice of Ancient Greek Science.* Berkeley.
Lloyd-Jones, H. 1999a. "The Pride of Halicarnassus." *ZPE* 124: 1–14.
———. 1999b. "The Pride of Halicarnassus (*ZPE* 124 [1999] 1–14): Corrigenda and Addenda." *ZPE* 127: 63–65.
Louden, B. 2011. *Homer's Odyssey and the Near East.* Cambridge, U.K.
Luraghi, N. 2003. "Dionysios von Halikarnassos zwischen Griechen und Römern." In *Formen römischer Geschichtsschreibung von den Anfängen bis Livius: Gattungen, Autoren, Kontexte,* edited by U. Eigler, 268–86. Darmstadt.
MacArthur, E. 1990. *Extravagant Narratives: Closure and Dynamics in the Epistolary Form.* Princeton.
Maclean, J., and Aitken, E. 2001. *Flavius Philostratus: Heroikos, Translated with Notes.* Atlanta.
Macleod, M. D. 1967. *Lucian.* Volume 8. Cambridge, MA.
Malkin, I. 1998. *The Returns of Odysseus: Colonization and Ethnicity.* Berkeley.
Mandilaras, V. 1995. Φιλόστρατος, Νέρων—Ἡρωικός. Athens.
Mantero, T. 1966. *Ricerche sull' Heroikos di Filostrato.* Genoa.
Marinčič, M. 2007. "Advertising One's Own Story: Text and Speech in Achilles Tatius' *Leucippe and Clitophon*." In *Seeing Tongues, Hearing Scripts: Orality and Representation in the Ancient Novel,* edited by V. Rimell, 168–200. Groningen.
Martin, R. P. 2002. "A Good Place to Talk: Discourse and Topos in Achilles Tatius and Philostratus." In *Space in the Ancient Novel,* edited by M. Paschalis and S. Frangoulidis, 143–60. Groningen.
Mason, H. J. 1971. "Lucius in Corinth." *Phoenix* 25: 160–65.
———. 1983. "The Distinction of Lucius in Apuleius' *Metamorphoses*." *Phoenix* 37: 135–43.
———. 1994. "Greek and Latin Versions of the Ass-Story." *ANRW* 2.34.2: 1665–707.
Massenzio, M. 1997. "Prefazione." In *Filostrato: Eroico,* edited by V. Rossi, 9–16. Venice.
McClure, L. 1999. "'The Worst Husband': Discourses of Praise and Blame in Euripides' *Medea*." *CPh* 94: 373–94.
McCoskey, D. E. 2012. *Race: Antiquity and Its Legacy.* London and New York.
McKeown, J. 1989. *Ovid, Amores: Text, Prolegomena and Commentary.* 4 vols. Vol. 2, *A Commentary on Book One.* Leeds.
Mendels, D. 1987. *The Land of Israel as a Political Concept in Hasmonean Literature.* Tübingen.
Merkelbach, R. 1947. "Pseudo-Kallisthenes und ein Briefroman über Alexander." *Aegyptus* 27: 144–58.
———. 1954. "Anthologie fingierter Briefe." In *Griechische Papyri der Hamburger Staats- und Universitätsbibliothek,* edited by B. Snell, 51–74. Hamburg.
———. 1962. *Roman und Mysterium in der Antike.* Munich and Berlin.
———. 1977 (1954). *Die Quellen des griechischen Alexanderromans.* 2nd ed. Munich.
———. 1989. "Der Brief des Dareios und Alexanders Wortwechsel mit Parmenion." *ZPE* 77: 277–80.

Merkelbach, R., and Stauber, J. 1998–2004. *Steinepigramme aus dem griechischen Osten.* 5 vols. Stuttgart.
Merkle, S. 1994. "Telling the True Story of the Trojan War: The Eyewitness Account of Dictys of Crete." In *The Search for the Ancient Novel*, edited by J. Tatum, 183–96. Baltimore.
Merritt, B. D. 1946. "Greek Inscriptions." *Hesperia* 15: 169–263.
Mestre, F. 1996. *Filóstrato, Heroico, Gimnastico, Descripciones de cuadros; Calístrato, Descripciones.* Madrid.
Mestre, F., and Gómez, P., eds. 2010. *Lucian of Samosata: Greek Writer and Roman Citizen.* Barcelona.
Millar, F. 1966. "The Emperor, the Senate and the Provinces." *JRS* 56: 156–66.
Moles, J. 1995. "Dio Chrysostom, Greece, and Rome." In *Ethics and Rhetoric: Classical Essays for Donald Russell on His Seventy-Fifth Birthday*, edited by D. Innes, H. Hine, and C. Pelling, 177–92. Oxford.
Möllendorff, P. von. 2009. "Bild-Störung: das Gemälde von Europas Entführung in Achilleus Tatios' Roman Leukippe und Kleitophon." In *Europa—Stier und Sternenkranz: von der Union mit Zeus zum Staatenverbund*, A.-B. Renger and R. A. Issler, 145–64. Bonn.
Momigliano, A. 1975. *Alien Wisdom: The Limits of Hellenization.* Cambridge, U.K.
Morales, H. 1999. "Gender and Identity in Musaeus' *Hero and Leander*." In *Constructing Identities in Late Antiquity*, edited by R. Miles, 41–69. London.
———. 2004. *Vision and Narrative in Achilles Tatius' Leucippe and Clitophon.* Cambridge, U.K.
———. 2009. "Challenging Some Orthodoxies: The Politics of Genre and the Ancient Greek Novel." In *Fiction on the Fringe: Novelistic Writing in the Post-classical Age*, edited by G. Karla, 1–12. Leiden.
Morgan, J. R. 1989. "The Story of Knemon in Heliodorus' *Aithiopika*." *JHS* 109: 99–113. Repr. in *Oxford Readings in the Greek Novel*, edited by S. C. R. Swain, 259–85. Oxford, 1999.
———. 1993. "Make-Believe and Make Believe: The Fictionality of the Greek Novels." In *Lies and Fiction in the Ancient World*, edited by C. Gill and T. P. Wiseman, 175–229. Exeter.
———. 1994. "The *Aithiopika* of Heliodorus: Narrative as Riddle." In *Greek Fiction: The Greek Novel in Context*, edited by J. R. Morgan and R. Stoneman, 97–113. London and New York.
———. 2007. "Kleitophon and Encolpius: Achilleus Tatios as Hidden Author." In *The Greek and the Roman Novel: Parallel Readings*, edited by M. Paschalis, S. Frangoulidis, S. J. Harrison, and M. Zimmerman, 105–20. Groningen.
Morgan, K. A. 2000. *Myth and Philosophy from the Pre-Socratics to Plato.* Cambridge, U.K.
Morgan, L. 2010. *Musa Pedestris: Metre and Meaning in Roman Verse.* Oxford.
Morgan, T. 2007. *Popular Morality in the Early Roman Empire.* Cambridge, U.K.
Mossman, H. 2006. "Narrative and Cultural Memory in Post-classical Representations of the Black Sea." Diss., University of Exeter.
Most, G. W. 1995. "Reflecting Sappho." *BICS* 40: 15–38. Rev. and repr. in (and cited from) *Re-reading Sappho: Reception and Transmission*, edited by E. Greene, 11–35. Berkeley.
Mullen, W. 1982. *Choreia: Pindar and Dance.* Princeton.
Müller, R. J. 1993. "Überlegungen zur Ἱερὰ Ἀναγραφή des Euhemeros von Messene." *Hermes* 121: 276–300.

Mulvey, L. 1975. "Visual Pleasure and Narrative in the Cinema." *Screen* 16: 6–18. Variously repr. Cited from *Film Theory and Criticism*, edited by L. Braudy and M. Cohen, 833–44. 5th ed. New York.

Murray, O. 1971. "περὶ βασιλείας: Studies in the Justification of Monarchic Power in the Hellenistic World." Diss., University of Oxford.

Musso, O. 1998. "La Sfinge di Mesomede alla luce di un mosaico del Monferrato." *ZPE* 120: 35–38.

Myers, K. S. 1990. "Ovid *Amores* 2.6: Programmatics and the Parrot." *EMC* 34: 367–74.

———. 2002. "*Psittacus redux*: Imitation and Literary Polemic in Statius, *Silvae* 2.4." In *Vertis in Usum: Studies in Honor of Edward Courtney*, edited by J. F. Miller, C. Damon, and K. S. Myers, 189–99. Munich and Leipzig.

Nagy, G. 1979. *The Best of the Achaeans: Concepts of the Hero in Archaic Greek Poetry*. Baltimore.

———. 1987. "Herodotus the Logios." *Arethusa* 20: 175–84.

———. 1990. *Pindar's Homer: The Lyric Possession of an Epic Past*. Baltimore.

———. 2001. "The Sign of the Hero: A Prologue." In *Flavius Philostratus: Heroikos, Translated with Notes*, by J. Maclean and E. Aitken, xv–xxxv. Atlanta.

Nasrallah, L. S. 2010. *Christian Responses to Roman Art and Architecture*. Cambridge, U.K.

Nauta, R. 2002. *Poetry for Patrons: Literary Communication in the Age of Domitian*. Leiden.

Neef, E. 1940. *Lukians Verhältnis zu den Philosophenschulen und seine μίμησις literarischer Vorbilder*. Greifswald.

Neimke, P. 1889. "Quaestiones Heliodoreae." Diss., Universität Halle-Wittenberg.

Newlands, C. 2002. *Statius' Silvae and the Poetics of Empire*. Oxford.

———. 2005. "Animal Claquers: Statius *Silv.* 2.4 and 2.5." In *Defining Genre and Gender in Latin Literature: Essays Presented to William S. Anderson on His Seventy-Fifth Birthday*, edited by W. W. Batstone and G. Tissol, 151–73. New York.

Newsom, R. 1988. *A Likely Story: Probability and Play in Fiction*. New Brunswick.

Newton, R. M. 1987. "Odysseus and Hephaestus in the *Odyssey*." *CJ* 83: 12–20.

Nicolet, C. 1991. *Space, Geography and Politics in the Early Roman Empire*. Ann Arbor.

Niehoff, M. 2011. *Jewish Exegesis and Homeric Scholarship in Alexandria*. Cambridge, U.K.

Nietzsche, F. 1993 (1872). *The Birth of Tragedy: Out of the Spirit of Music*. Trans. S. Whiteside. London.

Ní Mheallaigh, K. 2008. "Pseudo-documentarism and the Limits of Ancient Fiction." *AJPh* 129: 404–26.

———. 2010. "The Name of the Game: Onymity and the Contract of Reading in Lucian." In *Lucian of Samosata: Greek Writer and Roman Citizen*, edited by F. Mestre and P. Gómez, 83–94. Barcelona.

Nimis, S. 1994. "The Prosaics of the Ancient Novel." *Arethusa* 27: 387–411.

———. 2004. "Egypt in Greco-Roman History and Fiction." *Alif* 24: 34–67.

Nisbet, G. 2003. *Greek Epigram in the Roman Empire: Martial's Forgotten Rivals*. Oxford.

Norden, E. 1898. *Die antike Kunstprosa vom 6en Jahrhundert vor Christus bis in die Zeit der Renaissance*. 2 vols. Leipzig.

Nünlist, R. 2009. *The Ancient Critic at Work: Terms and Methods of Literary Criticism in Greek Scholia*. Cambridge, U.K.

Oliver, J. H. 1979. "Flavius Pantaenus, Prince of the Philosophical Muses." *HThR* 72: 157–60.

Orsini, P. 1968. *Musée, Héro et Léandre*. Paris.
Ortner, S. B. 1974. "Is Female to Male as Nature Is to Culture?" In *Woman, Culture, and Society*, edited by M. Z. Rosaldo and L. Lamphere, 68–87. Stanford.
O'Sullivan, J. N. 1995. *Xenophon of Ephesus: His Compositional Technique and the Birth of the Novel*. Berlin.
O'Sullivan, L.-L. 1997. "Athenian Impiety Trials in the Late Fourth Century B.C." *CQ* 47: 142–46.
Packman, Z. 1991. "The Incredible and the Incredulous: The Vocabulary of Disbelief in Herodotus, Thucydides and Xenophon." *Hermes* 199: 399–414.
Panayotakis, S., Zimmerman, M. and Keulen, W., eds. 2003. *The Ancient Novel and Beyond*. Groningen.
Paschalis, M., and Frangoulidis, S., eds. 2002. *Space in the Ancient Novel*. Groningen.
Paschalis, M., Frangoulidis, S., Harrison, S. J., and Zimmerman, M., eds. 2007. *The Greek and the Roman Novel: Parallel Readings*. Groningen.
Pavel, M. 1989. *Fictional Worlds*. Cambridge, MA.
Payne, M. 2007. *Theocritus and the Invention of Fiction*. Cambridge, U.K.
Perkins, J. 2010. *Roman Imperial Identities in the Early Christian Era*. London.
Pernot, L. 2008. "Aelius Aristides and Rome." In *Aelius Aristides between Greece, Rome, and the Gods*, edited by W. V. Harris and B. Holmes, 175–202. Leiden and Boston.
Perry, B. E. 1967. *The Ancient Romances: A Literary-Historical Account of Their Origins*. Berkeley.
Peterson, A. 2010. "Innovative Traditionalism: Lucian's Invention of the Comic Dialogue." Diss., Ohio State University.
Pfeiffer, R. 1949. *Callimachus*. Vol. 1. Oxford.
———. 1968. *A History of Classical Scholarship from the Beginnings to the End of the Hellenistic Age*. Oxford.
Philonenko, M. 1968. *Joseph et Asénath: introduction. texte critique, traduction et notes*. Leiden.
Pier, J., and Schaeffer, J.-M., eds. 2005. *Métalepses: entorses au pacte de la representation*. Paris.
Pieraccioni, D. 1951. "Lettere del ciclo di Alessandro." In *Papiri greci e latini: Pubblicazioni della società italiana per la ricerca dei papiri greci e latini in Egitto XII*, edited by M. Norsa and V. Bartoletti, 166–190. Florence.
Platt, V. 2011. *Facing the Gods: Epiphany and Representation in Graeco-Roman Art, Literature and Religion*. Cambridge, U.K.
Pöhlmann, E. 1970. *Denkmäler altgriechischer Musik*. Nuremberg.
Poliakoff, M. 1980. "Nectar, Springs, and the Sea: Critical Terminology in Pindar and Callimachus." *ZPE* 39: 41–47.
Porter, J. I. 2000a. *The Invention of Dionysus: An Essay on the Birth of Tragedy*. Stanford.
———. 2000b. *Nietzsche and the Philology of the Future*. Stanford.
———. 2001. "Ideals and Ruins: Pausanias, Longinus, and the Second Sophistic." In *Pausanias: Travel and Memory in Roman Greece*, edited by S. E. Alcock, J. Cherry, and J. Elsner, 63–92. New York.
———. 2010. *The Origins of Aesthetic Thought in Ancient Greece: Matter, Sensation and Experience*. Cambridge, U.K.

Pratt, L. 1983. *Lying and Poetry from Homer to Pindar: Falsehood and Deception in Archaic Greek Poetics*. Ann Arbor.
Pummer, R. 1982. "Genesis 34 in Jewish Writings of the Hellenistic and Roman Periods." *HThR* 75: 177–82.
Pummer, R., and Roussel, M. 1982. "A Note on Theodotus and Homer." *JSJ* 13: 177–82.
Purves, A. C. 2010. "Wind and Time in Homeric Epic." *TAPhA* 140: 323–50.
Rabel, R. 1999. "Impersonation and Representation in the *Odyssey*." *CW* 93: 169–83.
Radermacher, L. 1940. "Phidias in einem übersehenen Zitat aus Dionysius von Halicarnassos περὶ μιμήσεως?" *RhM* 89: 78–80.
Radici Colace, P. 1976. "Choeril. Sam. Fr. 4 Naeke." *RFIC* 104: 15–20.
Rajak, T. 2009. *Translation and Survival: The Greek Bible of the Ancient Jewish Diaspora*. Oxford.
Reardon, B. P. 1991. *The Form of Greek Romance*. Princeton.
Reeve, M. D. 1989. "Conceptions." *PCPhS* 35: 81–112.
Reichel, M. 2010. "Xenophon's *Cyropaedia* and the Hellenistic Novel." In *Oxford Readings in Classical Studies: Xenophon*, edited by V. Gray, 418–38. Oxford. Repr. from *Groningen Colloquia on the Novel* 6 (1995): 1–20.
Rimell, V. 2007. "Petronius' Lessons in Learning—the Hard Way." In *Ordering Knowledge in the Roman Empire*, edited by J. König and T. Whitmarsh, 108–32. Cambridge, U.K.
Ringer, M. 1998. *Electra and the Empty Urn: Metatheater and Role-Playing in Sophocles*. Chapel Hill.
Robert, L. 1980. "Deux poètes grecs à l'époque impériale." In *ΣΤΗΛΗ: Mélanges Kontoleon*, 1–20. Athens.
Robinson, C. 1979. *Lucian and His Influence in Europe*. London.
Rodríguez Adrados, F. 1999–2003. *History of the Graeco-Latin Fable*. 3 vols. Leiden.
Rohde, E. 1876. *Der griechische Roman und seine Vorläufer*. 1st ed. Leipzig.
———. 1886. "Die asianische Rhetorik und die zweite Sophistik." *RhM* 41: 170–90.
———. 1914. *Der griechische Roman und seine Vorläufer*. 3rd ed., revised by W. Schmid. Berlin. Repr., Hildesheim, 1960.
Romm, J. 1992. *The Edges of the Earth in Ancient Thought*. Princeton.
———. 1998. *Herodotus*. New Haven.
Rommel, H. 1923. *Die naturwissenschaftlich-paradoxographischen Exkurse bei Philostratos, Heliodoros und Achilleus Tatios*. Stuttgart.
Rosenmeyer, P. A. 1992. *The Poetics of Imitation: Anacreon and the Anacreontic Tradition*. Cambridge, U.K.
———. 2001. *Ancient Epistolary Fictions: The Letter in Greek Literature*. Cambridge, U.K.
Rösler, W. 1980. "Die Entdeckung der Fiktionalität in der Antike." *Poetica* 12: 283–319.
Rossi, V. 1997. *Filostrato: Eroico*. Venice.
Ruiz Montero, C. 2003. "Text and Context in Plutarch's *Amatoriae narrationes* and Xenophon of Ephesus' *Ephesiaca*." *Invigilata Lucernis* 25: 221–33.
Russell, D. A. 1979. "De imitatione." In *Creative Imitation in Latin Literature*, edited by D. West and T. Woodman, 1–16. Cambridge, U.K.
———. 1990a. *Dio Chrysostom, Orations VII, XII, XXXVI*. Cambridge, U.K.
———. 1990b. "Aristides and the Prose Hymn." In *Antonine Literature*, edited by Russell, 199–219. Oxford.

———, ed. 1990c. *Antonine Literature*. Oxford.
Russell, D. A., and M. Winterbottom. 1972. *Ancient Literary Criticism: The Principal Texts in New Translations*. Oxford.
Russo, J., Fernández-Galiano, M., and Heubeck, A. 1992. *A Commentary on Homer's Odyssey*. Vol. 3, *Books XVII–XXIV*. Oxford.
Rusten, J. S. 1982. *Dionysius Scytobrachion*. Opladen.
———. 2004. "Living in the Past: Allusive Narratives and Elusive Authorities in the World of the *Heroikos*." In *Philostratus's Heroikos: Religion and Cultural Identity in the Third Century* C.E., edited by E. B. Aitken and J. K. B. Maclean, 143–58. Atlanta.
Rutherford, I. 2000. "The Genealogy of the *Boukoloi*: How Greek Literature Appropriated an Egyptian Narrative-Motif." *JHS* 120: 106–21.
———. 2001. *Pindar's Paeans: A Reading of the Fragments with a Survey of the Genre*. Oxford.
———. Forthcoming. "Greek Fiction and Egyptian Fiction: Are They Related, and If So, How?" In *The Romance between Greece and the East*, edited by T. Whitmarsh and S. Thomson. Cambridge, U.K.
Rutherford, R. B. 2012. *Greek Tragic Style: Form, Language and Interpretation*. Oxford.
Sacks, K. S. 1990. *Diodorus Siculus and the First Century*. Princeton.
Saller, R. 1982. *Personal Patronage under the Early Empire*. Cambridge, U.K.
Sartre, J.-P. 1967. *What Is Literature?* Trans. B. Frechtman. London.
Schäfer, P. 1997. *Judeophobia: Attitudes toward the Jews in the Ancient World*. Princeton.
Scharffenberger, E. W. 2007. "*Deinon eribremetas*: The Sound and Sense of Aeschylus in Aristophanes' *Frogs*." *CW* 100: 229–49.
Schäublin, C. 1985. "Konversionen in antiken Dialogen?" In *Catalepton: Festschrift für Bernhard Wyss zum 80. Geburtstag*, edited by Schäublin, 117–31. Basel.
Schibli, H. 1990. *Pherekydes of Syros*. Oxford.
Schirren, T. 2005. *Philosophos Bios: Die antike Philosophenbiographie als symbolische Form. Studien zur Vita Apollonii des Philostrat*. Heidelberg.
Schissel von Fleschenberg, O. 1913. *Entwicklungsgeschichte des griechischen Romanes im Altertum*. Halle.
Schmeling, G., ed. 2003. *The Novel in the Ancient World*. 2nd ed. Leiden.
Schmid, W. 1887–96. *Der Atticismus in seinen Hauptvertretern von Dionysius von Halikarnass bis auf den zweiten Philostratus*. Stuttgart.
Schmitz, T. 1997. *Bildung und Macht: zur sozialen unde politischen Funktion der zweiten Sophistik in der griechischen Welt der Kaiserzeit*. Munich.
———. 2010. "A Sophist's Drama: Lucian and Classical Tragedy." In *Beyond the Fifth Century: Interactions with Greek Tragedy from the Fourth Century* BCE *to the Middle Ages*, edited by I. Gildenhard and M. Revermann, 289–311. Berlin.
Schnepf, M. 1887. "De imitationis ratione, quae intercedit inter Heliodorum et Xenophontem Ephesium, commentatio." Diss., Hochschule Kempten.
Schofield, M. 1991. *The Stoic Idea of the City*. Cambridge, U.K.
Schröder, S. 1990. *Plutarchs Schrift De Pythiae oraculis: Text, Einleitung und Kommentar*. Stuttgart.
Sedley, D. Forthcoming. "The Atheist Underground." In *"Politeia" in Greek and Roman Philosophy*, edited by V. Harte and M. Lane. New York.

Seeck, G. A. 1990. "Lukian und die griechische Tragödie." In *Theater und Gesellschaft im Imperium Romanum*, edited by J. Blänsdorf, J.-M. André, and N. Fisk, 233–41. Tübingen.

Segal, C. 1983. "Sirius and the Pleiades in Alcman's Louvre *Partheneion*." *Mnemosyne* 36: 260–75.

Selden, D. L. 1994. "Genre of Genre." In *The Search for the Ancient Novel*, edited by J. Tatum, 39–64. Baltimore.

———. 1998. "Alibis." *ClAnt* 17: 289–412.

———. 2010. "Text Networks." *Ancient Narrative* 8: 1–24.

Silk, M. S. 2000. *Aristophanes and the Definition of Comedy*. Oxford.

Silk, M. S., and Stern, J. P. 1981. *Nietzsche on Tragedy*. Cambridge, U.K.

Sironen, E. 2003. "The Role of Inscriptions in Greco-Roman Novels." In *The Ancient Novel and Beyond*, edited by S. Panayotakis, M. Zimmerman, and W. Keulen, 289–314. Groningen.

Smallwood, E. M. 1981. *The Jews under Roman Rule: From Pompey to Diocletian—A Study in Political Relations*. 2nd ed. Leiden.

Snowden, F. M. 1970. *Blacks in Antiquity: Ethiopians in the Greco-Roman Experience*. Cambridge, MA.

Sorabji, R. 1993. *Animal Minds and Human Morals*. London.

Sourvinou-Inwood, C. 1989. "Assumptions and the Creation of Meaning: Reading Sophocles' *Antigone*." *JHS* 109: 134–48.

Speyer, W. 1970. *Bücherfunde in der Glaubenswerbung der Antike*. Göttingen.

Stallybrass, P., and White, A. 1986. *The Politics and Poetics of Transgression*. London.

Stanton, G. R. 1973. "Sophists and Philosophers: Problems of Classification." *AJPh* 94: 350–64.

Starr, C. P. 1952. "The Perfect Democracy of the Roman Empire." *American Historical Review* 58: 1–16.

Stavrakopoulou, F. 2010. *Land of Our Fathers: The Roles of Ancestor Veneration in Biblical Land Claims*. New York and London.

Stephens, S. A. 2003. *Seeing Double: Intercultural Poetics in Ptolemaic Alexandria*. Berkeley.

———. Forthcoming. "Fictions of Cultural Authority." In *The Romance between Greece and the East*, edited by T. Whitmarsh and S. Thomson. Cambridge, U.K.

Stephens, S. A., and Winkler, J. J. 1995. *Ancient Greek Novels: The Fragments*. Princeton.

Stock, B. 1996. *Augustine the Reader: Meditation, Self-Knowledge and the Ethics of Interpretation*. Cambridge, MA.

Stoneman, R. 1995. "Riddles in Bronze and Stone: Monuments and Their Interpretation in the *Alexander Romance*." *Groningen Colloquia on the Novel* 6: 159–70.

———. 2003. "The Metamorphoses of the Alexander Romance." In *The Novel in the Ancient World*, edited by G. Schmeling, 601–12. 2nd ed. Leiden.

———. 2007. *Il romanzo di Alessandro*. Vol. 1. Milan.

Strobach, A. 1997. *Plutarch und die Sprachen. Ein Beitrag zur Fremdsprachenproblematik in der Antike*. Stuttgart.

Strohmaier, G. 1976. "Übersehenes zur Biographie Lukians." *Philologus* 120: 117–22.

Stronk, J. P. 2010. *Ctesias' Persian History: Introduction, Text and Translation*. Düsseldorf.

Swain, S. 1996. *Hellenism and Empire: Language, Classicism, and Power in the Greek World, AD 50–250*. Oxford.

———, ed. 1999. *Oxford Readings in the Greek Novel.* Oxford.
———. 2007. "Polemon's Physiognomy." In *Seeing the Face, Seeing the Soul: Polemon's Physiognomy from Classical Antiquity to Medieval Islam,* edited by Swain, 125–201. Oxford.
Szarmach, M. 2003. *Flawiusz Filostratos, Dialog o herosach: Przełożył, wstępem i przypisami opatrzył.* Toruń.
Tatum, J., ed. 1994. *The Search for the Ancient Novel.* Baltimore.
Taussig, M. 1993. *Mimesis and Alterity: A Particular History of the Senses.* New York and Abingdon.
Tcherikover, V. 1999 (1959). *Hellenistic Civilization and the Jews.* Peabody, MA.
Thomas, R. 2000. *Herodotus in Context: Ethnography, Science, and the Art of Persuasion.* Cambridge, U.K.
Tilg, S. 2010. *Chariton of Aphrodisias and the Invention of the Greek Love Novel.* Cambridge, U.K.
Too, Y. L. 1995. *The Rhetoric of Identity in Isocrates: Text, Power, Pedagogy.* Cambridge, U.K.
———. 2001. "Losing the Author's Voice: Cultural and Personal Identities in the *Metamorphoses* Prologue." In *A Companion to the Prologue of Apuleius' Metamorphoses,* edited by A. Kahane and A. Laird, 177–87. Oxford.
———. 2010. *The Idea of the Library in the Ancient World.* Oxford.
Trapp, M. B. 1990. "Plato's *Phaedrus* in the Second Century." In *Antonine Literature,* edited by D. A. Russell, 141–73. Oxford.
———. 1995. "Sense of Place in the Orations of Dio Chrysostom." In *Ethics and Rhetoric: Classical Essays for Donald Russell on His Seventy-Fifth Birthday,* edited by D. Innes, H. Hine, and C. Pelling, 163–75. Oxford.
Turner, J. G. 1990. "The Poetics of Engagement." In *Politics, Poetics, and Hermeneutics in Milton's Prose,* edited by D. Loewenstein and J. G. Turner, 257–75. Cambridge, U.K.
Usener, H., and Radermacher, L. 1965. *Dionysii Halicarnasei quae extant.* Vol. 6, *Opuscula II.* Stuttgart.
Usher, M. D. 2007. "Theomachy, Creation, and the Poetics of Quotation in Longinus Chapter 9." *CPh* 102: 292–303.
Van der Louw, T. 2007. *Transformations in the Septuagint: Towards an Interaction of Septuagint Studies and Translation Studies.* Leiden.
Van der Paardt, R. 1981. "The Unmasked 'I': Apuleius *Met.* XI.27." *Mnemosyne* 9: 96–106. Repr. in *Oxford Readings in the Roman Novel,* edited by S. J. Harrison, 237–46. Oxford, 1999.
Van Mal-Maeder, D. 2007. *La fiction des declamations.* Leiden.
Van Nuffelen, P. 2011. *Rethinking the Gods: Philosophical Readings of Religion in the Postclassical Period.* Cambridge, U.K.
Van Thiel, H. 1971. *Der Eselsroman.* Vol. 1, *Untersuchungen.* Munich.
Venuti, L. 1995. *The Translator's Invisibility: A History of Translation.* London and New York.
Vermeer, H. J. 1992. *Skizzen zu einer Geschichte der Translation.* Vol. 1, *Von Mesopotamien bis Griechenland, Rom und das frühe Christentum bis Hieronymus.* Frankfurt.
Vernant, J.-P. 1980. *Myth and Society in Ancient Greece.* Trans. J. Lloyd. Hassocks.
Versini, L. 1998. *Le roman epistolaire.* 2nd ed. Paris.
Veyne, P. 2005. *L'empire gréco-romain.* Paris.
Vidal-Naquet, P. 2007. *The Atlantis Story: A Short History of Plato's Myth.* Exeter.

Walbank, F. 1960. "History and Tragedy." *Historia* 9: 216–34.
Walker, A. D. 1992. "*Eros* and the Love-Letters of Philostratus." *PCPhS* 38: 132–48.
Wallace-Hadrill, A. 1981. "The Emperor and His Virtues." *Historia* 30: 298–323.
———, ed. 1989. *Patronage in Ancient Society*. London.
Walsh, R. 1997. "Who Is the Narrator?" *Poetics Today* 18: 495–513.
Wardy, R. 1996. *The Birth of Rhetoric: Gorgias, Plato and Their Successors*. London.
Watson, N. 1994. *Revolution and the Form of the British Novel, 1790–1825: Intercepted Letters, Interrupted Seductions*. Oxford.
Webb, R. 1997a. "Mémoire et imagination: les limites de l'*enargeia* dans la théorie rhétorique grecque." In *Dire l'évidence: philosophie et rhétorique antiques*, edited by C. Lévy and L. Pernot, 229–48. Paris.
———. 1997b. "Imagination and the Arousal of the Emotions in Greco-Roman Literature." In *The Passions in Roman Thought and Literature*, edited by S. Braund and C. Gill, 229–48. Cambridge, U.K.
———. 1999. "Ekphrasis Ancient and Modern: The Invention of a Genre." *Word and Image* 15: 7–18.
———. 2006. "Fiction, *Mimesis* and the Performance of the Greek Past in the Second Sophistic." In *Greeks on Greekness: Viewing the Greek Past under the Roman Empire*, edited by D. Konstan and S. Saïd, 27–46. Cambridge, U.K.
———. 2009. *Ekphrasis, Imagination and Persuasion in Ancient Rhetorical Theory and Practice*. Farnham.
Webber, A. 1989. "The Hero Tells His Name: Formula and Variation in the Phaeacian Episode of the *Odyssey*." *TAPhA* 119: 1–13.
Weber, G. 1993. *Dichtung und höfische Gesellschaft: die Rezeption von Zeitgeschichte am Hof der ersten drei Ptolemäer*. Stuttgart.
Weinreich, O. 1928. *Studien zu Martial: literargeschichtlichen und religionsgeschichtliche Untersuchungen*. Tübingen.
Weissenberger, M. 1997. "Der 'Gotterapparat' im Roman des Chariton." In *Der antike Roman und seine mittelalterliche Rezeption*, edited by M. Picone and B. Zimmermann, 49–73. Basel, Boston, and Berlin.
West, M. L. 1982. *Greek Metre*. Oxford.
———. 2011. "Poseidon's Viewpoint (*Od*. V 283)." *Eikasmos* 22: 11–14.
West, S. 1974. "*Joseph and Asenath*: A Neglected Greek Romance." *CQ* 24: 70–81.
———. 1992. "Sesostris' Stelae (Herodotus 2.102–106)." *Historia* 41: 117–20.
White, P. 1993. *Promised Verse: Poets in the Society of Augustan Rome*. Cambridge, MA.
Whitmarsh, T. 1998. "The Birth of a Prodigy: Heliodorus and the Genealogy of Hellenism." In *Studies in Heliodorus*, edited by R. Hunter, 93–124. Cambridge, U.K.
———. 1999. "Greek and Roman in Dialogue: The Pseudo-Lucianic *Nero*." *JHS* 119: 142–60.
———. 2000. "The Politics and Poetics of Parasitism: Athenaeus on Parasites and Flatterers." In *Athenaeus and His World: Reading Greek Culture in the Roman Empire*, edited by D. C. Braund and J. M. Wilkins, 304–15. Exeter.
———. 2001. *Greek Literature and the Roman Empire: The Politics of Imitation*. Oxford.
———. 2002. "Written on the Body: Perception, Deception and Desire in Heliodorus' *Aethiopica*." *Ramus* 31: 111–24.

———. 2003. "Reading for Pleasure: Narrative, Irony, and Erotics in Achilles Tatius." In *The Ancient Novel and Beyond*, edited by S. Panayotakis, M. Zimmerman, and W. Keulen, 191–205. Groningen.
———. 2004a. *Ancient Greek Literature*. Cambridge, U.K.
———. 2004b. "The Cretan Lyre Paradox: Mesomedes, Hadrian and the Poetics of Patronage." In *Paideia: The World of the Second Sophistic*, edited by B. E. Borg, 377–402. Berlin.
———. 2005a. *The Second Sophistic*. Oxford.
———. 2005b. "The Greek Novel: Titles and Genre." *AJPh* 126: 587–611.
———. 2005c. "Quickening the Classics: The Politics of Prose in Roman Greece." In *Classical Pasts: The Classical Traditions of Greco-Roman Antiquity*, edited by J. I. Porter, 353–74. Princeton.
———. 2006. "The Sincerest Form of Imitation: Plutarch on Flattery." In *Greeks on Greekness: Viewing the Greek Past under the Roman Empire*, edited by D. Konstan and S. Saïd, 93–111. Cambridge, U.K.
———. 2007a. "Josephus, Joseph and the Greek Novel." *Ramus* 36: 78–95.
———. 2007b. "Prose Literature and the Severan Dynasty." In *Severan Culture*, edited by S. Swain, S. Harrison, and J. Elsner, 29–51. Cambridge, U.K.
———, ed. 2008. *The Cambridge Companion to the Greek and Roman Novel*. Cambridge, U.K.
———. 2009a. "Reframing Satire: Lucianic Metalepsis." In *Uluslararası Samsatlı Lucianus sempozyumu*, edited by M. Çevik, 69–75. Adıyaman.
———. 2009b. "Performing Heroics: Language, Landscape and Identity in Philostratus' *Heroicus*." In *Philostratus*, edited by E. Bowie and J. Elsner, 205–29. Cambridge, U.K.
———. 2009c. "An I for an I: Reading Fictional Autobiography." *Cento Pagine* 3: 56–66. Available online at http://www2.units.it/musacamena/iniziative/SCA2009_Withmarsh.pdf (*sic*). Repr. in *The Author's Voice in Classical and Late Antiquity*, edited by A. Marmodoro and J. Hill, 233–47. Oxford, 2013.
———. 2010a. "Thinking Local." In *Local Knowledge and Microidentities in the Roman Greek World*, edited by Whitmarsh, 1–16. Cambridge, U.K.
———. 2010b. "Domestic Poetics: Hippias' House in Achilles Tatius." *ClAnt* 29: 327–48.
———. 2010c. "Metamorphoses of the *Ass*." In *Lucian of Samosata: Greek Writer and Roman Citizen*, edited by F. Mestre and P. Gómez, 73–81. Barcelona.
———. 2010d. "Prose Fiction." In *A Companion to Hellenistic Literature*, edited by J. Clauss and M. Cuypers, 395–411. Oxford.
———. 2011a. *Narrative and Identity in the Ancient Greek Love Novel: Returning Romance*. Cambridge, U.K.
———. 2011b. "Hellenism, Nationalism, Hybridity: The Invention of the Novel." In *African Athena: New Agendas*, edited by G. Bhambra, D. Orrells, and T. Roynon, 210–24. Oxford.
———. 2011c. "Pharaonic Alexandria: Ezekiel's *Exagoge* and Political Allegory in Hellenistic Judaism." In *The Space of the City in Graeco-Roman Egypt: Image and Reality*, edited by E. Subias, P. Azara, J. Carruesco, I. Fiz and R. Cuesta, 41–48. Tarragona.
———. 2011d. "Greek Poets and Roman Patrons in the Late Republic and Early Empire: Crinagoras, Antipater and Others on Rome." In *The Struggle for Identity: Greeks and Their Past in the First Century BCE*, edited by T. Schmitz and N. Wiater, 189–204. Stuttgart.
———. 2012. "Joseph et Aséneth: réligion et érotisme." In *Les hommes et les dieux dans l'ancien roman*, edited by B. Pouderon and C. Bost-Pouderon, 229–43. Tours.

———. Forthcoming a. *Hellenism and Hybridity: The Earliest Greek Novels.* New York.

———. Forthcoming b. "Radical Cognition: Metalepsis in Classical Drama." *Greece and Rome.*

———. Forthcoming c. "Addressing Power: Fictional Letters between Darius and Alexander." In *Epistolary Narratives in Ancient Greek Literature,* edited by O. Hodkinson, P. Rosenmeyer, and E. Bracke. Leiden.

———. Forthcoming d. "The Erotics of *Mimēsis*: Gendered Aesthetics in Greek Theory and Fiction." In *The Construction of the Real and the Ideal in the Ancient Novel,* edited by M. Paschalis and S. Panayotakis. Groningen.

Whitmarsh, T., and Thomson, S., eds. Forthcoming. *The Romance between Greece and the East.* Cambridge, U.K.

Wiater, N. 2006. "Geschichtsschreibung und Kompilation: Diodors historiographische Arbeitsmethode und seine Vorstellungen von zeitgemäßer Geschichtsschreibung." *RhM* 149: 248–71.

———. 2011. *The Ideology of Classicism: Language, History, and Identity in Dionysius of Halicarnassus.* Berlin.

Wilamowitz-Möllendorff, U. von. 1900. "Asianismus und Atticismus." *Hermes* 35: 1–52. Repr. in *Kleine Schriften* 3, 223–73. Berlin, 1969.

———. 1921. *Griechische Verskunst.* Berlin.

———. 1956. *Der Glaube der Hellenen.* 2 vols. Basel.

Williams, D. S. 1994. "The Date of Ecclesiasticus." *Vetus Testamentum* 44: 563–66.

Wills, L. M. 1995. *The Jewish Novel in the Ancient World.* Ithaca.

———. 2002. *Ancient Jewish Novels: An Anthology.* New York.

Winiarczyk, M. 1976. "Der erste Atheistenkatalog des Kleitomachos." *Philologus* 120: 32–46.

———. 1981. "Theodorus ὁ ἄθεος." *Philologus* 125: 65–71.

———. 1991. *Euhemeros Messenius, reliquiae.* Stuttgart and Leipzig.

———. 2002. *Euhemeros von Messene. Leben, Werk und Nachwirkung.* Munich and Leipzig.

Winkler, J. J. 1982. "The Mendacity of Kalasiris and the Narrative Strategy of Heliodoros' *Aethiopica*." *YCS* 27: 93–158. Repr. in *Oxford Readings in the Greek Novel,* edited by S. C. R. Swain, 286–350. Oxford, 1999.

———. 1985. *Auctor and Actor: A Narratological Reading of Apuleius' "The Golden Ass."* Berkeley.

Winston, D. 1976. "Iambulus' *Islands of the Sun* and Hellenistic Literary Utopias." *Science Fiction Studies* 3: 219–27. Available online at www.depauw.edu/sfs/backissues/10/winston10art.htm.

Wiseman, T. P. 1993. "Lying Historians: Seven Types of Mendacity." In *Lies and Fiction in the Ancient World,* edited by C. Gill and T. P. Wiseman, 122–46. Exeter.

Wright, M. 2005. *Euripides' Escape Tragedies: A Study of Helen, Andromeda and Iphigenia among the Taurians.* Oxford.

Yatromanolakis, Y. 1990. Ἀχιλλέως Ἀλεξανδρέως Τατίου ΛΕΥΚΙΠΠΗ ΚΑΙ ΚΛΕΙΤΟΦΩΝ: εἰσαγωγή—μετάφραση—σχόλια. Athens.

Zaczek, B. M. 1997. *Censored Sentiments: Letters and Censorship in Epistolary Novels and Conduct Material.* Newark and London.

Zadorojnyi, A. 2006. "King of His Castle: Plutarch, *Demosthenes* 1–2." *CCJ* 52: 102–27.

Zanker, G. 1981. "*Enargeia* in the Ancient Criticism of Poetry." *RhM* 124: 297–311.

Zeitlin, F. I. 1990. "The Poetics of Eros: Nature, Art and Imitation in Longus' *Daphnis and Chloe*." In *Before Sexuality: the Construction of Erotic Experience in the Ancient Greek World*, edited by D. M. Halperin, J. J. Winkler, and Zeitlin, 417–64. Princeton.

———. 2001. "Visions and Revisions of Homer." In *Being Greek under Rome: Cultural Identity, the Second Sophistic and the Development of Empire*, edited by S. Goldhill, 195–266. Cambridge, U.K.

Zimmermann, B. 1997. "Die Symphonie der Texte: zur Intertextualität im griechischen Liebesroman." In *Der antike Roman und seine mittelalterliche Rezeption*, edited by M. Picone and B. Zimmermann, 3–13. Basel, Boston, and Berlin.

INDEX

Achilles Tatius, *Leucippe and Clitophon,* 43–45, 123–25, 132–33
Aeschylus: *Persians,* 218; *Suppliant Women,* 218
Alexander Polyhistor, 216
Alexander Romance, 30–31, 86–100
animal rationality, 77–79
Antipater of Thessalonica, 139–42, 149–50
Apuleius, *Metamorphoses,* 64–66, 68, 77
Aristides (Aelius), *Hymn to Sarapis,* 199–200, 204–5
Aristides, *Milesian Events,* 25
Aristophanes, *Frogs,* 241
Aristotle: *Poetics,* 188; *Rhetoric,* 192, 201
art. *See* paintings; statues
Asianism, 205–6
Ass, story of, 75–85
assimilation, 222–23
Assmann, Jan, 217, 222, 235
astrology, 165–66
atheism, 50, 55, 178
Atlantis, myth of, 50–51
Atticism, 109, 112–13
Augustine, *City of God,* 64–66
authorial intention, 102, 198–99
autobiography (fictional), 63–74

Barthes, Roland, 115
belief, 103–6, 182
Ben Sirach, 213–15

Bible, 221–22, 232–47
boundaries, 110–11
Bourdieu, Pierre, 129–30, 148–49, 206
Bowie, Ewen, 72, 173–74
Brooks, Peter, 208
Bundy, Elroy, 148
Burstein, Stanley, 91–92
Byblis and Caunus, 27–28

Calligone, 31
Callimachus, 203; *Aetia,* 150, 224–25, 241; *Hymn to Apollo,* 242; *Hymn to Zeus,* 18, 19–20; *Iambus* 1, 54–55; *Pinakes,* 194
Catullus: Poem 16, 64; Poem 68, 113
Celer, *Araspes in Love with Panthea,* 26
Chariton, *Callirhoe,* 41–45
Choerilus of Samos, 233–36
choruses, 159–60, 163–68
Cicero, *Pro Archia,* 138–39
circumcision, 235
citharodic poetry, 159–60
comedy, and fiction, 14–15
commerce, 112, 118
comparison. *See* syncrisis
cosmic themes in poetry, 144–46, 163–68
Crinagoras, 142–44, 146, 152–53
Ctesias, *Persian history,* 22–23, 25–26, 44, 47, 61, 231
Culler, Jonathan, 39

INDEX

D'Angour, Armand, 28
Darius II, 86–100
Derrida, Jacques, 87, 196, 198
description, 117–18
dialogue, 102–4
Dictys of Crete, 232
digression, 117–18
Dio Chrysostom: *Oration 7* (*Euboicus*), 107, 111–13; *Oration 11* (*Troicus*), 18
Diodorus (epigrammatist), 143–44, 147–48
Diodorus of Sicily, 52
Dionysius of Halicarnassus, *Dinarchus*, 127–28; *On Imitation*, 126–34
Dionysius of Miletus. *See* Celer
Dionysius Scytobrachion, 18
Doulamis, Konstantin, 44
Duris of Samos, 131

Ecclesiasticus. *See* Ben Sirach
Ecphrasis, 168–71, 225–27
education, 128, 214, 222
Egypt, representation of in Jewish thought, 217, 219–20
Egyptian literature, 29–31
Eikos, to. See plausibility
Enargeia. See visualization
Ephorus, 21
epic poetry, 16–20, 228–47
epigram, 137–53
epistolography. *See* letters
Eratosthenes, 191
Euhemerus of Messene, 16, 31–32, 49–62
Euripides, *Bacchae*, 218–19
exchange, 147–50
Exegetes (local guides), 24
Ezekiel, *Exagoge*, 211–27

fables, 171–74
Fanon, Frantz, 151, 213
feet, 184–85, 202–4
fiction, 11–34
first-person narration, 63–74
Fish, Stanley, 102
flattery, 149
Foucault, Michel, 190
Fowler, Alastair, 37–41

gaze, 123–34
gender, 123–34
genre, 37–41
Gesner, Konrad von, 85
gifts, 147–50

glass-working, 168–69
Gorgias, 14, 70, 192

Hadrian, 143, 154–75
Hall, Edith, 83
Halliwell, Stephen, 129
Halperin, David, 117
Heath, Jane, 225
Hecataeus of Miletus, 20
Hegesianax of Alexandria Troas, 19
Heliodorus, *Charicleia and Theagenes*, 45–47, 115, 133–34
Hellenism, 109–10
Henderson, John, 173
Henrichs, Albert, 50
herms, 114–15
Herodotus: on autopsy, 104–5; on Jews, 234; on myth, 17, 20, 26; on Protesilaus, 105, 109; as source for Euhemerus, 59–56
Hesiod, *Theogony*, 14, 224–25, 231, 241
Heubeck, Alfred, 238
hexameter, 146
history, and fiction, 20–23, 59–62
Holzberg, Niklas, 53
Homer, 102–3, 228–47; *Iliad*, 111, 119–22, 125; *Odyssey*, 14, 56–59, 77, 82–83, 112
Honigman, Sylvie, 51, 53
hospitality, 245
hymns, 160–63

Iamblichus, *Babyloniaka*, 83
Iambulus, *Islands of the Sun*, 31
imaginary worlds, 31–32
impersonation, 63–74
intermarriage, 223–24, 245–46
Isocrates, *Evagoras*, 193, 196

Jerusalem, 233–39, 244–45
Jewish literature, 28–29, 211–47
Jewish Sophistic, 212–15
Jews, negative depiction of, 222
Johansen, Thomas, 51
Joseph and Aseneth, 28–29
Josephus, *Against Apion*, 216, 233–36

Kerkhecker, Arnd, 54

Lada-Richards, Ismene, 69–70
Laetus, *Phoenician Events*, 27
landscape, 106–11
Lessing, Gotthold, 119–20
Letter of Aristeas, 100, 216

letters, 86–100
liminality. *See* boundaries
Lloyd, Geoffrey, 192
local history, 23–25
Longinus (?), *On the Sublime*, 28, 70
Longus, *Daphnis and Chloe*, 215
Lucian (?): *Ass*, 75–85; *Gout*, 182–85; *How to write history*, 201–2; *True stories*, 72–73; *Zeus the tragedian*, 177–82
Lucius of Patrae, 65, 75–77
Lucretius, 215

Maccabees (3), 217
maternity, 133–34
Maximus of Tyre, 196–97
Memnon, 229–30, 237–39
Merkelbach, Reinhold, 89–92
Mesomedes, 154–75; parodied by Lucian?, 182
metalepsis, 53, 71–74, 77, 179, 181, 183
meter, in poetry, 146, 156, 179–80, 184–85
mimesis, 123–34
Morales, Helen, 38–39
Mulvey, Laura, 124

Nagy, Gregory, 69
names, 82–84, 93–95
narratology, 63–74
nature and culture, 127–34, 144–46
Near Eastern stories, 25–29
Neoptolemus (son of Achilles), 143–44, 147–48
Ní Mheallaigh, Karen, 73
Nicolaus of Damascus, *Universal History*, 47
Nietzsche, Friedrich, 187–88
Ninus and Semiramis, 22, 29

paideia. *See* education
paintings, 123–34
Palaephatus, 17–18
Pancrates (Egyptian poet), 143
parrots, 152–53
Parthenius, 25
pastiche, 98
pastoral, 106–8, 243–44
patronage, 137–75
Pausanias, 108–9
penis, 114–15
pentameter, 146
phallus, 127. *See also* penis
phantasia. *See* visualization
Philip of Thessalonica, 138–53
Philo (epic poet), 239–43

Philostratus: *Heroicus*, 19, 101–22; *Lives of the Sophists*, 113
Phoenicians, 231
phoenix, 225–27
Photius, *Library*, 64–65, 75–77
Phylarchus, 21
Pindar, 144, 148, 150
Piso, Lucius Calpurnius, 140
Plato, 104; *Phaedrus*, 57; *Timaeus-Critias*, 50–51
plausibility, as criterion for fiction, 18
Plutarch: *How to tell a flatterer from a friend*, 154–55; *On the Pythian oracles*, 197–99, 204
Polus (actor), 15, 69–70
Porter, James, 109, 241
postclassicism, 1–2
postmodernism, 189
Pound, Ezra, 186
Prodicus, 50
prose poetry, 200–206
prose, 186–208
Protesilaus, 101–22
pseudo-documentarism, 60–61

Quintus of Smyrna, 237–39

Radici Colace, Paola, 235
reproduction, 129–30. *See also* maternity
resistance literature, 151
rhetoric, and fiction, 15
riddles, 171–72
Rohde, Erwin, 3, 12–13, 50, 122, 189
Roman Empire, 137–53
romance, Greek, 35–48; 113–14, 123–34

Second Sophistic, 2–3, 188–89, 212
Sedley, David, 62
Selden, Daniel, 76
Semiramis, 22
Septuagint, 242
Sesonchosis, 29–30
sex and luxury, 170
sexual transgression, 245–46
Shechem, 243–46
Sibylline Oracle (4), 237
simile, 141–42
Sisyphus fragment, 50
Solymoi, 233–39
sophists, and fiction, 16, 19
Sosates "the Jewish Homer," 239
Soterichus of Oasis, 26
Sourvinou-Inwood, Christiane, 219
split personalities, 81

statues, 114–15, 119–20
Stavrakopoulou, Francesca, 221
Strabo, 191, 195–96
Stratonice romance, 27
subelite literary production, 155
sublimity, 240–43
Swain, Simon, 191
syncrisis, 142–44

Tacitus, *Histories*, 236
Taussig, Michael, 129
technology, 168–71
textuality, 115–20, 123–34
thaumata. *See* wonders
Theocritus, *Idyll* 7, 71–72
Theodorus of Cyrene, 55
Theodotus, 243–46
Theopompus, 21
Thucydides: on authentication, 104–5; on myth, 17, 20
thunder, 241
Tiberius (Roman emperor), 143–44, 147–48
Tilg, Stefan, 41
titles, of Greek romances, 36
tonsuring, 234

touch, 116–17
tragedy, 176–82, 218–27, 228
translation, 213–15, 242–43

utopias, 50–51

Venuti, Lawrence, 242
visualization, 115–16, 118–19, 123–34

West, Martin, 233
Wilamowitz, i.e. von Wilamowitz-Möllendorff, Ulrich, 106, 173–74
womb, 129–30
wonders, 20–21
work, 168–71

Xenophanes, 54–55
Xenophon of Cyprus, 27
Xenophon of Ephesus, *Anthia and Habrocomes*, 41–43, 45–47
Xenophon, *Cyropaedia*, 26

Zeitlin, Froma, 121, 211
Zeuxis, 130–31
zooming, 219–20

www.ingramcontent.com/pod-product-compliance
Lightning Source LLC
Chambersburg PA
CBHW030528230426
43665CB00010B/804